# Fort Wayne Sports History

Blake Sebring

Published & distributed by:

Bauer Communications
Fort Wayne, IN
www.amauth.com

ISBN 978-0-9895149-0-3
First Edition

Edited by Sheryl Krieg, Laura Stuckey and Don Graham.

Cover illustration by Ken Dutton

Printed in the United States of America.

## Also by Blake Sebring

*Tales of the Komets*
*Legends of the Komets*
*Live from Radio Rinkside* (with Bob Chase)
*The Biggest Mistake I Never Made* (with Lloy Ball)
*The Lake Effect*
*Homecoming Game*

**visit www.blakesebring.com**

Dedicated to Bud Gallmeier, Jim Costin, Kerry Hubartt, Steve Warden and Bill Scott who told me so many of these stories in the first place, and to Don Converset, Reggie Hayes, Pete DiPrimio, Tom Davis, Rick Rimelspach, Brett Hess, Jonathan Batuello and Justin Kenny who continue to tell them every day in The News-Sentinel.

Special thanks to Arthur Alcid, Matt Bair, Dave Benson, Mark Bradley, Ashley Michael Brouwer, Dana Caldwell, Dan Cortez, Larry Everhart, Jenna Everson, Tom Gaffney, Rich Griffis, Robin Hartman, Dave Haynes, Brian Hedger, Terry Hutchens, Marc Johnson, Bob Jonason, Michael Kahn, Kent Kasey, Dave Luegring, Jeff Lockridge, Vinnie Lopes, Monica Denney Markel, Greg Mengelt, Mandy Miller, Marlon W. Morgan, Casey O'Boyle, Aaron Organ, Maria Burns Ortiz, Matt Pallister, Len Pasquarelli, Erik Pupillo, Chad Ryan, Duane Schuman, Frank Smith, Elbert Starks, Nate Trela, Scott Warden and Cam Weprin.

Also thanks to Don and Marge Graham, Carl and Carol Bennett, Bob and Murph Chase, Ken Ullyot, Phil Olofson, Len Davis, Hilliard Gates, Art Saltsberg, Mike and Laura Stuckey, Betty Stein, Ruth Wiegman and, as always, Doug and E.J. Sebring.

Some of these stories appeared originally in The News-Sentinel.

# Foreword

As you read through these pages, you'll realize this book has been a long time coming, probably for the reason it took a special person with compassion, understanding and dedication to research, compile and prioritize the materials in a logical manner.

Blake has done that with great restraint, which was also needed to cover the vast historical period the research covered. Northeastern Indiana has always been an incredible contributor to Indiana sports history and lore from the moment that recorded documentation has preserved the basics for someone with both the curiosity and compassion it took to get it right.

In all truth, this book could have encompassed many more pages than it presents. The secret of a good author is to know what to take, what to use as secondary material and what just can't be included at all. Blake has done an exceptional job of culling and selecting the jewels included herein.

Many present generation readers will not be able to identify with many of the incredible athletes and teams described within. Their mere mention should give you perspective on what you are reading.

I've spent the past 61 years covering all matter of sports in Indiana. Many of these stories I have personally been acquainted with in varying degrees. Even armed with that knowledge, I found a wealth of excitement in every story. It provided me with a wonderful stroll down memory lane. It also verified for me why I chose to pursue my entire career in the Hoosier state, especially northeastern Indiana.

If I would have a special wish for Blake for this wonderful sports history book and what it means to everyone in any way associated with it (including you, the reader), it would be to allow Bud Gallmeier to peruse the pages. He would be proud of his protégé who learned his lessons well. I'm sure he's smiling right now.

Thanks, Blake. You hit another home run. Congratulations.

Bob Chase
April, 2013

# JANUARY

## January 1

**In 1939, distance runner Don Lash is presented with the James E. Sullivan Award as the nation's top amateur athlete.**

As Don Lash was growing up in Auburn, he loved running. He eventually ran into history.

A 1988 Sports Illustrated article called Lash, "the first great American distance runner," and "possibly the best U.S. cross country runner ever."

Lash's career started with a 1933 state high school championship in the mile with a time of 4:30.5. After leaving Auburn, he went to Indiana University, where he persuaded coach Billy Hayes to give him a chance.

During Lash's first cross country meet in 1933, he finished third. It was the last time he would ever lose a cross country race. In 1934 he started a streak of seven consecutive AAU national championships. The streak finally ended in 1940 with his 12th national title in running overall. Pat Porter broke the record with his eighth national cross country title in 1989.

While at IU, Lash broke two of Paavo Nurmi's records for the indoor and outdoor two-mile run. He also anchored the Hoosiers' medley and four-mile relay teams to world records and became the first American to finish the two-mile run in less than nine minutes. From 1935-1937, he held several national records from 3,000 to 10,000 meters.

About the only time Lash failed in an event came during the 1936 Olympics in Berlin. Lash had qualified in the 5,000- and 10,000-meter events but finished 13th in the 5,000 and eighth in the 10,000. Lash blamed his failure on the 10-day ocean ride to get to the games, saying he had gained 10 pounds. His dream was to come back for the 1940 Olympics in Tokyo, but the event was canceled by World War II.

Lash's cross country title-streak ended after winning in 1940. In 1941 he left his job with the State Police and joined the FBI, where he stayed for 21 years.

He was a charter member of the Indiana University Hall of Fame in 1982.

Though he died Sept.19,1994, Lash was inducted into the Amateur Athletics Union Hall of Fame and the U.S. Track Hall of Fame in 1995.

**January 2**

**In 1963, Notre Dame beats Indiana 73-70 in basketball after trailing big in the first half.**

This was a huge win for the fighting Irish and the series in Fort Wayne because Notre Dame had been pounded the previous two seasons in Memorial Coliseum against the Hoosiers and also by Purdue in 1962.

It looked like the same thing would happen again as the Hoosiers led 46-30 at halftime behind the play of former Mr. Basketball Jimmy Rayl who scored 20 points. After chewing his team out at halftime, Notre Dame coach Jimmy Jordan inserted Sam Skarich into the lineup to take on Rayl.

Skarich scored six points in the second half but more importantly, he held Rayl to one free throw as the Irish rallied. Walt Sahm shut down the inside by grabbing 23 rebounds. Notre Dame out-scored Indiana 43-24 in the second half.

The crowd of 9,790 saw South Side's Tom Bolyard score 19 for IU, while Jay Miller led Notre Dame with 19 and John Andreoli scored 16. Oddly, Indiana coach Branch McCracken never substituted in the game, relying on the Hoosiers' 1-3-1 zone defense to keep them fresh.

Notre Dame improved to 8-2 early in the season, and the Hoosiers fell to 3-6.

**Also, in 2010, Bishop Luers basketball player Deshaun Thomas scores 52 points against Muncie South Side.**

**Also, in 2008, Huntington University basketball guard Tyler Shively starts an NAIA record string of making 70 consecutive free throws.**

The streak ended Nov.19 after 20 games over two seasons.

## January 3

**In 1993, the Komets tie the IHL record with their 10<sup>th</sup> straight road victory.**

The Komets started the season 1-6 on the road before going 10-0-2 over their next 12 games. They tied the International Hockey League mark with a 4-2 win at Indianapolis as Bob Lakso, Peter Hankinson, Joel Savage and Colin Chin scored. The Ice led 2-0 before the Komets got going.

Kalamazoo won 10 consecutive games from Oct. 5 to Nov. 25, 1990; Muskegon won its last five regular-season road games and its first five playoff road games from April 1 to May 8, 1985. The Komets' previous record of seven consecutive wins was set in 1980, and the K's tied it in 1984. The 1980 team actually went 9-0-1 on the road before it lost in regulation.

"I'm more proud of this team than I have been of any team in my coaching career, mainly because we did it the hard way on the road," Komets coach Al Sims said.

During the most-dramatic game of the streak, the Komets trailed at Kalamazoo 6-3 in the third period on Dec. 26 before Scott Gruhl scored twice as Fort Wayne forced a shootout before winning.

Goaltender Pokey Reddick won seven games during the streak, Dave Gagnon two and Mark Richards one.

**January 4**

**In 1995, the CBA's Fury win their seventh home game in a row.**

Fort Wayne scored a franchise-record 70 first-half points on the way to a 118-108 win over Rapid City before 3,082 Memorial Coliseum fans. The Fury had won nine of 12 games overall to take over the Continental Basketball Association's Eastern Division lead.

The Fury were led that season by the two best scorers in the CBA, Lloyd Daniels and Jerome Harmon, but they also had strong players such as Mark Strickland and Nikita Wilson. Harmon scored 37 points in this game as Daniels notched 18 with 11 assists.

Strickland scored 25 and was the CBA's Player of the Week after scoring 19.3 points over four games.

The streak reached eight two days later with a 118-108 win over Oklahoma City as Harmon scored 28 and Daniels 23.

The Tri-City Chinook came in the next night to end the streak with a 136-113 wipeout despite 42 points and seven assists from Daniels. Tri-City shot 63 percent from the floor.

Fort Wayne finished the season 24-32 to place second behind Pittsburgh in the Eastern Division and was swept by Rockford in two games in the first round of the playoffs.

**January 5**

**In 1966, Len Thornson scores his 1,000ᵗʰ point for the Komets.**

While Don Graham and Ryan Taylor were researching their book "50 years of Komets Hockey" in 2001 and 2002, they talked to more than 75 former Komets and asked almost all of them, "Who is the greatest player you ever played with?"

Every player from the 1950s and 1960s had the same answer, except one, the player everyone else identified.

"We had a lot of great players," Len Thornson said.

Except none were able to match Thornson's statistics or individual accomplishments. He finished his 13-season International Hockey League career in 1969 with a league record 1,382 points. From his first Fort Wayne season in 1958-59 until his next-to-last year in 1967-68, Thornson scored more than 100 points seven times and had three other seasons of 99, 93 and 97 points. During the 99-point season, Thornson reached that total in 52 games before being knocked out for the season with a broken leg.

During this game, Thornson scored a goal and an assist to become the first and so far only Komet to reach 1,000 career points. Unfortunately, Fort Wayne blew a 5-2 lead with eight minutes remaining and lost 6-5 to Port Huron in overtime. Thornson scored his milestone point on a slap shot for a power-play goal 24 seconds into the second period.

Despite being 33, Thornson finished this season with 105 points and came back the next year to set career-best totals with 46 goals and a Komets-record 139 points.

## January 6

**In 1993, the IPFW men's basketball team climbs to No. 4 in the NCAA Division II poll.**

The Mastodons were coming off a dominating 105-88 home win over Northern Kentucky as Scott Simmons scored 17 points.

At 9-0, IPFW was off to its best start since going 11-0 at the beginning of the 1990-91 season. At the time, IPFW was the only undefeated team in the Great Lakes Valley Conference, shooting an amazing 57 percent from the floor under coach Andy Piazza.

The Mastodons were led by Sean Gibson's 22.7 points per game and guard Andre Walton's 12 points and 7.3 assists per game. Shane Gibson scored 13 points per game, Simmons 10 and Lan Bullard nine. IPFW was averaging 95 points per game.

The No. 4 ranking was an all-time high for the IPFW men's basketball program, but it didn't last long. The Mastodons went on a two-game road trip to Kentucky Wesleyan and lost 69-66 and then to Southern Indiana and lost 107-96. IPFW trailed Kentucky Wesleyan by eight points with seven minutes left and lost on a three-pointer at the buzzer. Southern Indiana led 85-65 before IPFW rallied to make the score respectable.

Still IPFW rebounded to make its first appearance in the NCAA Division II National Tournament with a 23-5 mark. The Mastodons finished 14-0 at home, won 11 of their last 12 regular-season games, tied the school record with 23 wins overall and set another mark with 13 GLVC wins.

They drew Wayne State in the first round of the tournament and lost 78-72 despite 19 points and 18 rebounds from Sean Gibson, who was the GLVC Player of the Year.

**January 7**

**In 1992, it is announced that figure skater Kim Seybold has a brain tumor.**

A 1988 Olympic participant with her brother Wayne in pairs figure skating, but the tumor put her professional skating career on hold for a while.

The dime-sized tumor was originally diagnosed as benign, but it was also located next to the brain's main artery.

"It is kind of scary knowing that one of these days, I will have to have surgery to remove it," Seybold, 25, said. "At least I will still be able to skate."

Doctors told her she could return to skating.

"When you hear about it — 'brain tumor' — you think immediately you are going to die, but when you learn more about it, you learn that you can live with anything, really," Kim Seybold said. "Life is precious because at 26, I didn't think I was going to make it through the night. When I first learned about it, I was scared, and I didn't know what I was dealing with. Seeing the best specialists in the U.S., if they weren't too worried about me skating and moving on with my life, then I guess I shouldn't be. Now I usually worry about it once a year, and if the doctor says, 'you're fine,' I'm OK for another year."

Eventually, doctors recommended surgery in 1995 to remove the tumor when it grew to the size of a gumball. Kim was able to resume her professional career after taking a year off.

When more tumors developed, Seybold required more surgeries in 2003 and in 2007.

**Also, in 1992, the Komets' Steve Fletcher is suspended for eight games against the Indianapolis Ice.**

**January 8**

**In 2002, IPFW beats Chicago State 79-62 for its first NCAA Division I men's basketball victory.**

Everyone associated with IPFW was delighted the Mastodons had a chance to compete on the NCAA Division I level – until they actually had to do it.

The Mastodons under coach Doug Noll were scrappy but out-manned during their first few seasons competing with the big boys. IPFW opened with an 82-73 loss against Morehead State on Nov. 16, 2001, before 2,392 Memorial Coliseum fans. Then IPFW had to start trying to pay for everything.

That meant taking long road trips for guarantee money games. An 0-8 start included losses at Toledo, Florida International, Michigan State, Michigan and Ball State. A quick trip home for wins over Indiana Tech and Trine was followed by a five-game road trip that took the Mastodons to Colorado State, Montana State, Oregon State, Long Beach State and San Diego State.

Good thing the North Pole didn't have a Division I team with an opening in the schedule. Noll could have used the recruiting pitch "Come to IPFW and see the world."

Despite the ridiculous travel, Noll and his team kept a positive attitude and was rewarded against Chicago State. Nick Wise scored 24 points, Jeremy King 18 and Brad Noll 10 as the Mastodons won 79-62.

"Playing the tough schedule we faced the last couple of months really helped us down the stretch," Wise said. "We just picked things up intensity-wise. I'm thrilled. It feels real good. It feels real good to come home and get a win."

After getting its first significant win, IPFW was definitely more competitive after that, losing at Eastern Kentucky in overtime a week later.

The Mastodons finished their first NCAA Division I season with a 7-21 record, including 1-16 on the road. But they paid the bills.

**January 9**

**In 1994, the Steve Alford-coached Manchester men's basketball team wins its ninth of eventually 31 consecutive games in a row.**

After a four-year playing career in the NBA, Alford started his coaching journey by taking the job at Manchester in mid-December 1991. The Spartans were 0-8 and in their 15th consecutive losing season. They finished 4-16 under Alford, but the next year went 20-8 and made the NCAA Division III National Tournament for the first time. The 20 wins broke the school record of 18 set in 1966.

That record improved to 23-4 in 1993-94 and then 31-1 in 1994-95 and a third trip to the NCAA Division III National Tournament. The Spartans reached the championship game in Buffalo, N.Y. before finally losing to fellow undefeated Wisconsin-Platteville 69-55.

"It used to take Manchester College four years to get 15 wins," Alford told The News-Sentinel's Larry Everhart. "It's hard to be down after what we've done. I wish we could have felt the feeling of being champions, but we are champions to me. It would be hard to have more fun than we have all year. I'll never forget these guys – their integrity, their character, love for one another, camaraderie."

Wisconsin-Platteville was coached by future Wisconsin coach Bo Ryan.

The Spartans went 74-13 over Alford's last three seasons, and within 10 days of the championship game, Southwest Missouri State had hired him to replace Mark Bernson who had replaced Bears' legend Charlie Spoonhour.

Alford stayed at SWMS (which later became Missouri State) four seasons, going 78-48, including 22-11 in his last year when he led the Bears to the Sweet 16. That led to eight seasons at Iowa, six at New Mexico and then his current posting at UCLA.

**Also, in 1991, the Komets lose their 11th consecutive game at Salt Lake.**

**January 10**

**In 1958, Notre Dame beats Valparaiso 94-69 behind Tom Hawkins' 24 points.**

Ever wonder why Notre Dame played so many men's college basketball games in Fort Wayne throughout the 1960s? Notre Dame's home gymnasium held only about 4,000 fans, and this was the only way to get a decent crowd. It was also the only way Purdue and Indiana would regularly play the Irish on the road.

From 1962 to 1964, Notre Dame would play Indiana and Purdue each in Fort Wayne, one in the first half of the season and the other in the second. That ended in 1964 when Notre Dame and Indiana played single games in Fort Wayne through the 1967 season.

How did this all start? When this Notre Dame game against Valparaiso drew 6,574 fans for a doubleheader that included the Concordia Lutheran and Central Catholic boys teams playing the opener. The Irish, 6-7, upset the 10-1 and No. 21-ranked Cadets 55-53 to prime the crowd.

The Crusaders never had a chance in this one, though Concordia product senior Neil Reincke led them in scoring with 15 points. The Irish were just too strong, particularly 5-foot-6 guard Gene Duffy who scored 22 points. All five Notre Dame starters hit double figures.

**Also, in 1994, the Fury's Myron Brown wins the CBA's slam dunk contest.**

At 6-2, Brown was shorter than any other competitor in the prelude to the next night's Continental Basketball Association All-Star Game, but he also had the home-crowd advantage along with his 45-inch vertical leaping ability. Brown caught a break when fellow-finalist George Ackles of Fargo-Morehead missed his final dunk before Brown's last attempt.

## January 11

**In 1890, Baseball Hall of Fame inductee Max Carey is born.**

You may look up Max Carey biographies and see that he was born in Terre Haute which is also listed as his hometown and wonder why he's included in this project.

His formative years were actually spent in Fort Wayne. Maximillian George Carnarius came to Fort Wayne when he was 13 years old to attend Concordia Seminary with the dream of becoming a Lutheran pastor. The program lasted six years, and Carey then went to St. Louis to continue his studies, and his name was changed to maintain his amateur eligibility. When the Pittsburgh Pirates signed him in 1910, he was stuck with the new name.

When Carey retired after the 1929 season, he had 2,665 hits, 738 stolen bases and a .285 lifetime batting average. He hit over .300 six times, led the National League in steals 10 times and was a spectacular defensive center fielder. He still ranks ninth in career stolen bases in Major League history.

Carey was also a World Series champion in 1925 and was elected into the Baseball Hall of Fame by the veterans' committee in 1961.

After he retired as a player, Carey was also manager of the Fort Wayne Daisies in 1950 and 1951.

**Also, in 1994, the Fury host the CBA All-Star Game.**

Jeff Martin of Grand Rapids was named the Most Valuable Player after scoring 20 points and grabbing nine rebounds. The Fury was represented by Travis Williams who scored 15 points and Jay Edwards who scored 10. The crowd was 6,324.

## January 12

**In 1988, DeKalb's girls basketball star MaChelle Joseph scores 57 points against Bluffton to set the area scoring record.**

Less than a week after scoring 40 points and grabbing 14 rebounds in the Northeastern Indiana Athletic Conference championship game, the DeKalb senior made 25 field goals and seven of eight free throws against the visiting Tigers in a 114-27 win.

Joseph's total broke the DeKalb school record but it was not the high score in the state that season. Two days before, North Judson's Debbie Bolen scored 65 in a game against River Forest.

Joseph finished her high school career with 1,633 points and led the state as a senior with 35 points per game.

Continuing her scoring exploits at Purdue, Joseph set a Boilermakers record with 37 points against Michigan State on Feb. 17, 1991. The 5-foot-8 guard averaged 18.9 points as a freshman, 19.4 as a sophomore, 20.3 as a junior and 22.2 as a senior. She became the all-time leading women's scorer in Purdue and Big Ten history with 2,405 points, and Purdue's all-time assists leader with 628. She was also the highest-scoring basketball player ever at Purdue, edging Rick Mount.

After her senior season, Joseph was named the Big Ten's Player of the Year and Female Athlete of the Year as well as a consensus All-American. She was also elected to the Big Ten's All-Decade team for the 1980s and was the first player to rank in the top 10 on the conference's all-time lists for points and assists. When she graduated in 1992, Joseph held 33 Purdue records.

Joseph later became an assistant coach at Illinois, Purdue and Auburn before becoming head women's coach at Georgia Tech in 2003. She has a 193-122 record in her first 11 years in Atlanta through the 2012-13 season.

**January 13**

**In 1953, Fort Wayne hosts the third NBA All-Star Game which is also the first nationally televised pro basketball game.**

A record crowd of 10,340 showed up to see the best basketball players in the world put on a show. The first two all-star games had been played in Boston, drawing a crowd of 10,094 the year before.

With a population of approximately 135,000 at the time, Fort Wayne was the smallest city in the league. Pistons owner Fred Zollner paid about $18,000 for a chance to show off the new Memorial Coliseum.

The game itself featured 14 future Hall of Famers, including greats Bob Cousy, Bill Sharman, George Mikan, Ed Macauley and Vern Mikkelsen. The Pistons were represented by Andy Phillip and Larry Foust.

The game was also historic because Don Barksdale became the first African American to play in an NBA All-Star Game.

Barksdale was used to breaking barriers, as he was the first consensus African-American All-America player while at UCLA and later became the first African American to play on the United States Olympic basketball team, earning a gold medal in 1948.

At the time, Barksdale was one of four African-American players in the NBA along with Chuck Cooper, Nat "Sweetwater" Clifton and Earl Lloyd. Ironically, Lloyd became the first African American to play in an NBA game on Oct. 31, 1950, and during that same week Cooper and Clifton both made their NBA debuts on different nights in Fort Wayne.

Barksdale scored one point, pulled down three rebounds and passed two assists in the all-star game.

The West won 79-75 as Mikan was named the Most Valuable Player after scoring 22 points and grabbing 16 rebounds. Phillip set up Mikkelson on the two baskets that decided the game.

## January 14

**In 2006, the New York Rangers decide to send Dale Purinton to the minors, effectively ending his National Hockey League career.**

Purinton was recalled by the Rangers from their American Hockey League farm club in Hartford five times during the 2005-06 season, but he never got into another NHL game. After the 2006-07 season in Hartford, he signed as a free agent with Colorado but was sent to the Avalanche's farm team in Lake Erie after training camp.

The son of former Komets great Cal Purinton, Dale Purinton was really known for was his penalty minutes and fighting. Purinton earned 578 penalty minutes in the NHL, including 74 fights, and another 2,590 minutes and 112 fights during his minor league career.

Ironically, his father went to four training camps with the Rangers and never got a chance to stick.

"I run into guys all the time here who knew him or played against him," Dale said in 2000. "I think this is pretty special for him."

Dale Purinton was born in Fort Wayne on Oct. 11, 1976, three years following his father's retirement after helping the Komets win the 1973 Turner Cup. He lived in Fort Wayne until he was 4 years old.

"You always dream and hope that your kid will make it, in anything," Cal said. "It's not only my dream but it's his. If he didn't have that dream, no matter how much you push a kid, if he doesn't want it, he's not going. This is his dream, too."

Dale retired as a player after the 2007-08 season with 181 NHL games, scoring four goals and 20 points. He coached the Cowichan Valley Capitals for three seasons in the British Columbia Hockey League until his contract was not renewed following the 2011-12 season.

**Also, in 1975, Fred Zollner is proclaimed Mr. Pro Basketball at the NBA's 25th anniversary all-star game in Phoenix.**

## January 15

**In 2011, Guy Dupuis plays in his 1,000th game as a Komet.**

Dupuis's career is remarkable in so many ways, but maybe nothing is more amazing than he played more than 1,000 games in Fort Wayne with a six-year hiatus in the middle. Dupuis played with the Komets from 1991 to 1999. When the Komets dropped from the AAA International Hockey League to the AA United Hockey League, the defenseman continued his career with six teams before coming back to Fort Wayne in 2005 where he stayed until he retired at the end of the 2010-11 season.

His total included 945 regular-season games and 95 playoff games over 14 seasons. His career-total of 1,324 regular-season games is believed to be the fourth-most in minor league hockey history according to hockeydb.com.

He holds the Komets' defenseman records for most games, goals, assists and total points as a defenseman and ranks second in career penalty minutes. He also played an amazing 311 games consecutively.

After starting his second Komets career in 2005, 497 games ago at age 35, Dupuis missed only 10 games because of injury or just to rest – and he'd argue that he could have and maybe should have played a few of those.

Dupuis broke Eddie Long's record of 866 Komets games on April 8, 2009, a week after he topped Terry Pembroke's mark of 864 games for second place. Dupuis is also one of only 15 people who have won four Turner Cups as IHL playoff champions, and he was captain of three of those teams.

Dupuis became the 11th Komets player to have his jersey retired on Oct. 29, 2011 when his No. 2 was raised to the Memorial Coliseum rafters.

**January 16**

**In 1995, Lloyd "Sweet Pea" Daniels and Jerome Harmon are named starters in the CBA All-Star Game.**

Harmon scored 16 points in Hartford, Conn., on Jan. 23, but Daniels missed the game with a knee injury.

For many Fury fans, this half season will always be their favorite memories. Under coach Bruce Stewart, the team was off to a 19-16 start as Daniels and Harmon battled for the Continental Basketball Association scoring lead. With help from Mark Strickland, the Fury could score with anyone, and they were fun to watch every night.

Then within five late-January days, Daniels was called up by the Los Angeles Lakers and Harmon by the Philadelphia 76ers.Two weeks after that, Strickland was driving to Indianapolis to join the Pacers. Then Nikita Wilson, Leonard Harris and Ron Matthias all suffered serious knee injuries.

At the time of their call-ups, Harmon was averaging 29 points and Daniels 28 and 7.4 assists. Strickland was averaging 16 points and 7.3 rebounds when he was called up.

The Fury fell apart after that, losing 16 of its last 21 games, including eight in a row, and then both playoff games to Pittsburgh even though Harmon and Strickland both came back late in the season.

Harman ended up leading the CBA in scoring 28.8 points per game, and Daniels was second at 28.7.

**January 17**

**In 2005, Leland Etzler announces his retirement as Woodlan's football coach after 40 years.**

Etzler retired after the 2004 season with a career mark of 287-117-2 after 40 years and still ranks ninth on the state's all-time wins list. When he retired, Etzler's .710 winning percentage was sixth among Indiana prep football coaches with 200 or more wins

Etzler's teams won 12 Allen County Athletic Conference championships, including six in a row 1970-75. He has a 25-23 playoff mark, which includes three sectional titles, two regional crowns and a state runner-up finish in Class A in 1981.

More than 1,300 players suited up for Etzler at Woodlan.

After serving as an assistant for three seasons, Etzler took over as head coach for the 1965 campaign, the first season Woodlan did not have a junior varsity team on its schedule. Darrell Casey had gone 6-1-1 the year before, playing among others South Side's junior varsity squad. That season ended with Woodlan owning a modest seven-game unbeaten streak. Etzler's teams then went 15-1-2 over the next two years, with the only loss coming to Concord in the eighth week of the 1966 season. The defeat ended the Warriors' unbeaten string at 23 games.

Only three times in Etzler's 40 seasons as head coach did Woodlan post a losing record. The first came more than 20 years into his tenure. He finished the 2004 season second among active state high school football coaches in total wins with 287, eight fewer than Sheridan's Larry Wright.

Etzler was inducted into the Indiana Football Coaches Hall of Fame in 2001.

## January 18

**In 1984, Former Leo basketball star Tonya Burns scores 42 points against Nebraska to set the Iowa State single-game scoring record.**

The former Leo center made 18 of 25 shots in setting her high game in what was a brilliant college career.

Burns finished with 33 Iowa State records, including 23 rebounds in a game, career scoring with 1,789 points and career rebounding with 921 boards. She was as three-time all-Big Eight selection. She scored double digits in 92 of her 114 games.

Burns became the first Iowa State women's basketball player to have her number retired, which was announced at the post-season team banquet after her senior year in 1985. She was inducted into the Iowa State Hall of Fame in 2000.

During her high school career, Burns scored 1,059 points and grabbed 785 rebounds before she graduated in 1981 and was inducted into the Indiana Basketball Hall of Fame in 2010.

Following her career at ISU, she played one year of professional basketball for the Virginia Express of the NWBA professional league.

After her playing career, Burns became a very successful high school coach, going 103-137 in 13 seasons at North Side. In 2000, she moved to Woodlan where the Warriors have gone 113-163 through the 2012-13 season.

**Also, in 1992, the Komets rally to beat the Indianapolis Ice 7-5 in the infamous ice-scraper game.**

**Also, in 2011, South Side center Raphael Davis scores 53 points in a 79-72 loss to Northrop.**

## January 19

**In 1980, North Side boys basketball's homecourt winning streak reaches a remarkable 38.**

Led by guard Tony William and forward Sim Nelson, the Redskins shut down a powerful Harding offense 59-55. William, who later played at Florida State, scored 22 points and held Harding star Jim Master to 23 points. Future Michigan football star Nelson controlled the inside with 18 points.

The next week the streak would end on Jan. 26 as DeKalb won 71-70 behind 20 points from Dave Hathaway and 16 from Brett Hughes. The Barons hit 19 of 23 free throws to overcome 19 points from Nelson. William was held to 14.

The Redskins also lost their six-year, 20-game SAC home winning streak to Bishop Dwenger a week after losing to DeKalb.

"I don't know whether we lost more than one or two home games all throughout the 1970s," North Side coach By Hey said. "Those losses were shocking to us."

What's remarkable about the streak is it was maintained during what was arguably Fort Wayne's greatest era of boys basketball.

Harding, South Side, Northrop, Bishop Dwenger, Concordia and North Side were all ranked at some point during the season. In the Dec. 11, 1979, poll, South Side was ranked No. 2, Northrop No. 6, Harding No. 9, Concordia No. 18 and Bishop Dwenger No. 20.

Interest was so high that schools were selling tickets during the week leading up to games. Gyms were full for reserve games because fans were wary of missing a seat for the varsity contests.

Attendance was strong throughout the season. More than 5,000 watched Harding and South Side battle for the SAC Holiday Tournament title, more than 4,000 people came for a Memorial Coliseum doubleheader, and more than 28,000 attended the five-session sectional basketball tournament, including more than 6,000 for the two title games.

At the end of the 1979-80 season, long-time News-Sentinel sportswriter Jim Costin wrote, "Overall, it was probably as good or better than any Fort Wayne has ever had. Had they not been forced to play each other, the records would have been much better. But, not the financial intake or the interest."

21

**January 20**

**In 2008, the Fort Wayne Sports Corporation displays its Sports Heritage Project for the first time.**

After eight years of discussion, planning and preparation, the Fort Wayne Sports Corporation unveiled its Fort Wayne Sports Heritage project at the organization's banquet at the Grand Wayne Convention Center.

The project is a DVD of 32 vignettes reflecting on Fort Wayne's sports history. The run time is roughly an hour and 20 minutes, and the material can be displayed in an interactive kiosk.

"I think it will give visitors to the community a feel for the exciting sports history of Fort Wayne and our heritage," project co-chairman Art Saltsberg of Federated Media said. "And I think it's going to be great for people in the community to take a look at as well."

The project cost about $65,000, paid for by a grant from Sports Corp. member Dick Waterfield and the Waterfield Foundation.

**Also, in 1982, Hamilton's Tom Heitz scores a career-high 15 points in Kentucky's basketball win over Florida.**

A 6-9 forward, Heitz averaged 27.5 points and 17.8 rebounds as a senior at Hamilton in 1980. Playing behind such players as Sam Bowie, Melvin Turpin and Kenny Walker, he saw limited playing time at Kentucky, scoring 143 points and grabbing 86 rebounds in 73 games. His best game was likely against Auburn on Jan. 6, 1982 when he had 12 points and six rebounds against Charles Barkley.

## January 21

**In 2007, Indianapolis coach Tony Dungy suggests the Colts and Bears play the Super Bowl in Fort Wayne.**

The Colts had just beaten the New England Patriots 38-34 for the AFC title after the Chicago Bears had beaten the New Orleans Saints 39-14 for the NFC title earlier in the day. As he was being interviewed on CBS, Dungy said, "It's a shame we have to go to Miami. We should just go to Fort Wayne and play it off there."

What was funny about the comment was that all the Fort Wayne media were in Indianapolis for the game and missed it. Back home, phones were ringing like crazy with everyone asking, "Did he just say what I thought he said?"

Sports Illustrated even wrote a story about the comment, written by Steve Rushin whose father grew up in Fort Wayne. Rushin interviewed Fort Wayne natives Eric Wedge and Rod Woodson and Fort Wayne Convention & Visitors Bureau president Dan O'Connell who was quoted, "We don't have the hotel rooms for tens of thousands of people, but I guarantee you, we'd put everybody up in our homes. And they'd all get a hot meal, family-style."

"I know Tony was joking," Woodson said, "but the Super Bowl gives kids a once-in-a-lifetime opportunity to see the big hoo-rah in their own town."

**Also, in 1970, the Komets draw a record crowd of 8,537 to Boy Scout night.**

This was the night when Komets Business Manager and future co-owner Colin Lister was hiding from the fire marshal. Many fans who were there claim there were actually over 9,000 people in the building. It was the Komets' largest attendance until the Memorial Coliseum was renovated in 2002.

**Also, in 1963, Purdue beats Notre Dame 112-103 in double overtime as Dave Schellhase scores 43.**

**Also, in 1992, Terri Lydy breaks the Indiana Tech women's basketball scoring record with 44 points in a win over IUPU-Indianapolis.**

**January 22**

**In 2004, one of Fort Wayne's greatest all-time athletes dies, Bob Cowan of North Side.**

Cowan is the first and so far only athlete to be inducted into Indiana's high school halls of fame for track, football and basketball.

During his North Side athletic career, Cowan earned 11 letters, consistently leading the Redskins to titles. During his senior year in 1940, Cowan scored 155 points in eight games to set a state record as North Side won the mythical state football title, and he helped the Redskins reach the semistate level in basketball. In track, he won the 220-yard dash, finished second in the 440 and anchored the winning relay team as North Side won the state title.

Cowan then attended Indiana University, lettering in basketball in 1943 and in football in 1942 and 1946 with time off in between to join the Air Force. He started at right halfback his sophomore and junior seasons in football before signing a contract his senior year to play with the Cleveland Browns. He played two years with the Browns before being traded to the Baltimore Colts.

The Browns and Colts were both members of the All-American Football Conference, and the Browns won the league title both years Cowan played for them.

**Also, in 1994, No. 1-ranked defending national champions UCLA escapes with its life against IPFW's men's volleyball team and 2,770 fans.**

The No. 4-ranked Volleydons pushed the Bruins to play their best in a rocking Hilliard Gates Sports Center. Though IPFW led 10-8 in the first game, 11-6 in the second game, was tied 6-6 in the third and led 11-5 in the fourth, UCLA won the match 15-11, 10-15, 15-9, 17-15. IPFW had three serves and two swings to win the fourth game and push the match to five games, but the Bruins' experience was the difference.

This was the first time a local network television affiliate (WKJG) had ever aired live a men's college volleyball match.

## January 23

**In 1954, WKJG televises the championship game of the ACAC Tournament.**

Hilliard Gates was always a mainstay at the Allen County Tournament, beginning as a radio broadcaster with WOWO in 1941. He always said New Haven's gym was the loudest building in the state, and everyone knows how he loved "the beautiful Allen County War Memorial Coliseum" when the tournament moved there in 1953.

He later founded WKJG with William Kunkle of the Journal Gazette, and in 1953 they applied for a television license which they received in November. Two months later, WKJG broadcast the ACAC Tournament title game, which was the first televised game in northern Indiana and possibly the state.

With the exception of two years during World War II, Gates was at the mike for every ACAC Tournament title game from 1941 until he retired in 1993, usually with Dick DeFay at his side. Gates passed away in 1996, and DeFay in 2007.

Huntertown won the first televised game, beating Elmhurst 65-63. It was the Wildcats' third title in four years under coach Terry Coonan. As a reward, Principal Edwin Prible gave everyone an extra day off school.

1954 was a particularly tough year for Huntertown which beat defending champion Leo 50-49 in the first round and Harlan 61-59 in the semifinals.

**Also, in 1943, South Side graduate Ralph Hamilton sets the IU single-game basketball scoring record with 31 points in a win at Iowa.**

Hamilton might have been Fort Wayne's best high school player from the first half century, earning all-state honors as a junior and senior and first-team all-American honors at IU. He also set a state tournament scoring record in leading the Archers to the 1940 final four. He was named to the Indiana Basketball Hall of Fame in 1990.

**January 24**

**In 1985, No. 1 Marion beats No. 2 Northrop 64-63 in boys high school basketball.**

A crowd of 8,940 fans came out to see the top-ranked showdown as the Giants were 13-0 and the Bruins were 14-0.

The Giants were loaded with players like seniors Jay Teagle, Lefon Bowens and Nikki Mallory and a pair of sophomores named Lyndon Jones and Jay Edwards. Northrop was paced by future Purdue player Tony Jones, Bruce Brineman and Dan O'Reilly.

Behind Jones' 18 points, Northrop built a 12-point lead late in the third quarter, but then the Giants went on a 16-2 run to take a 53-51 lead with 5:34 left. The lead see-sawed until Daric Keys hit a three-pointer with 1:19 remaining, and then O'Reilly tied the game at 63-63 with a minute left. Northrop tried holding the ball for a final shot before turning it over with nine seconds remaining. Marion's Jones missed a pair of shots before Keys was fouled by Northrop's Jones on a rebound with no time remaining.

Keys hit the first free throw to end the game and give the Bruins their first loss of the season. Edwards led the Giants with 23 points, and Keys added 14.

Marion later beat defending state champion Warsaw 70-65 in the Fort Wayne Semistate. That Tigers' team included 1985 Mr. Basketball Jeff Grose and future NBA player Rick Fox. Northrop stayed No. 2 all season but lost to Michigan City Rogers 60-59 in the other semifinal of the Fort Wayne Semistate.

The Giants then beat North Central Conference rival Richmond 74-67 in the state championship game to finish 29-0. It was the first of three straight state titles for Bill Green's Giants.

**Also, in 1950, ground is broken on the Memorial Coliseum.**

The idea for the building actually started in 1944. The original cost was $3 million, and the project had to pass a county-wide referendum. The vote was 25,705 for and 7,720 against.

Dedicated Sept. 28, 1952, the building quickly became Northeast Indiana's mecca for sports, hosting NBA games from the Fort Wayne Pistons and International Hockey League games from the Fort Wayne Komets.

## January 25

**In 1957, construction continues on McMillen Park's new ice rink.**

When McMillen Park Ice Rink started in 1956 as the state's first artificial ice rink, there were cooling pipes laid over the tennis courts and then the area was flooded. Developers basically used instructions out of a library book.

After the tennis courts were torn up, different kinds of stone were spread into the hole, piping was added and sand was used to hold the pipes in place. Then trucks poured on the cement. While the floor cured for a year, the metal building was erected around the rink.

There was no roof until 1968, meaning teams often switched sides several times a period so one wouldn't have too big an advantage with the wind. They also played no matter what the conditions because the schedule was too full to make changes.

Mitzi Toepfer was there for almost all of it as the rinks' general manager, den mother and chief protector. In many ways, she held the building together when it should have been falling apart.

The building was eventually closed in 2010 when the new Canlan rink opened on the north side of town.

The original cost of $300,000 for McMillen Park Ice Arena may be the best investment the city has ever spent on a project.

**Also, in 1993, Hall of Famer Rick Barry agrees to become coach of the Fort Wayne Fury.**

Barry led the Fury to a 19-37 record in one season.

**January 26**

**In 2003, Rod Woodson plays in his third Super Bowl, this time with the Oakland Raiders.**

Though he was 38, Woodson was coming off one of his best NFL seasons. He tied for the
league-high with eight interceptions and was named to his 11th Pro Bowl appearance in his 16th season.

This was probably not one of Woodson's favorite days as a pro as the Tampa Bay Buccaneers beat the Raiders 48-21 in San Diego. The Raiders had been favored by four points going into the game. Woodson played very well with an interception and eight tackles.

Woodson finished his career with a 1-2 record in Super Bowls, losing with Pittsburgh in 1996, winning with Baltimore in 2001 and losing with Oakland in 2003.

**Also, in 1973, the Komets Oldtimers beat the Detroit Red Wings Alumni.**

After whipping the Glenbrook Komets 11-2 and 18-6, the Komets Oldtimers figured they'd try someone a little tougher in their third-annual game for charity. The Red Wings Alumni had never lost to an amateur team in 13 years of organized play.

Playing in front of 6,682 Memorial Coliseum fans, the Komets Legends beat the Red Wings Alumni 11-8 in a benefit game for the Allen County Crippled Children Society. Montreal Canadiens great John Ferguson made a successful return to Fort Wayne with a hat trick and Len Thornson and Merv Dubchak each scored twice as the Komets dominated. Thornson also passed four assists Chuck Adamson finished 20 saves and Gerry Randall made 18 saves in the Fort Wayne goal.

**January 27**

**In 2004, John Grantham retires from Wildcat Baseball after 40 years.**

Mr. Mac was the founder of Wildcat, but John Grantham was the man who made the program the success it became.

Grantham joined the league in 1964 as a site director and in 1965 was appointed as Wildcat's president, a position he held for 39 years before retiring in 2004. Among his many highlights, Grantham used to take 4,000 children on train trips to games in Chicago or Detroit. He brought in stars, such as Jackie Robinson, Bob Feller, Carl Erskine and Ted Williams, to speak to the players on Mr. Mac Day, the league's annual season-ending celebration. The Wildcat League earned national publicity in Sports Illustrated and in an NBC story narrated by Tom Brokaw.

Grantham made sure to develop Wildcat sites that touched all parts of the city. Wildcat League records showed more than 180,000 players came through the program while Grantham was in charge.

In 1994, he organized a Wildcat Reunion at the Grand Wayne Center, where he displayed some 1,500 photos and artifacts from more than 30 years of Wildcat.

He passed away on July 1, 2009 at age 74.

**Also, in 1966, Bill Russell and the Boston Celtics beat the Detroit Pistons 131-112.**

Only 3,890 fans showed up as Russell scored 21 points and grabbed 21 rebounds, Sam Jones scored 32 points, Mel Counts 23 and Don Nelson 22 to lead the Celtics. Player-coach Dave DeBusschere led the Pistons with 32 points.

**January 28**

**Bob Pelkington grabs 30 rebounds for Xavier against Canisius in college basketball.**

A Central Catholic product, Pelkington wasn't the biggest center around at 6-foot-7, but no one could out-rebound him. In fact, he led the NCAA in rebounding as a senior at Xavier, grabbing 21.8 per game after finishing eighth the season before with a 16.2 average. He had a high of 31 against St. Francis (Pa.) on Feb. 18, 1964. His career rebounding average was 16.6.

During his career at Xavier, Pelkington grabbed 1,325 rebounds which still ranks second on the Musketeers' all-time list behind Tyrone Hill who played four seasons. During Pelkington's era, freshmen were ineligible, but he started as a sophomore and grabbed 11.7 rebounds per game. He still holds the Xavier records for top average for juniors and seniors.

Pelkington could also score a little. He averaged 13.4 points during his career and scored 1,075 points, shooting 46 percent from the field. He scored a career-high 29 points against Western Kentucky on Dec. 30, 1961. He also averaged 3.2 assists per game during his career.

The rough part of Pelkington's career is that he never got to play in an NCAA Tournament or National Invitational Tournament game as the Musketeers went 14-12, 12-16 and 16-10 during his three seasons. Pelkington was drafted in the eighth round (67th pick) of the 1964 NBA draft but never played in the league.

**Also, in 1996, Rod Woodson becomes the first NFL player to return from an ACL tear in the same season to play in the Super Bowl against Dallas.**

**Also, in 2001, Woodson wins his Super Bowl ring with Baltimore.**

## January 29

**In 1995, Lindy Jones leads IPFW women's basketball to upset of No. 3 Southern Indiana 104-94.**

The Eagles were 15-1 coming in, but Lindy Jones scored a school-record-tying 40 points. Leah Sheets scored 23 points and grabbed 12 rebounds and Tara Muzzillo scored 17 points. Southern Indiana's LeAnn Freeland scored a conference record 50 points in the loss.

Jones became one of the most prolific scorers in IPFW and Great Lakes Valley Conference history. She led NCAA Division II in scoring as a senior when she averaged 26 points and helped lead the Mastodons to the NCAA Tournament with a 23-5 record.

She finished her IPFW career with 2,107 points to rank second all-time and was inducted into the IPFW Hall of Fame in 2006.

**Also, in 1987, Northrop tries to stand up to Marion senior Lyndon Jones and Jay Edwards in boys basketball.**

After the Bruins upset the Giants on their homecourt the previous year, the Giants came in and dominated, winning 77-46 in front of 3,741 fans at Memorial Coliseum. The duo of IU-bound Jay Edwards and Lyndon Jones led the No. 1-ranked Giants with 27 and 18 points. The No. 17 Bruins didn't have any player who scored more than six points.

The defeat was Northrop's worst since Jan. 30, 1982 when the Bruins lost to Marion 84-52.

**Also, in 1949, sports broadcaster Len Davis arrives at WGL radio.**

**January 30**

**In 1982, the Komets hang their retired numbers for the first time, adding Robbie Irons and Terry Pembroke.**

For more than 13 years, the Komets only had two retired numbers, No. 11 for Len Thornson and No. 16 for Eddie Long. This was the only time the team retired the numbers of two players at the same time, and the Komets also named the 5-30 Unsung Hero Award after Pembroke and Irons.

Irons and Pembroke played together for seven seasons and their names cover the Komets record book. Irons played 573 games in net, more than double the next-closest Komet. Though he retired in 1982 after playing in three decades, Irons still holds franchise records for career assists by a goaltender, 65 playoff games and five all-star game appearances.

Pembroke played 864 games in Fort Wayne, third-most of any player, and he set a franchise mark with eight all-star game appearances.

Irons has continued to work with the Komets as Bob Chase's color commentator for all Fort Wayne home games.

**Also, in 1971, Huntington College basketball player Steve Platt grabs 33 rebounds against Bethel.**

## January 31

**In 1957, George Yardley sets a Fort Wayne Pistons' record by scoring 40 points at the Minneapolis Lakers in a 111-107 win.**

After playing on an AAU national championship team and missing the 1952 Olympics because of a broken hand, Yardley finally signed with the Pistons in 1953. Because he hated training camp, Yardley ignored the Pistons' offer of $6,000, playing beach volleyball in California and becoming the first rookie to hold out, until the Pistons' offer reached $9,500.

Though Yardley had broken all of Hank Luisetti's scoring records at Stanford, his professional career started slowly. As a rookie he averaged nine points and 6.5 rebounds per game, but he became a starter the next season and averaged 16 points and nine rebounds per game in 1954-55.

A 6-foot-5 forward, Yardley specialized in out-jumping opponents and was one of only a handful of players who dunked regularly in games. Yardley played four years in Fort Wayne, scoring 4,380 points. Other than his rookie season, Yardley averaged more than 17 points in his final six seasons. He made the All-NBA first team once in 1958 and the second team in 1957.

During an era when teams regularly scored between 70 and 80 points, Yardley's NBA career averages are 19.2 points and 8.9 rebounds per game, while playing in six NBA All-Star games. Twice he scored more than 50 points in a game.

Yardley had his best season in Detroit in 1957-58. At age 29, he played 39.5 minutes per game, and late in the season he was closing in on George Mikan's league record of 1,932 points in a season set in 1950-51. He broke that with a few games left and then became the first NBA player to score 2,000 points in a season. He finished the season averaging 27.8 points per game.

Yardley played two more seasons in Detroit, averaging 19.8 points in 1958-59 and 20.2 in 1959-60 before abruptly retiring.

**Also, in 1973, Jim Hrycuik scores the fastest goal in Komets' history, six seconds after the opening faceoff.**

**Also, in 1963, Elgin Baylor scores 49 points and Jerry West 36 as the Los Angeles Lakers beat the Detroit Pistons 127-122.**

# FEBRUARY

## February 1

**In 1986, Northrop stuns host Marion in boys basketball.**

This might have been the best game of Tony Jones' excellent high school career, and it might be one of the best performances ever by a Fort Wayne high school player. The 6-2 senior guard put up 35 points, nine assists and five rebounds as the No. 19-ranked Bruins upset the No. 1 Giants 77-75 on their home floor in front of 7,600 fans.

Over the game's last four minutes, Jones scored 14 straight points. His 16-foot jumper tied the game with 20 seconds left. After the Giants threw the ball away, they denied Jones the ball for a last shot, but Vonnie Williams hit a jumper as time expired to give the Bruins the win.

Williams finished with 17 points and nine rebounds, and Ernie Davis passed a school-record 15 assists. Jay Edwards led Marion with 29 points and Lyndon Jones scored 16.

**Also, in 2009, Harding's Trai Essex wins his second Super Bowl championship ring with the Pittsburgh Steelers.**

Essex was the utility man on the Steelers' offensive line, helping protect Ben Roethlisberger as Pittsburgh beat Arizona 27-23 in Tampa. Originally picked by the Steelers in the third round of the 2005 draft out of Northwestern, Essex played in three Super Bowls with Pittsburgh.

**Also, in 1992, IPFW sweeps No. 4 USC 3-0 in men's volleyball.**

The Volleydons were ranked No. 10 nationally before this signature win before 2,600 fans at Gates Sports Center. IPFW won an even more significant match later in the season when they went to USC and stomped the Trojans in four games.

**February 2**

**In 1961, on his birthday Komets forward Len Thornson breaks his leg to end the season at 99 points.**

Thornson broke every record the Fort Wayne Komets ever even thought about. He finished his 13-season International Hockey League career in 1969 with a league record 1,382 points. From his first Fort Wayne season in 1958-59 until his next-to-last year in 1967-68, Thornson scored more than 100 points seven times and had three other seasons of 99, 93 and 97 points. During the 99-point season, Thornson reached that total in 52 games before being knocked out for the season with a broken leg.

Thornson's start of 35 goals and 99 points was remarkable as Ken Yackel of Minneapolis won the IHL scoring title with 114 points – playing 20 more games than Thornson.

Thornson came back the next season to win his second scoring title with 122 points. He also started a remarkable string of five straight MVP awards, sharing the 1962-63 honor with teammate Eddie Long.

"He reminded me of Jean Beliveau," Long said. "Lennie was smooth and really very deceptive. He was faster than people thought he was. He'd do the same move and these guys would go for it every time. Pull the puck back and go. He was an all-around player really. If you played the position with Lennie, he knew where you were. He knew where everybody was on the ice, too. The one thing he didn't do, and he probably would have gotten more goals was shoot the puck. He had a good shot, but he didn't shoot."

Seven times Thornson was named the league's most valuable player, and The Hockey News named him the IHL's all-time greatest player in 1997.

"He brought up the level of the league," long-time Komets coach Ken Ullyot said. "His talent was on display every game because he played hard. The challenge was to opponents to stop him, and they couldn't."

Thornson's IHL scoring record lasted an amazing 32 years before Cleveland center Jock Callander passed him in February of 2000. Callander broke the record at age 38 by playing in nearly 300 more games.

## February 3

**In 2013, South Side graduate Bernard Pollard wins a Super Bowl with the Baltimore Ravens.**

Pollard made two tackles in the Super Bowl win over San Francisco despite playing with six cracked ribs. He had played most of the season with the injury, missing the final three regular-season games to heal up.

After playing three years at Purdue, Pollard was in his seventh NFL season during the Super Bowl run, playing three years with Kansas City, two with Houston and two with Baltimore. He had nine tackles and a forced fumble during the Raven's AFC title game win over New England.

**Also, in 1973, Steve Platt scores 57 points for Huntington College against Goshen College in men's basketball.**

Before there was Larry Bird as a small-town Indiana legend, there was Steve Platt.

Platt was a three-year starter at Union Township High School in Huntington County during the early 1960s, scoring 1,270 points before taking five years off to concentrate on farming and his young family. Then new Huntington College coach Keith Spahr persuaded Platt to give basketball another try.

The 6-foot-5 Platt's accurate jumper and continual drives to the basket helped him score 3,700 points during his career with Huntington – the most by any Indiana college player. He led the nation in scoring with 36 points per game his junior year and came back to score 38 points per game as a senior. Platt also grabbed 1,917 rebounds during his career.

Platt still ranks as the seventh-leading scorer in NAIA history, and he was inducted into the NAIA Hall of Fame in 1987. He was drafted by the Washington Bullets but was the last player cut in the fall of 1974. He then signed with the Fort Wayne Hoosiers of the International Basketball Association where he scored 34.1 points to lead the league.

He later returned to Huntington University and became the men's coach until he retired in 2008, finishing with a 329-123 career record. He was inducted into the Indiana Basketball Hall of Fame in 1996.

## February 4

**In 1963, Tom Bolyard scores 35 points for Indiana basketball against No. 4 Illinois.**

It would be amazing to see what Tom Bolyard could do on a basketball court today because he'd be a superstar. Bolyard was a standout player at South Side, helping the Archers to the 1958 state title and to the 1959 semistate after the other four starters had graduated.

A 6-foot-4 forward, Bolyard scored 1,420 points in his three years at South Side High School and then 1,299 points at IU. He was the Hoosiers' Most Valuable Player in 1963.

As a high school senior, Bolyard was named to the Parade All-America team and was the Most Valuable Player in the Indiana-Ohio All-Star game. He had a high game of 48 points against Gary Froebel, and averaged nearly 30 points for his senior season to end with 17 points per game for his high school career.

"In my senior year (1959) I thought we would be just average," said Bolyard in 1991 when he was inducted into the Indiana Basketball Hall of Fame, "but things went together very well and we made it to the semistate, where we lost on a last-second long bomb by Kokomo's Jimmy Rayl. But then, if I had not missed a free throw a bit earlier, we would have won."

Bolyard wasn't a one-sport athlete at South Side. He anchored the state championship mile relay team, finished second in the state in the half-mile and played football.

At Indiana, he was a three-year starter, averaging 18 points per game. When he graduated he was Indiana's No. 10 all-time scorer, earning All-Big Ten honors in 1963, averaging 18 points per game for his career. After graduating from IU, Bolyard signed with the Baltimore Bullets, then decided instead to return to graduate school. He was an assistant at North Side High School for one year and an assistant for five years at IU.

## February 5

**In 1994, Tiffany Gooden's spectacular high school basketball career ends.**

Fort Wayne first became aware of Gooden's abilities when she teamed with Leslie Johnson to help the Decatur Thunderbirds win the 13-and-under national AAU title in 1989. That began a dominating decade for girls basketball in Fort Wayne, and Gooden led the way.

A few years later, Gooden and company won three AAU national titles in four years as part of Mohr Magic.

Gooden's high school career was the best individually in northeast Indiana basketball history. She scored 2,198 points to break the area's career scoring record, including 29.9 points, 13.5 rebounds per game her junior year, and 29.9 points and 9.5 rebounds per game as a senior.

At the culmination of her high school career in 1994 as Indiana's Miss Basketball, Gooden led a late Indiana rally as the Hoosier girls completed a two-game sweep of the Kentucky All-Stars with a 100-92 victory. Gooden's 24 points, coupled with her record 31 points a week earlier, broke the 17-year-old two-game series mark of 54 points.

She was selected as the National Player of the Year by Parade magazine and the Naismith Foundation.

That led to her career at the University of Iowa, where she earned all-Big Ten honors as a sophomore and senior, and conference Freshman of the Year honors. She finished with 1,024 career points, overcoming a second knee injury in her junior year.

After a 13-game stint with the ABL's Colorado Xplosion in 1998, Gooden's pro career ended when the league folded. She's now a successful lawyer in Fort Wayne and president of the Fort Wayne Sports Corporation.

**Also, in 2006, Harding's Trai Essex wins a Super Bowl ring as the Pittsburgh Steelers beat the Seattle Seahawks.**

**February 6**

**In 2005, Jim Steeg retires as the NFL's special events director after 26 years of running the Super Bowl.**

The 1968 Snider High School graduate was the National Football League's vice president for special events from 1979 to 2005, meaning he was in charge of everything around the event - everything.

"Super Bowl XIII was the first one I ever worked with the league," Steeg recalled. "Of all the things, it was supposed to rain that day, and it was a downpour in the morning. I remember going out running around and trying to buy every raincoat we could find in ... town. Everybody was concerned, but magically the rain stopped two hours before kickoff."

Steeg started in the NFL with the Miami Dolphins as an accountant in 1975, the season Pittsburgh and Dallas played Super Bowl X in Miami. NFL Commissioner Pete Rozelle hired him away from the Dolphins in 1979.

During Steeg's 29 years with the NFL, including the final 25 years in charge of the league's special events, the Super Bowl grew from a championship football game to a four-day extravaganza. He has been responsible for all aspects, including stadium and practice-site preparation and build-out; pregame and halftime shows, National Anthem performers; team, media, corporate and fan accommodations, corporate hospitality and everything else imaginable.

Steeg left his position to become executive vice president and chief operating officers of the San Diego Chargers.

**Also, in 2008, Bishop Dwenger gymnast Alicia Roche scores a perfect 10 on the bars.**

Because she was battling the flu, the Saints senior competed only in the bars and floor events during a home meet against Concordia.

Asked what Roche did right, judge Nan Durant, a veteran of more than 30 years, said, "Every single thing. There wasn't a twitch, a moment's hesitation. The other judge (Cristie Slane) and I looked down at our papers, and we looked at each other.

"You can't take what isn't there. Everybody starts with 10 and if you make a mistake we have to deduct, and she didn't make any mistakes – absolutely, breathtakingly perfect."

## February 7

**In 1951, the Zollner Pistons honor Paul "Curly" Armstrong with the first night given to a Fort Wayne athlete.**

Wherever Armstrong played basketball, and later softball, his teams won. He started at St. Paul's Lutheran Grade School where Armstrong began his lifelong friendship with Herm Schaefer. The two grew up together on Madison Street and played together in grade school, high school at Central, college at Indiana University and later in the pros with the Fort Wayne Zollner Pistons.

The two helped lead Central High School to back-to-back appearances in the state Final Four in 1936 and 1937. They lost to Frankfort in the 1936 championship game and to Huntingburg in the 1937 semifinals. Armstrong and Schaefer then helped Indiana win its first national title in 1940. Armstrong scored 10 points as IU beat Kansas 60-42.

In the pros, Armstrong was a 5-foot-11 guard. He signed with the Pistons in 1942 and averaged 8.3 points as a rookie. After his second season, he joined the Navy and played for the Great Lakes Navy team coached by Tony Hinkle.

Armstrong returned to the Pistons in 1946 and continued to average about eight points per game as the team won the world championship. During his 11-year career he averaged 7.4 points per game, and he also coached the Pistons to a 22-32 record in 1948-49.

Armstrong was also a strong player on the Pistons' softball team, helping them win three world championships.

A knee injury eventually led to Armstrong's retirement in 1951. In 1969, he bought the Curly Armstrong Village Inn on Bluffton Road and he died June 6, 1983, at age 64.

**Also, in 2013, South Dakota State's Nate Wolters scores 53 points against IPFW to break the Memorial Coliseum basketball scoring record.**

Wolters made 17 of 28 shots overall, including 9 of 14 from three-point range, and 10 of 11 free throws to break Wilt Chamberlain's record of 51 points set March 8, 1963 against the Detroit Pistons. He out-scored IPFW by himself 38-37 in the second half.

**February 8**

**In 2003, Kendallville's Brad Miller plays in his first NBA All-Star Game**

The East Noble and Purdue product was named as a reserve to the East team while representing the Indiana Pacers. In 17 minutes of playing time, Miller scored five points, grabbed six rebounds and passed three assists as the West won 155-145 in Atlanta.

Amazingly, Miller was not drafted after his senior year at Purdue. The 7-foot center improved each season in West Lafayette, averaging 14.1 points and 8.3 rebounds as a junior and 17.2 points and 8.8 rebounds as a senior. He played in four consecutive NCAA Tournaments and was the first Boilermaker to score 1,500 points, grab 800 rebounds and pass 250 assists.

Because he was undrafted and because of the NBA lockout, Miller started his pro career in Italy before he was signed as a free agent by the Charlotte Hornets. He played two seasons in Charlotte before signing with Chicago where he also played two seasons.

In February 2002, Miller was traded to Indiana where he and Ben Wallace became the first two undrafted players to be named to play in the NBA All-Star Game. The next summer he was part of a sign and trade deal with Sacramento where he had the best years of his career. He averaged 14 points and 10 rebounds during his first season with the Kings, earning another All-Star Game appearance, and a career-high 15.6 points during his second season. After five-and-a-half seasons in Sacramento, he was traded back to Chicago.

Miller played a year-and-a-half with the Bulls before signing with Houston. After one season with the Rockets, he was traded to Minnesota where he played one season in 2011-12.

Miller's NBA career totals included 14 seasons, 868 games, 11.2 points, 7.1 rebounds and 2.8 assists per game. He also played in 50 playoff games.

**Also, in 2001, Isiah Thomas folds the Continental Basketball Association, killing the Fort Wayne Fury.**

## February 9

**In 1966, Merv Dubchak scores his 50th goal in the Komets' 48th game of the season.**

Maybe the most amazing stat about Merv Dubchak's career is that he only played in two all-star games. That was the only way to stop him from scoring.

During his seven years as a Komet, Dubchak scored 321 goals in 437 games. In today's game, a player like that would be an all-star averaging that many points, let alone goals.

What's amazing about this season is that Dubchak kept going and scored 72 goals in 70 games and finished with 117 points. He got help from center Bobby Rivard who passed 91 assists and scored 133 points and linemate John Goodwin had 79 assists and 114 points. That was the top-scoring line in Komets and International Hockey League history.

"'It was one of those years when everything was going in from behind the net, that the puck was bouncing off players," Dubchak told The News-Sentinel's Steve Warden in 1994. "That's all. And I also had two pretty good players with me in Johnny Goodwin and Bobby Rivard."

What's even more amazing about scoring 50 goals in 48 games is that Muskegon's Gary Schall scored his 51$^{st}$ goal in his 47$^{th}$ contest for the Mohawks in the same game. Schall finished with 71 goals in 68 games.

**Also, in 1959, for the first time since they moved to Detroit the Pistons return to Fort Wayne and beat Cincinnati 122-97.**

**February 10**

**In 2011, Erica Cutler sets the women's city bowling record with an 864 series.**

A week before this big night, Doug Cutler had bought his wife a new pair of bowling shoes as a Valentine's Day gift. She decided to try them out early, and what happened was truly magical, as Erica Cutler set the women's city record for a three-game series with an 864 series. Cutler, 28, was competing in the Ladies Minor League at Pro Bowl West. She rolled 32 strikes for a 290, 277, 297 series.

"The first game I missed the first frame, the second game I missed two frames and in the third game I missed the last frame," said Cutler, who is an insurance worker for Pediatric Associates. "The entire bowling alley had stopped bowling and was watching, and I was very nervous."

According to Pro Bowl West, Cutler's series was the third-highest ever by an Indiana woman and the sixth-highest ever in the nation. Cutler's previous high game was a 298 two years ago at Village Bowl, and her previous high series was a 783 in September. Her 224 average was raised three pins by her record-breaking performance.

On her next outing, a week later, Cutler rolled a 641 with a high game of 245.

Cutler's 783 series in September broke the city record, but was topped by Sandy Hall's 785 at Westwood on Jan. 31. Charles Holiness has the overall city record with an 886 set in 2000 when he bowled a pair of 300 games at Westwood. Leo Schweyer previously held the men's record with an 867 set during the 1995-96 season.

Cutler began bowling at age 9 in the junior program at Pro Bowl West. She now competes in two leagues and has won individual, doubles and team championships throughout the city.

"I told him it was because of the new shoes," Erica said of Doug. "Everybody says they are going to go buy new shoes."

## February 11

**In 1991, Indiana Tech basketball player Richard Rutland scores 54 points in a loss to IU-South Bend.**

Rutland hit 21 of 40 from the field, including 9 of 13 from three-point range to set Indiana Tech records for points in a game and most three-pointers, while tying the mark for field goals in a game. Amazingly, the Warriors lost 122-120 to stop a 10-game winning streak.

IU-South Bend's Greg Hitchens, who scored 37 points, hit two free throws with six seconds left to put his team up by five points before Rutland hit one last three-pointer at the buzzer.

Rex Carroll also scored 29 points for Indiana Tech, 18-6.

Rutland finished his career as Indiana Tech's all-time career scoring leader with 2,659 points, breaking the mark of 2,394 set by Ron Ziegler who graduated in 1965.

After averaging 20 points as a senior at Indianapolis Chatard, Rutland's best scoring Indiana Tech season came as a freshman when he averaged 27.2 points. He scored 21.9 as a sophomore, 21.1 as a junior and 22.2 as a senior.

Rutland was inducted into Indiana Tech's Hall of Fame in 1998.

**February 12**

**In 1992, Wayne grad Nate Tubbs scores 10 points and plays strong defense as Minnesota upsets IU in basketball.**

After leaving Wayne, Tubbs was always known more for his defense than his offense, but he hit two big late shots against the Hoosiers to help the Gophers avenge a 46-point loss in Bloomington on Jan. 9.

Minnesota was struggling when Tubbs, a senior, was inserted into the starting lineup. He sank two baskets with five minutes left to give Minnesota a 64-58 lead in a game it won 71-67. He also helped hold Indiana star Damon Bailey scoreless in the game.

Later that season, Tubbs scored his career-high 16 points in a win against Purdue.

Tubbs played 113 games at Minnesota, averaging 3.9 points. He took a fifth year of eligibility to play football at Minnesota as a free safety in 1993 before embarking on a professional international basketball career.

While a senior at Wayne, Tubbs averaged 22.5 points and 10 rebounds to become an Indiana All-Star.

## February 13

**In 1999, Snider swimmer Michala Kwasny wins her fourth straight state title in the 100 butterfly to finish with seven state titles.**

Kwasny won in a season-best time of 55.63 seconds after setting a state record in the 200 individual medley in 2:00.99. She also swam on Snider's fifth-place 200 medley relay team and the second-place 400 freestyle relay team.

At the time, Kwasny was only the seventh Indiana girls swimmer to win a state title in an event all four years, and the second from Fort Wayne after Bishop Dwenger's Lia Oberstar completed a sweep of the 500 freestyle in 1994.

A four-time News-Sentinel PrepSports Swimmer of the Year, Kwasny received a standing ovation from the crowd at the Indiana University Natatorium after her last individual race.

During her college career at Southern California, Kwasny was a 13-time all-American, four-time Pac 10 conference champion and holder of school records in eight events.

**Also, in 1999, 2,653 fans cram the Gates Center as IPFW men's volleyball beats Lewis 3-1 for its first win ever over a No. 1-ranked team.**

IPFW, ranked No. 7 coming into the match and off to its best start in school history at 7-0, used the victory to start a run to another NCAA Tournament berth. The Volleydons tied a school record with 13 aces to drive the home crowd into a frenzy.

After the victory, IPFW jumped to No. 4 in the national polls and eventually beat Lewis three times, including twice on the Flyers' home court.

**February 14**

**In 1957, Fred Zollner announces he will move the NBA Pistons to Detroit.**

For several months, the move had been rumored, and finally confirmation came during the NBA All-Star Game that Fred Zollner was negotiating to move the Pistons to Detroit.

Some fans argued that the NBA was trying to pressure the small-market teams such as Fort Wayne, Syracuse and Rochester to move to bigger markets where they would be more appealing to the growing television market. Actually, the Pistons simply weren't drawing enough fans in Fort Wayne. Fort Wayne had the highest per capita attendance in the NBA at the time, but still averaged only 3,859 fans during their final season in Fort Wayne. Their all-time high average attendance had been 4,745 the season before. The Pistons averaged just 4,024 their last four years in Memorial Coliseum with teams that reached the NBA Finals twice and made the playoffs the other two seasons..

"Let's say that we have been division champions for two years and are now leading the league and still have 6,000 empty seats," Zollner said. "What would happen if we were trailing?"

Zollner had the option of taking some of his final regular-season or even playoff games to Detroit for a test run, but he kept the rest of the schedule in Fort Wayne, where, ironically, the NBA was born.

Some blamed coach Charley Eckman for the move, and were somewhat pleased when he was fired after the Pistons got off to a 9-16 start in their first Detroit season. Others, perhaps correctly, realized Zollner needed to move some of his business interests closer to Detroit where his pistons were in great demand from the automobile industry.

**Also, in 2003, Elmhurst ends Bishop Luers' run of four straight girls basketball state titles.**

**February 15**

**In 1924, New Haven wins the first Allen County Tournament basketball title.**

The longest-running high school conference basketball tournament in Indiana continues every January, culminating with the championship games at Memorial Coliseum.

The Allen County Tournament actually started in 1924 at New Haven High School. The first schools participating were Arcola, Elmhurst, Harlan, Hoagland, Huntertown, Leo, Lafayette Central, Monroeville, New Haven and Woodburn.

In the final day of play, New Haven beat Leo 15-14 and Monroeville beat Lafayette Central 46-17 in the semifinals before New Haven won the championship game 22-7, holding the Cubs to only two field goals.

New Haven went on to win five tournament titles over the first 10 years. Since the beginning, 21 schools have participated and 19 have won championships.

The tournament was held at New Haven, Monroeville and Woodburn's gyms until moving to Central High School's gym in 1931. The New Haven Community Building became the tournament home in 1937 and it stayed there until the coliseum opened in 1952.

The championship game was broadcast on radio starting in 1941 and was televised from 1954 to 1994 on WKJG. In 1968, color cameras were used for the first time to broadcast a ballgame.

The first girls tournament was held in 1974.

In 1989 and 1991, New Haven hosted the Allen County Nostalgia Tournament to raise money for the New Haven Little League.

**Also, in 2004, East Noble product Brad Miller plays in his second NBA All-Star Game.**

**February 16**

**In 1988, figure skaters Wayne and Kim Seybold finish 10th in mixed pairs at the Calgary Olympics.**

Though the Seybolds were from Marion, for almost 10 years Jean Seybold drove her children 500 miles per week to practice at McMillen Park Ice Arena under Nancy Ruedebusch. The Seybolds competed in four U.S. Nationals championships, earning three medals, and competed in four World Championships where they earned a bronze medal in 1986. The highlight of their career was qualifying for the 1988 Olympics in Calgary where they finished 10th.

After the 1988 Olympics, the Seybolds retired from competitive skating, but continued as professionals with the Ice Capades and on various tours. In 1994 they were leading cast members of the "Nutcracker on Ice."

**Also, in 1991, IPFW's men's basketball team wins its biggest game ever to that point, beating Division II No. 7-ranked Bellarmine 92-89 before a packed house.**

Sean Gibson scored 23 points and grabbed 12 rebounds, and Duane Shears scored 22 points as coach Andy Piazza became the winning basketball coach in IPFW history.

**February 17**

**In 2007, Megan King's spectacular high school basketball career ends.**

King completed her Canterbury career as the state's second-leading scorer this past season and the third-leading all-time scorer with 2,652 points behind Shanna Zolman's 3,085 and Stephanie White's 2,869.

Along with her 27 points per game as a senior, King also averaged four assists and four steals. She finished second in the state in scoring that season, leading the Cavaliers to the No. 3 ranking.

During her last three years, King finished second in the state in scoring twice and led the state as a junior. She averaged 26.2 points for her high school career, at the time becoming the all-time leading scorer in Allen County for girls or boys.

Her high game was 43 points to open her senior season against Wayne.

King continued her college career at the College of Charleston in South Carolina and eventually came home to become an assistant coach at Canterbury.

During her career at the College of Charleston, King played 50 games, scoring 114 points and grabbing 37 rebounds.

**February 18**

**In 1965, a boys basketball showdown between Ossian and Garrett draws 8,013 fans to the Memorial Coliseum.**

Both teams were 17-1 and were led by some excellent individual players. The "big" draws were Garrett forwards Jim Heitz and Chuck Bavis. Heitz, a senior, measured 6-10, a Bavis, a junior, measured 6-11. Because Garrett games were so popular to casual fans, four games that year were moved to the coliseum. This game turned out to be the second-largest crowd ever to see a high school basketball game in Fort Wayne behind the 1958 sectional game between Central and South Side.

After losing their second game of the season at Waterloo, the Railroaders had a 15-game winning streak heading into Fort Wayne. They easily made it 16 straight with an 87-56 win. The streak eventually reached 21 games before the Railroaders lost in the semistate.

Bavis was a major star who eventually topped 7-feet and earned a scholarship to Purdue after scoring 1,463 points during his high school career, averaging 33 points as a senior. Six of the Railroaders' 1965-66 games were played at the coliseum. Garrett completed the regular season during his senior year undefeated, and the streak reached 24 games before it was ended with a loss to South Side and Willie Long in the regional.

Bavis had a strong career at Purdue, starting at center in the 1969 season that saw the Boilermakers win the Big Ten title and advance to the NCAA Tournament final against Lew Alcindor and UCLA. The only problem was that Bavis had suffered a broken shoulder in the regional. That injury and an automobile accident ended Bavis's career.

**Also, in 1957, the Detroit Red Wings play the IHL All-Stars in Fort Wayne.**

**Also, in 2004, Elmhurst's James Hardy breaks Tom Baack's all-time Allen County basketball career scoring record.**

**February 19**

**In 1983, the coliseum hosts its first girls basketball semistate.**

This came about because of the popularity of the Heritage and Bishop Luers girls basketball teams in the early 1980s which regularly sold out the Harding Sectional.

There had been speculation the tournament would move to another city if a gym with a larger capacity than Northrop's 3,200 seats could not be found. Hundreds of fans were turned away from the 1982 semistate when it was held in the Bruins' gym.

The move led to some fantastic showdowns for fans as first Heritage and then Northrop and Snider represented Fort Wayne teams in the semistate against such powers as Kokomo, Warsaw, Huntington North and Columbia City.

Northrop (1986), Snider (1988), Huntington North (1990), Kokomo (1992), Kokomo (1993) and Huntington North (1995) were all state championship teams that came through the Fort Wayne semistate at the coliseum. The crowds were massive and often out-drew the boys tournament which would be held a month later.

Among the great games was a No. 2 vs. No. 1 meeting between Northrop and Kokomo in 1993. Northrop had beaten Kokomo 54-50 in 1991, but the Wildkats came back to win 70-62 in 1992 on their way to the state title. In 1993, the No. 2 Bruins were 24-0 and the No. 1 Wildkats were 25-1 with their only loss coming to a Chicago team. Kokomo raced out to a 27-9 first-quarter lead and won 78-58 as Miss Basketball Tiffany Longsworth scored 26 points..

**Also, in 1962 Terry Dischinger scores 34 as Purdue beats Notre Dame 115-64.**

**February 20**

**In 1959, Sammy Kreigh of Lafayette Central establishes an Allen County basketball scoring record with 51 points against West Union High School.**

At the time of Kreigh's senior season, Lafayette Central held fewer than 100 students, and there were only 21 in the graduating class. Coached by Max Amstutz, the Pirates were pretty good despite their lack of numbers. After going 21-21 during Kreigh's sophomore and junior seasons, the Pirates were 14-6 during his senior year.

Though only 5-foot-9, Kreigh was a gifted shooter and ballhandler, scoring 1,254 points during his career. He also led the team in assists.

Kreigh's record of 51 points lasted better than 40 years, until Dec. 9, 2002, when Elmhurst's James Hardy scored 57 against Harding.

After high school, Kreigh played one season at Nebraska before coming home to finish up at Huntington College.

**Also, in 2007, longtime WKJG broadcaster Dick DeFay passes away.**

DeFay came to Fort Wayne in 1955 as a booth announcer for WKJG radio and television. He eventually became a sports anchor and later sports director for WKJG television until he retired in 1996.

In 2004, DeFay was inducted into the Komets Hall of Fame. He later called the induction the biggest honor he received in his broadcasting career.

**Also, in 1993, Leslie Johnson ends her Northrop career as Allen County's all-time leading basketball scorer.**

## February 21

**In 1987, Northrop's girls basketball team wins the semistate for another trip to state and a state-record 57th game in a row.**

During the 1980s, winning the Northrop Sectional and regional for girls basketball were like trying to survive a gauntlet. First, in the sectional, Northrop, Snider and Bishop Dwenger were always ranked, which meant two ranked teams were going home during the first week of tournament play. The regional was just as difficult as Heritage in 1982, Northrop in 1986 and Snider in 1988 went on to win the state championship, the only regional in the state to produce three champions during the 1980s.

Coached by Dave Riley, Northrop was always in the title mix. The Bruins put together two remarkable seasons, going 29-0 in 1986 and 28-1 in 1987. Northrop crushed Indianapolis Roncalli 50-36 in the semifinals before edging Scottsburg 58-55 in the 1986 finals to become the sixth girls team to finish undefeated.

The Bruins were loaded with talent that season, led by 1987 Miss Basketball Lori Meinerding, Jenny Bull, Jill Ramsey, Vanessa Williams, Cindi Westendorf, Regina Johnson and Michelle Starks.

Riley went 346-87 from 1979 to 1998 at Northrop with 10 SAC titles, seven sectional championships, seven regional crowns and two semistate titles. That earned him induction into the Indiana Basketball Hall of Fame in 2008. He's the 2011 recipient of the Nancy Rehm Award, which goes to those who have excelled in women's athletics.

Meinerding averaged 17.7 points and 12.6 rebounds as a junior, and 17.7 points, 10 rebounds and four assists during her senior season when she actually got less playing time because the Bruins were so dominant.

**Also, in 1998, Bishop Dwenger's Anton Talamantes wins his second state wrestling title.**

**February 22**

**In 1980, Komets Mark Wells and Steve Janaszak help the United States hockey team upset the Russians in the Olympics.**

Wells was the last man named to the team that created history, and scored two goals and played a vital defensive role in the Olympics. Janaszak backed up starting goaltender Jim Craig.

Both men were highlighted in the movie "Miracle" which came out in 2004. In particular, Wells said the movie helped him come to peace with the way coach Herb Brooks used him during the run up to the Olympics. Brooks sent Wells to the minor leagues several times before naming him to the team just before the games started in Lake Placid, N.Y.

"The movie was so accurate that it made me feel like I got a monkey off my back," Wells said. "I understand him more so now than I ever did, even though I talked to him for years. Once you see the movie, you'll understand where I come from and what we went through as players. He tried to push us to a level beyond what we knew, and the results show what happened."

A goaltender with the Komets during the 1980-81 season, Janaszak was 9-5-1 in pre-Olympic play but sat the bench in Lake Placid behind Jim Craig.

"I know the ending, we all know the ending, but even more than that I know the process," Janaszak said. "I lived through how that was all put together, and they take this story and in two hours pull all those emotions out of me."

**Also, in 1997, Bishop Dwenger's Anton Talamantes wins the first of his two state wrestling titles.**

The Bishop Dwenger product had a remarkable high school career, finishing second in the state as a sophomore and winning state titles as a junior at 215 pounds and as a senior at 189 pounds. As a junior and senior, he won his last 67 consecutive matches and was 108-1 over his last three years. He won a junior college national championship at Lasson, Calif. before going to Ohio State where he qualified for the NCAA Tournament twice.

**February 23**

**In 1985, Elmhurst's Oliver Richmond wins the second of his back-to-back state wrestling titles.**

After choosing wrestling over basketball, Richmond won an amazing 64 consecutive matches during his two-year run, but almost lost at the last second in his attempt for a second title.

During the championship match against Merrillville junior Tom Magiers, Richmond led 5-4 with 19 seconds remaining when Magiers executed a takedown that would have given him a 6-5 lead. The referee ruled the move was legitimate, but the two mat judges overruled the call, saying the move came out of bounds.

With two seconds remaining when he was called for stalling. That gave a point to Magiers and tied the score, but Richmond somehow scored a takedown in those final moments to win the match 7-5.

Richmond finished his senior year with a 33-0 record. He won his first title in the 105-pound division and came back the next year to claim the 112-pound championship. He finished with a 110-10-1 career record.

He went on to wrestle at Ferris State University in Big Rapids, Mich., where he was a two-time letter-winner and made the All-America team in the 188-pound division.

Richmond was inducted into the Indiana Wrestling Hall of Fame in 2001.

**February 24**

**In 1996, gymnast Laura Szczepanski of Bishop Dwenger scores a perfect 10 on the balance beam.**

This came during the Summit Athletic Conference meet, and the odd thing was Szczepanski said that during warm-ups she had no feel for the beam at all. It might have been the defending state champions all-time best meet, too, as she also scored a 9.95 on the floor exercise, won all four events and posted a 38.85 to win the all-around competition.

"She was always just beautiful," Rose Nix said. "In 1996 she was the last one up on beam at state and it was almost like there was an aura around her. She was very graceful, very poised and there was not a flaw. She brought you into her routine. You couldn't look away because everything was so precise and perfect and beautiful. Every little detail was perfect."

Long-time gymnastics judge Nan Durant had the honor of evaluating both performances.

"When she stepped on the floor, she owned it," Durant said. "In gymnastics we want to see people who can take it to the edge and control it. Our job is that everybody starts at a 10 and you pick away at it as they make mistakes, if their amplitude isn't complete, if they aren't stretched enough. If you sit there and watch someone who never makes a mistake, how can you take that away from them?"

Szczepanski had also earned a perfect 10 on the floor exercise at the 1995 SAC meet.

**Also, in 1999, Bishop Dwenger gymnast Betsy Minix scores a perfect 10 on the vault.**

During a meet at Homestead, Minix, a sophomore, executed a perfect handspring into a front tuck, and then rotated 1½ times before sticking her landing. If that wasn't enough, she did it again on her second vault and received another 10!

"Betsy was this bundle of energy," Saints coach Rose Nix said. "I remember when she was running down that runway and literally exploded off the vault and then she came down and planted that landing. It was just crazy, crazy good."

## February 25

**In 1974, Eugene Parker scores 45 points against Wayne in the boys basketball sectional opener.**

Parker made 18 of 32 shots from the field and nine of 12 from the free throw line to break the sectional record of 39 points set by South Side's Tom Bolyard against Central in 1959. He scored 30 points in the second half as Concordia won 73-61 to advance to a game two days later against South Side. This time Parker scored 37 but the Cadets lost 81-79.

Parker finished his high school career with 1,503 points.

**Also, in 1984, Ricky Hall and Greg Eifert help Purdue beat Illinois on the way to the Big Ten basketball title.**

The Boilermakers were picked to finish ninth in the Big Ten, but Jim Rowinski, Mark Atkinson, Steve Reid, Hall and Eifert surprised everyone. Hall and Eifert were outstanding defensive players in college. In fact, Hall was named the Big Ten Defensive Player of the Year that season. After a 7-3 non-conference record, the Boilermakers won the title with a 15-3 mark.

**Also, in 1988, Churubusco basketball player Jeff Perlich scores 54 points in a game against Fort Wayne Christian, less than a month after he scored 52 against West Noble.**

Perlich finished his career with 2,019 points.

**February 26**

**In 1941, the Zollner Pistons basketball team begins to become a national force by winning a spot in the upcoming World Championships in Chicago.**

The Pistons beat a scrappy International Harvester team 37-35 in overtime at the G.E. Club Gym. IH led the entire game until Zollner rallied to tie at 31 and force the overtime. Dale Hamilton and Hans Dienelt led the Pistons with nine points while Bob Irons led International Harvester with 14 points.

This was the start of Fred Zollner's dream to build a basketball powerhouse in Fort Wayne. There were 16 teams competing in the national tournament, including the Harlem Globetrotters, the New York Rens and the Philadelphia Hebrews. The Pistons lost their first game to the Oshkosh All-Stars 47-41. Oshkosh made it all the way to the championship game before losing to the Detroit Eagles 39-37.

What's ironic is that many of the players in this tournament eventually became Pistons, players like Ed Sadowski, Buddy Jeannette and Carlisle (Blackie) Towery.

The next year the Pistons joined the National Basketball League and two years later were playing in the league finals. In 1944 they won their first world championship.

**Also, in 1995, Laura Szcezpanski of Bishop Dwenger earns her first perfect 10 on the floor exercise at the Summit Athletic Conference gymnastics meet.**

## February 27

**In 1982, Heritage wins the girls state basketball title.**

The impact of one title run has reverberated throughout history as a group of girls from Heritage made it OK to watch, and even like, girls basketball.

People who never gave the girls game a chance were lining up to buy tickets to the Harding Sectional. Many scoffed, claiming too many turnovers and airballs and not enough defense and athletic ability, but the fans were turned on to the game by the Patriots' underdog story.

The Patriots were unranked as they started their state title run. They beat Summit Athletic Conference champ Bishop Luers in the sectional, breaking the Knights' 16-game winning streak; Norwell and DeKalb in the regional; and No. 2 Columbia City and No. 5 Marion in the semistate. At state, they beat Sullivan 66-55, but fell behind early to Valparaiso before winning the title 52-45. Heritage finished 24-2.

"'We were just at the right time, and girls basketball took off," said Heritage Coach Cheri Gilbert. "A lot of it had to do with the girls because they were athletic and very personable."

As Northrop Coach Dave Riley said, "They gave us all the idea that maybe the dream could be accomplished up here. We knew they were very good and (if) we got up there to that kind of level we would have a chance to do what they did."

The Patriots' winning streak reached 35 games the next year before they lost to Crown Point in the state semifinals.

The next year, the girls semistate moved from Northrop to the Memorial Coliseum.

**Also, in 1988, Snider wins the state girls basketball championship.**

LaMar Kilmer's Panthers were loaded with talent and they needed all of it to beat Noblesville 60-58 in the state title game. Individual stars included Donna and Bonnie Gill, Lori Stinson, Yalonda Naylor, Jenny Herman, Missy Conrad and Trisha Patterson.

The Panthers finished 27-1 as Donna Gill blocked a Noblesville shot with one second left.

**February 28**

**In 1948, Monroeville becomes the first county school to win a basketball sectional.**

More than 60 years after their accomplishment, the Monroeville Cubs' legend continues to grow.

For decades the Fort Wayne city schools dominated the boys basketball sectional until the Cubs became the first county school to win the title in 1948. They beat Central Catholic, Woodburn and North Side to improve to 21-3 and set up a battle with city champion Central, led by Johnny Bright and Dick Miller.

Coach Bill Milliner's Cubs used only six players in the final two games of the sectional, starters Dick Reinking, Roland Lee Merritt Myers, Don Lehrman and Gene Rhodes were backed up by Byron Beucler after Reinking fouled out. Lehrman was the only senior. The other team members were Bob Hullinger, Tom Brown, Jim Giant and Stan Shaffer.

Central took a 20-19 halftime lead. Just as it did against North Side in the semifinals, Monroeville took the lead in the third quarter with a 13-4 run and won 38-32. Myers led the Cubs with 11 points followed by 10 from Lee and nine from Rhodes.

After a big celebration in North Side's gym, the Monroeville fans returned home for a bonfire that lasted until 3 a.m. The celebration continued the next week when the Cubs beat Milford and Garrett to win the regional title. Monroeville's run ended the next week as Muncie Central took the semistate.

The next year the Cubs went undefeated until they lost to Central in a sectional rematch.

Monroeville's miracle lasted as the only county sectional victory until 1979, when Jim Master and Harding won.

**Also, in 1990, the Fort Wayne Sports Corporation is formed.**

**Also, in 1987, the Northrop girls basketball team loses in the state semifinals to end its record 57-game winning streak.**

## February 29

**In 1996, the CBA's Fury pull off the Memorial Miracle, beating Yakima 103-98**

The Fort Wayne Fury usually played better at home, something coach Gerald Oliver used to call "Memorial Magic," but on this night they needed something more. With 6:42 left in the third quarter, the Fury trailed 70-49 after the Sun Kings finished off a 17-6 run. Then, thanks mostly to Evric Gray, Fort Wayne started to turn things around.

Though he didn't start the game, Gray finished with 39 points, hitting 16 of 24 from the field and 7 of 8 free throws. After the Fury cut the Yakima margin to 14 points at the end of the third quarter to bring the crowd back into the action, Gray scored 14 points in the fourth quarter on a variety of drives, tip-ins and jump shots. As a team, Fort Wayne hit 15 of 19 shots in the fourth quarter while holding the Sun Kings to 7 of 19.

The Fury tied the game at 90 with 5:16 remaining on a Duane Cooper layup off a fastbreak, and Gray put them ahead on the next possession. A pair of free throws each by Damon Bailey and Cooper in the final minute gave the Fury a little cushion. When Gray blocked a shot by Yakima's Willie Sims with 16 seconds remaining, the Memorial Coliseum fans could start celebrating the 103-98 win and the biggest comeback in Fury history. It was Fort Wayne's seventh win in a row at home and ninth in 10 games.

After the Yakima lead got to 21 points, the Fury out-scored the Sun Kings 54-28 the rest of the game. Eric Anderson added 20 points and 13 rebounds for Fort Wayne.

This was just the start of good things happening for the team this season, as they finished second to Grand Rapids in the division to make the playoffs.

# MARCH

## March 1

**In 1958, South Side and Central play what many say is the greatest high school basketball game in Fort Wayne history.**

The game pitted No. 1-ranked South Side against No. 3 Central in the 1958 sectional semifinal. It also matched two hall of fame coaches, three Mr. Basketballs and seven Indiana all-stars. It was played before 9,418 Memorial Coliseum fans in an atmosphere so intense that a number of people fainted. And it went into overtime, and the winner went on to easily win the state title.

The first time South Side and Central played that season, Jan. 15, a record crowd of 9,012 crammed into the coliseum on a Wednesday. Trailing by 10 at halftime, No. 8 South Side rallied to beat No. 4 Central 72-63 and climb to the top of the polls the next week.

When the teams met for the rematch Feb. 14, the Archers were still ranked No. 1, but the Tigers had climbed to No. 2. This time a "disappointing" Friday night crowd of 8,412 watched as South Side's balance out-dueled Central's duo of John Kelso and Ben Hawkins.

Central coach Herb Banet had a wonderful 18-3 squad led by Parade All-American Kelso, still considered by many – including many of the Archers – to be Fort Wayne's best basketball player ever. He was joined in the Tigers' rotation by Tharnell Hollins, Bill Boyd, Ron Brubaker, Steve Hatch, Norm Beers, T.C. Williams, Frank Smith, Percy Moore and Hawkins.

Don Reichert's South Side squad, 20-2, countered with an iron-man five of Mike McCoy, Tom Bolyard, Carl Stavreti, Rich Miller and Dan Howe. All five starting Archers were named all-city that season and averaged in double figures.

The sectional game was tied 56-56 at the end of regulation before Bolyard scored all four South Side points in overtime as the Archers won 60-56. Kelso finished with 21 points and 14 rebounds, Bolyard scored 22 points.

South Side went on to crush Crawfordsville 63-34 in the state title game, still the second-largest margin in championship game history, on their way to a 28-2 record.

**Also, in 1986, Northrop wins the girls basketball state title.**

## March 2

**In 2002, Bishop Luers wins a girls state basketball title for the fourth straight year.**

After winning the first three titles in Class 2A under coach Gary Andrews, the Knights came back under Teri Rosinski to win the Class 3A title by beating Gibson Southern 51-37 at Conseco Fieldhouse. Senior Megan Dossen won her fourth individual title, and junior Michelle King and senior Michelle Hamlin each won for the third time.

It's the first time in IHSAA history that a school won four straight titles in either the boys or the girls state tournaments.

The Knights' starting lineup was Dossen, Hamlin, King, sophomore Jessica Hathaway and freshman Stephanie Gerardot. Individually, all five players are among the best in Bishop Luers history.

Besides playing for a new coach, moving up a class and adding some new players, this title was also unique because this squad lost five games, more than the previous three teams combined, finishing with a 21-5 record. The Knights lost to Leo, Northrop, Snider, Huntington North and Concordia during the regular season.

The biggest test of this season came against Concordia in the regional. The Cadets had beaten the Knights 71-54 at Bishop Luers to win the Summit Athletic Conference title, but the Knights won the rematch in the state tournament, 51-26, in the regional.

The 2002-03 Knights finished 22-3 and won the SAC tournament and regular-season titles, but lost to NorthWood 50-40 in the regional championship game.

**Also, in 1991, the boys sectional basketball title games are held at the Memorial Coliseum for the last time.**

**Also, in 1991, New Haven's boys basketball team wins its first sectional title.**

## March 3

**In 1980, Jim Master scores 38 and Greg Eifert 37 as Harding beats Bishop Dwenger 79-77 in the sectional.**

Two of the great players in Fort Wayne history went head-to-head before a large Memorial Coliseum crowd. The Saints led early, but Master got hot in the second half to lead the Hawks to the victory, icing the game at the free throw line.

Master scored 611 points as a senior, averaging 27.8 points to break the city single-season scoring record on his way to winning Mr. Basketball honors. No one could stop him from outside, and he scored 30 points in a half against South Side during the Summit Athletic Conference tournament.

Eifert was just as good from the inside. He averaged 26.8 points per game, including scoring 46 one night against Northridge. By the time his career was over, he held 11 Bishop Dwenger records.

Master hit 15 of 30 shot in the battle, while Eifert made 10 of 23. Steve Driver added 16 for the Hawks, and Casey Newell scored 11 for the Saints. The crowd for the game was 4,721.

The sectional was a culmination of a fantastic year in Fort Wayne basketball as Harding, Bishop Dwenger, Concordia, Northrop, North Side and South Side were all ranked at some point during the season. More than 28,000 fans attended the five-session sectional basketball tournament, including more than 6,000 for the two title games. Northrop and South Side won the sectional titles, with the Archers taking the regional crown.

Both Eifert and Master were named all-state and led Indiana against Kentucky in the all-star series.

Master played college basketball at Kentucky, where he became the last Fort Wayne player to participate in a Final Four in 1984. Eifert went to Purdue where he helped the Boilermakers win the 1984 Big Ten title after being picked to finish ninth in the preseason.

## March 4

**In 1978, the Purdue careers of Eugene Parker and Walter Jordan come to an end.**

Though they often do not receive the recognition for it, the senior class of Parker, Jordan and Wayne Walls was a very important one in the history of Purdue basketball.

Before they arrived, the Boilermakers had not made the NCAA Tournament since their runner-up season in 1969. Purdue finished 17-11 during their freshman season as Jordan averaged 14 points. Purdue went 16-11 during their sophomore season followed by 19-9 and 16-11. By the time they graduated, Jordan ranked fourth among Purdue's all-time leading scorers with 1,813 points and Parker was sixth with 1,430 points.

Parker was Purdue's Most Valuable Player during their sophomore season, and then Jordan won the honor the next two years. The Boilermakers won three of their last four games against Indiana.

Jordan and Parker led Purdue to one NCAA Tournament appearance when the Boilermakers lost in the 1977 first round to North Carolina 69-66 in Raleigh, N.C.

As Jordan's scoring average increased to 18.6 points as a junior and 17.0 as a senior, Jordan was twice named all-Big Ten. By the time he graduated, he ranked in Purdue's top 10 career lists in almost every category including scoring, rebounds and games played.

Parker, a second-team all-Big Ten performer in 1976, was one of the first combo guards who could run the offense from the point but also score. He also ranks seventh all-time on the Purdue career assists list.

Both Parker and Jordan were drafted by the NBA, and both have been inducted into the Indiana Basketball Hall of Fame.

**Also, in 1999, Sam Gensic of Carroll scores 41 points in a sectional win over Peru.**

## March 5

**In 1931, WGL broadcasts the first professional basketball game.**

When the Fort Wayne Hoosiers made the American Basketball League playoff finals in 1931, it was big news, especially since the Hoosiers were playing in the finals for the third time in four years. In fact, the Fort Wayne Basketball Association sponsored a radio play-by-play of the first game at Brooklyn, including pre-game interviews. It is believed to be the first time ever a professional basketball game was broadcast live on radio.

There had been previous games where reporters would call in reports while the contest had been in action. One of those reporters was Gunnar Elliott, who made the live calls on this game. According to reports, Elliott sat in a small booth at one end of the 23rd Armory in Brooklyn.

According to Todd Gould's book "Pioneers of the Hardwood," "the broadcast was unrefined and filled with static, but it was live."

Fort Wayne lost the game and the series. Led by Homer Stonebraker and Benny Borgman, they turned Fort Wayne into a basketball hotbed. Stonebraker, a 6-foot-4 center, was called the best basketball player alive by Abe Saperstein of the Harlem Globetrotters, and Borgman led the ABL in scoring five times, with a high of 11.2 points in 1927. Future Indiana coach Branch McCracken was also a member of the 1931 team.

Maybe the highlight for the Hoosiers was beating the world-famous New York Rens on Jan. 27, 1929, a shocking upset at the time.

Shortly after the 1931 series, the Hoosiers and the league disbanded, ending a near decade-long run as one of the nation's best pro teams. Most of the teams returned to barnstorming.

## March 6

**In 2010, Fort Wayne hosts the IHSAA Girls Basketball state finals for the first time and Concordia and Canterbury win titles.**

When Indiana High School Athletic Association officials first approached Fort Wayne and Memorial Coliseum about the possibility of hosting the girls basketball state finals, it was supposed to be a filler year. The Big Ten Tournament had knocked the state finals out of Conseco Fieldhouse, and the IHSAA needed someone to fill in.

This was a lot better than that.

The coliseum hosted 12,564 fans who watched three terrific basketball games and one horrific blowout. Fortunately for the home crowd, the three great games involved Fort Wayne schools. Canterbury won its third straight Class A title, beating Vincennes Rivet 69-65. Concordia Lutheran won its first Class 3A title over No. 1 Rushville, 59-48. Bishop Luers came up a couple of plays short in a 70-65 overtime loss to Austin in Class 2A. Ben Davis romped over Merrillville 99-52 in the Class 4A game.

Complaints were few and far between, and limited publicly to Vincennes Rivet coach Tim Young. Canterbury beat previously undefeated Vincennes Rivet for the second straight time in the title game. The Rivet fans had the farthest to travel at 262 miles.

"I liked it; it just felt homey to me," Rushville coach Melissa Marlow said. "Our home crowd was pretty much on top of us. The cheer block was able to be close by. I love the coliseum."

The Fort Wayne-Allen County Convention and Visitors Bureau, Fort Wayne Sports Corp., Gym Rats and Vera Bradley teamed up to organize Fan Fest, a free event to help local and visiting fans celebrate the Friday before the tournament at Spiece Fieldhouse.

Dan O'Connell, president and CEO of the Visitors Bureau, estimated before the tournament the economic impact of Fort Wayne playing host to the finals at $300,000 to $400,000.

The tournament came back the next year, but Bishop Luers was the only local team competing and attendance dropped to 8,019 for the four games. Bishop Luers won the Class 2A title with a 59-46 win over Brownstown Central.

## March 7

**In 1999, baseball manager John "Red" Braden dies.**

If "Red" Carrington was Fort Wayne's godfather of baseball, then Braden was its patron saint.

A Wells County native, Braden was asked to take over the General Electric semi-pro team 1942. The Voltmen won the 1945 state championship but that was just the start of their title runs.

Braden managed teams sponsored by Capehart, GE, North American Van Lines and Allen Dairy and scheduled 12 major league teams into Fort Wayne during this time, including the Phillies, St. Louis Browns, the Senators, the Reds, the Boston Braves and the White Sox, and won six of these exhibition games. He is enshrined in the Fort Wayne and National Baseball Congress halls of fame.

When the GE sponsorship ended in 1949, Capehart-Farnsworth eventually took over, and the Capes went on to win the 1950 world championship. It won the title in Tokyo at a stadium packed with 60,000 fans. Mrs. Douglas MacArthur, wife of the great army general, threw out the first ball.

Braden broke the color barrier by hiring black players Pat Scantlebury and Jim LaMarque for the simple reason that they were great players. The 1950 squad had won Braden's fourth consecutive national semi-pro championship.

Maybe Braden's greatest accomplishment was directing the Allen Dairy team to the 1956 world title. After winning a fifth national title, the team advanced to and won the World Series in Milwaukee County Stadium.

Braden was inducted into the Fort Wayne Oldtimers Baseball Association Hall of Fame in 1965, and in 1993, at the age of 82, he purchased the first season ticket to the new Fort Wayne Wizards.

Braden passed away March 7, 1999, at the age of 89.

**Also, in 2009, Elmhurst girls basketball wins the school's first state title.**

**Also, in 1993, Tiffany Gooden and Leslie Johnson are both named Parade All-Americans.**

## March 8

**In 1922, the Fort Wayne Caseys upset the New York Celtics traveling basketball team.**

The barnstorming Celtics had an incredible record, but the Caseys shocked the nation by winning 21-17 at the Concordia College gym. The Caseys were led by 6-foot-4 Homer Stonebreaker who scored 16 points.

Before the contest, Stonebreaker told the local media he had dreamed the Caseys would win the game, so forever after Stonebreaker's nickname was "The Big Dreamer."

Stonebreaker was possibly the state's first big man star. He led Wingate High School to a pair of state championships in 1913 and 1914, scoring 18 points of Wingate's 36 points in the 1914 title game. Stonebreaker, who also starred as a three-time all-American at Wabash College, was also part of the inaugural Indiana Basketball Hall of Fame class in 1962, and was also named one of Indiana's 50 greatest players in 1999.

The Fort Wayne Knights of Columbus formed a professional team in 1919 known as the Caseys. Teams played in wire or rope cages about 12 feet high that surrounded the court and had a door at either end. Cages were predominant on the East Coast but not in the Midwest, but this is how basketball players came to be known as "Cagers."

The Celtics won the rematch a night later 48-23 as Stonebreaker was held to nine points.

According to Todd Gould's book "Pioneers of the Hardwood," the Caseys put up $2,500 to host the games and tickets cost $1.50 but the games sold out in two days.

The Celtics, not related to the NBA franchise in Boston, were credited with bringing basketball to national attention during a 205-game barnstorming tour across the country when they went 193-11-1. They went 67-4 the next year, 94-6 in 1924-25 and 90-12 in 1925-26, According to the Basketball Hall of Fame, the Original Celtics are credited with many innovations, including the post play, zone defenses, and switching man-to-man defenses.

The Celtics also beat the Fort Wayne Hoosiers 3-1 in the finals of the American Basketball League championships in 1928, winning the final game 27-26.

**Also, in 1956, the Pistons clinch the Western Division title with a win over the Minneapolis Lakers.**

**Also, in 1963, Wilt Chamberlain scores 51 points in Philadephia's win over the Detroit Pistons.**

## March 9

**In 1963, Tom Bolyard ends his brilliant basketball career at Indiana.**

As Central Catholic coach Terry Coonan once said, "Bolyard can tie his shoestrings without bending over."

And Tom Bolyard knew how to use those long arms. At 6-foot-4, he was a force inside on a basketball court. Bolyard scored 1,420 points in his three years at South Side High School and then 1,299 points at IU.

He was also a starting forward on South Side's 1958 state champions as a junior. That team -- which also featured Dan Howe, Mike McCoy, Rich Miller and Carl Stavreti in its starting lineup -- lost only to Muncie Central and Michigan City before winning its last 20 games in a row.

As a senior, Bolyard was named to the Parade All-America team and was the Most Valuable Player in the Indiana-Ohio All-Star game.

"In my senior year (1959) I thought we would be just average," said Bolyard in 1991, "but things went together very well and we made it to the semistate, where we lost on a last-second long bomb by Kokomo's Jimmy Rayl. But then, if I had not missed a free throw a bit earlier, we would have won."

Bolyard wasn't a one-sport athlete at South Side. He anchored the state championship mile relay team, finished second in the state in the half-mile and played football.

At Indiana, he was a three-year starter, averaging 18 points per game. When he graduated, Bolyard was Indiana's No. 10 all-time scorer, earning all-Big Ten honors in 1963. After graduating from IU, Bolyard signed with the Baltimore Bullets, then decided instead to return to graduate school. He was an assistant at North Side High School for one year and an assistant for five years at IU.

**Also, in 1954, Notre Dame beats Loyola, (La.) 80-70 and Penn State beats Toledo 60-52 in an NCAA Tournament doubleheader.**

**Also, in 1996, Lisa Winter of Huntington North is named Miss Basketball.**

## March 10

**In 1961, Wilt Chamberlain scores his 3,000th point of the season before 10,018 Memorial Coliseum fans.**

During his rookie season the year before, Chamberlain scored 2,102 points in only 56 games to break the all-time regular season scoring record of Bob Pettit, who once scored 2,101 points in 72 games.

Chamberlain shattered that record the next season, averaging a record 38.4 points per game to finish with 3,033. His record has lasted ever since. In fact, the next and only player to ever score at least 3,000 points in a season was Michael Jordan who set the new record with 3,041 in 1986-87.

After moving to Detroit in 1958, the Pistons sometimes played two or three games a season in Fort Wayne, including this one. Despite 32 points and 35 rebounds from Chamberlain, the Philadelphia Warriors lost to the Pistons 120-103. After scoring 67 points the night before against New York, Chamberlain needed 16 points to hit the mark and scored a turnaround jumper from 15 feet with 36 seconds remaining in the first half to reach the milestone.

Chamberlain's final points of the night came when he tipped in a basket off a jump ball with 35 seconds left.

This was the next-to-last regular-season game of the year, and Chamberlain scored 17 points the next night in St. Louis.

Bailey Howell scored 32 and Gene Shue 27 points for the Pistons.

During the 1962-63 season, Chamberlain averaged 50.4 points to score an all-time record 4,029 points.

This was the largest crowd ever to see a regular-season pro basketball game in Fort Wayne, and about 1,000 fans had to be turned away. The 1953 NBA All-Star Game drew 10,332 fans.

**Also, in 1953, Notre Dame beats Eastern Kentucky 72-57 and DePaul beats Miami of Ohio 74-72 as part of an NCAA Tournament doubleheader.**

Not many people remember that the Memorial Coliseum once hosted the first round of the NCAA Men's Basketball Tournament for two years. In this initial year, the Irish were led in part by Dick Rosenthal's 17 points. Rosenthal went on to play with the Pistons, and was Notre Dame's athletic director when the Irish football team sealed a deal to have its home football games televised by NBC. Attendance at the doubleheader was 6,043.

## March 11

**In 1911, Crawfordsville wins the first state basketball title, but not before beating Bluffton 42-16 in the semifinals.**

According to Indiana basketball historian Herb Schwomeyer, IU's physical director requested the organization of the first state high school tournament, which was neither endorsed nor opposed by the Indiana High School Athletic Association Board of Control. The IU Boosters Club conducted that first tournament March 10 and 11, 1911, at Assembly Hall. The best teams from each of the state's 13 congressional districts were invited to compete. One district was not represented.

According to a story by Kerry Hubartt in The News-Sentinel on March 2, 1999, Bluffton represented the Third District, comprising Allen, Wells, Steuben, DeKalb, White, Whitley, Huntington and Adams counties. The members of that team were Doster Buckner, Claude Ware, Dwight Fritz, Homer Brumbaugh and Homer Marshall.

Twelve teams played in Bloomington on March 10, 1911, including Bluffton, which lost to Crawfordsville 42-16 in the semifinals. Crawfordsville won the first state championship on March 11, beating Lebanon 24-17. The 1911 tournament had never been formally endorsed by the IHSAA, and Crawfordsville's title was not recognized officially until 1957.

From that humble beginning Hoosier Hysteria blossomed into a phenomenon recognized throughout the country for its uniqueness. The tourney grew to 13 teams in 1912. District tournaments were held at four sites on March 9 with the state finals again at IU on the 16th. By 1913, the field had grown to 38 teams. There were 77 a year later, 155 by 1915 and 301 by 1918.

The first Fort Wayne team to win a state title was South Side in 1938, though Central finished second to Everett Case and Frankfort in 1936.

The tournament maintained a single-class format until 1998.

**In 2000, Steve Smith of Saint Francis scores 53 points in an NAIA Tournament win over Newman.**

## March 12

**In 1994, Leslie Johnson is named NCAA Freshman of the Year for women's basketball, and Tiffany Gooden is named Miss Basketball.**

This is somewhat appropriate because their careers were so intertwined as the best female basketball players Fort Wayne has ever produced. Their competition drove each other to greater heights, and they were at the forefront of a fantastic era of female athletics. They were also exceptional role models for the female athletes to come.

Gooden, who graduated from Snider in 1994, finished her career with 2,198 points, fifth all-time in Indiana among girls players. She averaged 26.2, 29.9 and 28.7 points during her last three seasons.

Gooden, attended the University of Iowa on a basketball scholarship, also owned several prestigious basketball awards, including Kodak All-American, USA Today Super 25, Parade All-American and Player of the Year and Naismith Player of the Year.

At the culmination of her high school career in 1994 as Indiana's Miss Basketball, Gooden led a late Indiana rally as the Hoosier girls completed a two-game sweep of the Kentucky All-Stars with a 100-92 victory. Gooden's 24 points, coupled with her record 31 points a week earlier, broke the 17-year-old two-game series mark of 54 points.

That led to her career at Iowa University, where she earned All-Big Ten honors as a sophomore and senior, and conference Freshman of the Year honors. She finished with 1,024 career points.

Johnson had an outstanding high school and college career. scoring 2,045 points during her Northrop career to become the all-time northeast Indiana scoring leader (Gooden broke the record the next year). During her senior year in 1992-1993, she averaged 28.4 points and 13.9 rebounds per game while shooting 75 percent from the field.

After that she played one year at Purdue University, earning National Freshman of the Year honors while leading the Boilermakers to the Final Four. She scored 10.9 points per game as a sophomore before she decided to transfer to Western Kentucky. In two years with the Hilltoppers, she averaged 16.9 points and 7.4 rebounds per game and earned All-Sun Belt Conference honors both times.

## March 13

**In 1981, Al Gooden plays in the NCAA Tournament for Ball State.**

The Wayne graduate scores 23 points on 5 of 7 shooting from the field and hitting all 13 free throw attempts while grabbing six rebounds, but the Cardinals lose to Boston College 93-90. It was Ball State's first-ever NCAA Tournament appearance.

One of the most-underrated high school players in Fort Wayne history while he played at Wayne, Gooden was a monster presence inside even though he was only 6-5.

At Ball State, he was undersized as a power forward and sat the bench for his first two years before becoming an all-Mid-American Conference player as a junior and senior. As a junior, he averaged 12.5 points and 5.6 rebounds while setting a league record by hitting 60 percent of his shots from the field.

As a senior, he hit 58 percent from the field and averaged 14.4 points and 5.4 rebounds to finish his career with 10.6 points in 80 games played. He made 58 percent of his shots from the field and 82 percent from the free throw line.

Gooden's best performances game late in his senior season at Ball State. The Cardinals were part of a five-way tie for first place in the regular-season standings. In the MAC Tournament semifinals, he scored a career-high 33 points, hitting 14 of 17 from the field on his 23rd birthday as the Cardinals beat Toledo 79-77.

Gooden was inducted into the Ball State Hall of Fame in 1991. He became a great high school coach at Harding, leading the Hawks to 321 wins, 10 sectionals, eight regionals, five semistates and one state title.

**Also, in 1992, Lisa Miller's career as IPFW's all-time leading scorer comes to a close.**

Miller scored 34 points, but IPFW lost to Washburn, Kan., in the first round of the NCAA Division II National Tournament. Miller completed her career with 2,358 points, and 937 rebounds. She was the Great Lakes Valley Conference Player of the Year as a senior when she averaged 26 points. The school also retired her No. 24 jersey.

## March 14

**In 1959, Kokomo and South Side play the best game in Fort Wayne Semistate history.**

South Side was the defending state champion, but returned only one starter, Tom Bolyard, while the Wildkats were led by Mr. Basketball Jimmy Rayl, a sharp-shooting guard who would fire from anywhere.

They put on one of the best duels in Memorial Coliseum history as Bolyard scored 38 points and Rayl 40. Unfortunately for South Side, Rayl had the last shot.

After Bolyard missed a potential game-leading free throw, Rayl crossed midcourt and let fly from 25 feet to just beat the buzzer as Kokomo won 92-90.

"In my senior year (1959) I thought we would be just average," said Bolyard in 1991, "but things went together very well and we made it to the semistate, where we lost on a last-second long bomb by Kokomo's Jimmy Rayl. But then, if I had not missed a free throw a bit earlier, we would have won."

Despite drawing all the extra defensive attention during his senior year, Bolyard, a 6-4 forward, averaged 30 points a game. He was also named the Parade All-America team and was the Most Valuable Player of the Indiana-Ohio All-Star Game. He finished with 1,420 points during his South Side career.

About the only thing he would want to do differently was the end of that one game.

"As a spectator's game, it must have been unbelievable," Bolyard said. "But that's a game we should have won."

Rayl finished with 1,632 career points and the Mr. Basketball award, but the Wildkats lost the state title game the next week to Indianapolis Attucks 92-54.

**Also, in 1964, in the semistate tournament tiny Swayzee outlasts Liberty Center 64-61 after nine overtimes.**

## March 15

**In 2011, St. Francis loses to Cornerstone in its bid for back-to-back NAIA titles.**

All year long, the members of the Saint Francis men's basketball team took everyone else's best shot, always getting their opponents' best effort. And all year long, the Cougars always found a way to retaliate and win, all the way until the end.

After DeJovaun Sawyer-Davis hit a free throw with 6;52 remaining to tie the game, it looked like Saint Francis was on its way to a second consecutive NAIA Division II National Championship. Instead, Cornerstone got hot at the right time, going on an 11-3 to take control and beat the Cougars 80-71.

The Golden Eagles finished 34-4, and the Cougars 28-10. Saint Francis had all but one player back from the team that won the title in 2010.

Sawyer-Davis finished the championship game with 20 points, 11 rebounds and two steals to earn all-tournament honors with teammate Qadr Owens who averaged 20 points during the tournament. He scored 19 points and grabbed six rebounds during the title game.

The four Cougars seniors, Sawyer-Davis, Austin Leisure, Ferdinand Morales-Soto and Matt Edmonds, combined for an 87-49 record during their careers at St. Francis, including 57 wins as juniors and seniors.

**Also, in 1992, Harding graduate Craig Riley scores 15 points to help Purdue upset Indiana.**

## March 16

**In 2010, Saint Francis wins the NAIA Division II national title in basketball.**

Sometimes an underdog wins a game or two, but the University of Saint Francis men's basketball team became the alpha dog at the NAIA Division II men's national basketball championships last spring. The Cougars started the tournament in Point Lookout, Mo., as the No. 15 seed and then beat five teams that were ranked in the top 12 nationally.

Their final victory was a stunning 67-66 upset of No. 1-ranked Walsh University in the national title game March 16. Before the tournament, Saint Francis (28-9) lost four of its five games.

"I'm just so proud of what those guys accomplished this year," Saint Francis coach Jeff Rekeweg said. "Part of that is that we've played as an underdog a lot of the time."

The Cougars, who became the second-lowest seed ever to win this tournament, played 16 teams ranked in the NAIA top-25 poll this year and won 11 of those games, including beating Walsh twice and a second-ranked Oregon Tech team in the tournament semifinals. Part of their tournament run included trailing defending national champion Oklahoma Wesleyan by 13 points before fighting back to win.

"There's nobody (who) thought we would be able to get this done," Rekeweg said. "I'd even say that we knew we were going to have to be pretty special if we were able to get it done."

All-American forward DeJovaun Sawyer-Davis led the Cougars in the title game with 22 points. Matt Edmonds scored 14 points, and Ferdinand Morales-Soto grabbed seven rebounds, scored 10 points and passed four assists.

**Also, in 1985, Homestead wins its third consecutive state gymnastics title.**

**Also, in 1999, the Saint Francis women finish second in the NAIA Tournament.**

## March 17

**In 1871, the Fort Wayne Kekiongas are among the original members of the National Association of Professional Baseball Players which later became the National League.**

During the Civil War, in April 1962, some young men formed the Summit City Club to play baseball on that land that is today covered by the Fort Wayne Community Schools' Grile Administration Center. After the war, the club disbanded and another team was formed, the Kekiongas.

In 1870, a team from Baltimore, called the Marylands, had disbanded right in the middle of a tour of the Midwest, and several of the best players ended up on the Kekiongas. One of them was the pitcher, Bobby Mathews, who some say invented the curveball.

The National Association of Professional Baseball Players was started during a meeting in New York. Representatives from Philadelphia Athletics, Brooklyn Eckfords, Chicago White Stockings, Boston Red Stockings, Washington, D.C. Olympians, Troy, N.Y. Haymakers, New York City Mutuals, Cleveland Forest Cities, Rockford, Ill., Forest Cities, and Fort Wayne were present. The entry fee was $10 per team.

Each team was to play the others in a best-of-five series. The team with the best record at the end of the season was entitled to fly the championship streamer, or pennant, at its ballpark for a year. The teams tossed coins to see who would play the first game.

The Kekiongas and Cleveland won the flips and the first game was scheduled for May 4, 1871 at Kekes Park in Fort Wayne. Fort Wayne won 2-0.

The National League was founded Feb. 2, 1876.

It's something of an urban legend that the Kekiongas evolved into the Brooklyn Dodgers, but actually the Fort Wayne team folded in July after a 7-21 start and was replaced in the league by the Brooklyn Eckfords team which chose not to pay the initial $10 entry fee. That team eventually became the Dodgers.

## March 18

**In 2006, Bishop Dwenger wins a second consecutive state gymnastics title.**

This was the year where the Dwenger gymnastics team really proved to be a dynasty. This was the Saints' second title in a row, third in four years and fourth overall. And they did it with six sophomores and six freshmen on the roster.

The lead gymnast was Jeanna Van Hoey who won the uneven parallel bars title, and freshmen Alicia Roche and Michelle Sordelet were also key competitors. The only seniors were Rebecca Trahin, Juanita Nix and Kristie Koczor.

Nix had perhaps the toughest performance during the state meet, as she had to finish up on the balance beam. Everyone in the Perry Meridian gym knew she needed a good score for the Saints to edge second-place Center Grove. Bishop Dwenger scored 113.3 points to nip Center Grove's total of 113.1. It was also the best score ever at the state meet to that point, topping the Saints' previous year's total of 112.825.

"To repeat is just the best thing that can happen to these girls," Saints coach Rosemarie Nix told The News-Sentinel. "That shows that it wasn't just a fluke that they won. They've worked very hard right up until yesterday. It wasn't like, `OK, we've made it this far. Let's see what happens.'

"And it came down to the last event, and once again, beam, a pressure event," Nix said. "We were like, `Oh, man,' but they came out tough as nails and three of the four stayed on the beam and even the fourth one scored a high score. That shows what they're made of. They're solid, strong competitors. We can't ask for more."

**Also, in 1994, Tiffany Gooden is named Naismith Female Prep Basketball Player of the Year.**

**Also, in 2000, Homestead's Shellen Goltz wins the state all-around gymnastics title.**

## March 19

**In 1957, the Pistons played their final game as Fort Wayne's team, losing to the Minneapolis Lakers 110-108 before 2,212 fans at Memorial Coliseum.**

After making the NBA Finals in 1955 and 1956, the Fort Wayne Pistons were not quite as strong the next season, finishing 34-38, but they still qualified for the playoffs against the Minneapolis Lakers. The only problem was, negotiations to move the team to Detroit has already been revealed in the media coming out of the NBA All-Star Game.

Even before that, the Pistons were averaging only 4,300 fans during their first 15 home games. When the Pistons played Rochester at home on Dec. 9 with a chance to take over first place, only 3,006 fans were in attendance. After an appeal for more fan support, only 3,100 showed up for a Sunday game against the New York Knicks. Only 2,730 fans showed up on Jan. 2 to see George Yardley scored 33 points in a win over Minneapolis. A nationally televised game on Jan. 5 against the Knicks drew 4,360 fans.

There were few good nights at the box office, such as when 8,108 fans showed up to watch Bill Russell make his Fort Wayne debut, but most of the crowds were slim, especially considering the Pistons had the league's cheapest tickets with a high of $2.50.

After the speculation started, the Pistons' next home game on Jan. 22 against St. Louis included all tickets being sold for $1. The smallest home crowd of the season to that point, 2,315, showed up.

On Feb. 14, 1957, Fred Zollner announced he was moving the team to Detroit. The Pistons still somehow managed to qualify for the playoffs, but they lost in two straight games to Minneapolis. Larry Foust scored the final basket in Fort Wayne as part of his 30-point effort.

## March 20

**In 1943, Central wins the state boys basketball title.**

The 1943 tournament was a very important one for the state as it was the first that included private, parochial and black schools, the first all-inclusive state tournament. So it was appropriate that Central was such a balanced team and didn't have true superstars.

The Tigers finished 27-1 after their 45-40 win over Lebanon. Central's only loss that season came against South Side, a loss the Tigers avenged in the second meeting. The third meeting was one of best games in Fort Wayne history, with Central winning 25-24 in overtime in the sectional as Tom Shopoff hit the winning free throw.

Central was coached by the great Murray Mendenhall, and his team included Murray Mendenhall Jr., Bob Armstrong, Bob Van Ryn, Shopoff, Jim Blanks, Charlie Stanski, Max Ramsey, Ray Chambers, Ed Lindenberg, Bob Doty and Ron Lewton. Shopoff led the team in scoring during the state tournament with 83 points, followed by Mendenhall Jr. with 81, Blanks with 66, Stanski with 62, Armstrong with 55 and Van Ryn with 53.

That balance was also evident during the title game as Mendenhall scored 10 points, Stanski, Blanks and Van Ryn nine each. The Tigers were also great defensively, holding Lebanon to 13 of 55 shooting from the field. Lebanon star Pete Mount made just 3 of 21 shots. Stanski scored the finishing basket with about 30 seconds left.

Mendenhall Sr. eventually became coach of the Fort Wayne Pistons, Mendenhall Jr. coached some excellent South Side teams in the 1970s and 1980s and Murray Mendenhall III became an excellent coach at Wayne. The Mendenhall coaches combined for 747 career wins.

**Also, in 1954, Bob Chase and Hilliard Gates broadcast the Milan-Muncie Central state championship game, the inspiration for the movie "Hoosiers."**

## March 21

**In 1973, Komets captain Bob Fitchner challenges the Flint bench to fight.**

With 22 games left in the regular season, the Komets were coasting in second place with a 31-19-2 record when they caught fire, going 17-4-1 to capture the Huber Trophy as regular-season champs.

Despite their record, no Komet was named on the postseason all-star teams, and Ted Garvin of Port Huron was named the all-star coach. None of the Komets scored 40 goals or 100 points, but eight scored at least 20 goals and nine at least 50 points.

The Komets' hot streak continued into the playoffs. In the first game of the semifinals against Flint, the Komets pounded the Generals 9-0 on the scoreboard and also in a bench-clearing brawl with 2:50 left. Flint's Laurie Yaworski slashed Bob Fitchner from behind. Yaworski refused to fight so Fitchner skated over and challenged the Flint bench. Rodney Cox came off to fight him and begin the brawl.

Two nights later in Flint, the Generals were talking again, this time with tough guy Doug Kerslake in the lineup. Several Generals said Fitchner would not have challenged the Flint bench had Kerslake been on it. When the two finally met on the ice, Fitchner broke Kerslake's nose. The Komets won the game 4-2 and the series 4-1.

"One thing people don't know about that fight is that on the bench Boileau had a hold of (Cal) Purinton and (D'Arcy) Keating from the back," Robbie Irons said. "He told them, 'If Fitch gets beat, that guy doesn't get back to the bench unless it's through one of you.'"

The Komets went on to sweep Port Huron in the Turner Cup Finals.

**Also, in 2009, Snider graduate Kaleigh Schrock captains Neumann College to the NCAA Division III title in men's hockey.**

**Also, in 1987, Marion wins its third consecutive semistate title behind Jay Edwards and Lyndon Jones.**

**Also, in 2012, one-time city scoring record holder Tom Baack is inducted into the Indiana Basketball Hall of Fame.**

**March 22**

**In 1958, South Side wins the boys state basketball title.**

South Side coach Don Riechert was known for playing his starting five until the game was over or until they collapsed. This time the Archers were far enough ahead that everyone got to play.

South Side beat Crawfordsville 63-34 to win the area's second boys basketball state championship, the second-greatest margin of victory in state finals history.

Ranked No. 1 most of the season after winning sectional and regional titles in 1956 and 1957, the Archers finished 28-2 in 1958, losing only to Muncie Central in a holiday tournament and to Michigan City in overtime. Their toughest test was a 60-56 overtime heartstopper against Central in the sectional semifinals.

The Archers also won the city series title in a season where four teams were ranked among the top 15 in the state.

The championship game was close for a half, as the Archers led 28-22 at the break before breaking things opening the second half. Mike McCoy had 24 points and 20 rebounds, Dan Howe 13 points and 10 rebounds and Carl Stavreti 12 points and 10 rebounds.

The other starters were Rich Miller and Tom Bolyard. The other team members were Jim Vachon, Larry Miller, Bill Meyers, Mike Simmons, Teddy Lebrecht, Ken Howe and Nick DeMetre.

McCoy was named Mr. Basketball that season, and Stavreti also played on the Indiana All-Stars. Miller and Howe were named to an all-star team that faced Ohio. Bolyard came back to be named Mr. Basketball in 1959 for the Ohio games.

**Also, in 2003, the Freedom win their first-ever indoor football game 41-40.**

**Also, in 1998, Kelley Racing gets its first victory as Scott Sharp wins at Phoenix.**

**Also, in 2004, Chris Thomas scores 39 points as Notre Dame beats St. Louis 77-66 in an National Invitational Tournament game in front of a crowd of 11,074.**

## March 23

**In 1974, Northrop wins the boys state basketball title.**

One loss made all the difference for Northrop. Bitterly disappointed after an early-season one-point loss to South Bend Adams, the Bruins resolved to play harder and smarter the rest of the season. They went on to win 26 games in a row and the state title.

The Bruins finished 28-1 after beating Wayne Walls and Jeffersonville 59-56 for the state title in Bloomington. Walter Jordan led the Bruins with 18 points, Tom Madden 16 and Mike Muff 10.

All season long, teams had a hard time matching up with Muff, Jordan, Madden, Maurice Drinks and James Wimbley. Though Jordan became the better-known player at Purdue and later in the NBA, he was the second-leading scorer that season behind Muff.

Maybe the Bruins' best game came in the semistate when they dominated No. 1-ranked Anderson 67-53 with Drinks shutting down Indians star Tony Marshall. The Bruins beat the top three ranked teams – Anderson, Lafayette Jefferson and Jeffersonville – on their way to the title.

The amazing thing about the Bruins' title was that Northrop was only three years old, but Bob Dille and assistant A.C. Eldridge were amazing coaches. Dille's combined record at Northrop and Central was 223-96 (.699) when he retired in 1978 to be replaced by Eldridge.

Northrop was the last Fort Wayne boys team to win a state title in the one-class system, but was also the last team to even reach the final four. That drought didn't end until Harding won the Class 2A state title in 2001.

## March 24

**In 1994, Fred Knipscheer becomes the first Fort Wayne native to score a National Hockey League goal in only his second game.**

Fred Knipscheer never listened to anyone who ever said he couldn't and just kept going until he proved he could.

A star on the Snider High School club team, he played junior hockey for one year to earn a scholarship to St. Cloud State where he scored 34 goals and 60 points over 36 games in his final season. That earned him a free agent contract with the Boston Bruins in 1993, and he scored 26 goals for their American Hockey League club in Providence before earning a late-season call-up.

He made the most of it, scoring a goal in his second game, against Anaheim, and stuck for the last 11 games of the regular season and all 12 Boston playoff games. Later that spring he scored the game-winning goal in Game 7 of the playoffs for Boston against Montreal. He still has the puck.

Another souvenir is a picture of Knipscheer standing at the blue line with Ray Bourque, Cam Neely, Don Sweeney and Adam Oates in the last hockey game ever played at Boston Gardens.

Knipscheer left the Bruins in 1995 in a trade with St. Louis. He played one game with the Blues to bring his NHL totals to 44 games with eight goals and 12 points. Knipscheer started his trek as primarily a minor-league player in 1995, playing in seven cities over the next five years, and becoming a thorn in the side to the Komets. He scored nine goals and 12 points in 11 career games against the K's.

A series of three concussions in three months finally ended his career in 2000.

**Also, in 1945, the Pistons basketball team repeats as world champions.**

## March 25

**In 1944, the Zollner Pistons win their first World Basketball title.**

After losing in the semifinals of the world tournament the year before to Oskosh, the Pistons loaded up for the 1943-44 season, signing star Buddy Jeannette to team with backcourt ace Bobby McDermott. They ran through the National Basketball League season and playoffs to win their first league title.

Playing at the Herald-American World Basketball Tournament in Chicago Stadium, the Pistons faced the surprising Brooklyn Eagles in the championship game. The Eagles, group of former Army players, had upset the Harlem Globetrotters in the semifinals. The Pistons also had to play without Jeannette who sprained his ankle in Fort Wayne's 42-38 win over the New York Rens.

The championship outcome was almost anti-climactic, as the Pistons cruised to a 50-33 win before nearly 15,000 fans. Big man John Pelkington led Fort Wayne from the pivot with 19 points and McDermott scored 14 from outside. The Pistons led 28-11 at halftime, and Fort Wayne's biggest lead in the second half was 23 points.

McDermott's defense was really the key to the game. Brooklyn's Bob Tough had scored a tournament-record 32 points against the Globetrotters, but he was held us just 11 points on 14 shots against the Pistons. McDermott was named the tournament's Most Valuable Player.

The season was completed two days later when the Pistons blasted the National Basketball League All-Stars, giving Fort Wayne the sweep of the NBL regular-season and playoff titles, the world title and the all-star game title.

Besides Pelkington, Jeannette and McDermott, other team members were Chick Reiser, Dale Hamilton, Carlyle Towery, Jerry Bush and Paul Birch. The Pistons finished 42-10.

**Also, in 1955, the World Bowling Congress takes over the Memorial Coliseum for 72 days.**

## March 26

**In 1938, South Side wins the state basketball title.**

During the first 27 years of the Indiana High School Basketball State Tournament, teams from small towns dominated, creating the mystique upon which much of Hoosier Hysteria is based – that the teams from little schools can and should compete with the big schools.

That started to change in 1938 when South Side became the first team from a city of more than 50,000 to win the tournament.

Jim Glass, a 6-foot-8 center, Jim Roth, Bob Bolyard, Dale Hamilton and Jimmy Hines were the stars for coach Burl Friddle, whose team lost only three games that season.

As was often the case, sometimes the best team from Fort Wayne didn't make it out of the super-competitive sectional. After losing a heartbreaker in the 1937 sectional to Central, the Archers were hungry for redemption. They cruised through the sectional by an average of 25 points before out-lasting Muncie Central 37-33 in the semistate. In the state finals, South Side beat Columbus 40-34 in the afternoon and then Hammond 34-32 to bring home Fort Wayne's first state title.

Hamilton scored 12 points and Hines nine in the championship game. Hines made three consecutive long shots to keep the Archers in front late in the fourth quarter. Hamilton, Hines and Roth were named to the all-tournament team.

While Roth and Hines both started for three years at Alabama, Friddle coached the Toledo University men's team to the championship game of the National Invitation Tournament in 1943. Fort Wayne's Bolyard and Dallas Zuber were on that team. Friddle, who also coached the 1930 champion Washington team, was inducted into the Indiana Basketball Hall of Fame in 1969.

The odd thing about South Side's win was that big schools started to dominate the tournament and it would be 16 years until the Milan Miracle.

**Also, in 2011, IPFW's Arnie Ball becomes just the fifth NCAA men's volleyball coach to win 500 career matches.**

**Also, in 1939, Central Catholic wins the national Catholic basketball championship.**

**March 27**

**In 1964, the Komets hold "Eddie Long Night."**

When the Fort Wayne Komets first came to town in 1952, they held a free exhibition two nights before their first game to introduce the sport to the fans.

Then-News-Sentinel Sports Editor Ben Tenny wrote, "It didn't take me long to see that the young short skater who was wearing No. 16 on his white jersey had that desire to win and get ahead that makes some athletes outstanding. If the play of this youngster is typical of the play fans will see in the International Hockey League, hockey will make it in Fort Wayne."

Hockey made it, and so did Eddie Long. Long played 14 seasons for the Komets, and his No. 16 became the first Komets' jersey to be retired on March 27, 1965. The Komets shocked Long by sneaking his mother into town for the event.

During his playing days, Long scored 459 goals, 465 assists and 924 points while earning 845 penalty minutes in 858 games. He retired as the IHL's all-time leading scorer.

He ranks second in games played, goals, assists and points and is ninth in penalty minutes on the Komets' all-time lists.

"But Eddie Long is more than a statistic — he's a spirit, the spirit of competition," former News-Sentinel Sports Editor Bud Gallmeier wrote at Long's retirement in 1965. "He only knew one way to play the game — as hard as he could. Eddie would burn more energy during one shift on the ice than many players do in an entire game."

During his career, "Tiny Mite" as he was first known, became "Mr. Komet."

Long was part of two Turner Cup championship teams, played in four IHL All-Star games, was the league's MVP in 1963 and was named all-league three times.

## March 28

**In 1977, Teri Rosinski of Norwell is named the area's first Miss Basketball.**

Teri Rosinski was a true pioneer for female sports. The IHSAA first started sponsoring girls basketball in 1974, and Judi Warren of Warsaw was the first Miss Basketball. Rosinski was the second after leading Norwell to the final four in 1977. Rosinski averaged 25 points per game and also won the state's mental attitude award as the Knights finished 20-4.

Rosinski was northeast Indiana's first superstar. She'd practice against the boys, adults, whomever she could entice into a game. Holidays? She'd find a place to shoot, and rain or snow was irrelevant.

Girls basketball was so new, Rosinski remembers buying boys shorts for the girls team so they didn't have to practice wearing cutoff jeans shorts, even though the boys shorts hung past the girls' knees.

Along with players such as Harding's Linda Hege, Wayne's Linda Stadler and East Noble's Susie Thrapp, Rosinski started the foundation for this area's outstanding girls hoops tradition. Heritage followed that up behind Jody Beerman by winning the 1982 state title.

Though she only played varsity for two years, Rosinski finished with 1,210 career points.

After her college career at Illinois State, Rosinski became a coach, working at Bishop Luers, IPFW and Homestead before coming back to Bishop Luers in 2001. She compiled a 128-24 record at Bishop Luers, winning state titles in 2002 and 2006.

Rosinski retired as coach in 2007 and moved to Southern California.

**Also, in 1992, IPFW's Lisa Miller's is named a Kodak all-American after ending her career with 2,358 points.**

**Also, in 1955, Fort Wayne makes the cover of Sports Illustrated for the American Bowling Congress national tournament.**

## March 29

**In 1958, John Kelso of Central is named a Parade All-American, the first time a Fort Wayne player was so honored.**

Many people believe Kelso was the best basketball player to come out of Fort Wayne, and possibly the city's best athlete during the 1950s.

He was a star at Central High School in football, basketball and track,

In 1997, The News-Sentinel named him Allen County's sixth-greatest basketball player of all time. During his senior season at Central, five Fort Wayne teams were ranked among the state's top 15 with South Side at No. 1 and Central at No. 2 for a large part of the season. The teams met three times at Memorial Coliseum, averaging 9,000 fans per game.

Because of his 40-inch vertical leaping ability, Kelso was nick-named "Jumpin Johnny." The 6-foot-4 forward was named a first-team all-American by Parade Magazine after the season, the first time anyone from Fort Wayne had received such an honor. He was also named Mr. Basketball for the Indiana-Ohio series, leading the Hoosiers against the Buckeyes who were led by Jerry Lucas.

Kelso died at age 60, Jan. 2, 2000, in Lansing, Mich.

**Also, in 2002, Heritage graduate Bryan Enterline works his first NCAA Women's Final Four as a referee.**

Enterline also called Final Four games in 2003 and in 2004 called the title game between Connecticut and Tennessee. He's also one of the top officials in the WNBA.

**Also, in 1956, the basketball Pistons draw 9,261 fans to watch the team clinch a playoff series win over St. Louis.**

**Also, in 1980, play-by-play man Len Davis calls his last game for WGL radio.**

**March 30**

**In 1940, Fort Wayne's Curly Armstrong and Herm Schaefer help IU win its first national championship.**

Almost every Indiana University basketball fan knows the Hoosiers won their first NCAA Tournament title in 1940. Very few know the Hoosiers owe thanks for that title to Purdue.

Purdue actually won the Big Ten title in 1940, but coach Ward "Piggy" Lambert didn't believe in post-season play, so Indiana represented the conference in the tournament. The Hoosiers had also beaten the Boilermakers twice during the season.

The Hoosiers were led that season by Marv Huffman, Jay McCreary, Bill and Bob Menke and Berne-native Bob Dro. Two of their starters were Central graduates Curly Armstrong and Herm Schaefer who had helped the Tigers to the 1936 and 1937 state finals. Armstrong and Schaefer ended up leading the 1939-40 Hoosiers in scoring as juniors, with Armstrong earning all-Big Ten honors.

During the national tournament, only eight teams were invited, and Indiana easily dispatched Springfield and Duquesne to face Kansas for the title. With Armstrong scoring 10 points, the Hoosiers ran the Jayhawks off the floor 60-42. Schaefer led IU in scoring during the tournament.

Though Armstrong was 5-foot-11, and Schaefer was 6-0, both players often played forward for coach Branch McCracken.

Armstrong's career at Indiana ended the next season when he was declared academically ineligible for the second semester. Schaefer finished the season averaging 5.6 points,

**Also, in 1990, the Indiana Kick play their final indoor soccer game.**

**Also, in 2000, Steve Smith of Saint Francis wins the national collegiate slam dunk contest.**

## March 31

**In 1940, Central Catholic wins the second of back-to-back Catholic national championships.**

Before 1943, parochial schools were prohibited from playing in the Indiana High School boys basketball tournament. While every other team played in the sectionals, Central Catholic would participate in the Catholic state tournament, and when the Irish won, they'd advance to the National Catholic High School Basketball Championships in Chicago to play in the field of 32.

The Irish won their first national title in 1939, beating Leo of Chicago 44-37 at Loyola University to finish 25-4. Ed Stanczak led the scoring with 19 points, Jim Boedecker scored nine and George Bitler seven.

Central Catholic scored more than 40 points in all five tournament games. For the season the Irish averaged 41 points and allowed only 28. Central had beaten Leo 27-17 during a regular-season tilt.

The other starters were Bob Heiny and Gene Maxwell with John Falvy, Nick Leto, Ed Gorman, Ed Klotz and Ed Dehner coming off the bench.

Coach John Levicki's Irish survived a 29-27 barnburner the next year against Indianapolis Cathedral in the state tournament.

The national tournament was also much closer as Central Catholic beat Chicago St. Phillips 33-31 in the third round, Leo of Chicago 51-42 in the semifinals and finally beat Santa Fe, New Mexico 35-33 for the championship. Stanczak had 15 points this time and Klotz nine. Stanczak scored seven of his points in the fourth quarter, including the game-winning basket.

The other starters that year were Harold Morthorst, Dick Krouse and Ed Dehner, with Nick Leto, Bob Walker and Bob Heiny coming off the bench.

**Also, in 1956, the Pistons lose the first game of the NBA Finals to Philadelphia 98-94.**

# APRIL

## April 1

**In 1967, South Side's Willie Long is named Mr. Basketball.**

The Archers' senior averaged 25.6 points and 16 rebounds per game, leading South Side to the 1967 Final Four in Indianapolis. There, the Archers lost 79-70 in the semifinals to Lafayette Jeff to finish 24-4.

Long was the second player from Fort Wayne and South Side to earn Mr. Basketball honors, following Mike McCoy in 1958.

The 6-foot-7 forward averaged 23.2 points per game as a junior and 25.6 as a senior to earn Mr. Basketball honors and finish his high school career with 1,606 points. His single-game high was 44 points.

Then he went to the University of New Mexico and established new records in almost every scoring category the school had. He averaged 23.8 points per game as a junior and 23.9 as a senior, earning All-Western Athletic Conference honors both years. As a senior, he led the WAC in scoring and earned All-America honors as the Lobos climbed as high as No. 5 in the national rankings.

His 1,542 points was the New Mexico career scoring record for 17 years. He was the second Lobo ever to score at least 1,500 points and grab 800 rebounds. Long finished with a 19.8 scoring average and 10.3 rebounds for his college career.

Long was a second-round draft choice of the NBA's Cleveland Cavaliers (35th overall) but played three years in the American Basketball Association. With Florida as a rookie, he averaged 11.7 points and then he scored 9.0 and 12.6 points per game in two seasons with Denver. His career totals were 11.4 points and 6 rebounds per game as a pro.

A restaurant executive with Taco Bell Inc., Long rarely visits Fort Wayne and currently lives in Atlanta.

Long was inducted into the Indiana Basketball Hall of Fame in 1999.

**Also, in 1988, the Flames drop the final game of the indoor soccer playoffs to Canton 5-4 before 8,032 at Memorial Coliseum.**

## April 2

**In 2000, Hector Soto becomes first IPFW volleyball player to hit 2,000 kills.**

Arnie Ball's program has had some wonderful hitters over the last four decades, including Loren Gebert, Jay Golsteyn, Fred Malcolm, Jeff Ptak, C.J. Macias, Norman Almodovar and Craig Collins, but Soto was the best. That's partly because he could jump higher than any blocker.

His teammates called Soto "Peeke" because he could peak over the blockers with his 51-inch vertical jump. As a freshman in 1997, he led the nation with seven kills per game. One night, he hit 50 kills in only 67 swings against Wisconsin-Milwaukee to set the IPFW single-match record.

"When somebody jumps that high with those long arms and hits the ball that high, you have to wonder how you prevent him from scoring whenever he wants to," Penn State Coach Mark Pavlik said. "It's got to be nice to have a player who can jump double the height of his coach. The more he figures things out, the scarier he's going to be."

When he was 17, the 6-6 native of Arroyo, Puerto Rico, could touch 12-6. Most people would be afraid to even land from that high. Soto could touch a basketball rim with his head, or touch the top of the box over a basketball goal with his hand. While in high school, with no coaching and little technique, he cleared 6-7 in the high jump.

The top of the antenna on a men's volleyball net is 10 feet, 8 inches off the floor, and Soto once leaped to put his hand over the top five times in a row.

A two-time first-team all-American, Soto finished his career with 2,193 kills and was inducted into the IPFW Hall of Fame in 2006.

## April 3

### In 2010, Deshaun Thomas of Bishop Luers is named Mr. Basketball.

After scoring more points in Indiana high school basketball history other than Damon Bailey and Marion Pierce, Deshaun Thomas was an easy selection for Mr. Basketball in 2010. Thomas finished his career with 3,018 points and helped Bishop Luers win a pair of Class 2A state titles.

Maybe his most impressive performance wasn't scoring but turning the Knights into a basketball powerhouse. For decades Bishop Luers had been known strictly as a football school, regularly finishing last in the Summit Athletic Conference basketball standings.

During his senior season, Thomas averaged 31.8 points, 15.3 rebounds and three assists per game.

Thomas went on to help Indiana beat Kentucky twice, scoring 18 points and grabbing 13 rebounds in the first game and scoring 28 points and grabbing 12 rebounds in the rematch.

### Also, in 1983, Jody Beerman of Heritage is named Miss Basketball.

Beerman transformed the sport, making girls basketball a spectator sport. Her Heritage team was so popular, some games were sellouts and there was talk about moving sectional and regional contests to Memorial Coliseum.

Beerman finished with 1,616 career points, which at the time was second in Indiana history, and only seven points behind the Allen County record for boys or girls. During her senior season, she averaged 19.7 points, hitting 56 percent from the floor, and four assists.

She scored in double figures 85 of her 87 high school games, and was a two-time first-team all-state selection. She also helped Heritage win the 1982 state title.

Throughout her career, Beerman averaged 18.6 points and shot 53 percent from the floor.

## April 4

**In 2003, Homestead grad Amy Waugh celebrates winning the national college basketball three-point shooting contest.**

Very few people were ever dumb enough to challenge Waugh to a shooting contest. She scored 1,326 points during her career at Homestead, and then had a great career at Xavier where she set several school records, including for three-pointers in a season with 107. As a senior, she led the Atlantic 10 in scoring with 19 points per game and led the nation in three-point shooting with 3.6 per game.

After making a record score of 24 earlier in the competition, Waugh beat Vanderbilt's Ashley McElhiney 19-14 to win the women's title before knocking out men's champion Darnell Archey of Butler 17-15 to win the overall title at the men's Final Four in New Orleans.

After leading Xavier to three NCAA Tournament appearances, Waugh's playing career was over but not her basketball career. She was an assistant coach at Youngstown State for a season, and then at Wake Forest for five years before joining the staff at Xavier. After two seasons as a Musketeers' assistant, Waugh was named the head coach on April 20, 2011, replacing Kevin McGuff who took the head coaching job at Washington.

As a senior at Homestead, Waugh averaged 16.1 points per game and led the Northeast Hoosier Conference in three-pointers made (57) and three-point percentage (.442). She also averaged 4.2 assists per game.

## April 5

**In 1987, Northrop's Lori Meinerding is named Miss Basketball.**

During her senior season, Meinerding averaged 17.7 points, 10.1 rebounds, 3.7 assists and 2.9 steals for Northrop, helping the Bruins continue a state-record 57-game winning streak, the longest winning streak ever for a Northeast Indiana basketball team. That streak ended in the state finals as the Bruins attempted to repeat as state champions.

"With any other team, I doubt whether I would have gotten this award," Meinerding told The News-Sentinel's Steve Warden. "I couldn't have played so well without them. And that's not just the other four starters, who often gave the ball up to me to score, but also the other players who pushed the starters every day in practice."

Meinerding finished her Northrop career with 1,352 points, 882 rebounds, and 322 steals. As a junior, she averaged 17.7 points and 12.6 rebounds, grabbing 27 rebounds during the two games at the state finals. Because the Bruins were so dominant, Meinerding rarely played four quarters. Meinerding also received the mental attitude award at the 1987 state finals.

She continued her career at Indiana where she averaged 5.2 points and 1.6 rebounds per game in 79 career games. She had a career-high of 33 points in a 1989 game against Houston.

**Also, in 2013, the NBDL's Mad Ants qualify for the playoffs for the first time in six years as Tony Mitchell scores 49 points against Sioux Falls.**

**April 6**

**Also, in 1958, South Side's Mike McCoy is the city's first Mr. Basketball.**

Amazingly, McCoy was cut from his seventh grade basketball team.

McCoy became the first Mr. Basketball from Fort Wayne and only the third Indiana All-Star from the Summit City following Central's Bobby Milton in 1946 and North Side's Charley Lyons in 1955.

McCoy clinched the award by scoring 24 points and grabbing 20 rebounds in the state championship game against Crawfordsville which the Archers won 63-34. He averaged 18 points per game as a senior on a very balanced team.

Allegedly, McCoy was the first 7-footer to play Indiana high school basketball.

After leaving South Side, McCoy first went to Northwestern University and eventually played college ball at Miami University. He led the Hurricanes in scoring and rebounding for three years, scoring 1,231 points and grabbing 857 rebounds during his career. He averaged 19.1 points and 12.6 rebounds during his junior and senior seasons.

He was inducted into the Miami Hall of Fame in 2007 and into the Indiana Basketball Hall of Fame in 1998.

**Also, in 1971, Fort Wayne's Steve Hargan pitches for the Cleveland Indians against Detroit on baseball's opening day.**

Pitching against Mickey Lolich and a crowd of 54,089, the largest to see a Tigers game in 10 years, Hargan never had much of a chance in an 8-2 loss. Facing 13 hitters, he gave up four hits and four runs and walked two on 45 pitches. He was pulled after facing two hitters in the third inning.

Hargan was the Tribe's second pick to start but Sudden Sam McDowell had to miss the game because of a family illness. Hargan had started slow the season before but came up halfway through to finish 11-3 with a 2.90 earned run average and eight complete games.

The 1971 season didn't get much better for Hargan who was 0-5 on May 4 when he suffered a hairline fracture on his right ankle while covering first base and missed six weeks. He ended the season with a 1-13 mark and a 6.19 ERA.

## April 7

**In 1955, the Pistons beat Syracuse 74-71 to go up 3-2 in the NBA Finals.**

This might have been the high point for the Pistons' entire tenure in Fort Wayne.

Playing before about 4,000 fans, Frankie Brian hit two free throws in the final seconds to cement the win for the Pistons.

Because of the American Bowling Congress national tournament taking over the Memorial Coliseum, the Pistons had to play their home games in Indianapolis, but they still won all three. The problem was, they had a six-year losing streak going in Syracuse and lost all four games there.

The Pistons led Game 6 84-78 going into the fourth quarter, but lost 109-104. The Pistons led by 17 points in the first half of Game 7 but lost 92-91 when George King hit a free throw with 12 seconds left.

In 1955-56, Fort Wayne was paced by its big front line of Larry Foust (6 feet, 9 inches), Mel Hutchins (6-6) and future Basketball Hall of Famer George Yardley (6-5), who all played in the NBA All-Star Game. Yardley averaged 17.4 points, Foust 16.2, Hutchins 12.0 and Houbregs 11.1. Guards Chuck Noble, who averaged 9.5 points, and Andy Phillip, at 5.9 assists, also did their part.

**Also, in 1956, the Pistons lose to Philadelphia 99-88 in the deciding Game 5 of the NBA Finals.**

After winning the Western Division title with a 37-35 record, the Pistons fell behind St. Louis 2-0 in the best-of-five semifinals before rallying to win the series in the fifth game 102-97 before a Fort Wayne regular-season record crowd of 9,261. The Pistons were the first NBA team to rally from a 2-0 deficit to win a five-game playoff series.

Things never worked out in the finals as the Warriors won the first game in Fort Wayne to take control early.

Pistons owner Fred Zollner had come close once again, but eventually became the longest-tenured owner (34 years) never to win an NBA championship.

**Also, in 1980, Harding's Jim Master is named Mr. Basketball.**

Master scored 28 points per game for the Hawks.

**April 8**

**In 1946, the Zollner Pistons win their third and last world basketball title.**

Bobby McDermott was easily recognized as the best shooter in basketball over the first half of the century, and he always came up with his best in the biggest games. McDermott scored 20 points at Chicago Stadium as the Pistons won their third straight World Professional Basketball Tournament title.

Firing set shots from long range, McDermott hit eight of 17 shots as the Pistons beat Oshkosh 73-57 and earned a standing ovation from the crowd. The Pistons led 39-32 at the half and 53-41 after three quarters. Fort Wayne's defense allowed Oshkosh to hit only 20 of 90 shots from the field.

This title was different from the first two Fort Wayne championships for a couple of reasons. The Pistons had lost the National Basketball League playoffs to Rochester a few weeks before, and then they lost the first game of the best-of-three finals to Oshkosh.

The final game was a total team effort as Ed Sadowski scored 14, hitting all seven of his shots in the second half, and Bobby Tough scored 10. John Pelkington, Curly Armstrong, Charley Shipp, Bob Kinney, Chick Reiser, Jerry Bush and Buddy Jeanette also played for Fort Wayne.

This turned out to be the last championship the Pistons ever won. Early the next season, McDermott was released after an altercation on the train ride home from a game. He had averaged about 20 points per game over the previous five seasons to lead the team in scoring. McDermott retired as a player in 1950, and died in a 1963 auto crash at age 48.

**Also, in 2000, Dale Purinton gets called up by the New York Rangers to make his NHL debut.**

## April 9

**In 1963, the Komets rally from a 6-1 deficit to beat Muskegon in their greatest playoff comeback.**

Muskegon joined the IHL in 1963 and became an immediate thorn in the Komets' side, taking a 2-0 lead in the semifinals before the Komets rallied to take the series 4-2. Game 6 turned out to be the largest playoff comeback in Komets history, as they gave up six consecutive goals to fall behind 6-1 early in the second period. But a goal by Gary Sharp and a pair of short-handed tallies by Len Thornson before the period ended gave the Komets hope.

"We knew we were that good that we could come back," defenseman Lionel Repka said. "Sometimes when you don't have the team, you get your head down, but that year we were able to scramble back."

Bobby Rivard and Norm Waslawski scored in the third period to force overtime. After a shaky start, goaltender Chuck Adamson finished with 38 saves, but Eddie Long may have made the largest stop. In overtime, Muskegon's Larry Lund tried a shot from 10 feet, which Adamson blocked, but the puck trickled through his legs toward the goal line. It was halfway across the goal line when Long popped into the crease to slap the puck away.

Adamson made great saves on Joe Kiss and Joe Kastelic to keep his team alive until Waslawski won three straight power-play face-offs back to Roger Maisonneuve. Maisonneuve buried the third at 5:28 to win the game 7-6 and send the Komets to the finals.

"I think the big comeback and how we related to it was the turning point for us," Waslawski said. "The guys really got motivated. After we won that game, it was like we figured nobody could beat us. There was always someone taking up the slack."

During the finals, the Komets beat Minneapolis in five games to win their first title.

**April 10**

**In 1955, the Pistons lose Game 7 of the NBA Finals to Syracuse 92-91.**

The Nationals won when George King hit a free throw with 12 seconds left and then stole the ball from Andy Phillip in the final seconds.

King scored 15 points to lead the Nats, who had seven players score in double figures and hit 40 of 49 free throws. Larry Foust scored 24 points to lead the Pistons who attempted 34 free throws.

Fort Wayne led 31-21 after the first quarter and 53-47 at halftime, but the Nationals tied the score 74-74 after three quarters. At one point, the Pistons had a 17-point lead, 41-24, in the second quarter.

Dolph Schayes hit two free throws with a minute left to give Syracuse a 91-90 lead, but the Pistons' George Yardley answered with a free throw. The Pistons had a chance to take the lead, but Yardley turned the ball over on a palming violation with 18 seconds left. Then King was fouled and missed the first free throw but hit the second before stealing the ball from Phillip with three seconds remaining.

Schayes finished with 19 points and 12 rebounds per game in the series. Foust, Brian and Yardley all averaged 16 points per game for the Pistons, and Mel Hutchins scored 14. Phillip set a record with 7.1 assists per game. The Pistons shot 79 percent from the free throw line compared to 75 percent for the Nationals, but Syracuse had 30 more attempts in the series.

This was the first NBA Finals to use the 24-second shot-clock.

The Pistons had defeated the Minneapolis Lakers in four games during the semifinals, twice playing into overtime.

**Also, in 1993, the Class A minor league baseball Fort Wayne Wizards begin play on the road in Waterloo, Iowa.**

**Also, in 1998, the Wizards score 12 runs in an inning in a game at South Bend.**

## April 11

**In 1978, Snider graduate Andy Replogle makes his Major League pitching debut.**

Replogle was called in to pitch in relief by the Milwaukee Brewers against the New York Yankees at County Stadium in Milwaukee. Replogle faced one batter and gave up a hit. The Brewers beat the Yankees that day, 9-6, and Replogle went on to pitch in 32 games that season.

Replogle pitched for two seasons for the Milwaukee Brewers, compiling a 9-5 record with a 3.92 ERA in 1978. Replogle, a 6-5, 205-pound right hander, started 18 games that season with three complete games and two shutouts. He struck out 41 batters in 149 1/3 innings.

His athletic career actually started in South Bend where he came to prominence during his sophomore year when he pitched Clay High School of South Bend to the state championship in 1970. After one more season at Clay, he and his family moved to Fort Wayne where he attended Snider and graduated in 1972. He was an all-city performer in basketball and on the mound for the Panthers.

After graduating from Snider, he was selected by the New York Mets in the fourth round of the 1972 amateur draft. Replogle did not sign, however, choosing to attend Kansas State University where he continued his baseball career.

Replogle was drafted again in the 1975 amateur draft by the St. Louis Cardinals and played in their minor league system for three seasons. In December 1977, Replogle was drafted by the Baltimore Orioles from St. Louis in the Rule 5 draft. He was waived by the Orioles in 1978 and picked up by the Brewers.

His final game in the majors was September 30, 1979, when the Brewers lost to Minnesota 5-0. Replogle pitched 2 1/3 innings of shutout ball, allowing two hits. He was released by Milwaukee in 1982 and signed as a free agent by the Cincinnati Reds. He was released in spring training by the Reds after tearing a rotator cuff. He retired from baseball shortly thereafter.

**Also, in 1997, Tiffany Gooden was named the Naismith Award winner for being the nation's top girls prep basketball player.**

**April 12**

**In 1965, swimmer Judy Humbarger comes home after finishing third in the 200-meter backstroke at the AAU Nationals.**

Humbarger was a prodigy, making the AAU Nationals and finishing third in the 200-meter backstroke in 1964 and 1965. She qualified for the United States Olympic Trials in 1964. At the age of 13, she finished eighth in the 100-meter backstroke and sixth in the 200-meter backstroke even though she was the youngest swimmer in the competition.

Here's how much of a pioneer Humbarger and her peers were: In order to simulate competing in an Olympic-sized pool, they often practiced in gravel pits around the newly built I-69 highway on the west side of town.

As a 14-year-old, she set records for the 100-meter and 200-meter backstroke during an AAU meet at the McMillen Park Pool. From 1964 to 1966 she competed twice a year in national championships and regularly won backstroke titles, including setting the national record for the 200-meter backstroke in 2:28 in 1965.

Eventually, Humbarger held more than 40 age-group records and competed on three tours throughout Europe, winning several championships.

Because of various reasons, Humbarger eventually burned out and lost her drive for national competition and did not attend the 1968 Olympic trials. After graduating from South Side in 1968, she swam at Indiana as a freshman in 1969, winning two national championships at the Association for Intercollegiate Athletics for Women national meet and then stopped swimming for many years.

She came back to the sport in 1986 while living in Florida.

While competing in a World Masters Swimming national meet in Indianapolis in 1992, she won three individual events and set two more world records. She also was part of two first-place relay teams.

She finally stopped competing in 2010 and works as a commercial realtor in St. Petersburg, Fla.

**Also, in 1997, DeKalb's Luke Recker is named Mr. Basketball.**

## April 13

**In 1999, Luke Recker sends a fax in the middle of the night to announce he's leaving IU's basketball team.**

In a shocking development, Indiana's leading scorer, a former Mr. Basketball and a Parade All-American, announced his decision by sending a fax. The DeKalb High School graduate had been taking part in offseason workouts in Bloomington, but he came home to send out his decision.

"It is with sincere regret that I am announcing today my decision to transfer from Indiana University," Recker's statement said. "This is the toughest decision I have ever made. I love the state of Indiana, and playing for IU was always my lifelong dream.

"It is not easy to leave my friends, my family, and my home state. I love to play basketball, and the thought of sitting out a year kills me. I appreciate the opportunity given to me by coach Knight, however, I have not been satisfied with my development as a player. I blame no one but myself for this, and believe my development will best be served in another program."

The IU Athletic Department issued a statement that included, "We are very sorry that Luke has decided to leave Indiana University. He has been an integral and important part of our basketball program the last two years. We will miss him. We wish him much success as he goes forward."

Recker had committed to IU as a high school sophomore. He averaged 12.8 points and 2.8 assists as a starter during his freshman year with the Hoosiers, and 16.1 points, 4.0 rebounds and 2.3 assists as a sophomore.

In May, Recker announced he was transferring to Arizona, but soon after he suffered many injuries in a horrific Colorado car accident. Then, after one semester at Arizona, he transferred again to Iowa where he would play two years for IU legend Steve Alford. Recker averaged 18.1 points as a junior and 17.1 as a senior, including hitting a game-winning jumper against the Hoosiers in the Big Ten Tournament.

## April 14

**In 1960, the Komets play their longest game ever, losing to the St. Paul Saints in 4 overtimes.**

The 1959-60 Komets posted the best record in franchise history, 50-16-2, finishing 14 points ahead in the race for the Huber Trophy.

But they did not win the Turner Cup because of this game, possibly the most-famous in franchise history. Game 4 of the 1960 Turner Cup Finals, lasted four overtimes and finally ended at 1:25 a.m. April 15 on a goal by an ineligible player.

The Komets seemed to have won when Eddie Long scored with 4:41 left in regulation, but St. Paul's Aggie Kukulowicz beat Fort Wayne goalie Reno Zanier with a 40-foot slap shot with 2:10 left. Kukulowicz's shot would be replayed later.

The teams were tied 4-4 at the end of regulation. The Komets had the best chance to win it 55 seconds into the second overtime when they were awarded a penalty shot after St. Paul's John Bailey threw his stick at Komet Con Madigan. Len Ronson had scored 62 goals that season and two earlier in the game, but the puck rolled on him at the last instant.

The two goaltenders were spectacular. Earlier that summer, Ullyot had traded Glenn Ramsey to St. Paul, deciding Reno Zanier was the better goaltender. Ramsey haunted his former teammates throughout the series and held them scoreless for 62 minutes and 53 seconds. He made 72 saves in the game, including 46 during overtime. Zanier made 52 saves, including 28 in overtime.

The two teams missed playing a doubleheader by only 1:31. St. Paul's Elliott Chorley rifled a long shot past Zanier after the two teams had played for 118:28. Only about half the crowd of 3,512 remained.

Trailing three games to one, the Komets rallied to force a seventh game, but lost 3-1.

The disappointment tripled when the Komets discovered that Chorley, who scored three game-winning goals in the series, was actually ineligible. Ullyot went to the league meetings that June and protested, but the league said the series was over, and nothing was going to change.

## April 15

**In 1973, the Komets beat Port Huron 5-1 to clinch their third Turner Cup and the only one they clinched on the road.**

The only time the Komets clinched a playoff championship on the road, there were so many Fort Wayne fans present it sounded like Memorial Coliseum. The McMorran Arena attendance on April 15, 1973, in Port Huron, Mich., was announced as 3,046, but that included 15 busloads of Fort Wayne fans on a Sunday afternoon.

Early that season, General Manager Ken Ullyot and coach Marc Boileau used their connections with Pittsburgh of the NHL to get a new crop of quality players. Brian Walker, Jimmy Pearson, Don Atchison, Jeff Ablett, Jim Hrycuik and Bob Fitchner were the main baby Penguins. By the time everyone settled in, the season was three-fourths complete. The Komets were 31-19-2 and in second place with 22 games left when they got hot, finishing 17-4-1 to storm past Dayton.

Despite their record, not one Komet was named first or second team on the postseason all-star teams, and Ted Garvin of Port Huron was named the all-star coach. None of the Komets scored 40 goals or 100 points, but eight scored at least 20 goals and nine at least 50 points.

That balance continued in the playoffs as the Komets beat Flint 4-1 and swept Port Huron 4-0.

**Also, in 1997, Henry James sets an NBA record with seven 3-pointers in a quarter for Atlanta against New Jersey.**

The Hawks trailed 80-61 after three quarters before James, a North Side product, came into the game with 10 minutes left. He scored 24 points on seven three-pointers and three free throws as the Hawks out-scored the Nets 48-21 to win 109-101.

**April 16**

**In 2009, the TinCaps start play at Parkview Field.**

A controversial project when it was proposed, the Harrison Square project initially cost $120 million, including $31 million for the 8,100-seat ballpark. The team drew more than 400,000 fans in its initial season and won the Midwest League title.

The opening night crowd of 8,206 meant there was a little waiting in line for the concession stands and the bathrooms, but that was to be expected. Mayor Tom Henry threw out the first pitch, Tom Didier sang "God Bless America" and the Voices of Unity Choir sang "The Star-Spangled Banner" before a flyover by F-16s.

The TinCaps did their part by beating the Dayton Dragons 7-0. It was also the TinCaps' seventh consecutive win to start the season after they won the first six on the road, the best start in the team's 17-year history.

Dayton lead-off hitter Dave Sappelt got the new park's first hit, TinCaps pitcher Nick Schmidt threw the first strike out and Fort Wayne's James Darnell belted the first home run in the second inning.

**Also, in 2003, Scott Sharp wins his final race for Kelley Racing, the Japan 300.**

This was the Indy Racing League's first race held outside the United States, and there was plenty of excitement thanks to several wrecks.

After Tony Kanaan and Scott Dixon combined to crash on lap 178, Sharp moved into first place. Dixon had attempted to pass Kanaan on the inside during the third turn, but the cars smacked tires and ended up in the wall. Except for the 45 laps when Dixon was in front, Kanaan had led most of the race.

Another crash helped Sharp stay in front as with seven laps to go, Shinji Nakano wrecked causing another yellow flag which Sharp finished under.

The win tied Sharp with Buddy Lazier and Sam Hornish Jr. for the career IRL wins lead with eight.

## April 17

**In 1996, Summit City native Henry James scores 33 points as Sioux Falls beats Fort Wayne in Game 1 of the CBA Finals.**

Usually, the first game of a championship series is decided by defense, but the Skyforce outshot the Fury 131-123 in South Dakota. Former Fort Wayne resident Henry James scored 23 of his 33 points in the second half, including a run of four-straight jumpers to help Sioux Falls pull away before a crowd of 6,087 fans..

The CBA's top-scoring team during the regular season, the Skyforce shot 55 percent from the field, while the Fury shot 52 percent.

Sioux Falls 7-foot-2 center Rich Kelley opened the Skyforce push with 15 points in the first half, scoring over 6-7 Evric Gray. Kelley was double-teamed by Greg Kite and Jimmy Carruth in the second half and was held to four points.

The Fury tried to keep it close behind 40 points from Gray and 23 from Jaren Jackson, but Sioux Falls never trailed in the second half. The Fury cut the Sioux Falls lead to 125-121 with a 6-0 run with a minute left, but Jackson missed a running jumper with 35 seconds left.

The Fury regrouped to slow down the pace and win the second game 113-105 as Jackson scored 15 of his 22 points in the fourth quarter. He hit a trio of three-pointers in a row to give Fort Wayne its biggest lead 101-87 in the fourth quarter.

James was held to 14 points in the loss. The Fury out-rebounded the Skyforce 68-47.

**April 18**

**In 2000, Charles Holiness sets the Fort Wayne city bowling record with an 886 series.**

Just a month before this, Holiness just missed a personal goal with a 799 series.

"It just motivated me even more because I knew I was so close," Holiness said. "I didn't get upset at all."

On his perfect night at Westwood Lanes, Holiness rolled a 300, 300, 286 series to attain his first 300 games and his first 800 series, breaking the previous mark of 867 set by Leo Schweyer set during the 1995-96 season.

"I just knew something great was going to happen," Holiness said. "I've been so close so many times lately that it just had to happen. But two 300s is more than I ever thought possible."

Holiness was actually competing in a nine-pin no tap tournament, but the Fort Wayne Bowlers Association and the American Bowling Congress recognized the scores because there were no nine-pin strikes and the Westwood score sheets differentiated between regular and nine-pin strikes. All of his strikes were verified as legal strikes.

"I was right in the pocket every time," Holiness said. "Every ball was the same. When I got that first 300 I wasn't too excited; I was more relieved. It was about time. But then a second one? I got the pressure out of the way right away in the third game with an eight in the first frame."

Holiness recovered by picking up his spare, then rolled nine more strikes. Holiness then left four pins on a split and picked up two of those with his last ball. It surely didn't dampen the evening.

"I wasn't even thinking about a city record," Holiness said. "When you bowl back-to-back 300s, you don't think about records."

## April 19

**In 1993, the Fort Wayne Wizards open play in the Midwest League at home.**

When the Kenosha Twins moved to Fort Wayne, everyone had high hopes, but no one really knew what to expect. The players didn't know anything about Fort Wayne and vice versa.

It also didn't help when the Memorial Stadium dedication was snowed out two days before the home-opener, and there was rain in the forecast for that night.

Except for the breezy chill in the air, opening night was perfect as the Wizards beat the Peoria Chiefs 7-2 in front of 6,316 fans. Shortstop Ramon Valette smacked three hits, including a two-run home run, and four runs batted in and pitchers Scott Moten and Kevin LeGault combined to shut down the Chiefs. Valette was off to a hot spring already after he turned a triple play in Fort Wayne's first game on April 10.

The Wizards lost the momentum to their hot start and finished 68-67 in their first season, they sold almost 2,000 season tickets and attracted 318,506 fans to Memorial Stadium.

**Also, in 1998, Jason Fabini is drafted by the New York Jets.**

When Jason Fabini was a senior at Bishop Dwenger two years ago, he was a 6-7, 235-pound guard. He had the height but not the weight and strength to attract Big Ten teams.

By the time he was a junior at Cincinnati, Fabini had added 50 pounds of muscle and had made himself into a prospect. As a senior, Fabini was a dominating player who helped the Bearcats go 8-4, including a 35-19 victory over Utah State in the Humanitarian Bowl. He started 44 consecutive games and became an all-USA Conference selection.

Fabini was selected in the fourth round with the 111th overall pick by the Jets.

**April 20**

**In 1971, Wildcat Baseball League founder Dale "Mr. Mac" McMillen dies at age 91.**

The eldest of six children, Dale W. McMillen was born in 1880 to a farm family in Van Wert, Ohio. His father owned a grain elevator and wholesale feed and hay business, where Dale worked as a boy. In 1900, he went to Oberlin College in Ohio to study law, but left in 1901 to earn a business degree from Eastman College in Poughkeepsie, N.Y. He returned to Ohio to operate his father's business, and in 1906 he married Agnes Stewart of Battle Creek, Mich.

At age 54, McMillen founded the Central Soya Co. in Decatur.

Legend says Mr. Mac was driving through a park in 1961 when he saw the disappointed faces of boys who were told they weren't good enough to play in another league. He formed the Wildcat Baseball League as "one in which every boy makes the team and plays in every game." He later called it "the greatest thing I ever did."

"He had many, many avenues that he could share his good fortune and influence, and Wildcat was one of his favorites because it just gave so many kids, now over 200,000 in the 50 years, something," said Bill Derbyshire, the Wildcat League president in 2010.

The first year nearly 900 young boys came out, according to Guenther Herzog, who served as director at McMillen Park in the league's first year. The league had nearly 6,000 participants by the mid-1960s and gained national attention through an article in Parade magazine. It was eventually featured in Sports Illustrated.

An endowment through the McMillen Foundation continues to fund the program including the staff and equipment.

**Also in 1991, IPFW's men's volleyball team wins 3-2 at Ball State to earn its first NCAA Tournament appearance.**

After years of coming close, the Volleydons finally beat their arch-rivals for their first trip to the final four where they finished third behind seniors Fred Malcolm and Tony Luhning and freshman setter Lloy Ball.

## April 21

**In 1952, Hall of Fame baseball player Jimmie Foxx begins managing the Daisies.**

After completing his playing career with the Philadelphia Phillies in 1945, Foxx had totals of 2,646 hits and 534 home runs, but what he didn't have was a job or much money, thanks to a divorce. The next season he briefly tried working in the Red Sox radio booth, but then he bounced around minor league coaching jobs before coming to Fort Wayne the year after he was inducted into Cooperstown.

Foxx did a pretty good job, leading the Daisies to the playoffs where they lost in the first round 2-1 to the Rockford Peaches. He did not return the next season.

Supposedly, Tom Hanks role in "A League of Their Own" was loosely based on Foxx. Unlike Hanks' character, the Daisies all remember Foxx as being involved with the team and easy-going to work with.

**Also, in 1991, Lonnie Loach cements the Komets' comeback season with a Game 7 overtime goal against Indianapolis.**

Loach slipped the puck through the pads of the Indianapolis Ice's Jimmy Waite at 18:29 of overtime in Game 7 of the International Hockey League playoff series. Loach quieted the sellout Fairgrounds Coliseum crowd with perhaps the most important Komets goal of the last 40 years as it sparked the Komets' rebirth after the original franchise moved to Albany, N.Y., the summer before.

Taking a pass from Robin Bawa to get deep in to the Indianapolis zone, Loach somehow scored before defenseman Cam Russell could get across the crease to bury him. Instead, Loach and the Komets buried the Ice.

"I was just trying to get something away before he got me to the point where I couldn't shoot," Loach said. "He didn't get enough of me. I just tried to get it on net. I didn't see it go in, but I heard everybody start screaming."

The goal ended an epic series that saw five of the seven games decided by one goal, including the last three that were played on successive nights with the road team winning each time.

## April 22

**In 1990, wax figures from North Webster's International Palace of Sports are auctioned off as the museum closes.**

In an effort to attract more of the tourism trade which seemed to be passing through on the way to lake properties, North Webster leaders broke ground June 23, 1972 on the International Palace of Sports. When the building was dedicated two years later, 50,000 people watched the three-hour Little Mermaid Festival Parade and the crowning of O.J. Simpson as the 1973 King of Sports.

Simpson was not the only attraction, either, as ABC sportscaster Chris Schenkel, tennis great Pancho Gonzalez, bowler Dick Webber and Olympic track star Jesse Owens were also present.

Olympic swimming Mark Spitz great had been named the first King of Sports in 1973, but the building was not completed so the ceremony was held at the Tippecanoe Valley Country Club.

Each year the 7,600 member of the National Sportswriters and Sportscasters Association choose the King of Sports, inviting the stars to come to North Webster to take part in the parade and see a life-size wax replica costing $2,500 be unveiled. An oil painting would go on the wall, and a plaster checker with the person's likeness would be placed on a massive checkerboard.

Sports celebrities such as two-time Heisman Trophy winner Archie Griffin, Olympic decathlon champion Bruce Jenner, race car driver A.J. Foyt and basketball's Larry Bird came to town. NFL running back Walter Payton and IU basketball coach Bobby Knight did not.

When the museum closed permanently in 1990, there were 27 wax figures which were auctioned. The low price was $150 for Griffin's figure to $1,500 for Wayne Gretzky. Some of the other figures were of Gordie Howe, Red Grange, Muhammad Ali and Babe Didrickson Zaharias. The auction raised $51,000, including $14,000 for a championship belt from boxer Rocky Marciano.

The building itself was turned into a shoe store.

## April 23

**In 1963, the Komets win their first Turner Cup.**

Next year finally arrived for the Fort Wayne Komets in 1963. After bitter disappointments in 1959, 1960 and subpar seasons in 1961 and 1962, the Komets finally won their first Turner Cup championship in 1963.

Except it wasn't that easy. No one would have predicted this would have been the team to break through. The Komets earned 75 points to win the regular-season title by a point over Minneapolis, finishing 3-7 over their last 10 games, including losing four of the last five.

They also had to deal with history.

"The longer you go and you don't win, the harder it is because you have to start all over again from Game 1 the next year," Komets forward Eddie Long said.

The nucleus included Len Thornson, Reggie Primeau, John Goodwin, Lionel Repka and Long. Coach Ken Ullyot added Bobby Rivard, Roger Maisonneuve, Norm Waslawski and goaltender Chuck Adamson. Gary Sharp was added for the playoffs.

"We used to get together as a group away from the rink every once in a while and everybody got along together well," Thornson said.

They needed that camaraderie to come back and beat Muskegon in six games in the first round before taking on Minneapolis in the finals. The Komets lost the second game at home 6-1 to Minneapolis, but won the next three games, including two at St. Paul.

The Komets won the series 4-1 as 5,026 people joined them at Memorial Coliseum to celebrate. Finally, "next year" had arrived.

**Also, in 2008, Indiana Tech cornerstone Dan Kline announces his retirement.**

Kline served 30 years at Indiana Tech as men's basketball coach, athletic director, women's basketball coach and as vice president for student life. His men's teams were 274-243 in 18 seasons and made 14 trips to postseason tournaments.

**Also, in 1999, the Komets play their final game in the original International Hockey League.**

**April 24**

**In 1994, Alex Rodriguez hits his first professional baseball home run at Wizards Stadium.**

The No. 1 selection by the Seattle Mariners in the 1993 June amateur draft, Rodriguez held out until he received a $1.3 million contract on Aug. 30, which meant he didn't get to start his pro career until the next summer. Then he went 16 games with the Appleton Foxes without hitting a home run.

That ended in the ninth inning against the Wizards, with the Foxes trailing 7-5. Rodriguez stroked a solo home run over the right field wall to spark a five-run, six-hit inning as the Foxes came back to beat the Wizards 10-7.

"Where I see my improvement is my mental approach, the late at-bats in the game," Rodriguez told The News-Sentinel's Marlon Morgan. "It's hard when you're coming from high school where you get two and three at-bats a game. Here you may have five and six."

He figured it out pretty quickly, though, hitting 21 home runs that year in the minors and was playing with Seattle before the end of the season. Heading into the 2013 season, Rodriguez has hit 647 home runs in the Major Leagues.

**Also, in 1998, IPFW volleyball beats Ohio State to win a trip to the NCAA Tournament in Los Angeles.**

As Hector Soto crumpled to the practice floor March 20 with a severely sprained ankle, everyone on the IPFW men's volleyball team thought their season had crumpled, too. Sure, they all said the ultimate sports cliché, someone would have to step up, but no one really believed it.

Except this time everyone stepped up. The No. 6-ranked Volleydons stunned the volleyball nation by first beating No. 7 Lewis University on its home floor and then by beating a No. 5 Ohio State team to win the Midwest Intercollegiate Volleyball Association Tournament title and the region's berth in the NCAA Tournament.

Though Soto came back to play on a gimpy leg in Los Angeles, the magic ended there as Long Beach State beat the Volleydons in four games.

## April 25

**In 1992, LPGA star Cathy Kratzert Gerring is severely injured during a hospitality tent accident at the Sara Lee Classic.**

Gerring had just finished her second round at the Sara Lee Classic, a 1-over-par 73, when she was serving herself at a post-round buffet. As two workers tried to refill an alcohol-burning warmer, it exploded, setting Gerring on fire from the waist up. She suffered second-degree burns on her hands and face.

In 1995, Gerring settled a lawsuit with the catering company whose employee caused the fire to start.

Gerring, who won three times in 1990 and was fourth on the LPGA money list with $487,326, didn't play golf for nearly two years after the 1992 accident. But she had one main goal, to not let the Sara Lee be her last tournament.

She did much better than that. The Elmhurst High School graduate first returned to competitive golf at the JC Penney Classic in December, 1995, when she teamed with old friend Jay Haas and finished tied for 17th. She missed the cut May 3 in the Sprint Titleholders Championship, her first official event since the accident, and then in the Women's U.S. Open.

Gerring came back to play 10 tournaments in 1996, placing in two tournaments. She played in 58 tournaments after that, including 18 in 2000 and 14 in 2001. She finished her career in 2006 with more than $800,000 in career earnings.

**Also, in 1996, the Fury falls to the Sioux Falls Skyforce 118-117 in the CBA Finals to lose the series 4-1.**

Rookie Devin Gray hit a running jumper at the buzzer to end the Fury's best playoff run ever. Fort Wayne had lost Game 4 on another buzzer-beating shot the night before 123-122.

Former Fort Wayne resident Henry James scored a combined 61 points in the last two games to crush the hometown fans and win the Most Valuable Player Award.

The Fury were led by coach Gerald Oliver, Jaren Jackson and Carl Thomas. Fort Wayne won 15 of its last 17 home games to make a playoff push and then lost the last four home games in the playoffs.

**April 26**

**In 1992, Vaughn Dunbar is taken in the NFL draft's first round by the New Orleans Saints.**

As a junior at Snider High School in 1985, the tailback rushed for 1,646 yards and 20 touchdowns. During his senior season, he rushed for 2,568 yards and 40 touchdowns, including 252 on 28 carries against Carmel in the state championship game.

Dunbar played his first two seasons of college football at Northeastern Oklahoma A&M before transferring to Indiana where he finished his senior season with 1,805 yards, which led the nation. It was also the most in a single season by an IU player and 11th best in the history of the NCAA. His career total for rushing yards is 3,029, third in IU history behind Anthony Thompson and Mike Harkrader, who both played four seasons to Dunbar's two. Dunbar ranked second among Big Ten rushers for a single season.

Dunbar was a first-team all-American and finished sixth in the Heisman Trophy voting. He also helped IU do something incredibly rare, win a bowl game. Dunbar rushed 28 times for 106 yards and was the most valuable offensive player as the Hoosiers dominated Baylor 24-0 to win the Cooper Bowl.

Dunbar was picked with the 21st pick overall by the Saints where his career never really got started. He played in 39 NFL games, starting 14 times, and rushed for 935 yards and five touchdowns.

**Also, in 2008, Elmhurst graduate James Hardy is taken in the second round by Buffalo.**

As a red-shirt freshman at Indiana in 2005, Hardy caught 61 passes for 893 yards and 10 touchdowns, and then followed with 51 catches for 722 yards and 10 more touchdowns. As a junior, he caught 74 passes for 1,075 yards before declaring himself eligible for the draft. He finished at IU's all-time leader in career touchdowns with 36, catches with 186 and in yards with 2,690.

The Bills picked him with the 41st pick overall in the second round. He played 16 games with Buffalo, catching 10 passes for 96 yards and two touchdowns.

## April 27

**In 1965, the Komets win their second Turner Cup by beating Des Moines.**

It's amazing how close the Komets came to winning three consecutive championships. After finally winning their first Turner Cup in 1963, they almost came back for a repeat in 1964 but lost to Toledo in the finals.

"We had an offsides that was called when (Merv) Dubchak scored a goal and there was no way it was offsides," Len Thornson said. "Then we turned around and went back to their building and lost 2-1."

They rebounded the next season to beat Des Moines in a six-game Turner Cup Finals.

After finishing 40-25-5 and in second place during the regular season behind Port Huron, the Komets matched up again with Toledo in the first round of the playoffs. This time, the Komets crushed the Blades in four straight games. Then they caught a break as fourth-place Des Moines upset Port Huron in seven games, winning two games in Port Huron.

That meant the Komets had to sit around for 10 days, and they were a little rusty in Game 1 of the Turner Cup Finals before winning 2-1 at home. After winning Game 2 at home 6-4, the Komets lost Game 3 at Des Moines 6-3 but won Game 4 5-3 to take control of the series. After a 7-6 loss in the final game at Des Moines, the Komets came home to beat the Oak Leafs 7-5.

Bobby Rivard was the team leader that season with 116 points, followed by Merv Dubchak's 101, including 52 goals. Len Thornson scored 93 points. There was incredible balance as Norm Waslawski scored 86 points, Reg Primeau and John Goodwin 84 each and Lionel Repka led the defensemen with 57 points.

Thornson and Goodwin were the leading scorers during the playoffs with 18 points, but eight players scored at least 10 points in the postseason and two others scored nine and eight points. Chuck Adamson was once again the mainstay in goal, playing all 10 playoff games.

**April 28**

**In 2007, Anthony Spencer is a first-round NFL draft pick by the Dallas Cowboys.**

The Cowboys picked the Bishop Luers and Purdue graduate with the 26th pick.

Spencer had emerged at Purdue during his junior season when he started 11 games. Of his 33 tackles, 7.5 were sacks and 9.5 were for losses. He also forced three fumbles and knocked down six passes.

He was even better as a senior, as his 26.5 tackles for loss were second in the nation and the fifth-best total in conference history. His 93 tackles were second on the team, and his 10.5 sacks and five forced fumbles earned him all-Big Ten honors and the Purdue Most Valuable Player Award.

Spencer had a credible rookie season in 2007, starting the first six games, played in all 17 games and finished with 28 tackles.

The outside linebacker finally became a full-time starter in his third season and he hasn't come off the field since. He earned his first Pro Bowl selection in 2012. The Cowboys put their franchise tag on him in 2012, good for $8.9 million. He led the team with 95 tackles and 11 sacks and was the only NFL player with 90-plus tackles and 10-plus sacks.

The Cowboys again put the franchise tag on Spencer for the 2013 season, worth $9.6 million.

**Also, in 1985, Robbie Laird scores three goals and two assists as the Komets beat Salt Lake 6-2 in Game 7.**

The Komets led the series 3-0 after winning the first two games at home and Game 3 in Salt Lake. Then the Golden Eagles got hot to force a seventh game in Fort Wayne, and Laird put on one of the best individual playoff performances in franchise history.

## April 29

**In 1995, LaTroy Hawkins becomes the first Fort Wayne Wizard to make it to the Major Leagues.**

Hawkins was the Wizards' pitcher of the year in 1993, posting a 15-5 record and leading the Midwest League in strikeouts and with a 2.06 earned run average. He also won 12 straight games.

Hawkins was followed to the Twins by former Wizards Scott Watkins, Matt Lawson, Dan Naulty, Dan Serafini, Travis Miller, Shane Bowers, Torii Hunter and Javie Valentine. Other famous former Wizards to make it to the show with the Twins include Corey Koskie, A.J. Pierzynski, Matt LeCroy, Jaun Rincon and Michael Cuddyer.

The 1993 team, the first Wizards team, featured nine players who eventually made it to the Major Leagues, and the 1994 squad had seven such players.

Among the more famous future San Diego Padres who have come through Fort Wayne are Sean Burroughs, Jake Peavy, Josh Barfield, Matt Latos, Nick Hundley and Will Venable.

As compiled by Chad Gramling's website "Baseball in Fort Wayne," there are more than 112 former Wizards and TinCaps who have made it to the Major Leagues.

**Also, in 2006, South Side's Bernard Pollard is drafted in the second round by the NFL's Kansas City Chiefs.**

**April 30**

**In 2005, Nancy Rehm is inducted into the Indiana Basketball Hall of Fame.**

An all-city basketball and volleyball player at Bishop Luers and a starting guard at Indiana Tech, Rehm was killed Feb. 3, 1982, when she attempted to stop a thief from stealing her snowmobile after a basketball practice.

The leading scorer in Bishop Luers history at the time, Rehm averaged 17.8 points and 6.2 assists while leading the Knights to the Summit Athletic Conference, sectional and regional titles in 1980. She played one semester at William Penn College in Iowa before transferring home to Indiana Tech where she helped the Warriors win a state title in 1981 with 13 points and 6.4 assists per game.

Following her death, the Nancy Rehm Invitational started with a softball tournament in 1982 and became a girls basketball showcase in 1983. The Fort Wayne Women's Bureau began presenting the Nancy Rehm Award for significant contributions to women's sports in the city in 1982.

**Also, in 2001, Tony Gwynn and the San Diego Padres play the Wizards in an exhibition game.**

This was the Padres' second trip to Fort Wayne for an exhibition game and they won the game 8-7 despite getting out-hit 10-9 and giving up six extra-base hits while tagging only three of their own.

Because he had been put on the disabled list the week before with a hamstring problem, Gwynn did not play in the game but he spoke with many fans and signed hundreds of autographs for at least 45 minutes. Rickey Henderson skipped the game for personal reasons, but Padres regulars like Ryan Kelsko and Phil Nevin played.

# MAY

## May 1

**In 1993, the Komets win at Atlanta 2-1 to take the most intense playoff game from their 1993 run.**

Because this game was played on the road, it doesn't rank as highly in most Komets' fans memories as the Game 3 overtime win against San Diego in the Turner Cup Finals, but every Komets player will say this was the game that convinced them they could win the championship.

"That's one of the greatest periods I've ever been in," Komets captain Colin Chin said, gasping. The Komets had just pulled off one of their typical nail-biting, fist-clenching, muscle-cramping third-period comebacks. Except this wasn't typical by any hockey standards.

The Komets trailed 1-0 after two numbing periods, but they came back to win and go up 2-0 in their Eastern Conference Finals playoff series. When it looked like they were beaten, the Komets found the energy and the execution to come back and win their sixth straight playoff game. The Komets were battered and bruised in the locker room after the game, but they weren't beaten.

The Komets looked as though they were going to lose after Herb Raglan snapped a slap shot past goalie Pokey Reddick in the second period. Playing their second game in two nights, the Komets' legs were dead. The specialty teams had to kill off four Atlanta power plays in the first period, and they were sucking wind.

Bob Wilkie and Joel Savage gave the Komets a big boost when Wilkie took a pass from Savage and tried to beat Atlanta goalie David Littman between the legs. The puck hit Littman's stick instead, but Savage smacked in the tying goal.

The goal gave the Komets' legs new life, and they forced an Atlanta penalty with 6:29 left. Nine seconds later, Colin Chin hit Jean-Marc Richard charging down the slot, and Richard beat Littman with a backhand to give Fort Wayne a 2-1 lead.

"It doesn't seem to matter if we're down or up," Komets coach Al Sims said. "These guys just won't take a loss. Atlanta probably played about as well as they could. I figured the next goal would win it, and we got it. I think everybody thought if we kept going, we'd be OK."

## May 2

**In 2006, DaMarcus Beasley is named to his second World Cup soccer team.**

Many Fort Wayne athletes have been trailblazers such as Johnny Bright, Lloy Ball, Nel Fettig, Bobbi Widmann-Foust and the Fort Wayne Daisies, but Beasley is another who has had a huge impact on the world stage.

After being named a Parade All-American and the national co-player of the year in 1999, the South Side product left Fort Wayne after his junior year to attend IMG Academy in Bradenton, Fla., and later became the youngest player ever to sign a Major League Soccer contract.

Beasley first broke onto the international scene in 1999 at the Under-17 World Cup in New Zealand where he was named the tournament's second-best player. He played his first game with the U.S. National team on Jan. 27, 2001 before playing on the under-20 team at the 2001 World Youth Championships. That led to his first World Cup team assignment in 2002 and return trips in 2006 and 2010.

His professional league career has had better success. He played four seasons with the Chicago Fire of the MLS, scoring 14 goals and 20 assists, and then the Dutch team PSV Eindhoven bought his rights for $2.5 million. Beasley helped PSV win its league title and scored a key goal in the Dutch Amstel Cup.

He also became the first American player to play in the semifinal stages of the UEFA Champions League, scoring four goals in 12 games. His European career concluded with stints with the Glasgow (Scotland) Rangers and the Hannover (Germany) 96. In 2011 he signed to play with the Mexican team Puebla F.C.

"At this point in my career, I'm not getting any younger," he told The News-Sentinel's Tom Davis in 2011. "I just want to play. The Mexican teams saw my desire and my effort to show I'm still the player (people) saw three years ago. Give me a chance and I'm going to perform."

## May 3

**In 2007, IPFW beats Pepperdine to play for the NCAA Tournament volleyball title.**

First, the Volleydons surprised everyone by sweeping No. 6-ranked Ohio State in Columbus to win the Midwest Intercollegiate Volleyball Association title to earn IPFW's sixth trip to the NCAA Tournament. The Buckeyes had their 19-match home winning streak ended.

Then, the Volley dons pulled an even bigger surprise, crushing top-ranked Pepperdine 3-1 to win their 10th straight match and advance to their first NCAA championship match. Besides the No. 1 ranking, Pepperdine's resume included five national titles and 13 NCAA Tournament appearances.

C.J. Macias belted 24 kills, Brock Ulrich 20 and Jason Host 18 as setter Colin Linden set up the hitters with 64 assists as IPFW hit 38 percent for the match compared to the Waves' 34 percent.

"If I had thought that (IPFW would never make the title game), I would have retired a long time ago," IPFW coach Arnie Ball said. "If you don't have that as your goal, you shouldn't be coaching."

The dream run came to an end in the finals as IPFW lost to UC-Irvine 3-1.

Macias and Linden were named to the all-tournament team, and Ball was named the American Volleyball Coaches Association Coach of the Year after leading IPFW to a 23-8 record.

**Also, in 1988, former Piston Bobby McDermott is selected for the basketball hall of fame.**

**Also, in 1998, Fort Wayne artist and baseball historian Bob Parker dies at age 82.**

**May 4**

**In 1871, the Kekiongas play the Cleveland Forest Citys in what is believed to be the first professional baseball game.**

After the Civil War, the Fort Wayne Kekiongas baseball team was formed in 1866. In 1869 the team played the Cincinnati Red Stockings who were believed to be the first team in the country of paid professional players. The Red Stockings won easily 86-8, and then won the rematch later that season 41-7.

The Kekiongas were actually a very good team, and won the state championship in 1870, and in 1871 the National Association of Professional Baseball Players was started at a meeting in New York. The teams tossed coins to see which squads would pay the first game, and Fort Wayne and Cleveland won.

The game was played in Fort Wayne, and the Kekiongas won 2-0.

**Also, in 2003, Dustin Virag scores in overtime as the Komets win the UHL's Colonial Cup.**

When Dustin Virag's wrist shot snapped over the left shoulder of Quad City goaltender Jeff Reynaert 39 seconds into overtime in Game 5, Virag skated to the corner with the biggest smile on his face. Then he stopped and his smile froze.

"I was like, `Crap, what do I do now?'" Virag said. "I thought I had to celebrate somehow, so I turned around, threw my gloves off and called the bench on."

His delighted teammates buried him in joy. The win ended a remarkable turnaround for the Komets who had missed the playoffs the season before. The only players who returned were Kevin Bertram, Michel Massie, Troy Neumeier, Kevin Schmidt, Ryan Severson and Virag. The team loaded up with new players like Colin Chaulk, Bobby Stewart, David-Alexandre Beauregard, Sean Venedam, Kevin Kotyluk and Kelly Perrault. Goaltender Tom Lawson was the playoffs' Most Valuable Player for coach Greg Puhalski.

The Komets beat Port Huron 3-0 in the first round and Elmira 4-0 in the second round of the playoffs. After splitting the first two games of the finals at home, the Komets won both games in Quad City to take control.

**May 5**

**In 1925, Everett Scott's Major League record consecutive games played streak ends at 1,307.**

Though not as well known as Lou Gehrig or Cal Ripken who held the record after him, the sure-handed "Deacon" became the first player to play more than 1,000 games consecutively from 1916 to 1925.

Born in Bluffton on Nov. 19, 1892, Scott graduated from Bluffton High School in 1909. His family moved to Auburn while Everett started his pro baseball career in Kokomo and then moved on to Youngstown, Ohio, to play in the Ohio-Pennsylvania League.

Though he was only 5-foot-8 and never weighed more than 148 pounds, Scott was an expert fielder. From 1916 to 1923 he led all American League shortstops in fielding. He once set the American League record for fewest errors in a season by a shortstop with 23 in a 154-game season in 1920.

Ironically, his consecutive-game streak started with an injury to Scott. According to a 1922 story in Baseball Magazine, Scott was spiked by Ty Cobb in 1916. He tried to play the next game wearing the larger spikes of his manager but suffered a sprained ankle, forcing him to sit out a few games. The streak began June 20, 1916, when Scott replaced a player in the ninth inning.

There was plenty of luck along the way to keep the streak alive. According to a 1922 story in the New York Tribune, Scott often played through injuries and illnesses. Scott often suffered from boils, and one time a boil almost forced one of his eyes closed.

Amazingly, Scott more than doubled the former record of 577 games by Dodgers third baseman George Pinkney. The streak didn't end until New York Yankees manager Miller Huggins benched him because of sore knees on May 5, 1925. Scott had played 1,307 consecutive games. Less than a month later, on June 1, 1925, Gehrig began his streak. He broke Scott's streak on Aug. 17, 1933, in a game against the St. Louis Browns.

Scott's record did not include 27 World Series games or about 200 exhibition games. He also played only 126 games in 1918 and 128 in 1919 because of World War I, during which baseball played fewer games.

**Also, in 1994, the Minnesota Twins play the Wizards in an exhibition game.**

**May 6**

**In 1927 Babe Ruth and the New York Yankees play the Lincoln Lifers.**

Fort Wayne has a fantastic baseball history, thanks in part to the Lincoln Lifers, a semi-pro team sponsored by Lincoln National Life Insurance Co. The squad regularly played exhibition games against Major League teams during the 1920s. Maybe the Lifers' biggest game ever came against the Yankees' "Murderers' Row" squad that featured Babe Ruth and Lou Gehrig. Ruth hit 60 home runs that season and Gehrig drove in 175 runs as the Yankees went on to win the World Series.

A standing-room-only crowd of more than 3,000 fans was on hand to watch the first-place Yankees who stopped off on their way to a series in Chicago.

The Lifers rallied to take a 3-2 lead in the top of the eighth inning before the Yankees tied it in the bottom of the inning.

The game was tied 3-3 in the 10th inning with a man on first when Ruth stepped to the plate for the fifth time. He had been held hitless in his first three at-bats along with a walk. With two strikes, Ruth belted the third pitch over the right field wall for a two-run home run that gave the Yankees a 5-3 win. As Ruth crossed home plate, he was mobbed by fans and members of both teams.

Legend says the Lifers catcher Bruff Cleary walked to the mound before the final toss to inform pitcher Chuck Noel that, "These fans came here to see Babe Ruth hit, not to see you pitch. So give them what they want and groove one."

That turned out to be the last season for the Lifers. A year later Fort Wayne rejoined professional baseball as the Chiefs played in the Central League.

The Yankees finished the 1927 season with a 110-44 record, sweeping the Pittsburgh Pirates in the World Series.

## May 7

**In 1994, Penn State ends the West Coast's NCAA Volleyball domination by beating UCLA as Fort Wayne draws a record 15,495 fans to the tournament.**

In a tournament that broke many traditions, Penn State broke the biggest, ending California's 24-year run of NCAA Men's Volleyball Championships. The Nittany Lions came back from an 11-4 fourth-game deficit to beat UCLA 9-15, 15-13, 4-15, 15-12, 15-12.

No one gave them any chance against what many consider to be the best college men's volleyball team in 10 years. There would be no excuses from the West. Penn State won the match, UCLA didn't lose it. This was no fluke against a weaker team, or with a home-court advantage. The Nittany Lions simply refused to give up when they probably should have, and the 14-time national champion Bruins didn't realize they were being beaten until it was too late to stop it.

Ramon Hernandez buried UCLA's defense with 17 kills and no errors in the fourth game, tipping the ball around three-Bruin blocks to open holes on the floor.

During the fifth game Hernandez, only belted two kills, but UCLA self-destructed. The best offensive team in the nation hit only 18 percent. UCLA had not been challenged all year, winning 27 straight matches, mostly by 3-0 scores. When the Bruins needed to dig deep to fight off a challenge, they didn't know how.

Before the title match, only two other non-California teams had ever played for the title, and no one had even come close even during semifinal matches in 10 years. These Penn State seniors were making their fourth appearance in the Final Four, but they had never won even a game in the semifinals before.

"'We've all endured the stigma of 'Do you guys belong here? Do you guys belong on a volleyball court with us?'" Penn State senior Ed Josefoski said. "I've endured it, and I'm not going to cover it up. H---, yes, we deserve it. We beat your best team. I think a lot of other schools had the feeling, that they didn't care who it was, but somebody had to beat these guys."

There were 7,587 tickets sold for the first night and 7,908 for the second – a total of 15,495. The old record of 13,102 was set in Muncie for the 1992 tournament.

**May 8**

**In 2009, the Komets beat Muskegon in five games to defend their Turner Cup.**

After 57 years as a franchise, there were not too many firsts remaining for the Komets, but they erased the biggest one left by successfully defending a playoff championship.

As 10,480 orange-and-black-wearing fans screamed their joy, the Fort Wayne Komets played keep-away from the Muskegon Lumberjacks just like they did the rest of the Turner Cup Finals. The Lumberjacks could never catch up to the speedy Komets, who won Game 5 of the International Hockey League playoff finals 4-1.

While everyone else was talking about a repeat title, the Komets never did.

"There are guys who were here last year and guys who weren't," defenseman Kevin Bertram said. "You really don't want to hear about what the team before you did. We wanted to win the championship for us, not for back-to-back or the guys who were here last year."

There really was very little doubt after the Komets took a 2-1 lead at 13:57 of the second period. After Leo Thomas knocked the puck away from a Muskegon defenseman, Colin Chaulk skated behind the net and tossed the puck to Mark Versteeg-Lytwyn for a tap-in.

With Versteeg-Lytwyn's goal giving them momentum, the Komets came out flying in the third period and pushed the margin to 4-1 on goals by Thomas and Justin Hodgman. By hooking Muskegon defenseman Darryl McArthur, Chaulk forced a turnover at the Muskegon blue line and fed Thomas for a goal at 4:45. Then the Komets' rookie line put a marker on the board when Sean O'Connor and Rick Varone set up Hodgman at 5:26.

The Komets wore down the Lumberjacks, outshooting them 38-23 in the game and 208-131 in the series. David Hukalo was named the playoffs Most Valuable Player after helping hold Muskegon scoring leader Todd Robinson to five points and Robin Bouchard to no goals. Hukalo, 30, led the Komets in scoring with eight goals and 14 points in 11 playoff games.

## May 9

**In 1990, Woodlan High School's Lloy Ball picks volleyball over basketball.**

Though he was 6-8 and had very good passing ability and outside range on his shooting, Lloy Ball was not a hot basketball recruit until after his senior season was completed. Then he played in a couple of all-star games and got hot to attract a lot of notice.

Louisville, Kentucky, Indiana, Southern California and Stanford all tried to recruit Ball, but his favorite team growing up, Purdue, wasn't interested. USC and Stanford wanted him to play basketball and volleyball, but he had already decided if he was going to play basketball he'd go to IU, and if he was going to play volleyball he'd stay at home and play for his dad at IPFW. His only recruiting trip was to Bloomington.

In his biography, "The Biggest Mistake I Never Made," Ball wrote, "But it was an excruciating decision, really the only hard thing I'd had to do with my life up until that moment because I was so torn. Every day at school I've got secretaries, teachers, friends and people who didn't even like me for four years telling me I had to go to IU. Most of the kids from my high school went to IU, and most of the staff had graduated from down there so it was a big IU place. Obviously, everyone supported Coach Knight and that program and it was just relentless. I'd find notes in my locker saying, `Go to IU.' Girls who would never even think about dating me would say, `Hey, I'm going there next year. Maybe you and I could date.' It was kind of like rock stars-type stuff. Teachers who I had to beg for B-minuses were asking if I needed extra help in school or tutoring and things like that to prepare for SATs. I went from being a good athlete and people knew me to sort of like the class president for a while."

The night before making his announcement, Ball went to bed totally undecided. It hadn't helped that his father told him he'd be crazy not to play for coach Bob Knight.

"I just woke up the next morning after about an hour's sleep, and I just knew.

"To some moans and groans, I said, `I'm going to sign with IPFW.' I'll bet there were 100 to 150 people there in the gymnasium, including all the teachers.

"To this day, people ask me if I could have that moment back, would I take it back? Never."

**Also, in 1980, the first Walter Jordan's Parade of Stars game is held at Northrop.**

The first game of a 10-year run featured local former high school stars. Jordan scored 29 points and former Northrop teammate Mike Muff 21. Eugene Parker also scored 15 for the North which won 134-120. Mr. Basketball Jim Master led the South with 24 points and former Wayne star Tim Smiley scored 19.

**Also, in 1993, Tom Knauss drives in eight runs for the Wizards in a game against Appleton.**

**May 10**

**In 2005, Jonathan Goodwin scores in overtime as the Komets win Game 7 against arch-rival Rockford.**

The Komets had never been able to come back from a 3-1 deficit to win a series before, but Kevin St. Pierre shaved his moustache, Colin Chaulk got hot and then Rob Guinn helped Goodwin become a hero. Oh, yeah, and it happened in overtime.

The Komets rallied to win Game 5 in overtime on a Chaulk goal, and then St. Pierre shut down the IceHogs with 35 games in Game 6 to send the series back to a deciding game in Fort Wayne. Then, regulation wasn't enough to decide things.

The end finally came 14:46 into overtime when defenseman Guinn took a faceoff from Colin Chaulk in Rockford's zone and skated wide around an IceHogs defender. Guinn had been planning to shoot, but when IceHogs goaltender Michel Robinson came out to challenge him he saw a white shirt out of the corner of his eye and heard Jonathan Goodwin yell.

"I didn't know if he heard me, but then I got the puck," Goodwin said. "There was no way Robinson could have been back in the net to save it. I just wanted to put something quick on goal."

After the puck dented the back of the net, the IceHogs defenders collapsed to the ice as the Komets swarmed over Goodwin and Guinn in the corner celebration.

"This is the most fatigued I've been in my entire life, but by the same token it's the happiest I've ever been in my life," forward Danny Stewart said. "I'm so proud of these guys it's unbelievable. They showed unbelievable character, unbelievable heart."

## May 11

**In 2002, Northrop softball pitcher Amy Kendall throws her fourth perfect game of the season.**

Though the season still had a month to go, Kendall had already thrown four no-hitters and eight shutouts. This time she beat East Noble 9-0.

The senior finished 29-5 that season and was named Miss Softball for Indiana.

"I never really thought about winning this until this year," Kendall told The News-Sentinel's Erik Pupillo. "My intentions, beginning my freshman year, (were) to make a name for myself and dominate the sport the way I know how, and it grew into something else.

"This is the kind of exciting award you always dream of winning because you're not just being named the MVP for your high school, but for the entire state of Indiana. It's so much greater than any other award because you're being singled out in the entire state as the greatest player for that season."

A four-time News-Sentinel PrepSports Player of the Year, Kendall finished with career state records of 106 wins, 1,543 strikeouts, 117 complete games, 72 shutouts and 33 no-hitters. She threw eight perfect games and had a career earned run average of .29. She also finished with the state's top four seasons for strikeouts.

As far as individual seasons, Kendall finished with state records for 29 wins, 399 strikeouts, 19 shutouts, and 11 no-hitters.

Kendall joined teammate Lori Melchi in playing college softball at Kentucky.

**Also, in 1997, Tom Knauss drives in four runs to become the Wizards' all-time leader in runs batted in.**

**May 12**

**In 2008, Justin Hodgman scores in triple overtime to give the Komets a Game 7 Turner Cup win against Port Huron.**

The season of a lifetime ended with a game that seemed to last a lifetime.

When Justin Hodgman grabbed Guy Dupuis' slap shot out of the air, dropped it to the ice beside the Port Huron net and shoved it behind goaltender Larry Sterling at 12:22 a.m., the Komets stopped feeling like dog-tired old men and turned into joyous little boys. They had finally beaten the Icehawks 3-2 at 23 seconds of the third overtime to claim the International Hockey League's Turner Cup 4-3 before a sellout Memorial Coliseum crowd of 10,462.

"I'm so tired right now I don't even want to wake up this afternoon because I know everything is going to hurt so bad," defenseman Kevin Hansen said. "The only thing that doesn't hurt is my smile."

It's the longest Game 7 in the 57-year IHL history and the third-longest game in the Komets' 56-year history. During a playoffs that was all about endurance and resiliency, the Komets were pushed way beyond what they thought their limits were, coming back from a 3-1 deficit to win three games in five days.

The Komets had some bounces early in the game and almost lost it. Fort Wayne led 2-0 halfway through the second period on goals by Hodgman and Dupuis, but Port Huron rallied on Jeff Zehr's back-door goal to give the Icehawks a chance in the third period.

That chance almost ran out. With Sterling pulled in the final minute, defenseman Joe Markusen fired a shot on net that forward Tab Lardner deflected with 52.2 seconds left in regulation.

"We tried to stay as loose as we could," Dupuis said. "It was ours to win. It wasn't that we were losing the cup, because we had never won it. It was just an opportunity for us to win it. That helped us stay loose."

**Also, in 2001, Scott Sharp wins the pole at the Indianapolis 500 for Kelley Racing.**

**In 1999, the Wizards host the San Diego Padres in an exhibition game.**

The Padres beat the Wizards 6-4 before 5,989 fans at Memorial Stadium.

Because of injuries, the Padres were short-handed so Wizards outfielder Jon Cook, infielder Alex Garcia, catcher Ron French and batting coach Eric Bullock all played for the Padres.

The three pitchers the Padres used were flown in from the Arizona extended spring training.

Phil Nevin drove in the first run of the game for the big club, but the Wizards tied it when Sean Burroughs doubled and scored on a Tony Lawrence groundout. All-time Padres great Tony Gwynn stroked the first of his two hits and then scored San Diego's third run on a Dave Madigan sacrifice fly to make it 3-1.

Jeremy Owens tripled and scored for Fort Wayne in the third inning, but San Diego scored twice in the sixth to go up 6-2. The Wizards scored twice in the bottom of the seventh for the final margin.

"I like 'em," Gwynn said of the exhibition games the Padres were playing that season with each of their minor-league affiliates. "It gives people from all over the chance to come out and see me play. And for me, this was a chance for me to see some family and play in front of them."

**Also, in 1979, the Fort Wayne Scouts softball team begins play.**

**May 14**

**In 1993, the Komets win Game 1 of the Turner Cup finals by crushing San Diego 7-1 on the Gulls' home ice.**

After sweeping Cleveland and Atlanta in the first two rounds, the Komets knew they could compete with the best regular-season team in minor league hockey history, but the San Diego Gulls didn't know that until this game.

San Diego was called for a team-record 22 penalties for 82 minutes and the Komets 12 for 27 minutes. Fort Wayne had 14 power plays, twice as many as the Gulls. After the Komets built a 4-0 lead halfway through the second period, the Gulls kept trying cheap shots and referee Steve Watson kept sending them to the penalty box.

"It was just a tremendous effort by our guys to keep their discipline, keep their cool," Komets Coach Al Sims said. "We're here to win hockey games and not get involved in any of that other stuff. I think they know that they're in for a series. I think San Diego realizes we're a good team now."

The Komets scored four power-play goals in the first two periods and knocked goalie Peter Ing out of the game with 1:44 left in the second period with the score 6-0.

The Gulls never recovered from the first minute of the game when the Komets pumped five shots at Ing. San Diego forward Daniel Shank picked up a slashing penalty 29 seconds into the game, and Paul Willett scored at 2:04 to give the Komets the lead.

The Gulls were held to one shot on goal in the first five minutes and two in the first 10 minutes. The second period was even more one-sided, as the Komets had five power plays and scored on three of them.

Willett scored the hat trick for the Komets, Joel Savage had three assists and Igor Chibirev had a goal and two assists.

**Also, in 2010, the IPFW women's tennis team loses to Notre Dame 4-0 in the NCAA Tournament.**

## May 15

**In 2010, the Komets win their third straight title in the IHL.**

For five years, the Cincinnati Mohawks' dominance was legendary. Since the Mohawks won five Turner Cups from 1953 to 1957, no other IHL team could win as many as three straight titles. Six times teams won back-to-back championships and then advanced to the finals again. All six lost.

The 2009-10 Fort Wayne Komets almost lost, too. The two-time defending IHL champions trailed a semifinal series against Port Huron 3-1 before rallying to win in seven games. Then they beat the Flint Generals in five games, winning a pivotal Game 4 before a standing-room-only crowd at Perani Arena. Playing before 10,480 Memorial Coliseum fans the next night, the Komets beat the Generals 3-2 in Game 5 to clinch three titles in a row.

"Our fans expect us to win, I expect us to win and the veterans expect us to win, and the rookies and all the other kids fall into line," Komets coach Al Sims said. "The cup becomes as important to them as it does to everybody else in the room. They want it just as bad as the rest of us do."

There were four one-goal decisions during the finals, and the Komets won three of them.

"We are used to winning, but we also know how hard it is to win," said veteran David Hukalo.

Nick Boucher became the first goaltender in the IHL's 59-year history to win three straight cups, Matt Syroczynski was the playoffs' Most Valuable Player after scoring 11 goals in 12 games and P.C. Drouin led the Komets in scoring during the playoffs with 18 points. The Komets scored nine power-play goals during the finals, and Drouin assisted or scored on eight of them.

"It just seemed that when the other team would throw a storm at us, everybody would get together and pull hard together," Komets captain Guy Dupuis said. "It always seems the last three years, whenever our backs were against the walls, we always came up with our best performance."

Dupuis, Drouin, Boucher, Hukalo, Kevin Bertram, Justin Hodgman, Brandon Warner and Colin Chaulk were part of all three championship teams. Chaulk, Bertram and Dupuis won their fourth titles as Komets, as did Sims.

"We appreciate as players that we're spoiled, but you know what, the fans of Fort Wayne have been a little spoiled, too," Chaulk said. "Both the players and fans have been spoiled."

**May 16**

**In 2003, Indiana Tech baseball earns its sixth-straight NAIA World Series appearance.**

As usual, the Warriors needed some stress to make sure they were in the right spot.

Indiana Tech lost a chance to win the Heartland Super Regional the easy way, blowing a 4-1 lead in the first game to lose 7-4 to force a winner-take-all rematch. This time the Warriors won easily 7-3 behind the hitting of Marcus Trujillo and the relief pitching of Shawn Kable.

Over the previous five years, the Warriors always had to come back through the loser's bracket to advance to the World Series, so they didn't freak out when faced with elimination.

"Guys in this program are just used to that," shortstop Jeff Wilson said. "I'm used to it, and the younger guys are getting used to it now so when they get up here it won't be a big deal. They'll bring the guys after them along."

Maybe this Indiana Tech team had to pull off the hardest comeback of the six teams. The Warriors were 40-18, but were unranked, receiving only five honorable mention votes from the national coaches poll. They were picked third in the region behind Spring Arbor and Bethel, two teams they clobbered last week in the regional.

Then they had to face No. 5 Olivet Nazarene, a team that already had at least an at-large bid to the World Series locked up.

"If you are prepared for it, you shouldn't be nervous," Indiana Tech coach Devine said. "Our kids don't get nervous or crack under pressure. If we fail, we fail, but it's not from being scared.

"That's a testament to the kids. Nothing comes easy and that's how it should be. Nothing comes easy in baseball or in the game of life."

**Also, in 2001, Concordia's Brian Reith makes this Major League debut with the Cincinnati Reds.**

Reith pitched in 73 games over three years, going 4-12 with a 5.92 earned run average.

**May 17**

**In 1991, John Anderson plays for the first time in a month and scores a hat trick.**

It still might be the most memorable game in Fort Wayne Komets history.

Other players have scored more goals or more points or put forth amazing efforts in key playoff moments, but none had the flair or the lasting legacy of Anderson's effort on May 17, 1991. Say "The John Anderson Game" and every Komets fan knows what it signifies.

Following a 5-4 overtime loss two nights before, the Komets trailed the Peoria Rivermen 3-0 in the Turner Cup Finals heading to Memorial Coliseum for Game 4. After upsetting defending champion Indianapolis and division winner Kalamazoo in the first two rounds, this was to be the end of the Komets' rebirth season. The Rivermen were the best-ever minor league hockey team, and the Komets were beat up and out of bodies. There were 8,025 fans showing up to say goodbye.

Then Anderson came out for warm-ups without his helmet, and the crowd started buzzing.

With 73 points, the 34-year-old right wing had been the International Hockey League's leading scorer through the first 51 games, but a deep thigh bruise on his right leg suffered Jan. 26 caused calcium deposits to form on top of the bone. X-rays later showed the buildup to be six inches long and about an inch thick, causing the muscle to snag on it.

"During those playoffs, in that final series, he could barely walk to the rink," said current Anaheim Ducks coach Bruce Boudreau, who was the Komets' second-leading scorer that season. "After we lost Game 3, I remember the morning skate, and John was flying. We couldn't believe that all of a sudden he felt so good. It was like a miracle."

Anderson's first goal beat Peoria goalie Pat Jablonski and the clock, lighting the lamp at 19:59 of the first period to give the Komets a 2-1 lead and a huge lift. His second tally shocked everyone, particularly Jablonski, as Anderson rifled in a slap shot from 25 feet. The third came off a rebound, scooped over Jablonski when his defensemen failed to clear the puck.

Anderson sat out the third period but the Komets had a 4-1 lead and they won 5-2.

**Also, in 1987, the final Fort Wayne Marathon is held.**

**May 18**

**In 1989, Matt Kinzer makes his Major League debut for the St. Louis Cardinals.**

St. Louis Cardinals Manager Whitey Herzog, his team down 3-2, handed the ball to the kid and said, "Get this guy so we can get you a win."

With three runs in and Astros on first and second and two outs in the bottom of the fourth, Matt Kinzer got the guy, but he didn't get the win.

The St. Louis victory came much later in the contest, a 4-3 decision in 10 innings after the Norwell High School graduate had contributed a successful 3 1/3 innings of relief. It was his first Major League appearance since being called up by the Cardinals from AAA Louisville two days before.

"I did what the definition of a long reliever says you're supposed to do. I held them," Kinzer said "It really helped getting that first pitch in for a strike."

Kinzer's line read 3 1/3 innings pitched, one hit, no walks, three strikeouts and no runs. He faced the minimum of nine hitters and retired the last eight straight.

"Being there sitting on the bench wasn't good enough," Kinzer said. "I wanted to play and prove what I could do. It's hard to have it really sink in because I feel like I could have made the team in spring training. It probably won't sink in until I read it in the paper."

**Also, in 1971, former Komet John Ferguson retires from the Montreal Canadiens after winning a fifth Stanley Cup.**

## May 19

**In 1950, Central graduate Paul Bienz wins the 100 and 200 dashes for the third straight year in the Southeastern Conference.**

Paul Bienz is likely the fastest person ever to come from Fort Wayne.

He first made his mark as part of Central High School's "Fearsome Foursome" with Max Ramsey, Bill Eschcoff and Bob Mugg who were the only four Tigers to compete in the 1944 state meet. Bienz won the 100 and 220 races, Ramsey won the 440 and finished second in the 220, and all four men combined to win the 880 relay. Central won the title with 29 points.

After two years in the U.S. Army Air Corps, Bienz played both football and track at Tulane. Though he was only 5-foot-8, 172 pounds, he had a muscular build, but his nickname was "Mr. No Legs" because he was usually shorter than anyone he ran against.

But no one could catch him. Three years in a row he won the 100 and 200 dashes at the Southeastern Conference meet before finishing third in each race three years in a row at the NCAA championships to earn all-American honors. He placed fourth at the 1948 U.S. Olympic trials.

Twice he tied world records, but each time the wind was too strong to allow him to qualify. On May 6, 1948, he ran a 9.4 100 yards in Baton Rouge against Louisiana State. A year later, he ran a 20.3 220 in Tuscaloosa, Ala.

He came back to Central in 1952, and eventually served as the Tigers' football coach for eight years, going 33-33-5. He was also the athletic director at Northrop and Elmhurst before he retired.

**Also, in 1994, the Komets lose 7-6 in the Turner Cup finals to Atlanta in three overtimes after leading 5-0.**

May

**May 20**

**In 2006, the Derby Girls host their first bout.**

In 2005, Danielle Abbott and Tonya Vojtkofsky were on vacation with their husbands in Seattle when they were hooked visiting a roller derby event. They came home and started a league that quickly grew to more than 50 skaters ages 22 to 45. Since then, the range of ages increased from 18 into the lower-50s.

There were two really cool things about the group. They came up with wonderful nicknames such as "Little D. Evil," "Go Go Beware," "Spuratik Payne," "Mali Bruise Barbie," "Baby Doll Beatdown," and "Bang, Bang LaDesh." The also came up with awesome event names such as "Derby Deeds Done Dirt Cheap," "Summer Shovin'" and "Apocalypse Pow."

The non-profit group also raised money for support groups that work with women and children. They raised $6,000 within their first year and have raised more than $110,000 for charity.

"Part of what drew us to this was the ability to raise money for these causes," Abbott said. "A lot of us have children or are close to nieces and nephews. Our practices are filled with women and children, and it just seemed natural to work with these charities. The girls really get a kick out of making a difference."

Skaters are encouraged to participate in community service and to bring worthy causes to the group for consideration. Some of the funds are raised through monthly dues to the skaters.

Their first event at Roller Dome South drew a sold out crowd of more than 1,200 people, and eventually the group grew enough that the Memorial Coliseum has hosted their events since 2008.

**Also, in 1998, the Indiana Tech baseball team makes its first NAIA World Series appearance.**

**Also, in 1987, high school sports' Northeast Hoosier Conference is formed.**

**May 21**

**In 1993, the Komets complete their 12-0 playoff sweep by beating San Diego.**

The Komets celebrated like little boys on the last day of school, leaping into each other's arms in a group hug. The San Diego Gulls were swept 4-0, losing 6-1 in Game 4 before a standing-room- only crowd of 8,154 at Memorial Coliseum.

After 20 years, the Fort Wayne Komets had won the Turner Cup.

This team's records will stand forever, a perfect 12-0 during the playoffs. Only two other teams - the 1988 Hershey Bears of the American Hockey League and the 1984 Edmonton Oilers - ever won 12 straight playoff games, and it has never happened before in the International Hockey League.

No team in any playoffs anywhere has given up only 18 goals in 12 games. Pokey Reddick stopped 95 percent of the shots against him in the playoffs, allowing only 1.49 goals against per game.

"They say the cream rises to the top, but Pokey was definitely the mist above the cream," Komets coach Al Sims said.

To make the feat even more amazing, the IHL is dominated by teams with National Hockey League affiliations, but the Komets are the first independent franchise in 10 years to win the Turner Cup. These are the players considered not good enough to make NHL farm clubs.

The Komets finished the season on a 27-2-1 run.

"What's funny is that Bobby Jay, Jean-Marc Richard and I went to dinner in Cleveland the night before the playoffs started, and we talked about how we thought it was possible that we could win 12 in a row," defenseman Grant Richison said. "We even talked about how it could happen even if we played San Diego. Who could ever have dreamed it would come true?"

**Also, in 2009, Northrop's Corey Shank wins his third straight state pole vault title.**

**Also, in 1964, Baer Field Speedway opens.**

**May 22**

**In 1962, Huntington's Gene Hartley qualifies for his 10th and last Indianapolis 500.**

Except for die-hard racing fans, most people have forgotten or never heard of Gene Hartley's accomplishments in the Indianapolis 500. Although today's drivers will do just about anything to earn a ride in the race, Hartley had to be persuaded in 1950.

"Some car owner (Joe Langley) built a car," Hartley said. "He had seen me run quite a bit. He contacted me, and I said he was out of his mind. I had never driven anything but midgets - nothing. I was on a half-mile track a couple of times. I turned him down, and he called me three or four more times and finally pestered me enough that I thought I would go try it."

Hartley qualified with the 32nd-fastest time and made the race thanks to rain on the last day of qualifying and some drivers who crashed. He wasn't awed by his new surroundings, and he became a regular at the speedway in May.

His career at Indy was steady, if unspectacular; he finished 10th in 1957 and 11th in 1956, 1959 and 1961. He is one of only 79 men to drive in the 500 at least 10 times. His cars were involved in only two wrecks, both on the same day in 1953, and he was not seriously hurt in either. Hartley said he had fun, and made a good living and great friends.

Hartley's career ended after 10 runs in the Indy 500 and more than 100 victories on the midget circuit. Hartley saw that the new style would change racing. The drivers were changing, too, and, after finishing 27th in 1962 with a steering problem, Hartley decided to get out.

He retired in Roanoke and died in 1994.

**Also, in 1989, Jodi Beermen finally gets her picture on the front of a Wheaties box.**

**May 23**

**In 1945, the Fort Wayne Daisies play their first-ever game.**

The All-American Girls Professional Baseball League started in 1943, but finally came to Fort Wayne in 1945 when the Minneapolis Millerettes moved here. One of the key players in the move was pitcher Dottie Wiltse who gave up only three hits and struck out 13 in the Daisies' first game, a 4-1 win over the Grand Rapids Chicks.

There were 1,799 fans at North Side Field to watch the game. The Daisies' offense was led by Margaret Callaghan, Lavone "Pepper' Paire, Vivian Kellogg and Lillian Jackson.

Fort Wayne's manager was former Major Leaguer Bill Wambsganss.

The other teams in the league were Rockford, Kenosha, Grand Rapids, South Bend and Racine.

"The fans seemed to enjoy their introduction to girls baseball, and many seemed amazed at the manner in which the girls threw, fielded, ran and batted," The News-Sentinel reported.

The players wore a one-piece uniform that included skirts similar to those worn by tennis, field hockey and ice skating participants of the time. The baseball they used started at 12 inches in 1943, and shrank to 9 inches by 1954.

The paper also reported, "The teams really talk it up from their bench, and the Daisies, happy over their lead, broke into some `beauty parlor' harmony a couple of times, with Pepper Paige, who is quite a singer and song writer, the director."

The highlight of the season was Wiltse, who later married Harvey Collins, throwing a pair of no-hitters within 17 days. She also once threw complete-game victories in both games of a doubleheader. She finished her Fort Wayne career in 1950 with a 117-76 record and a 1.83 earned run average.

Wiltse finished with a 29-10 record her first season in Fort Wayne, with 17 shutouts and 293 strikeouts.

**May 24**

**In 1998, Indiana Tech baseball finishes second in the NAIA World Series.**

Marking their first-ever trip to the World Series, the Warriors came up short because of one bad inning. Top-ranked Albertson College of Caldwell, Idaho, scored six runs in the fourth inning to beat Indiana Tech 6-3 in the championship game in Tulsa, Okla.

The Warriors, 48-21, hurt even worse because all six runs were unearned. Indiana Tech rallied with two runs in the top of the fifth inning and Jeremiah Deakins belted his third home run of the tournament in the seventh inning. Albertson pitchers struck out 10.

Indiana Tech pitcher Ken Fischer and third baseman Brad Casal made the all-tournament team. Fischer finished 12-7, taking the loss in the championship game. John Baum and Casal were named all-Americans after the season and Fischer and teammate Mark Baker received honorable mention.

What's amazing is that the Warriors started the season 12-9 before putting a run together to go 36-12. The Warriors were the No. 7 seed in the national tournament.

This was the first of six consecutive trips to the World Series by Indiana Tech, which also finished third in 2000 and fifth in 2003.

Deakins eventually re-wrote the Indiana Tech record book, setting new marks for career games played, at-bats, runs scored, hits, doubles, triples, home runs, runs batted in, total bases and walks. Fischer holds the marks for career appearances, games started, complete games, innings pitched and strikeouts. He's also second in career wings behind Jason Knowling.

**Also, in 2007, IPFW's Arnie Ball is named NCAA Men's Volleyball Coach of the Year.**

**May 25**

**In 1994, the Komets lose 3-1 to Atlanta to end their bid for back-to-back Turner Cups.**

This was the year no one expected, but everyone hoped for -- an encore to 1993's miraculous playoff run in which the Komets romped through 12 straight games to bring the Turner Cup back to Fort Wayne after a 20-year absence.

They were the lowest-seeded team, and the only eighth-seed ever to reach the Turner Cup Finals. They were the oldest team in the playoffs facing the greatest odds from Las Vegas.

It was a road they traveled well, upsetting Peoria and Cincinnati in the first two rounds to earn their third trip to the Turner Cup Finals in four years.

The Komets set IHL records this season for most franchise appearances in the Turner Cup Finals, most consecutive playoff appearances and most playoff appearances for a franchise. They also broke the record for most runners-up finishes with eight.

The killer was Game 4 as the Komets lost a 5-0 lead at home that would have tied the series 2-2.

After blowing a 5-0 lead, the Komets lost the second-longest game in International Hockey League history when Atlanta forward Steve Larouche intercepted a Danny Lambert pass, skated around the Fort Wayne net and pushed the puck through the legs of Komets goaltender Peter Sidorkiewicz at 1:55 of the third overtime.

It was Larouche's fifth goal and the Knights' 67th shot of the game, coming at 12:45 a.m.

## May 26

**In 2011, University of Saint Francis and Bishop Dwenger graduate Jean Marqueling wins her second straight NAIA national title in the hammer throw.**

Marqueling recorded a throw of 190-5 to easily beat the second-place toss of 176-0 at Indiana Wesleyan.

"I felt like there was more pressure this year because I won last year," Marqueling said in a university-released statement. "Everybody knew me, and you just never know what will happen at nationals, especially today with all the different weather elements."

Marqueling won the 2010 hammer title with a throw of 183-6 and was second in 2009 with a 179-10. Her victory makes her a three-time NAIA Outdoor All-American, and a six-time NAIA All-American in track and field competition, both record-setting marks for USF.

**Also, in 2002, Indiana Tech baseball coach Lance Hershberger resigns.**

After building the program from scratch into a five-time NAIA World Series participant over 12 years, Hershberger had to walk away because of a fear of flying. Despite counseling, he had been unable to force himself to leave to go to four of the Warriors' five World Series appearances.

Hershberger had a 407-309-2 record with the Warriors after starting the program in1991.

Hershberger became a very successful high school coach at Whitko and Concordia.

**Also, in 2009, an Edmonton, Alberta, school is named for Fort Wayne great Johnny Bright.**

## May 27

**In 2001, Kelley Racing's Scott Sharp crashes on the first lap after winning the pole position.**

This was probably the most discouraging day ever for Kelley Racing as Sharp slammed his pole-winning car into the outside wall of Turn 1 on the first lap and later Mark Dismore radioed to say his gearbox was broken.

"I went from being probably the happiest guy here to the saddest," team owner Tom Kelley told The News-Sentinel's Rich Griffis. "I felt so bad for Scott. It's almost more bearable when a part breaks. I'm sure Scott will regret that for the rest of his career."

Sharp became the fifth pole-sitter in Indy history to finish last while Dismore, who led 29 of the first 91 laps, settled for 16th place, five laps behind winner Helio Castroneves and runner-up Gil de Ferran. It was the worst combined finish at Indy for the 4-year-old Kelley Racing team.

Sharp joined Roberto Guerrero as the only pole sitters at Indy not to finish a lap.

"You wish you could hit the rewind button and do it again," Sharp said. "We talked about there are 800 turns in this race. We didn't want to throw it away on the first turn. I made the mistake and did."

The wreck ruined a near-perfect month that included his first Indy 500 pole and first pit stop challenge victory. Sharp's perfect start disintegrated when he roared into Turn 1 too fast and too low on tires too cold. His car veered into the outside wall, shattering the right front end. It took three trucks to haul the pieces.

"I can't put into words how disappointing it is," Sharp said. "There were so many expectations. The team did such a tremendous job."

**Also, in 1997, Kelley Racing takes part in its first Indianapolis 500.**

## May 28

**In 1993, Hilliard Gates retires from WKJG after 39 years.**

Hilliard Gates spoke the first words ever broadcast by a Fort Wayne television station. Gates began at WKJG, Channel 33, on Nov. 21, 1953. At 7:45 p.m., he introduced Fort Wayne viewers to a new communications medium.

"Good evening, ladies and gentlemen. You are watching history being made," he said. "These are the first words and pictures to emanate from WKJG-TV, Fort Wayne's first television station."

Gates came to Fort Wayne in 1940 from Muskegon, Mich., and began working at WOWO radio for $17 a week. On radio, he covered the Fort Wayne Pistons' NBA games, the 1967 and 1968 Rose Bowls, and the first NBA All-Star Game in 1950.

He was a broadcasting fixture at the Indiana High School Athletic Association's boys basketball state championship game, and played himself in the 1986 film "Hoosiers." The film was based on tiny Milan High School's 1954 state championship - a game Gates announced. He was the first broadcaster inducted into the Indiana Basketball Hall of Fame.

His last TV sports broadcast was the state boys basketball finals in March 1993 at the RCA Dome. For seven years, ending in 1981, he was the TV play-by-play voice for Indiana University men's basketball games.

"If you were 9 or 95 years old, you knew the voice of Hilliard Gates," longtime Fort Wayne Pistons executive Carl Bennett told The News-Sentinel's Duane Schuman. "You knew it and loved him. He was WKJG, as far as we were concerned in the city."

His influence was so profound, IPFW named its Multipurpose Building the Hilliard Gates Athletic Center in 1991.

Gates died Nov. 20, 1996.

**May 29**

**In 2004, the Three Rivers Volleyball Club is inducted into the YMCA Hall of Fame.**

During the 1980s and 1990s, the group played in 10 YMCA national tournaments, winning seven titles and finishing second twice and third once. The players also dominated the Hoosier State Games, winning 11 gold medals, two silvers and a bronze.

"When we all went on those trips, we were a unit on and off the court," Mark Hesterman said. "We were all just great friends. It was just a neat bunch of guys who got together because of volleyball."

Bob Michael, the team captain, started the squad because he wanted to compete in the YMCA National Tournament. He started gathering the best players in Fort Wayne who were Y members. Michael and Neal Arnold played with the team the longest, and were joined by Paul Wyss, Ron Dick, Dennis Shively and Hesterman the second year.

That was the nucleus of the team for several years, adding in Ojars Bertzins, Terry Crandall, Ry and Tolly Taliaferro, Tony and Tom Terrell, Jerry and Brad Beauchamp, Phil Bodine and Ric Grinsfelder along the way. Loren Gebert also played on the Hoosier State Games teams.

They kept winning so there was little need to change the roster. After finishing second to Youngstown, Ohio, in 1986, Fort Wayne hosted and won the title in 1987. The next year's YMCA tournament was held at Youngstown.

"When we were in Fort Wayne, they were like, 'We know we're hosting it next year so we'll look forward to seeing you then,'" Michael said. "That was an especially fun year because we clobbered them."

That was the middle of a string of six straight titles that ended in 1993 in Memphis. Michael and Hesterman were playing with bad backs, and Wyss had a terrible case of poison ivy.

The next year, the squad rebounded to win the title again, beating Dubuque, Iowa, which had won the year before.

The run ended in 1995, when Fort Wayne finished second to New Canaan, Conn.

**Also, in 1993, Rene Lopez sets a Fort Wayne Wizards' record with six hits in a game against Beloit.**

**May 30**

**In 1947, Zollner Stadium opens as a softball palace.**

Until 1947, the Pistons played their games at Municipal Beach (City Utilities Park) where there were no showers or locker rooms. Players would dress at home and then drive to the games.

Not all of the games were played at Municipal, though, as some had to be moved to Dwenger or Memorial parks because of schedule conflicts.

Construction on the new stadium started Jan. 12, 1946 at cost of $85,000. Completion was scheduled for the start of the 1946 season, but a shortage of steel bands pushed it back a year.

Zollner Stadium had everything a player could ask for, including 2,804 permanent seats in the grandstands around home plate. Bleachers along the foul lines pushed capacity to 5,000 seats.

The opening-night games, a doubleheader against arch-rival Midland Dow Chemicals, drew between 5,000 and 6,000 fans as the then two-time World Champion Pistons won both games.

More than 90,000 fans came out to see the new place during the 1947 season, including more than 7,500 over two nights when heavyweight champion boxer Joe Louis brought his Flint Punchers to town.

Concordia High School purchased the stadium in 1958 in a sweetheart deal from Zollner and converted it to a football configuration in 1962. The first football game was between Valparaiso University and Ohio University.

**Also, in 2003, Concordia and Bishop Dwenger combine to refurbish the entire Zollner Stadium complex to the cost of $2.4 million.**

Bishop Dwenger and Concordia have shared the facility for home football games since 1978.

## May 31

**In 1996, Lashanda Harper wins four more firsts to finish with 11 in her career as Harding wins state track title.**

In leading Harding High School to consecutive state championships in 1995 and 1996, Harper won 11 state titles: three in the 100-meter dash, three in the 200-meter dash, three in the long jump and two in the 400-meter relay.

That's 11 titles in 11 attempts.

The only Indiana high school track athlete, girls or boys, to come close to the achievement was North Central's Maicel Malone, who also won 11 titles. But Malone finished second in the 200 as a sophomore.

Harper is the only athlete in Indiana history to go undefeated in multiple state events. She accomplished her feat in three seasons, since she did not compete as a freshman. Malone's titles came over four seasons.

**Also, in 2001, East Noble's Amy Yoder-Begley wins the NCAA championship in 10,000 meters.**

Coming off an Achilles injury, the Arkansas senior was not looked upon as one of the face favorites, but she finished in 33:59.96 to earn her second NCAA titles. This race was held at Eugene, Ore.

On March 10, 2000, Yoder-Begley had won the 5,000 meters at the NCAA Indoor Championships in Fayetteville with a time of 15:46.89.

During her Arkansas career, Yoder-Begley was a 15-time all-American and a 15-time Southeastern Conference champion. She was also just the third track athlete to be named SEC Athlete of the Year.

Yoder-Begley qualified for the 2008 Beijing Olympics and finished 26th in the 10,000 meters.

# JUNE

## June 1

**In 1974, Northrop's Gary Hunter wins the high school state title to start Fort Wayne's pole vault dynasty.**

Hunter, who built a homemade practice pit in his back yard, invited all his friends to have fun.

Teammate Brian Kimball followed, winning titles in 1975 and '76 competing with Rick Rogers, who vaulted for North Side and Northrop. Ron Vernasco of Snider won in 1978 followed by Leo's Dale Gerke in 1983 and East Noble's Phil Yuska in 1984. Bobby Shank won in 1987 for North Side, setting a record of 16-6, before winning the Big 10 title for Illinois.

"That's kind of the way pole vaulting is," Hunter said in 1991. "In the past, we've had some pretty successful vaulters from Fort Wayne, mostly because we all work together."

Members of the group have set several state and national records over the years, and they've always helped train other pole vaulters.

The next generation started when Northrop's Jo'l Gerardot won the IHSAA title in 1997 and 1998, Bishop Dwenger's Ryan Schipper in 2003, Northrop's James Martzall in 2004, Homestead's Hunter Hall in 2006, and Northrop's Corey Shank in 2007, 2008 and 2009. Bishop Dwenger's Dave Schipper was second in 2011.

When the girls added the event in 2003, Homestead's Katie Veith won state titles in 2004, 2006 and 2007, losing only to Northrop's Brianna Neumann in 2005. Leo's Nina Gutermuth won the title in 2011, and twin sister Sophie finished second.

**Also, in 1987, Bob Knight and Steve Alford celebrate IU's last national championship at the Mad Anthonys.**

**Also, in 1998, the Lifetime Sports Academy opens.**

**Also, in 1979, Wayne edges South Side for the girls state track title.**

**June 2**

**In 1883, one of the first attempts at night baseball was played in Fort Wayne.**

Today there is some debate over when and where the first night baseball game was played. History says there was a game played Sept. 2, 1880 in Hull, Massachusetts between teams representing two prominent department stores.

Fort Wayne claims the first night game involving a professional team. In June 1883, the Jenney Electric Light Co. decided to try something very different, putting up 17 huge arc lights around League Park, providing 4,000 candlepower each. Three lamps were fastened to the grandstand; one was placed behind the pitcher's box and the rest were stationed along the baselines and in the outfield.

The opposing teams were the Quincys, a professional team from Illinois in the Northwestern League, and a local team from Methodist College. The college team lost 19-11 in seven innings under what were described as tough fielding conditions.

A crowd of 2,000 paid 25 cents per ticket to witness history. The game was originally scheduled for May 30 to include the Fort Wayne Professionals and Quincy but was rained out. There is no explanation for why the Professionals were replaced with the college team.

The event was covered by the media and three newspapers, and all three were very critical of the artificial light.

Despite the Jenney company's glowing reputation, it was in financial trouble by 1888 and was purchased by the Thomson-Houston Co. and renamed the Fort Wayne Electric Light Co. By January 1899, the company was taken over by the General Electric Co., and by 1916, Fort Wayne's electric works had become officially known as the General Electric Co., which still occupies some of the original Jenney buildings at its Broadway plant.

Night baseball games were considered gimmicks until the Cincinnati Reds played the Philadelphia Phillies under the Crosley Field lights on May 24, 1935. The Reds won 2-1 and within a few years were playing seven night games per season.

The first night All-Star Game was held at Philadelphia's Shibe Park in 1943.

## June 3

**In 1988, Snider's Donna Gill completes a dream senior season by winning the mental attitude award at the state track meet.**

Gill might have had the best senior year of any Fort Wayne athlete in history.

During the fall, Gill helped the Snider volleyball team win the state title with a 32-1 record as she hit a team-leading 14 kills in the championship match.

Over the winter, Gill was part of the Panthers' state championship girls basketball team and was named the Most Valuable Player of the state finals after joining teammate Jenny Herman with 21 points in the title game. Gill also blocked a potential-tying shot by Noblesville with two seconds left.

Gill then finished up in the spring by winning another state title, this time an individual award in track. She tossed the shot put 47-7¾ to win and was also named winner of the mental attitude award.

**Also, in 1990, Cathy Gerring wins the Lady Keystone Open for her first LPGA title.**

**Also, in 1990, Gregg Hart wins his third consecutive state discus title.**

**June 4**

**In 1999, Concordia wins the state track title with Northrop finishing second.**

Powered by sprinter Rolando Scott, the Cadets scored 42 points to hold off Northrop with 38 and Carroll with 32.

It was the second time in three years that a trio of Fort Wayne teams grabbed the top three spots.

Scott scored 30 of Concordia's points by winning the 100 meter dash in 10.78, anchoring the Cadets' championship 400 meter relay team and placing fifth in the long jump and the 200.

Gustin Smith also finished sixth in the 100 and helped with the 400 relay team which set a school record.

Northrop was led by senior Brett Tipton and junior Nathan Peffley who finished first and second in the 1,600.

**Also, in 1961, Ned Garver plays his final Major League game.**

Garver was 0-3 with a 5.59 earned run average in 12 games for the California Angels at age 35. He finished with 402 career games, going 129-157 with a 3.73 earned run average. In his final game, Garver threw two innings against the Cleveland Indians, giving up three hits, two walks and a run.

## June 5

**In 2005, Northrop wins its sixth consecutive girls state track title.**

Coach Tom Knudson's Bruins had one of the most dominant runs in state history, and their main challenge seemed to come from Fort Wayne teams. Concordia's 2004 squad gave Northrop its toughest test, losing 90-81. The streak ended in 2006 when Warren Central beat Northrop 47-41. The six-year streak was the longest of any girls Indiana high school program and the second-longest behind Gary West's nine-year run in boys track.

**Also, in 1955, the 72-day run of the American Bowling Congress Tournament ends.**

The 52nd annual event brought nearly 31,000 bowlers to the Memorial Coliseum as 38 alleys were constructed at a cost of about $200,000. The event started March 26 which caused a problem for the Fort Wayne Pistons who advanced all the way to the NBA Finals that year. They had to play their home games in Indianapolis. (Luckily, the Pistons won all three but lost the series in seven games.)

There were participants from 42 states, Canada, Alaska (which wasn't a state yet) and as far away as Saudi Arabia.

The tournament even received national recognition from Sports Illustrated which reported, "Colorfully uniformed contestants comprising 5,826 five-man teams, 11,312 doubles and 22,620 singles entries will roll for 72 consecutive days and nights (March 26 through June 5) before approximately 100,000 spectators, more than half of whom will accompany them from out of town. Bowlers and their rooters will spend an estimated $8 million for hotel rooms, food and entertainment and hundreds of thousands more for transportation."

**Also, in 2002, DaMarcus Beasley plays in his first World Cup match as the U.S. beats Portugal 3-2.**

## June 6

**In 1980, South Side edges Wayne to win the girls state track title.**

This meet should have been held in Fort Wayne.

South Side scored 34 points to beat Wayne's 29. Jeffersonville was third and Northrop was fourth. Wayne had won the year before with South Side finishing second, but this time the Archers had more depth.

Cathey Tyree won the high jump with a height of 5-8, and the Archers won the 800 medley relay. Sybil Perry continued her outstanding career for Wayne with championships in the 100 and 400 and also helped the Generals finish second in the 800 medley relay.

Northrop's Sherri Dunn repeated as the long jump champion, and Harding's Kristi Walker won the 1,600. Northrop's Lorna Russell was second in the 100 hurdles, Snider's Pat Jackson was third in the 800.

Perry finished her career the next spring with five state titles. She went to Purdue where she set 10 school records, won multiple Big Ten titles and was a five-time all-American.

**Also, in 1994, the Vera Bradley Classic is held for the first time.**

It started as a small golf tournament to benefit the American Cancer Society, and more than $60,000 was raised.

Now, almost 20 years later, the event is the largest women's amateur charity golf and tennis event in the country and has raised more than $10 million for cancer research. In recent years, there have been more than 600 participants and 400 volunteers. Included are 18- and 9-hole golf tournaments and a doubles tennis tournament.

Included in the benefit has been the endowment of the Vera Bradley chair in oncology at the Indiana University Cancer Center.

## June 7

**In 2007, Jarrod Parker is a first-round draft pick in the MLB draft.**

Parker was selected by the Arizona Diamondbacks with the ninth pick in the first round, the first high school pitcher selected in that year's draft.

After three years in the minors and a season off for Tommy John surgery, Parker made his Major League debut on Sept. 27, 2011, throwing 5 2/3 innings and not allowing a run in a 7-6 Arizona win over the Los Angeles Dodgers. He also pitched in one playoff game.

That winter, Arizona traded Parker to Oakland and he joined the A's starting rotation in April 2012. He started 29 games, going 13-8 with a 3.47 earned run average in 181 innings. Along with helping the A's win the division, the main individual highlight may have been no-hitting the Texas Rangers for seven innings on June 4. The Rangers' Michael Young broke up the no-hitter with a single leading off the eighth inning. Parker started two playoff games against Detroit, losing Games 1 and 5 to Tigers' ace Justin Verlander.

**Also, in 1989, Fort Wayne's Eric Wedge drives in the winning run to help Wichita State advance to the NCAA title game.**

On the same day he was drafted by the Boston Red Sox, Wedge belted a three-run homer to key Wichita State's 8-4 win over Arkansas in the semifinals of the College World Series. The home run was Wedge's 23rd of the season and 45th of his college career.

**June 8**

**In 1974, the first Midwest Meet of Champions track and field event is held.**

Originally called the Tri-State Meet, the event brought together the best seniors from Indiana, Michigan and Ohio. The meet was held at Northrop High School under the direction of honorary referee and former Olympic distance runner Don Lash.

Illinois soon joined the field in 1977 from 1996. The meet was held at Northrop for the first 12 years before moving to IUPU-Indianapolis from 1987 to 1995. Then Ohio Wesleyan hosted the meet from 1996 to 2005 before it moved to Jackson, Mich., from 2006-2009. Northrop became the home again in 2010.

The highlight of the first meet was a 13.3 time in the 110-meter hurdles by Gary West's Jimmy Williams. It would have smashed the national record but the breeze was too stiff to allow the time to qualify. Wayne's Willie Knox also won the 220 in 21.6.

**Also, in 1994, the Fort Wayne Aquatics swim club starts the Pete Johnston Memorial Scholarship.**

After Club Olympia was closed in 1990 and before the Brown Natatorium at South Side was opened in 1996, Fort Wayne Aquatics swimmers used to drive to Auburn's Eckhard Park for regular 6:30 a.m. practices.

On June 17, 1993, Johnston died and teammates Michael Leeper and Ryan Hambrook were injured in a car accident on Tonkel Road. FWA swimmers showed up the next morning for practice, saying that's what Johnston, 19, would have wanted.

"You have to do what it takes to be great, and that's what Pete would have wanted," former Snider and IU teammate Brian Kumfer said. "He wanted to be great."

Because Fort Wayne did not have a 50-meter pool they could use, 80-to-90 FWA swimmers had been driving to Auburn six days a week for summer workouts since 1967.

"Somebody asked one of the swimmers if he was coming home from a party or something like that," said teammate Julie Weaver. "No, he was up at 5:30 a.m. (going) to practice just like every day. He wasn't doing anything wrong."

Johnston had just been selected to compete at the Olympic Sports Festival later that summer.

## June 9

**In 2012, Leo runner Andy Bayer wins the NCAA title in the 1,500 meters for Indiana.**

With 300 meters to go in Des Moines, Iowa, Bayer raced to the front, just to the right of Oklahoma State's German Fernandez, but then Brigham Young's Miles Batty raced past him with 200 meters to go.

Instead of continuing to battle Batty, Bayer swung outside around Batty for the sprint to the finish line. It took 85 meters to Bayer to pull even with Batty who then dove for the tape. Bayer dove second but arrived at the line first to win the title in 3:43.82.

The win also meant the Indiana junior was named All-American for the eighth time.

**Also, in 1978, Walter Jordan, Mike Muff and Eugene Parker are drafted by the NBA.**

Jordan was picked in the fourth round with the 84th pick by New Jersey, Parker was tabbed in the fifth round with the 108th pick by San Antonio and Muff was selected in the 10th round by Golden State with the 193rd pick.

Jordan played 30 games for the Nets that season, averaging 6.9 points.

**Also, in 1986, after many years of trying, Fort Wayne obtains an expansion team in the American Indoor Soccer Association.**

**June 10**

**In 1989, Northrop's Eric Wedge helps Wichita State win the NCAA baseball title.**

Back in the days when the College World Series didn't last until July, Wedge was the heart and soul of a championship team at Wichita State.

The Northrop graduate earned first-team All-America honors as a junior and was named Missouri Valley Conference Player of the Year after hitting .380 with 23 home runs and 88 runs batted in. He also walked an NCAA record 88 times this season, led the Shockers to a school-record 24-game winning streak and also hit in 25 consecutive games.

During the postseason, Wedge was named the Most Valuable Player of the West II Regional and to the all-tournament team at the College World Series. While playing in Omaha, he had six hits in 17 at-bats and drove in eight runs. With the Shockers facing elimination, Wedge hit a three-run home run to beat Arkansas 8-4 and the next night drove in four runs to beat top-seeded Florida State and earn a spot in the finals against Texas. He also earned 11 walks during the six games.

"I look at that as respect," he said. "It's something that happened all year, and I have accepted that. I had to have faith in the other players and not get anxious up there and swing at bad pitches."

This was the second title for Wedge, who was a freshman on Northrop's 1983 state champions.

Because of injuries, the Shockers were limited to 10 position players in the final games of the tournament.

Wedge was inducted into the Wichita State Hall of Fame in 1996.

## June 11

**In 2005, the indoor football Freedom lose to the Omaha Beef 33-30 to break their 10-game winning streak.**

The frustrating thing about this game was that the Freedom had beaten the Beef 42-40 the week before in Fort Wayne. The Freedom also lost the next game, at home against Lexington 58-41, before rallying to win their final three games to finish 14-2.

Everything fell apart the next week, however. In the first round of the playoffs against a 6-9 Tennessee Valley team, the Freedom was embarrassed 57-22 in the Memorial Coliseum.

Making his first start, Tennessee Valley quarterback Ben Sankey looked like Peyton Manning playing the Indiana University defense. During the first three quarters, he completed 17-of-26 passes for 218 yards and five touchdowns.

The Freedom were even penalized for having an extra man on the field on a Tennessee Valley extra-point attempt. The Raptors scored 19 points in the second quarter after scoring 18 points total in the previous week's loss to Evansville.

Fort Wayne's offense was much, much worse, gaining only 100 yards in the final three quarters. Quarterback Bill Skelton was intercepted twice and there were also two fumbles.

Even when the Freedom did something right, it wasn't long before things went wrong. When Adrian Reese returned a kickoff for a touchdown with 10:32 left in the third quarter to cut the margin to 36-22, the Raptors' Luke McArdle ran the ensuing kickoff back to answer.

Later that winter, coach Matt Land left the Freedom to become head coach at Trine University.

**June 12**

**In 1990, David Welker moves the original Komets to Albany, N.Y.**

It's difficult to believe now, but the Komets did not make money throughout the 1980s. The team filed for bankruptcy in 1986 before Welker tried to save the team. Welker then lost an estimated $1 million in three years.

For three years attendance at games had dropped from 155,595 to 121,001, or a 2,813 average. After arguing with the Memorial Coliseum for years about the need for a better lease, Welker followed through on a threat and moved the team.

After 38 years, hockey in Fort Wayne got new life with new owners, some of the same players and a return to traditional colors and logos.

Things didn't turn out so well for Welker, though, as the Albany Choppers lasted only half a season before declaring bankruptcy.

Welker tried to sell the team before disbanding it after a group of businessmen declined to inject money. Playing in 15,000-seat Knickerbocker Arena, the team averaged a league-low 2,400 fans a game, less than 1,000 paid.

"It just didn't work out," Welker said. "I couldn't have gone another week. Everything I could beg or borrow was going into the team, but our attendance is so bad that our projected costs just kept going up."

**Also, in 2010, soccer player DaMarcus Beasley plays in his third soccer World Cup.**

**Also, in 2010, Bishop Dwenger's girls softball team wins the state title.**

## June 13

**In 1961, the Wildcat Baseball League opens its first season.**

The major purpose of the association was to give all boys who wanted to play organized baseball a chance to participate regardless of their skill, ability, race, creed or religion.

The first week was full of practices as everyone tried to get to know each other and understand this new league. There were 39 staff members at 10 sites, McMillen, Portage, Kekionga, Lakeside, Northwood, City Utilities, Franke, New Haven and St. Joe Center. The first game was played on June 19, 1961 at McMillen Park.

Since that first season, more than 205,000 children have played in more than 110,000 games on more than 15,000 teams. More than 40,000 baseballs have been used.

The original site directors included Bob Short, By Hey, Guenther Herzog, Norm Moser, Jack Massucci, Terry Coonan, Fred Parker, Robert Bragg and Nick Werling.

Among the longest-serving league officials include Massucci, John Grantham, Art Pinnow, Bill Derbyshire, J.R. Sinks, Gerry Tilker and Gary Rogers.

Site directors who have served 10 years or more include John Blad, Lance Hershburger, Dan Wilson, Ted Davis, Paul Felton, Dennis Patterson, Paul Kennel, Mark Fowerbaugh, Jim Rousseau, Sam Talarico, Jr., Fred Weiss, Bob Fox, Jeff Johnson, Mark Koos, Bob Short and Fred Cass.

**Also, in 1999, Mark Dismore wins his only race with Kelley Racing, taking the Longhorn 500.**

**June 14**

**In 2008, Bishop Luers completes a remarkable triple crown, adding the state baseball title to basketball and football championships.**

The 2008 Bishop Luers seniors might have been one of the best classes in state history.

The year started with a football state championship in Class 2A as the 11-4 Knights beat Heritage Christian 21-6. Then the Knights' basketball team finished 24-3, including winning the school's first state title with a 99-67 win over Winchester in the Class 2A championship game.

The Knights completed the sweep with a 14-8 win over Elwood in the Class 2A state baseball championship game to finish 30-3.

"We knew in each sport we could be very good if things went well, we worked hard, we played well and we got lucky," Bishop Luers Athletic Director and football coach Matt Lindsay said. "You do that and good things happen."

Bishop Luers became the first program in Indiana high school sports history to complete a state championship sweep in the three power sports - football, basketball and baseball - in an academic year. Only two other schools in the nation – one in North Carolina and one in Texas – had ever accomplished such a feat.

One interesting tidbit is that no one single athlete played on each team.

"Obviously, this is quite a special year that they have been able to put together," Lindsay said. "You may never see something like this again. We're fortunate to have these kinds of kids here, and we were fortunate to accomplish the things we have. It makes you really proud."

**Also, in 2001, the Wizards are no-hit by Kane County.**

## June 15

**In 1990, Vice President Dan Quayle participates in the Mad Anthonys.**

The 33<sup>rd</sup> edition of the Mad Anthonys was different from any tournament before or after it. The secret service showed up in 11 golf carts, as did about 10 times more media than usual. Oh, and the helicopters.

The Mad Anthonys was a little different with The Vice President of the United States playing. A Huntington native, Quale teed off at 8 a.m. With seven-time city champion Tom Kelley, PGA professional Bill Kratzert III, Magnavox President Jim Loomis and Mad Anthonys President Reed Silliman.

With the secret service, the helicopters and tons of media looking on, Quayle proved to be a pretty good golfer. He chipped in from a sand trap for a birdie on No. 12, and hit back-to-back birdies on No. 7 and No. 8.

"I hit it very well," Quayle told The News-Sentinel's Steve Warden. "I'm basically a very good golfer. I've been playing since I was 10 years old. Once you've got a good golf swing, you don't ever lose it."

The rest of the celebrity field was pretty spectacular, too, and included Bobby Knight, Lou Holtz, Gene Keady, Fred Akers, Scott Hamilton, Gene Okerlund and Steve Alford.

**Also, in 1988, Bob Knight, Fuzzy Zoeller and Gene Keady highlight the Mad Anthonys.**

**Also, in 1996, Lloy Ball and the U.S. men's volleyball team sweep France before 4,513 Memorial Coliseum fans.**

**June 16**

**In 2003, SportsTalk goes off WOWO after nearly 19 years.**

For a show that sometimes led to boisterous passion, a Fort Wayne tradition ended with a gentle whisper. The show ended with a small announcement on a Monday afternoon.

The first version of SportsTalk, starting in 1980, included WOWO's Ron Gregory and Art Saltsberg talking Monday through Thursday. Unfortunately, the show lacked support and died less than a year later.

WOWO Program Director Chris Roberts brought it back in September 1985 with Saltsberg and WPTA's Dean Pantazi battling for the microphone five nights a week. That worked perfectly until Saltsberg retired July 25, 2000. Dean McNeil replaced him, and Jim Shovlin took over for Pantazi in February 2002.

At its best, SportsTalk could entertain, inform and often inflame. The discussions about the Indiana-Purdue rivalry are legendary, and any discussion involving Bob Knight could fill up the board with calls pro and con.

Saltsberg had some pet peeves and some pet sayings, such as such as "Balderdash!," "Your point is well made," and "I see your point, I just don't agree with it." Pantazi would laugh along with anyone.

Their greatest strength is that they always knew what they were talking about because they had probably attended the event, or they knew someone who had been there who could come on and talk about it intelligently. They also preferred stressing the local over the national and always remembered that high school players were first and always kids.

They also always knew when to cut off a regular caller whose point was dragging on too long or who had called too often.

**June 17**

**In 2006, Blackhawk Christian's baseball team wins its third state title in five years.**

The Braves rallied from a 3-0 deficit in the third inning to win their second title in a row and beat Shakamak 7-4 in the Class 1A championship game.

"They won close ballgames all year - come-from-behind ballgames," Braves coach Mark Harmon told The News-Sentinel's Robin Hartman. "They're the kind of team that knew they weren't done until the very last out, and that was a credit to their heart and desire and determination."

Jon Ringenberg and David Ehmke each cracked four hits to lead the comeback, and Ringenberg was also the winning pitcher. Besides driving in the game-winning run, Andrew Nelson also received the Mental Attitude Award, matching the accomplishment of his father Charles who received it in 1967 as part of South Side's basketball team.

The Braves finished the season 25-2.

Ringenberg had also cracked two hits and drove in three runs in the 2005 title game as the Braves beat Hauser 7-0.

**Also, in 2006, Snider wins its first state baseball title by beating Indianapolis Cathedral 4-2 in the Class 4A championship game.**

**June 18**

**In 2011, the Carroll baseball team wins two state titles in a row.**

The Chargers won their second straight state title – the first Class 4A repeat baseball champion since the advent of class sports – and took down highly touted Indianapolis Cathedral pitcher Dillon Peters again.

Carroll won 5-3, topping the University of Texas recruit and Cleveland Indians draft pick Peters for the second year in a row. Peters had struck out 16 Chargers the previous year even though Carroll won 1-0 in nine innings. This time, Peters struck out 12 Chargers.

The Chargers finished 32-2, bringing their two-year run to 58-8.

The key hits this time were Austin Keathley's two-run triple in the third inning and Steve Remesnik's run-scoring double in the fourth.

Top-ranked Carroll's 5-3 Class 4A title-game victory over second-ranked Cathedral solidified the argument that Fort Wayne-area high school baseball is unrivaled in the state. Area teams have won nine state championships in the last 10 years, seven since 2005. Snider, Bishop Luers, Norwell and Blackhawk Christian won the others. Three other teams – Bellmont, Homestead and Norwell – were state runners-up.

**Also, in 1978, golfer Bill Kratzert finishes sixth at the U.S. Open.**

**Also, in 2007, the new NBA D-League basketball team is named the Mad Ants.**

## June 19

### In 2007, IU football coach Terry Hoeppner dies.

A 1965 Woodlan graduate, Hoeppner convinced IU Athletic Director Rick Greenspan to give him the job because he wanted it so much. Hoeppner, 57, was also ending a 19-year career at Miami, Ohio, the last six as head coach, where he was 21-5 over his last two seasons. In Hoeppner's final season, the RedHawks went 13-1 behind quarterback Ben Roethlisberger to push the coach's career mark to 49-24.

At the urging of Franklin alum and Woodlan assistant coach Ed DeLong, Hoeppner went to Franklin College. After college he tried out for the St. Louis Cardinals and Green Bay Packers, eventually playing in the World Football League for two years before beginning his high school coaching career at Eastbrook. He also coached for a year at East Noble before going back to Franklin as a defensive coordinator for seven seasons.

Hoeppner got his first big chance by going to Miami as a defensive assistant in 1987. When Randy Walker left Miami to take over Northwestern, Hoeppner finally got his chance at a head-coaching job.

During his first season, in 2005, he led the Hoosiers to their first 4-1 start since 1994. During his second season, in 2006, he pushed the Hoosiers to five wins, their most since 2001 despite having the youngest team in the Big Ten. The highlight was a 31-28 upset of No. 13 Iowa, IU's first win over a Top 15 team since 1987.

Hoeppner had a brain tumor removed near his right temple on Dec. 7, 2005. He had a second operation on Sept. 13, 2006, and took a medical leave from the Hoosiers on March 18, 2007.

**June 20**

**In 1983, Isiah Thomas accepts his red coat from the Mad Anthonys.**

When Isiah Thomas starts talking about things Indiana coach Bobby Knight had taught him by using three expletives, the audience at Orchard Ridge Country Club roars with laughter, Knight included. In fact, Thomas has to wait for the laughter to subside.

Then Thomas went too far, describing what he said were some other words Knight taught him, and everything got very quiet while his coach glared from the side. Thomas's entire speech lasted only 2 minutes, 41 seconds, but it is easily the worst moment in the history of a proud organization that has done so much good for the community.

"If Thomas, 22, meant to needle Knight in what he felt would be a humorous thrust, he missed the basket. The backboard, too," wrote News-Sentinel sports editor Bud Gallmeier.

Thomas left almost immediately after his remarks to return to Bloomington, and asked Master of Ceremonies Hilliard Gates to apologize for him to the Mad Anthonys. Gates said Thomas would have to make the apology himself.

The next day Thomas called Mad Anthonys president Walter Ainsworth. Two days later, Thomas told Gallmeier the incident did not go as he intended.

"On the way up to Fort Wayne Monday, I asked Coach Knight what I could talk about. He said, 'Why don't you poke a little fun at me.' I knew everybody knows Coach Knight swears, so I decided I would use that."

At the time, Thomas had just finished his second season with the Detroit Pistons.

**Also, in 1994, Rod Woodson hosts his first football camp at Snider High School.**

**Also, in 1916, Bluffton-native Everett Scott's long consecutive games streak begins.**

## June 21

**In 2000, the African-American Historical Society inducts its first Sports Hall of Fame class.**

After years of planning, the first class included 22 athletes that were as good as any Fort Wayne has ever produced.

Leading the way were National Football League star Rod Woodson, Canadian Football League star Johnny Bright and former American Basketball Association star Willie Long, along with National Basketball Association player Walter Jordan and Olympian DeDee Nathan.

Other inaugural inductees included former Central High School multi-sport stars Willie Curry, Nathaniel Buggs, James McDonald, Richard Warfield, Raymond Chambers, William Washington, John Kelso and Fitzhugh Lyons.

The remaining inductees were women's basketball stars Cathy Tyree, Tiffany Gooden and Leslie Johnson, longtime multi-sport referee Tom Knox, Metro Youth Sports coach Prince Chapman, Police Athletic League coach Tharnell Hollins, former Northrop coach A.C. Eldridge and former Harlem Globetrotter Bobby Milton.

Woodson was the keynote speaker, and each inductee received a commemorative replica of the plaque, which was placed in the African-American Historical Museum, at 436 E. Douglas Ave.

"Fort Wayne has a great tradition of sports, though a lot of people don't know it," Woodson said in his keynote address. "It's great that we can show the kids of today what the athletes of yesterday did. It's always good to bring people together."

Two more classes were inducted the next two years before the program ended.

**Also, in 1997, Luke Recker scores 39 points and the Indiana boys beat Kentucky in the basketball star-game series.**

**June 22**

**In 2009, the Fort Wayne Flash women's football team celebrates winning its final game.**

The Flash, 4-3, were led by Heather Anderson's 182 yards rushing and four touchdowns on 11 carries. Running back Tara Marble rushed eight times for 110 yards and two touchdowns, and quarterback Laura Kerr completed 3 of 6 passes for 58 yards. Jayme Neal, Kara Fultz and Kerr each scored one rushing touchdown.

Playing in the women's football alliance, the Flash lasted four years, starting with tryouts in 2005 and practicing to learn the game in the spring of 2006. They played their first official season in 2007 and finished 4-4, almost making the playoffs. The Flash came back the next year to make the playoffs and win the North Midwest Division title with a 5-3 record, but lost the first post-season game to Columbus.

The team finished 4-4 in 2009, winning its last two games. There was an attempt to return in 2010, but finances and a dwindling number of players meant the team had to fold.

Anderson was usually the team's best player and star. During the 2009 season, she ran for 902 yards and 10 touchdowns on 158 carries.

One of the neat things about the team is that none of the players were paid, but they'd raise money for field rental, officials, etc., through fundraising and sponsorship opportunities. Usually, there were between 30 and 40 players per season.

"I guess the challenge in Fort Wayne is that we are a women's sport, and that already hits roadblocks before we ever get started," Anderson said in 2008. "I find that ironic after everything we've been through, but it happens. It's the truth because a lot of people are like, 'Women playing football? Whatever.'

"The injuries that we face, the games and the preparation are all the same that the guys go through, and if anything it's more intense because we have to fit it in during our free time while we do a regular job and do everything else."

**Also, in 1971, Larry Hinson beats Don January in the pro match 68-69 at the Mad Anthonys.**

**June 23**

**In 1970, Lee Trevino loses 68-69 to Tommy Bolt at the Mad Anthonys.**

This match was remarkable for quite a few reasons as a huge, almost overflow crowd followed along at Fort Wayne Country Club to watch the two former U.S. Open winners. Trevino allegedly drank a beer per hole in what many longtime tournament watchers say is the most amazing performance they have ever seen.

Bolt finally won with an eagle on the last hole.

As The News-Sentinel's Jim Costin wrote, the crowd "... watched Bolt chip in for an eagle on the final hole to edge beer-drinking Lee Trevino by one shot.

"On the 18th he `chunked' his tee shot, proving it doesn't pay to drink beer and play golf at the same time."

Bolt, 57, surprised everyone by out-driving Trevino, 30, who still led by two shots at the turn. Trevino got his only bogey of the day on No.10. He still had a chance after a birdie on No.17 gave him a one-shot lead, but his poor tee shot on No.18 gave Bolt the chance for the birdie.

Bolt made it to 15 greens in regulation for the day and used 31 putts, while Trevino hit 13 greens in regulation and tried 29 putts.

When asked after the match about the age difference between he and Bolt, Trevino joked, "Yes, but counting all the miles I'm 63."

And then Trevino donated his playing fee back to the Mad Anthonys.

## June 24

**In 1994, the first Rod Woodson Football Camp ends.**

When Rod Woodson first tried running a football camp in Pittsburgh, he said it didn't feel right, and the program folded after one year. Then, he decided to try it again in Fort Wayne.

Almost everything worked perfectly as hundreds of kids from ages 8 to 18 showed up at Snider High School to work out with NFL superstars such as Tim Brown, Mike Tomczak, Vaughn Dunbar, Jeff Zgonina, Ray Buchanan, Lamar Smith, Ronnie Lott, Chris Dishman and Carnell Lake – and that was all just in the first year!

Not all the kids knew exactly who all the 18 NFL players were, but they listened to everything they said and tried to do everything, too. It seemed that everybody who ever owed Woodson a favor at some time showed up to help out.

The week-long event stressed fundamentals and education as Woodson and the other pros continually lectured the kids about the importance of schoolwork and listening to their parents and teachers. If anyone had a bad attitude and needed a lecture, All-Pro player was willing to step up and stress the importance of listening and make sure the message got through.

The camp also raised money for several local charities and organizations such as the Police Athletic League, Metro Youth Football, Catholic Youth Organization, the Euell Wilson Center and Community Harvest Food Bank.

In succeeding years, a basketball all-star game was added. Eventually, Fort Wayne pro Dunbar, Jason Baker and Jason Fabini all pitched in to help add their names to the event, but Woodson was always the main attraction.

"It wasn't about the parents or me or the guys who came to help out; it was about giving to the kids," Woodson told The News-Sentinel's Reggie Hayes in 2009. "Hopefully, they could see Rod Woodson, Deion Sanders, Marshall Faulk, Junior Seau and the guys who came through camp were just human beings. If we could make it to the National Football League, you never know, you could have that opportunity, too. I hope we made the professional football players human in their eyes and let them understand any dream was possible for them."

The camp ended in 2007 after serving more than 10,000 kids over 14 years.

**Also, in 1969, Tom Weiskopf defeats Chi Chi Rodriguez 69-75 during a match at the Mad Anthonys.**

**Also, in 2011, Josh Spence becomes the 100th player from the Wizards/TinCaps organization to make it to the Major Leagues.**

## June 25

**In 2007, the Mad Anthonys celebrate their 50th anniversary.**

Most people have forgotten that the Fort Wayne Open was a PGA Tour stop from 1950 through 1956, but they'll never forget what replaced it. Because the PGA prize money was getting too expensive (between $15,000 and $20,000), Indianapolis out-bid Fort Wayne for the 1957 tour slot.

Community leaders gathered to try to find a replacement, a tournament for charity featuring local, state and national celebrities. Notre Dame coach Terry Brennan was the first Celebrity of the Year, but the idea for the red coat presentation didn't come until a few years later.

The tournament's format has changed a few times over the years, but the primary function has been to raise money for local charities. In 2007, the Red Coat honorees were University of Saint Francis football coach Kevin Donley, IPFW men's volleyball coach Arnie Ball and the last original member of the Mad Anthonys, 91-year-old Carl Bennett.

"I had never even thought about receiving a Red Coat before this came up," said Bennett, a long-time Zollner executive and Pistons' softball player and basketball executive. "I can't believe this has happened, but I could not be prouder of what has become a great organization."

He was also president of both the National Fastball League and the National Basketball League. He later became a member of the NBA Board of Governors. He also played in nearly 40 Mad Anthonys tournaments before polio syndrome took away his golf game. The last time he played was April 24, 2003.

**Also, in 1992, the Fort Wayne Daisies attended a premiere for "A League of Their Own."**

More than 30 former All-American Girls Professional Baseball League players and more than 500 of their relatives watched the movie's premier in Fort Wayne.

**June 26**

**In 2010, DaMarcus Beasley scores the game-winning goal as the U.S. beats Algeria 1-0 in World Cup soccer.**

After coming in as a late substitution with about 10 minutes remaining, Beasley banged home a Landon Donovan rebound in the 91$^{st}$ minute to keep the United States' chances alive in the tournament.

Unfortunately, the U.S. lost to Ghana in the next round in South Africa. This was Beasley's third appearance for the Americans in a World Cup.

**Also, in 2004, the Freedom set an indoor football league record by drawing 10,225 fans to their last regular-season game.**

The Freedom averaged 8,061 fans per game this season to finish 8-6 and make the playoffs. Even better, the team had a 6-1 home record led by Adrian Reese, Rocky Harvey, Antoine Taylor, Luther Stroder, Dayna Overton and Rachman Crable.

During the playoffs, Fort Wayne beat the ShowMe Believers 45-48 at home but lost the next week at Ohio Valley 36-35.

**Also, in 1947, boxer Joe Louis appears at two Pistons' softball games.**

Louis owned the visiting Joe Louis Punchers team, and more than 7,500 fans showed up for the games over two nights which the Pistons won 3-1 and 2-1.

**June 27**

**In 1995, the Fort Wayne Volleyball Club wins fourth straight national title.**

Coached by Bryan Moore, Fort Wayne beat Chicago 15-7, 11-15, 15-9 in St. Louis to earn dynasty status.

For Belmont's Erin Heimann and Snider's Julie Fisher, it was their fourth straight AAU national title.

Teammates winning national titles for the third time were: Holly Schneider of Northrop, Jamie Hales of Homestead and Rachel Smith of Bishop Luers. Lori Kemerer of Antwerp, Ohio, and Dawn Leon of Wayne won their second national title, and club members Athena Sherwood from South Adams, Samantha Walker of North Side and Molly Ferber of Homestead won a national title for the first time. Schneider was named the tournament's Most Valuable Player.

"We were seeded first going into the tournament, and our goal was to win it," Moore said. "When it got tight, I told them I wanted to see smiles on their faces, and see them having fun. That's the difference between this group and other groups. They seem to play much better when I can get them to relax and just have fun."

The championship was the seventh AAU national title in four years for FWVC which was founded in 1990.

**Also, in 1973, at $10,000 purse draws a record number of fans to Avilla Speedway.**

**June 28**

**In 1991, Dale Jarrett wins a big-name race at Baer Field.**

Every once in a while, Baer Field Speedway would try to pull off a special night to give local fans a chance to meet and watch national drivers compete. No one was every disappointed.

On a night when Michael Waltrip, Davey Allison, Buddy Baker and Sterling Marlin were also racing at Baer Field, Jarrett won the biggest prize in the 25-lap feature. Waltrip, Allison and Marlin also led the race at some point.

Allison finished second and Baker third. All the NASCAR drivers used cars borrowed from regular Baer Field competitors. With less than half a lap remaining, Marlin and Waltrip tangled coming out of the third turn. Waltrip, driving Todd Oliver's car, hit the wall and the car sustained significant damage.

"It was a lot of fun," Jarrett told The News-Sentinel's Monica Denney. "But we hate it that we tore up the cars like that at the end."

This was Waltrip's fourth appearance at Baer Field, while Davey Allison used to come to Fort Wayne when his father Bobby often raced at Baer Field.

Allison finished third in the point standings that season, winning six races, and Marlin placed seventh.

## June 29

**In 1990, after borrowing Larry Zent's car, Dale Earnhardt wins a race at Baer Field.**

Maybe the biggest and best NASCAR driver field ever included Earnhardt, Rusty Wallace, Dick Trickle, Kyle Petty, Geoff Bodine, Michael Waltrip and Rick Wilson. This was a return trip for Wallace who won the 1978 Three Rivers Festival 100 and two other races at Baer Field, including his first as a professional. Trickle was also coming back after winning several races in Fort Wayne during the 1960s and 1970s.

At the time, Zent was dominating the local circuit so Earnhardt asked to borrow Zent's car, a 1990 Lumina that had won three consecutive races.

Make that four, as Earnhardt won the 25-lap feature by holding off Trickle by one car length. Rick Wilson was third, Bodine fourth and Waltrip fifth.

The most exciting part of the race came five laps in. Defending NASCAR Winston Cup champion Wallace was battling with Earnhardt for the lead when he suffered some trouble. As his back end came loose, so did the rest of the car from the track. Wallace flew off the track and into the shadows around Turn 1.

After a few moments of heart-racing drama for everyone else, Wallace climbed out of his car and gave a small wave to let everyone know he was OK.

Following the re-start and a few pointers from Zent, Earnhardt held onto the lead the rest of the way to get the checkered flag.

## June 30

**In 1998, Fort Wayne-native Don Shondell retires with the second-highest coaching wins in NCAA volleyball history.**

A 1946 graduate of Central High School and a Monroeville native, Shondell's 34-year Ball State career record finished 769-280-6, the second-highest number of wins in college history. His teams won or shared the Midwest Intercollegiate Volleyball Association championship 19 times.

Shondell, an eight-time MIVA coach of the year, took the Cardinals to the NCAA Tournament 14 times, and in 1995 became just the eighth coach in college volleyball history, and the second men's coach, to top 700 career victories.

Ironically, the volleyball bug almost skipped Shondell entirely when he went to work on the line at General Electric after graduating high school. One day a friend was promoted further up the line when he reached to flip out a piece of metal and lost two fingers.

"I was running an automatic punch press, and it was the most boring job in the world," Shondell said. "Jim Savio got transferred up the line, and that's where I'd be in 20 years if things went well. When he lost his fingers, I said, 'Hey, I'm getting out of here.' I saved all the money I could for six months."

At the behest of another Fort Wayne friend, Jim Hettler, Shondell left for Ball State, and started playing on the club volleyball team even though he had never seen or played in a match before. Shondell eventually graduated in 1952 and joined the Army where he played on his regimental volleyball team.

"A lot of it was just luck, and it turned out to be good luck," Shondell said. "I got a ton of breaks. I always talk about the people who made it possible for me. Everything you are is because somebody else has done something to make it possible for you. I'm very thankful for everything I've got."

Eventually, Shondell went back to Ball State in 1958 and started the varsity volleyball program, co-founded the MIVA with Jim Coleman in 1961, coached 30 All-Americans and was been inducted into numerous halls of fame.

**Also, in 1985, Bill Kratzert becomes the 52nd player in PGA history to clear $1 million in career earnings.**

**Also, in 1931, the Philadelphia Phillies come to town and lose to the Pennsy A.A. 8-4.**

# JULY

## July 1

**In 1953, Bob Chase starts his career at WOWO.**

Coming to Fort Wayne was a case of right place, right time for Chase.

A friend was getting married in Marquette, and Chase was part of his wedding party. The wedding was held at 11 a.m., and meaning Chase had to leave to deliver the noon newscast on WDJM. The groom's aunt was visiting from Fort Wayne and heard the broadcast while riding to the reception.

"When she got back to Fort Wayne she called the station manager, who was a good friend of hers, and said, `I heard this guy in Marquette, Mich., I think you better talk to him.' " Chase said in his biography "Live From Radio Rinkside" in 2008. "They called out of the blue. The fella says, `We've got a good report, send us tape, will you.' I say, `OK, fine.' "

Chase dismissed the opportunity completely.

"I go back to my job and spun my records and worked my job. About three days later, the phone rings and it's the same guy saying, I'm still waiting for that tape! All of a sudden I heard the station manager on the extension listening to my conversation which ticked me off. He's eavesdropping on my private conversation, so I said to the man, `I just sent that last night, it should be there in a day or two.' Then I promptly recorded what I was doing, put it on tape and sent it out. A week later they call and say come down for an interview, which I did. I got in on a Saturday in the middle of June, met with the people, had the audition and went back home. They call me and say, `Hey, hey, hey, come to work.' On July 1, I was here."

Ironically, Chase's first career plan was to work for the Cleveland Cliff's Iron Company setting up an educational program for the miners, except they went on strike and the job disappeared.

"I really had no formal training in broadcasting until I came to Fort Wayne and went to work for Westinghouse," Chase wrote. "After about a month, I began to realize what an incredible organization Westinghouse was. They were the hallmark of broadcasting, bar none, and as I grew into this thing and got to know the people, apparently I had a gift for the business that I wasn't even aware of."

## July 2

**In 1980, New Haven High School's Mark Virts qualifies for the Olympic team in diving but has to sit out because of the United States' boycott.**

After winning the 1972 state 1-meter diving title as a junior at New Haven with a score of 410.20, Virts attended Purdue where he was a three-time NCAA Championships competitor and held the school record in the 3-meter diving from 1977 until 2003. He was 25 in 1980 when he finished third at the U.S. Olympic Trials at Austin, Tex., in the 10-meter platform diving event behind Greg Louganis and Kevin Machemer.

Virts continues to live in Austin.

Fort Wayne also had some ties to divers in the 2008 and 2012 Olympics. Three-time Olympian Troy Dumais had aunts and uncles living in Fort Wayne, and 2012 10-meter platform Gold Medalist David Boudia is the son of 1977 Bishop Luers graduate Jim Boudia.

After graduating from Bishop Luers, Jim Boudia played football for two years at Hillsdale College before joining the Air Force. He met his wife, Sheilagh (from Torrance, Calif.), when they were stationed in Okinawa, Japan, and they were married in 1981. All three of their children were born when their parents were stationed in Abilene, Texas. Jim retired from the Air Force as a tech sergeant and Sheilagh as a staff sergeant.

David grew up playing soccer and gymnastics, but an injury before a regional meet when he was 11 forced him to re-evaluate his gymnastics career. A friend invited him to free diving lessons, where national team coach John Wingfield discovered Boudia in 2000.

**Also, in 2004, the local Connie Mack Baseball League is renamed for coaching legend Colin Lister.**

## July 3

**In 2000, the United States men's volleyball team beats Brazil 3-2 before heading to the Olympics.**

Before heading to Sydney, the U.S. Team and captain Lloy Ball spent a week in Fort Wayne getting ready. That included three matches against Brazil. The U.S. was ranked as the No. 5 team in the world at the time and Brazil was No. 4.

Well, the Brazilians were clearly ready for the Olympics, while the Americans had some work to do.

The Americans were 10-0 in World League play coming into the match and the Brazilians were 6-6 coming in, but the teams played as if their records were reversed. Brazil won the first match 25-21, 26-24, 25-18 before 2,800 fans in Memorial Coliseum, and then won the second 25-14, 27-25, 21-25, 25-20 in front of 900 fans two nights later.

The final match didn't count in the World League standings, but it counted for pride as the U.S. Won 25-23, 34-36, 26-24, 20-25, 25-8. Ball led the Americans with 49 assists, four aces and seven digs, and Erik Sullivan had 12 digs and Tom Sorenson 21 kills.

After these matches, the U.S. went to the Olympics and finished 0-5. Brazil won its pool with a 5-0 record but lost to Argentina in the quarterfinals and finished fifth.

Since that three-match series, neither the men's or women's U.S. National Teams have returned to Fort Wayne for a match.

**Also, in 2002, Jon Benick of the Wizards hits three home runs against Quad City.**

## July 4

**In 1946, pitcher Leo Luken's amazing 53-game winning streak with the Zollner Pistons ends.**

Over a span of three seasons, Luken was unbelievable. He and the Pistons lost to the Detroit Briggs 2-1, giving Luken his first defeat since midway through the 1944 season. It was also the Pistons' first loss in 15 games.

Luken gave up only three hits in the game, but both runs were the result of errors and a walk during the first two innings. The Pistons were limited to three hits by Detroit pitcher Hal Blumke.

The streak helped the Pistons win world championships Amateur Softball Association national championships in 1945, 1946 and 1947 before winning National Fastball League titles five years in a row, from 1949 through 1953. In national competition from 1945 to 1947, Luken won 12 games and lost none.

In 1992, Luken became the eighth Pistons player to be named to the Amateur Softball Association Hall of Fame, joining Bernie Kampschmidt, Hughie Johnston, Jim Ramage, Sam Lombardo, Elmer Rohrs, Bill West and Clyde (Dizzy) Kirkendahl.

Luken's career began with the Covington Kentucky Ward Boosters in 1937. In 1939 he pitched a perfect game against Cincinnati and in that game struck out the first 20 batters he faced. His last year with the Boosters he went 42-6.

After joining the Pistons in 1940, Luken went 29-2 with three no-hitters and 11 shutouts in 1942. In 1944 he was 30-2 and he followed that with a 35-0 season. It was 17-4 in 1947; 17-1 in 1949; 15-3 in 1950; 6-1 in 1951; and 9-1 in 1954, the year the team disbanded.

**Also, in 1861, future St. Louis Cardinals manager Louis Heilbroner is born in Fort Wayne.**

Louie Heilbroner managed the St. Louis Cardinals at the end of the 1900 season to a 23-25 record. Patsy Tebeau had resigned in the middle of the season, the Cardinals offered the job to third baseman John McGraw who declined. Then St. Louis named Heilbroner who was the team's secretary. The team went 23-25 under Heilbroner, and he was replaced the next season by Patsy Donovan.

Heilbroner remained with the Cardinals as a business manager until 1908.

He was more famous for founding Heilbroner's Baseball Bureau Service, the first commercial statistics service which included publishing the Baseball Blue Book.

Heilbroner died Dec. 21, 1933, in Fort Wayne.

## July 5

**In 1992, Mohr Magic wins its third AAU national basketball title in four years.**

This was essentially an all-star team of the area's best girls basketball players, and they turned out to be some of the nation's best basketball players. It was also likely the best AAU girls basketball team ever.

Snider's Tiffany Gooden and Kris Booker, Northrop's Leslie Johnson, Angie Harris of Bishop Luers and Bellmont's Krista Reinking were the cornerstones for Gary Andrews' AAU summer club. They won the 13 and younger national title in 1989 as the Decatur Thunderbirds, but they were just starting. The team also included future all-state players Tiffany Longsworth from Kokomo, Abby Conklin from Charlestown and Jennifer Howell from Mount Vernon.

They regularly played older teams led by high school stars or even college players during their warm-ups for tournaments, and usually lost by only a basket or two.

The group won six state championships and three national titles in six years. They might have won another title, but Gooden suffered a torn ACL injury early in the 1993 tournament and they finished third. They also finished fifth in 1990.

In their best season, in 1991, they won their second title by an average of 30 points per game. The next year Johnson and Harris decided not to play. Gooden was the only player to play in each tournament during the six-year run, and Booker played for five years.

Andrews later won three state titles at Bishop Luers before starting his college coaching career at Saint Francis. Gooden, Booker and Johnson were all NCAA Division I stars, and Harris was a volleyball star at Notre Dame.

**July 6**

**In 1982, Churubusco's Brent Gaff is called up to the New York Mets to pitch the next day.**

The Mets were playing a doubleheader against the Cincinnati Reds. After Ron Darling gave up four hits for a complete-game victory, Gaff pitched 1 2/3 innings in relief during the nightcap, giving up two hits and one run.

After being drafted by the Mets in the sixth round of the 1977 draft, Gaff pitched three years for the Mets from 1982 to 1984. He appeared in 58 games with a 4-5 record and 4.06 earned-run average. His career ended in 1985 when he missed the season with a partial rotator cuff tear in his right shoulder. He was released by the Mets on Nov. 13, 1985.

That Gaff made it to the big leagues is remarkable considering that during his first minor league season with Class A Wausau he went 1-13 with a 5.77 earned run average. He went 10-5 with a 2.98 earned run average the next summer with Wausau.

Gaff's best season was his last one in 1984 when he became a frequently-used reliever, appearing in 47 games and finishing 18 of them. It was the year that the Mets turned it around, improving from 68-94 in 1983 to 90-72.

Gaff was inducted into the Northeast Indiana Baseball Association's Hall of Fame in 2003.

## July 7

**In 1989, the Walter Jordan Parade of Stars play their last game with Ron Harper, Shawn Kemp and other former stars.**

There was no defense in this game, and everyone loved it.

The Blue beat the Gold 175-163 before more than 2,000 fans in the Memorial Coliseum Exposition Hall as more than $16,000 was raised for charity. There were 47 dunks in the game.

Ron Harper and Kenny Battle scored 41 points for the Blue, followed by 25 for Ray Tolbert, 23 by Todd Mitchell and 21 for Everette Stephens. Shawn Kemp scored 34 for the Gold followed by 33 by Tracy Foster, 32 by Ken Norman, 29 by Jay Edwards and 19 by John Flowers.

The halftime slam dunk contest was amazing as Tolbert, Harper, Battle, Kemp, Stevens and Mitchell battled. Harper, Kemp and Battle advanced to the finals where Battle won it with a 360-degree tomahawk.

The game was almost canceled by the NBA which withheld its sanction and threatened to fine players who participated. Future sanctions meant this was the last contest in the 10-year series.

"The NBA let us down today and we had to suck it up and go on with what we had," Jordan said. "We lost some players but the ones that were here wanted to play and made sacrifices. It's always a last-minute thing in dealing with these people. They don't think about the effort and commitment that goes into a game like this. I was going to go through with the game no matter what."

**Also, in 1952, the first AAGPBL All-Star Game is played in South Bend with Maxine Kline, Dottie Schroeder, Betty Weaver Foss and Jo Weaver representing the Daisies.**

## July 8

**In 1951, Ernie Berg, Harold Van Orman and Ramon Perry buy an IHL expansion franchise for $2,500.**

The Fort Wayne Komets have lasted more than 60 years, but they almost didn't last five minutes.

When plans for the new Allen County War Memorial Coliseum were announced, Ernie Berg, Harold Van Orman, and Ramon Perry figured maybe a hockey team would work in Fort Wayne, even though the building was to be used primarily for the NBA's Fort Wayne Pistons. Berg and Van Orman met with the International Hockey League's Board of Governors in Toledo.

At the end of the Fort Wayne presentation, some board members inquired about the Fort Wayne group's financial status. Van Orman assured the board that was no problem, pulling his wallet out and putting it on the table, backed with the bold statement, "Do you want a fee now?"

The cost for an expansion team was $2,500.

"Fortunately," Van Orman would say later, "they didn't ask to see our money. I think I had about $11 in my wallet. If they had asked to see our money, we were done."

**Also, in 1946, the G.E. Club beats the Cincinnati Reds 7-6.**

A crowd of 3,500 fans watched at Dwenger Park as the Electricians rallied in the bottom of the ninth to win. Bob Winters belted a bases-loaded triple to centerfield to drive in three runs and tie the game. Then Pete Chapman executed a perfect suicide squeeze to drive in Winters and end the game.

## July 9

**In 1985, Darrell Waltrip races at Baer Field and has to bow out after 35 laps.**

Baer Field Speedway has a long history of bringing the biggest names in racing to Fort Wayne. The tradition started in 1964 when eventual three-time Indianapolis 500 winner Bobby Unser raced there. Unser established a track record that would last for the next 12 years.

According to fwrace.com, the 1970s brought current-and future NASCAR stars such as David Pearson, Bobby Allison, Buddy Baker, Darrell Waltrip, Benny Parsons, and Rusty Wallace to the half-mile oval along with short track greats such as Dick Trickle, Ed Howe, Bob Senneker, Joe Ruttman, Tiny Lund, Bentley Warren, Johnny Rutherford, Gary Bettenhausen, Rich Vogler and Mel Kenyon.

A two-time NASCAR champion at that point, Waltrip was racing as part of the American Speed Association's new Gran Marque Series.

"Really, I love to race," Waltrip told The News-Sentinel's Bill Scott. "After the pressures of Grand National racing, this is the way I relax."

Waltrip had to drop out of the 100-lap race after 35 laps because a plug wire burned through.

**Also, in 1954, the Daisies host the last AAGPBL All-Star Game.**

The Daisies beat the All-Stars 10-8 at Memorial Park. Fort Wayne was led by Maxine Kline, Jean Geissinger, Jo Weaver and Betty Weaver were voted to the post-season all-star team.

This was the second year in a row that Fort Wayne had hosted the all-star game. On July 14, 1953, the Daisies beat the all-stars 4-3 in 11 innings. The Daisies had six players who had been named to the all-star team, Betty Weaver Foss, Jo Weaver, Jean Geissinger, Maxine Kline, Katie Horstman and Rita Briggs, and they were replaced on the all-star team by the players who had finished second in the voting.

**July 10**

**In 1982, the first time Walter Jordan's Parade of Stars Game featured NBA players.**

The game almost died after less than 300 fans came to watch the 1981 game. The first two years the format was based on a North vs. South match-up of former Fort Wayne high school stars.

Jordan changed everything in the third year and was rewarded as more than 4,000 fans crammed into IPFW's Multipurpose Building. The overflow crowd included fans stacked under the baskets at both ends and hundreds of fans were turned away.

Jordan later credited former IU star Wayne Radford for saving the event by recruiting Isaiah Thomas, Mike Woodson, Butch Carter and Ray Tolbert to play. Houston Rockets star Robert Reid also showed up.

The NBA stars beat the local team 168-157 as Carter scored 32, Woodson 31, Reid 30, Thomas 26, Tolbert 25. The Fort Wayne team was led by 25 from Mike Muff and Tim Smiley, Jordan 24 and Al Gooden 15. Other local players included Eugene Parker, Alonzo Craig, Rosie Barnes, George Sweigert and Craig Littlejohn.

**Also, in 1987, a record crowd of 7,939 watches the Walter Jordan Parade of Stars Game.**

Maybe the highlight of this game was watching Ron Harper beat Dominique Wilkins in the slam dunk contest. There were 49 dunks during the game, and more than $45,000 was raised for charity.

The lineup of stars included Wayman Tisdale, Chuck Person, Adrian Dantley, Johnny Dawkins, Spud Webb, Scott Skiles and Herb Thompson. Person scored 38, Harper 36 and Wilkins 28 during the game.

## July 11

**In 1951, The Lincoln Lifers beat the Washington Senators 1-0 behind the pitching of Philadelphia Phillies star Curt Simmons.**

Simmons had been called to Army service in September 1950 and was stationed at Camp Atterbury. To stay in shape, he'd occasionally pitch for semi-pro teams around the state. The corporal came up for this game and threw a two-hit shutout, striking out nine in front of a crowd of about 2,500 at Dwenger Park. Olin Smith had two hits for the local contingent.

Simmons was 21 years old and because he was called to active duty had to miss playing in the 1950 World Series which the Phillies lost to the Yankees in four games.

After his year-long absence, Simmons returned to the Phillies and continued his all-star career.

**Also, in 1986, Dominque Wilkins and Ron Harper highlight the Walter Jordan Parade of Stars Game.**

Wilkins scored 51 and Harper 49 as East beat the West 184-180 in overtime before more than 4,000 fans at IPFW. The duo also battled Fort Wayne's John Flowers in the slam dunk contest before Wilkins won.

**Also, in 1990, the Franke brothers purchase the defunct Flint Spirits and move the team to Fort Wayne as the new Komets.**

David Welker's transfer of the Komets to Albany, N.Y., proved to be a huge boon to the community because it made Fort Wayne realize how much the Komets meant to the city. There was intense speculation throughout the city after International Hockey League Commissioner Tom Berry promised there would be hockey in Fort Wayne the next season.

**Also, in 1967, Steve Hargan is named to the American League all-star roster but can't play because of an injury.**

## July 12

**In 1960, Jack Nicklaus sets the course record at Fort Wayne Country Club with a 66 at the Mad Anthonys.**

Though only age 20 and already the National Amateur Champion, the Golden Bear shot 5-under-par, including a 33 on the back nine. This was the third edition of the Mad Anthonys Tournament, and the crazy thing is, at that time no one knew who Nicklaus was.

Former Mad Anthony and Fort Wayne business legend Jim Kelley once said he at first through Nicklaus was a caddy because the young man's pants were wet when he approached. That's because Nicklaus had already been out playing on the course early that morning. That first tournament pairing started a great friendship between the men.

Two years later, after turning professional, Nicklaus returned and shot another 66 to beat Masters champion Gary Player's 69.

In 1985, Nicklaus was asked when he would return to play in the Mad Anthonys, and he quickly responded by asking if his record had been broken yet. When told the questioner did not know, Nicklaus reportedly joked, "Well, I guess there is no reason for me to come back to Fort Wayne then, is there?"

Actually, the course record has been tied a few times, and Nicklaus did come back, however, many times as he was the designer of Sycamore Hills Golf Club which opened in 1989. Kelley was the course's original owner until his death in 2005.

Ironically, Bill Kratzert III holds the Mad Anthonys record with a 63 set at Orchard Ridge Country Club in 1985.

**Also, in 1930, the Central League Baseball Park (League Park) on Calhoun Street burns down and arson was suspected.**

It was believed the fire was started by an irate fan who argued with park officials earlier in the day about returning two balls that were hit into the stands.

**Also, in 1975, Kenneth Ellingwood and Lora Cartwright win the first Three Rivers Festival marathon.**

**July 13**

**In 1931, Grover Cleveland Alexander pitches in Fort Wayne against the Pennsy A.A.**

One of the greatest pitchers in Major League history, Alexander won 373 big league games. But he lost one in his only appearance in Fort Wayne.

The Pennsylvania Railroad A.A. team was a semi-pro squad that won two league titles in a row and often took on Major League teams in exhibitions.

After ending his Major League career with the Philadelphia Phillies the year before, Alexander was 44 during a tour with the House of David barnstorming team. He was making the extravagant salary of $1,000 a month, but he was drawing big crowds and he had won 10 games in a row, five by shutout.

That streak ended in Fort Wayne. Though Alexander did not start the game, he came on to pitch in the eighth inning of a 1-1 contest. With a crowd of more than 3,000 watching at Pennsylvania Railroad Athletic Field, The Pennsys nicked Alexander for three hits and the game-winning run when "Old Pete" gave up a triple over the right fielder's head.

Chuck Noel, who always seemed to be pitching in exhibition games against Major League teams, gave up only five hits with five strikeouts and no walks.

**Also, in 1980, Bill Kratzert wins the Greater Milwaukee Open.**

This was the second tour victory for Kratzert after the 1977 Hartford Open. He scored very consistently 67, 66, 67, 66 for a 266 total and a four-shot victory over Howard Twitty and by five shots over Curtis Strange to earn $36,000.

**July 14**

**In 1955, Fort Wayne hosts the very first LPGA Championship at Orchard Ridge.**

Details about how the tournament came to be in Fort Wayne are a little sketchy. The LPGA, which was founded in 1950, came to Fort Wayne for a tournament in 1954, which Marilynn Smith won.

The players wanted to hold another major tournament in 1955 to go along with the United States Open, which started in 1946. Remembering how they were treated in 1954, the players chose Fort Wayne and worked with the Orchard Ridge members to promote the tournament.

"Back in those days, tournament sites were very sparse, and it looked like it would be a good promotion for Orchard Ridge," said Carl Bennett, who was in charge of promotion for the tournament. "I doubt if we made any money on it, but we had a good time for the club and the city."

There were only 18 players entered in the women's event, which ran July 14-17, 1955. The format was three rounds of medal play followed by a final round of match play, with the top two playing 36 holes, to determine the finishes. It was the first time such a format was tried in a major tournament, and it also turned out to be the last.

The LPGA didn't come back the next two years. The women did return in 1958 through 1960 to take part in the Hoosier Open, in conjunction with the first three Mad Anthony Hoosier Celebrity tournaments. During those weeks, they'd play a weekend tournament in French Lick or Youngstown, Ohio, play in Fort Wayne for two days and then another day in Leesburg before going to another tournament that weekend.

**Also, in 1953, the Daisies beat the AAGPBL All-Stars 4-3 in 11 innings.**

## July 15

**In 2000, DeDee Nathan wins the heptathlon at the Olympic track and field trials to qualify for the Sydney Olympics.**

After just missing making the U.S. Olympic team in 1992 and 1996, Nathan finally broke through in Sacramento. Her 6,343 points were short of her personal best of 6,577, but edged Sheila Burrell's 6339 in second. Kelly Blair-LaBounty finished third in 6,180 to clinch the other U.S. team position.

Nathan's key in winning the two day, seven-event competition was consistency. She took two firsts (shot put, long jump), two thirds (hurdles, high jump), a fourth (200 meters) and two fifths (javelin, 800 meters.)

he led the competition after the first day, and maintained her lead Saturday with a strong long jump (21 feet) and serviceable javelin (144-11) and 800 (2:16.33). In the 800, the heptathlon's final event, Nathan needed to stay within 5 1/2 seconds of Burrell to win the championship, and did so by half a second.

Nathan had finished fourth at the trials in 1992 and 1996.

"I knew what needed to happen would happen," she told The News-Sentinel's Reggie Hayes. "I was very confident that God would let me have this happen, and I would be where I needed to be."

Nathan, 32, went on to finish ninth in Sydney with 6,150 points.

**July 16**

**In 1952, Alex Wood signs to become the Komets' first coach.**

The Komets were very lucky to be able to sign Wood in a couple of ways. He had just led the Toledo Mercurys to the Turner Cup title, and he was the right man for the job.

"The one thing that this team always had was toughness, real competitive teams win or lose," said original Komet Eddie Long. "I credit Alex with a lot of that, and I think we set the tone for the franchise that year. There's no doubt Alex helped sell hockey in Fort Wayne."

The Komets finished 20-38-2 that season, but they had fun on and off the ice.

Wood had a little bit of devil in him, too, George Drysdale recalled. "Alex liked animals. He used to race pigeons, you know. And he liked dogs.

"I went to a dog show with him once and as the dogs were standing all groomed and quiet ready to be judged, Alex threw a ball into the ring. The dogs scattered all over the place."

Maybe Wood's greatest contribution to Fort Wayne was signing Long who was just 19 at the time and played in Fort Wayne for 14 seasons, becoming Mr. Komet along the way.

After signing as Komets' coach, Wood returned to Ottawa where he used to coach and asked some of his former players who some of the hot talent was. Some of Long's baseball teammates had played for Wood before and suggested the scrappy right wing.

"He came to the front door and came into the house and talked to my dad and me and offered me a contract," Long said. "That's how I came to Fort Wayne."

It could be argued that Long might have been the most important player in Komets history. As much as anyone, he gave the Komets their identity. Particularly at the start, Long's hustle, grit and ability were something that attracted new fans to the team and the game. Then he maintained that excellence during a 14-year career and retired as the IHL's all-time leading scorer at that time.

**July 17**

**In 1955, Bev Hanson wins the inaugural LPGA Championship in Fort Wayne.**

In developing the new major tournament, the LPGA decided on a format of three rounds of medal play followed by a final round of match play, with the top two players going at it for 36 holes. It was the first time such a format was tried in a major tournament,

"I think there was a little grousing on the part of some of the girls that didn't feel it was an adequate way to approach it," said eventual winner Bev Hanson Sfingi, now living in LaQuinta, Calif.

Hanson liked the format then just fine, especially after she used only eight putts for six birdies during one seven-hole stretch to clinch the title over Louise Suggs 4 and 3. Besides having a trophy awarded by St. Louis Cardinals great Dizzy Dean, Hanson won $1,200 plus a $500 bonus from MacGregor, where she also worked.

"The prize money is a laugh," she said. "Most of our financing came from the golf companies. Money wasn't flowing like water, but we did have a lot of camaraderie and a lot of fun. It's nice, and I wouldn't turn it down, but it wasn't all about money."

Suggs made $800 for finishing second, Fay Crocker got $650 for third and Jackie Pung $525 for fourth. Gloria Armstrong finished 16th and pocketed $75.

Hanson finished her career with 17 wins, including three majors. Suggs finished with 58 wins and 11 majors, earning a little more than $200,000 during her career.

**Also, in 1999, Scott Sharp wins his third race for Kelley Racing, this time at Atlanta.**

**July 18**

**In 1931, Butch Henline plays his last Major League game.**

Walter "Butch" Henline didn't make it to the Major Leagues until he was 26 years old, and then the New York Giants played the catcher only one game before trading him to the Philadelphia Phillies. Henline thrived with the Phillies, hitting .306 over the season's final 33 games to earn the starting catcher's spot.

The next season, he hit .316 with 14 home runs and 64 runs batted in during 125 games. He also led all National League backstops with a .983 fielding percentage. The next year he hit .324 with seven home runs and 46 runs driven in. Then the Phillies acquired all-star catcher Jimmie Wilson, a native of Philadelphia, and Henline never played 100 games in a season again.

Before the 1927 season, the Phillies traded him to the Brooklyn Robins where he remained a back-up catcher. He finished his career with a two-year stint with the Chicago White Sox. When he retired in 1931, Henline had a .291 career batting average with 40 home runs and 268 runs driven in. He also had a .971 career fielding percentage as a catcher.

Maybe the biggest day of his career was Sept. 15, 1922, when he hit three home runs against St. Louis. On March 9, 1925, he was named the Phillies' captain.

He stayed active in baseball as an umpire and even worked the 1947 Major League All-Star Game.  He died at age 62 in 1957 and was inducted into the Fort Wayne Baseball Oldtimers Association Hall of Fame in 1964.

**Also, in 1961, Arnold Palmer and Gary Player play a match at the Mad Anthonys.**

**July 19**

**In 1990, Gregg Hart of Homestead sets a national high school record in the discus.**

Hart actually broke the record in back-to-back years.

On June 10, 1989, using an Olympic-weight discus (4.41 pounds), Hart set the mark of 181-5 at the United States Junior Track and Field Championships at Ohio State.. Hart, who had just finished his junior season at Homestead, got the toss off on the second of his six attempts to break the record of 180-4 set by Charles Moye of Akron, Ohio in 1987.

"I was very surprised," Hart said. "I thought I'd only thrown 160 to 165 feet. I've never thrown this discus in competition before, although I've fooled around with it in practice."

A year later, he did it again, this time with a toss of 201-4 3/4 at an informal meet in Indianapolis. According to several online sources, Hart continues to hold the record using the 4.41-pound discus. Using a high-school sized discus (3.58 pounds), Hart's personal best had been a toss of 216-9 at the state high school meet in 1990. He had won the Keebler Classic in June with a toss ot 208-9.

"I was just trying to break my record. I never thought about throwing over 200 feet," Hart told The News-Sentinel's Reggie Hayes in 1990. "I was basically shocked more than anything else."

After winning three state titles at Homestead, Hart went to Indiana where he continued to set records and was a two-time Big Ten champion and a two-time all-American after finishing third at the NCAA meet as a junior and second as a senior.

He also finished 16th at the 1992 Olympic trails.

Hart retired after failing to make the Olympic team in 2004.

**July 20**

**In 1998, Scott Sharp wins his second race of the season for Kelley Racing at Dover.**

Somehow, Sharp kept his car in one piece to win the 248-lap Pep Boys 400K for Kelley Racing. Sharp survived a crash-filled race that saw only 10 of the 22 cars that started remained racing until the end.

After avoiding six wrecks and seven caution flags, Sharp beat Buddy Lazier by .689 seconds at the finish line to win $128,550. After charging to challenge Sharp at the finish line, Lazier almost rear-ended the winner after crossing the line but slammed on the brakes just in time. Lazier and Sharp were the only two drivers who were on the lead lap at the end.

"Two hundred and forty-eight laps, on any track going flat out the whole time is tough, let alone on a bumpy track like Dover," Sharp told The News-Sentinel's Rich Griffis. "I would have thought engines would have been a bigger factor. I'm surprised they held together."

Sharp caught a break when pole-sitter Tony Stewart experienced mechanical problems which stalled his chances after 100 laps. After leading 73 of the first 85 laps, Stewart ended up sitting 27 laps in the pits, before returning to finish eighth.

The victory marked the first time Sharp has ever led the most laps in a race, having shown the way on 145 of the 248 laps.

"This makes the first victory a little sweeter," team owner Tom Kelley of his team's second win of the season. "Scott went out and dominated this race. It's gratifying to know that it wasn't just luck."

## July 21

**In 1976, Matt Vogel wins a swimming gold medal in the 100-meter butterfly at the Montreal Olympics.**

When Matt Vogel swam for gold medals in the 1976 Montreal Summer Olympics, he was one of the first swimmers to shave his head before a competition. Vogel believed that the smooth, slippery feel gave him a psychological and physical advantage.

The advantage was enough as Vogel won gold medals in the 100-meter butterfly and the 400 medley relay. He then returned to the University of Tennessee for his sophomore season, but his remaining career could never live up to his expectations. So he quit several times and didn't return to Tennessee in the fall of '77. He worked several months on the graveyard shift at Scott's Food Store on Decatur Road.

Once while stocking shelves at 3 a.m., he decided he wanted to swim again, and he went back to Tennessee. That year the Volunteers won the national title as Vogel finished fourth in the 100 butterfly. Eventually, Vogel finished his eligibility but dropped out of school before graduating in 1980 to begin a coaching career in Maryville, Tenn.

He coached there five years before joining a club in Oak Ridge, Tenn. After 10 more years of coaching, he retired to buy a lawn-care service. The work was extremely difficult, and he then moved to California to begin coaching a club program in Visalia. Eventually, he came back to Fort Wayne to take over the Fort Wayne Aquatics swim team as head coach.

Vogel says he is still unable to put into perspective what it means to him to have won two gold medals, which his mother keeps for him in Fort Wayne.

"I don't think I'll be able to really fully access that until I can sit down and not have to worry about where my next paycheck is coming (from)," he said. "I was grateful to have the opportunity."

**Also, in 1961, Wildcat Baseball holds its first "Progress Day," later renamed Mr. Mac Day, with Jackie Robinson and Carl Erskine attending.**

**July 22**

**In 1993, the Wizards win their second-straight shutout.**

This new minor league baseball thing was turning out OK in Fort Wayne. The Wizards were proving to be a big hit at the box office, and the play on the field was doing OK, too.

Every day there was something new that hadn't been seen before in Fort Wayne, including back-to-back shutouts. LaTroy Hawkins improved to 10-4 with a three-hit 1-0 win over Madison. Hawkins won his eighth game in a row by striking out seven and walking just one.

Hawkins had allowed only one run in his last 29 innings over three starts.

Following Hawkins' example, Ron Caridad gave up only three hits over six innings the next night and won 3-0 at Appleton. While Hawkins hadn't lost in more than a month, this was Caridad's first win in more than two months as he struck out eight.

The shutout streak reached 28 innings as the Wizards won the next game 10-4. Scott Moten held Appleton scoreless through eight innings before the Foxes scored four in the bottom of the eighth.

Hawkins' streak eventually reached 13 wins in a row before it ended in the season's last game. He finished the season 15-5 to tie for the Midwest League lead in wins and led the circuit with 179 strikeouts and a 2.06 earned run average. Within two years, he was playing for the Minnesota Twins.

**Also, in 2010, Jonathan Galvez of the TinCaps belts three home runs in a game against Peoria.**

**July 23**

**In 1963, Sam Snead and Jimmy Demaret play an exhibition match at the Mad Anthonys.**

After sinking an eagle on No. 18, Demaret shot a 66 to beat Snead who shot a 69. Demaret needed only 27 putts on the day.

Demaret won 31 career PGA events including three Masters. He was inducted into the World Golf Hall of Fame in 1983.

Snead won a PGA-record 82 career tournaments, including seven majors. The only one he failed to win was the U.S. Open where he finished second four times. He was inducted into the World Golf Hall of Fame in 1974.

Pros who have appeared at the Mad Anthonys over the years include Jack Nicklaus, Gary Player, Arnold Palmer, Tony Lema, Julius Boros, Billy Casper, Ben Hogan, Tom Weiskopf, Chi Chi Rodriguez, Lee Trevino and Johnny Miller.

**Also, in 1998, Brad Miller is named to the U.S. National Team that will compete in the basketball World Championships in Athens, Greece.**

This was during an NBA lockout so the team was made up of players from the Continental Basketball Association, the European pro leagues and some college players. The U.S. won the bronze medal after losing to Lithuania in pool play and to Russia in the semifinals. Miller, who had been playing in Italy, was the only player from the team to go on to have a significant NBA career.

**July 24**

**In 1964, Avilla Speedway opens.**

The track lasted 31 years until it closed after a final show on Sept. 23, 1995. Among the notable drivers who regularly competed there are Moose Myers, Jess Jates, Little Joe Bennett, Hank Lower, Terry Fisher, Johnie Walker and Joe Wallace who won the first race ever held on the 3/8th mile track and was inducted with Clarence Schmuck into the Avilla Hall of Fame when it opened in 1978.

Under the direction of Owner Howard Bice, the track expanded from an original 2,500 seats to more than 6,000. After Bice died in 1984, the track was operated by his widow Barbara.

**Also, in 1995, Western Michigan star Sommer Stier rallies to beat former Homestead teammate Michelle Evans for the Women's City Tennis Tournament singles title 3-6, 6-3, 6-2.**

**Also, in 1995, United States Deaf Davis Cup team member Jay Smithley wins his first of two city tennis titles.**

**Also, in 2006, Michelle Smith wins her fourth Women's City Golf Championship by shooting a 72 to hold off Amber Sieber by one stroke at Brookwood Golf Club.**

**South Side grade Cathey Tyree wins a gold medal in the heptathlon at the U.S. Olympic Festival.**

Cathey Tyree was a two-sport star long before it was in vogue.

She didn't just run track, she excelled. Same with basketball.

In 1987, she was Purdue University's MVP in both sports, an unprecedented feat at the school. Her success led to an induction in the Purdue Hall of Fame in 1998. Tyree went on to place sixth in the 1988 Olympic Trials in the heptathlon, and in 1998 she tried out for the WNBA's Minnesota Lynx.

All of that took place after a stellar high school career for South Side that includes a 1,600-meter relay state record that still stands. Tyree was part of South's incredible 1983 relay team that included future Olympian heptathlete DeDee Nathan, former national triple jump contender Angela Goodman and sprinter Trudy McCloud.

"Sports were good to me, and the people in sports were good to me," Tyree said. "It gave me lots of experience, as far as life in general – meeting different people, dealing with people in different ways. Sports improved my life a whole lot."

Most of Tyree's time today in Alhambra, Calif., is spent with her boyfriend, actor Michael Taliferro, raising their 7-year-old daughter and 3-year-old son. Tyree also works occasionally as a model/actress in print and television advertising.

She moved to California to train as a heptathlete, and won a gold medal in the event at the 1989 U.S. Olympic Festival. She last competed in the javelin at the Olympic Festival in Los Angeles in 1991. Except for the brief tryout with the WNBA, most of her athletic work has been portraying athletes in advertising.

**Also, in 2005, Art Saltsberg retires from WOWO SportsTalk.**

**July 26**

**In 1994, Steve Beier wins his sixth men's city tennis singles title in a pressure-packed situation.**

Talk about pressure.

Steve Beier is marrying Ruth Hanlon in less than a week, but he didn't have much chance to think about that during the championship match against Luke Grossman. The pressure increased as some of Beier's future in-laws arrived in town early to meet him and watch him play for the city title.

Nothing like having your fiancé's brothers checking you out in a pressure situation. To increase the stress, Beier blew three break points and lost the first set 6-4.

"I never really thought about it before, but now that they've come I feel like I'd be letting them down if I lost," Beier said. "It's a different kind of pressure, because I, at least, wanted to give them a good show. If I had lost in two straight sets, that would have been embarrassing."

Nice first impression.

The Hanlons and about 40 weddings guests were relieved as Beier came back to beat Grossman 4-6, 6-2, 6-2 in a thrilling 2 1/2-hour match in the 84th men's City Tennis Tournament. The third set was much closer than the final score indicated, as five games went to deuce, but Beier won four of them.

Beier said it was the toughest of the 10 finals he has played.

"I felt I was hitting the ball, but that's the best I've seen Luke play," Beier said. "I thought Luke was playing really well, and if he continued to play that well I wasn't going to beat him. I felt that if I lost with him playing that way, I wouldn't feel bad because I was making him hit some shots."

Beier joined Grossman, Les Ortlieb, Miles F. Porter and Dudley Johnston as the only men to win six city singles titles.

## July 27

**In 2004, New Haven's Dave Doster sees his 32-game hitting streak with AAA Fresno end.**

Doster built the longest hitting streak in pro baseball in 2003 at the age of 33. When his streak began on June 21st, Doster was hitting .273, but the streak raised his overall batting average for the season to 333. Over the streak Doster hit .419 (57-136) with 26 runs, 15 doubles, 5 home runs and had 25 runs batted in. Five times during the streak he collected a base hit in his final plate appearance.

Doster established a new Fresno franchise record on July 11 after passing Wilson Delgado who had a 19-game hitting streak in 1998. On July 22, Doster passed Lansing's Brian Dopirak, who had the longest hitting streak in minor league baseball at 27 games, and on July 23 Doster surpassed Chicago White Sox' outfielder Carlos Lee for the longest hitting streak in baseball that season with his 30th game. Doster's hitting streak was the longest in the PCL since Lorenzo Gray hit in 40 consecutive games for the Edmonton Trappers back in 1982.

Doster ended a 13-year professional career in 2005 at age 36. The highlights were 137 games over two seasons as the Philadelphia Phillies' second baseman. He hit .267 in 105 at-bats in 1996. The New Haven High School graduate was drafted by the Phillies in 1993 after earning all-Missouri Valley Conference honors at Indiana State.

Doster also had a 30-game hitting streak during his college career at Indiana State.

He was inducted into the Northeast Indiana Baseball Hall of Fame in 2007.

**Also, in 2011, Bishop Luers graduate Kristi O'Brien rallies to win the Indiana Women's State Amateur golf title.**

**Also, in 2005, Fort Wayne is named the No. 7 minor league sports city in America by Street & Smith's Sports Business Journal.**

**July 28**

**In 1958, the Mad Anthonys begin hosting a golf tournament.**

The 1950s were tough on Fort Wayne sports fans as the Pistons softball team disbanded in 1954, the Daisies folded in 1954, the PGA's Fort Wayne Open ended in 1956, and then the NBA's Pistons left for Detroit in 1957.

Fort Wayne needed something good to happen, and the Mad Anthonys stepped up, hosting their first celebrity golf tournament in 1958 at Fort Wayne Country Club. The first event sold 1,200 tickets.

The event started with 20 stop ladies professional golfers and 30 other celebrities such as Notre Dame football coach Terry Brennan, Purdue football coach Jack Mollenkopf and Purdue basketball coach Ray Eddy. The goal was to pair one pro golfer and one celebrity with each group. The ladies finished up a tour event in French Lick the day before.

Despite a slight drizzle all day, the event was a big success. Marlene Bauer Hagge won the pro competition, shooting a course-record 72 to edge LPGA president Marilynn Smith's 73. Murle MacKenzie almost stole the highlights with a hole-in-one, using a 3-iron on the 156-yard No. 5 hole. The women split $2,000 in prize money.

Brennan was named the first Hoosier Celebrity of the Year and received a nice plaque. The Red Coat become part of the Mad Anthonys tradition three years later.

The tournament was also played at Fort Wayne Country Club every year until 1980 when it began a semi-regular rotation with Orchard Ridge Country Club and later with Sycamore Hills Golf Club.

## July 29

**In 1963, Chicago Cubs stars Ron Santo, Larry Jackson, Billy Williams and Bob Buhl entertain more than 5,000 Wildcat players.**

The Central Soya plane and huge Cubs fan Gint Herzog went to Chicago to pick up the stars and bring them to Fort Wayne. Long-time Wildcat supporter and former Dodgers great Carl Erskine also took part again. This was the third year in a row Eskine participated in Progress Day, and he also spent part of the summer presenting clinics for players.

As if to balance the Chicago representation, the next year a group of White Sox players came to Fort Wayne. Bill Skowron, Ron Hansen, Dave Nicholson, Pete Ward and Floyd Robinson joined Erskine at Progress Day.

Another great part of the early years of Wildcat Baseball were the annual trips to Major League games. The trips started in 1961 when about 700 Wildcat players, coaches and league officials went to Chicago to see the Yankees take on the White Sox. The next year the numbers increased to 1,500 to see the Tigers play the White Sox in Chicago. The total reached more than 2,000 for the first time in 1963 for a trip to Chicago to see the Yankees and White Sox again.

Over the next four years, Wildcat trips include trips to Chicago for the Giants against the Cubs two times, the Tigers against the White Sox and to Detroit for the Tigers taking on the Red Sox. The largest number on a trip was 2,642 in 1967.

The last trip required 17 train cars, but poor planning by the railroad line required the kids to be on trains for more than eight hours, making for a long day. This turned out to be the last Wildcat trip to a Major League game.

**Also, in 1993, Bruce Boudreau is named the Komets' new coach.**

After a year coaching Muskegon of the Colonial Hockey League, Boudreau came back to lead the Komets back to the Turner Cup Finals where they lost to Atlanta in six games. Boudreau was fired halfway through the next season, but he stuck with it and coached in the NHL with Washington and Anaheim.

**July 30**

**In 1931, Chuck Klein and the Philadelphia Phillies are beaten by the Pennsy AA Railroaders 8-4.**

Klein was an outfielder with the Fort Wayne Chiefs in the Central League in 1928 when his contract was picked up by the Phillies. He went on to play 16 years in the Majors with the Phillies, Chicago Cubs and Pittsburgh Pirates.

During his best seasons, he won four home run championships and two RBI titles and the triple crown in 1933. He also a superb defensive outfielder and had 44 assists in 1930 and was named the National League's Most Valuable Player in 1932. On July 10, 1936 he became the first National League player in the 20$^{th}$ century to slug four home runs in the same game against the Pirates, and he twice hit for the cycle.

Klein finished with a .320 career batting average and 300 home runs and was selected by the Veterans Committee for the Baseball Hall of Fame in 1980.

On his return to Fort Wayne, Klein had a great day with two home runs, but the Phillies lost 8-4 before about 2,000 fans. The Railroaders scored five runs in the bottom of the eighth inning to overcome a 4-3 deficit.

Chuck Noel was the winning pitcher for Pennsy, striking out five and also getting two hits.

**Also, in 1935, the Soap Box Derby draws more than 20,000 spectators.**

**Also, in 1999, Sean Burroughs extends his hitting streak to 20 games to tie the Wizards' team record set by Corey Koskie.**

**Also, in 1991, Northrop graduate and former Purdue player Tony Jones is named an assistant coach to Gene Keady.**

**July 31**

**In 1984, Bobby Allison wins a race at Baer Field Speedway.**

A crowd of more than 6,000 fans showed up on a Tuesday night to watch one of NASCAR's all-time best drivers. Other top drivers that night included Dick Trickle, Al Schill and Joe Shear who all challenged Allison in the 100-lap feature as part of a 21-car field.

Allison took the lead for the first time on the 22nd lap. He led through lap 38 when Trickle moved in front. It was Allison back in front again on lap 42 and he never trailed again. A car driven by Rich Bickle ran into the car driven by Steve Wallace on the 82nd lap, locking the drivers in their positions until the track was cleared. It gave Allison a breather.

When the green flag came out, Alison managed to fight off his challengers the rest of the way. Trickle made his final bid coming out of turn three on the 99th lap but Allision held him off. Trickle then got a little loose coming out of one which let both Schill and Shear zoom by him.

"You have to give Trickle, Schill and Shear a lot of credit," Allison said to the crowd following his exciting victory. "They put a lot of pressure on me."

This was the third time Allison had won a race at Baer Field, the first coming in 1971 and the second in 1974.

**Also, in 1962 Jackie Robinson, Carl Eskine, Ted Williams and Bob Feller appear at Wildcat Baseball's second "Progress Day."**

Before there was Mr. Mac Day, there was Progress Day. Jackie Robinson and Carl Erskine appeared at the first one in 1961 and brought back Feller and Williams the next year. After introductions by Mr. Mac, Erskine and Feller went to the mound and Robinson put on a bunting demonstration and Williams hit some towering drives. The Major Leaguers were feted at a Van Orman Hotel luncheon afterward.

# AUGUST

**August 1**

**In 1991, the NCAA rules preseason basketball scrimmages can no longer be held off-campus, killing IU's annual trip to Fort Wayne.**

For years, Indiana basketball fans would take over the Memorial Coliseum one night per year to watch coach Bob Knight's Hoosiers play an intrasquad scrimmage. The practice started in 1972 with less than 3,000 fans turning out, was halted for a few years after forward Scott May slipped on the coliseum floor and narrowly avoided injury in 1974, but returned as an annual event in 1984. It was an annual sellout from that point on.

Knight told coliseum officials in 1990 that the scrimmage may be ending because of NCAA rules.

"The thrust of this rule is to decrease the time away from campus by the student-athletes," said Dan Dutcher, NCAA director of legislative services.

Fans often camped out for seats, and as much as $30,000 was raised for area charities from the event.

"Bob said there was no way, unless he could bring in a team like the Czechoslovakia team or the Italian team, and he made an effort to do that," said Hilliard Gates of WKJG, the game's sponsor in later years. "But he found out it would be charged as a game against his schedule. He looked for an alternative and just couldn't find it."

**August 2**

**In 2010, Ryan Recht wins his record-breaking 10th men's city tennis tournament title.**

No one has ever dominated Fort Wayne tennis like Recht has. During his 10-year span, he beat eight different players in the championship match and never lost a set in any city tournament match. He passed Les Ortlieb's record of eight men's titles in 2009, and then Lee Ann Berning's mark of nine women's titles in 2010.

In this instance, he beat two-time city champion and former state high school champion Derek Carpenter 6-2, 6-2 at Swinney Tennis Center. Carpenter also lost to Recht in the 2008 city finals.

"It's special because it's the one that sets me apart from everyone else," Recht said. "Each one is another step forward. I kind of like this one a lot because it puts me more on top."

No one could match Recht's variety of shots, height or massive serve, and he always seemed to play stronger the longer a tournament lasted.

Recht also tied marks held by Dudley Johnston from 1964 to 1970 and Dr. Miles F. Porter Jr. from 1909 to 1915 with seven consecutive men's titles and won triple crowns in 2008 and 2009, also taking the doubles and mixed-doubles titles.

Recht moved to Texas for a tennis teaching job after 2010, and has not been eligible to extend his streak since.

**Also, in 1999, the Wizards' Sean Burroughs' hitting streak ends at 23 games.**

Perhaps the most famous Wizards' player while he was in Fort Wayne, Burroughs is the son of former Major League player Jeff Burroughs and also a part of a Little League World Series championship team.

## August 3

**In 1961, the first city swimming meet is held at McMillen Park.**

There's probably no more colorful or loud event in Fort Wayne each summer than the annual City Swim Meet. Each August, more than 1,000 screaming kids have their faces painted, wear funny hats and costumes for the annual march-in on that Sunday afternoon before the finals. And sometimes their parents look even more garish. Everyone is wearing homemade T-shirts and is encouraged to show their spirit in any way possible because noise makes for faster times.

That must mean Avalon has the loudest and strongest lungs because the outcomes of the city meet usually seem to be decided by dynasties. At one point into the early 1990s, Avalon won 22 titles in 25 years before Arlington Park ended the run. The two clubs battled back and forth for five years until Avalon won six titles in a row and then Arlington Park won three in a row from 1997 to 1999. Then Avalon won another eight in a row before Sycamore Hills won three in a row going into the 2011 meet.

Avalon also does extremely well in the City Diving Meet, winning 19 titles from the inaugural meet in 1979 to 2003, including twice winning seven championships in a row.

Usually the outcome is decided by depth as much as quality. The larger teams earn tons of points by placing as many swimmers as possible in the top eight of each event.

The meet was held at McMillen Park from 1961 to 1995. The next year it moved to the Brown Natatorium at South Side. Coming inside has only increased the noise and the pageantry.

**Also, in 1991, Mohr Magic wins its second AAU national championship in girls basketball.**

**August 4**

**In 1973, Bruce Miller makes his Major League debut for the San Francisco Giants.**

Though it was unspectacular, Bruce Miller had a solid major-league baseball career, including finally getting a shot in the show at the age of 26.

Born in Fort Wayne, Miller lived in Columbia City before playing baseball at Indiana University. There he hit .354 as a junior shortstop to earn all-Big Ten honors and IU's MVP award. The next year he signed with the Chicago White Sox and started his minor-league career with Duluth (Minn.) of the Northern League.

Miller led that league in defense at shortstop and was promoted to Asheville (N.C.) of the Southern League in 1971, where he became an All-Star, and to Tucson (Ariz.) of the Pacific Coast League in 1972. Then the White Sox traded him to the California Angels in 1972, and in 1973 he was sent to the San Francisco Giants.

It was with the Giants that Miller finally got his chance to make it to the majors. After he hit .313 and went 103 at-bats without striking out in Phoenix, the Giants called him up Aug. 4, 1973, and he hit .143 in 12 games.

Miller alternated between the majors and the minors the next season, hitting .278 with the Giants in 73 games, before sticking with San Francisco for the entire 1975 season. In 99 games that year, alternating at third base with Steve Ontiveros, Miller hit .239. His greatest attribute may have been the ability to play second, shortstop and third base.

Some of his highlights that year include a 13-game hitting streak, belting his first and only major-league home run on July 31 off Clay Kirby in Cincinnati, a 4-for-4 day in Montreal and five game-winning hits.

Unfortunately, Miller hit .160 the next season to end his major-league career. He returned to teach at North Side High School where he also coached for 24 years and was inducted into the Indiana High School Baseball Coaches Association Hall of Fame in 2012.

## Aug. 5

**In 1991, Lee Ann Berning becomes the first, and still so far only, person to win city tennis tournament titles in three decades.**

During her amazing career, Berning won a record nine women's city titles through the late-1970s, 1980s and early 1990s.

What's really amazing is that her career was almost permanently disabled. Berning was 18 when she was involved in a car accident that crushed her right leg. At the time she had the potential to turn pro, but the injury knocked those dreams down.

As a player, Berning won nine women's city singles tournament titles, and played in 12 finals. Both are city records.

"It serves as an example to all my students," she said of her record-breaking ninth singles title. "Fort Wayne has been good to me in terms of tennis, and being able to give something back is my goal. Teaching is a part of that, and these titles are a part of the teaching."

As a doubles player, Berning won 10 mixed doubles titles with six different partners and six doubles titles with six different partners. She never failed to win a city doubles tournament she entered. In 1972, 1973, 1979 and 1991, she won the singles, doubles and mixed doubles titles in the same year, and became the first player to win the triple crown more than once.

While playing at Concordia Lutheran High School, Berning won a state high school doubles title in 1972 and a state singles title in 1974. She also won the state Intercollegiate Singles Championship in 1975 at Valparaiso University.

For her accomplishments, Berning was inducted into the Fort Wayne Tennis Hall of Fame in 1989, and the Indiana Tennis Hall of Fame in 1993.

As a coach, Berning's high school teams at North Side, South Side and Bishop Dwenger won more than 200 matches. She became the first woman to coach a boys team in Fort Wayne.

Berning is the head professional at Wildwood Racquet Club where she has also been honored nationally for her coaching.

**August 6**

**In 1989, the Fort Wayne Flames go out of business only to be replaced by the Indiana Kick.**

What seemed like a second chance was really the beginning of the end of pro indoor soccer in Fort Wayne.

The Fort Wayne Flames played in the American Indoor Soccer Association in 1985 and 1986 before being replaced by the Fort Wayne Kick, which lasted until 1990 when financial problems finally killed the franchise. The highlight for indoor soccer came in 1988 when the Flames lost to Canton for the league title.

Attendance at games was loyal if sporadic, and constant money problems in the front office left everyone, players included, wondering every off-season if the team would return.

Kent Phillips made an unsuccessful attempt to buy the Flames in the summer of 1989, and eventually the team went defunct on Aug. 2 after a three-year run. Then Phillips introduced the Indiana Kick, which he tried to sell as Indiana's third major league team along with the Colts and Pacers. A flamboyant figure compared to most Fort Wayne pro sports owners, Phillips also challenged other teams to have the courage to face his new team.

Unfortunately, the lack of attendance and financial woes continued, and on Jan. 23, 1990, Phillips relinquished all affiliation with the franchise and returned it to the AISA.

**Also, in 2012, Homestead and IPFW grad Amy Recht wins her seventh Women's City Tennis Tournament title**

Recht beat former IPFW teammate Marcy Huck 6-0, 7-6 (7-2 in tiebreaker) for her seventh title in eight years.

During her high school career at Homestead, Recht compiled a 93-8 record in singles and was a three-time News-Sentinel PrepSports Player of the Year as she led the Spartans to the state finals her last three seasons. She was even better during her IPFW career, four times earning the Summit League Player of the Year Award. She never lost in 28 conference matches over four years and finished with a 106-20 career mark in singles while leading the Mastodons to the NCAA Tournament twice.

## August 7

### In 1946, coach Murray Mendenhall Sr. leaves Central High School

Mendenhall came to Fort Wayne from New Castle in 1924 and became the most successful and versatile coach in Summit City history. He signed a three-year contract to coach the Anderson Packers of the National Basketball League.

During his time guiding the Tigers, Mendenhall won a boys basketball state championship in 1943, a boys track state championship in 1944 and his football teams won 134 games in 22 years, including going 8-1 in 1929 and 1931 and 9-0 in 1939.

During his three years in Anderson, he led the Packers to the NBL title in his last season before coming back to Fort Wayne to coach the Pistons for two years. His first team went 40-28 before losing in the first round of the playoffs to the eventual champion Minneapolis Lakers. His second squad finished 32-36 before losing in the first round of the playoffs to Rochester.

Mendenhall then became athletic director and men's basketball coach at Indiana Tech.

### Also, in 2012, Rob Laird brings the Stanley Cup to Fort Wayne.

There are a million stories about the Stanley Cup, and a couple thousand Fort Wayne hockey fans got to add theirs to the tradition.

For 38 years as a professional hockey player, coach and scout, Laird's ultimate dream was to be part of a National Hockey League championship franchise, and when the Los Angeles Kings won in 2012, he wanted to share the victory with Fort Wayne. A former Komets player and coach, Laird had chosen to continue living in Fort Wayne.

Each member of the team gets to host the Stanley Cup for a day over the summer, and Laird and his wife Madeliene hosted a public party at her H.O.P.E. for Animals Spay and Neutering Clinic.

### Also, in 1977, Bill Kratzert wins the Greater Hartford Open.

### Also, in 1936, Don Lash finishes 13th in the 5,000 meters at the Berlin Olympics.

### Also, in 1924, Robert Juday of Geneva finishes fourth in the men's high jump at the Paris Olympics.

**August 8**

**In 2009 Rod Woodson is inducted into the Pro Football Hall of Fame.**

Woodson could do everything on a football field, and he often did.

A first-ballot Hall of Fame selection, Woodson, then 44, was inducted along with receiver Bob Hayes, offensive lineman Randall McDaniel, defensive lineman Bruce Smith, linebacker Derrick Thomas and owner Ralph Wilson.

"I love Fort Wayne, it was a great place to grow up," Woodson said during his induction speech. "It kept me rooted in reality and taught me what was truly real for me and important for me as a man. I really want to thank Fort Wayne for accepting me and embracing me throughout my career, and for accepting my family in Fort Wayne for who we were as people."

During his 17-year NFL career, the Snider graduate played for the Pittsburgh Steelers, San Francisco 49ers, Baltimore Ravens and Oakland Raiders as a cornerback, safety and kick returner. He's the only player in NFL history to be named to the Pro Bowl at three positions. In fact, he was an 11-time Pro Bowl selection. He played 10 of his 17 years with the Steelers.

He's also one of only four players to play in three Super Bowls with three different teams. In 1993, he was named the NFL's Defensive Player of the Year. He was named to the league's 75th anniversary team, and was ranked as the 30th-best player of all-time by Pro Football Weekly.

Among his classic achievements is holding NFL records for most career interceptions returned for touchdowns with 12, most career interception return yards with 1,482 and the third-highest career interceptions with 71.

"Choose to love rather than hate," Woodson said. "Choose to create rather than destroy. Choose to persevere rather than quit. Choose to praise rather than gossip. Choose to heal rather than wound. Choose to pray rather than curse. Choose to live rather than die. Choose Jesus Christ over the world. God bless you."

## August 9

**In 1989, Bishop Luers grad Mike Roesler makes his Major League debut with the Cincinnati Reds.**

In 1985, the former Bishop Luers star pitcher was a 17th-round selection by the Cincinnati Reds, beginning an up-and-down professional career that saw him play briefly with the Reds and the Pittsburgh Pirates.

Roesler fought his way through the minors as first a starting pitcher and then from the bullpen. He finally got his first chance in a regular season game against the San Francisco Giants, coming in during the third inning with the Reds already trailing 5-1. He gave up two hits, two runs and three walks while striking out two in three innings.

"I can't really say I was nervous, but I definitely wasn't as relaxed as I usually am out there," Roesler said. "I kept my composure and kept anything big from happening. This was a good one to build from."

Roesler finished the season with the Reds, going 0-1 with a 3.96 earned run average in 17 appearances as a reliever. After being traded with Jeff Richardson for Billy Hatcher, the next year Roesler pitched in five games for the Pirates, going 1-0 with a 3.00 earned run average. His last Major League appearance was April 23, 1990.

He bounced around the minors with the Pirates and Kansas City Royals before retiring in 1992. Roesler was inducted into the Northeast Indiana Baseball Association Hall of Fame in 2006.

**Also, in 2008, Carroll graduate Jon Fitch loses to George St-Pierre in the main event at UFC 87, Search and Destroy.**

Fitch walked onto the wrestling squad at Purdue and became team captain as a senior. After graduating, he worked his way up through the mixed martial arts circuit to earn the championship chance where he lost by unanimous decision.

**August 10**

**In 1995, Damon Bailey agrees to contract terms with the Fury.**

After being picked by the Indiana Pacers in the second round of the 1994 draft, the Indiana high school career scoring leader had to sit out his first season because of surgery on both knees. He came back the next year, but was cut by the Pacers at the end of training camp.

The Fury, however, had planned ahead, and signed Bailey to a contract worth between $40,000 and $50,000 with the promise of a solid chance to try out his knees.

Bailey scored just two points in his Fury debut on the road at Moline, Ill., but came back the next night to score 14 in Fort Wayne before a record crowd of 8,281. Jay Edwards led the way with 37 as Fort Wayne beat Quad City.

Along with a two-month trip to France at the end of his third season, Bailey played four seasons in Fort Wayne before retiring. During his final season, he averaged 15.1 points to finish second on the team, and 7.3 assists which was third in the league. He was named first-team all-Continental Basketball Association for that performance, but a groin injury hampered him the entire next season, his last in Fort Wayne. His starting spot was taken by Moochie Norris.

Despite some excellent statistics during his Fort Wayne career, Bailey never got another clear shot at the NBA. He signed with the Cleveland Cavaliers before the 1999-2000 season but was released early in training camp.

Among his career highlights in Fort Wayne were helping the Fury into the 1996 CBA Finals as a rookie, and scoring 38 points against Connecticut on Feb. 21, 1998 for his high game. He also once passed 18 assists against the Pride.

Bailey eventually announced his retirement in 2003.

**August 11**

**In 1997, WGL's "Golden Throat" Len Davis passes away.**

It's doubtful any coach, player or fan of high school sports attended as many events as Len Davis broadcast during his career.

From 1949 to 1980, Davis, known by his nickname "Golden Throat," called play-by-play for more than 4,000 high school sporting events on WGL, and then worked cable television for 10 years.

Besides calling high school basketball games, Davis also used to broadcast the Final Four of the junior high city championship at North Side. Davis also broadcast the Fort Wayne Daisies in the All-American Girls Professional Baseball League, and races at the Fort Wayne Speedway. But he was known best for basketball, including calling 29 state basketball championship games.

Known for his nasal pitch and businesslike attitude, David had very little flair to his call of a game, but he never missed anything. You knew if he criticized an official, that ref must have been having a bad night. Davis loved basketball so much, he even broadcast the final four of the city middle school tournament for a few years.

Besides the Phillies, Davis also loved Michigan football. He later worked for Fort Wayne Newspapers in sales and for Kroger's as a clerk.

During his life, Davis received many awards, including a Distinguished Media Service Award from the Indiana High School Athletic Association.

**Also, in 1991, DeDee Nathan wins the gold medal in the heptathlon at the Pan American Games.**

Nathan, a South Side High School and Indiana University graduate, edged fellow American Sharon Hainer of Houston for the gold in Havana, Cuba. Nathan, 23, scored 5,778 points to Hainer's 5,770. Magalys Garcia of Cuba was third with 5,690. The heptathlon consists of the 100-meter hurdles, 200-meter dash, 800-meter run, long jump, shot put, high jump and javelin.

**August 12**

**In 1991, Tom Kelley wins his final and record-breaking eighth men's city golf tournament.**

Kelley, who started playing in city tournaments at age 13 in 1966, played in five U.S. Amateurs, the British Amateur and national mid-amateurs. Five times he went to the final 16 in match play in national tournaments, including the finals of the U.S. Amateur in 1981.

After his first city tournament victory in 1974, shooting a 208 at Lakeside, Kelley won seven more titles. He won three in a row from 1977 to 1979, and his eight titles are three more than anyone else in the history of the tournament which started in 1926.

Consistency has also marked Kelley's play in the city tournament. From 1970 to 1993, he finished in the top 10 every year, including finishing second six times.

He also played on a Big Ten championship team at Indiana University in 1974 and had 14 top-10 finishes in the state amateur tournament.

Among other highlights: He beat Jack Nicklaus 75-79 in an exhibition at the grand opening for Sycamore Hills Golf Club in 1989, and he served as caddie for former President George Bush at the Bob Hope Classic.

He also competed three times in the Reno National Air Races, winning the Silver championship in 1985.

**Also, in 1932, Dan Zehr finishes fourth in the 100-meter backstroke at the Olympics.**

The 16-year-old South Side sophomore finished behind three Japanese swimmers in Los Angeles. He later won an NCAA title while swimming for Northwestern.

**Also, in 1926, the men's city golf tournament begins.**

## August 13

**In 1969, Pat Wright wins her ninth and last Women's City Golf Tournament title.**

No one dominated Fort Wayne city golf like Pat Wright did in the women's tournaments. Wright won nine titles from 1955 to 1969, winning in match-play format. Jean Saint held the previous mark of eight career titles and Pat McGary would eventually win six.

When the 1969 tournament started, it looked like Wright and McGary would play for the fourth time in the championship round, especially after Wright won medalist honors in the opening round with a one-over-par 80 at Brookwood. Wright had won two of the three title matches between the pair and everyone was looking forward to a rematch.

But this year there was a surprise as former Fort Wayne Daisies pitcher Dottie Collins shot an 81 in the opening round and then beat McGary in the semifinals. Wright continued her steady play in the final, playing even-par through 16 holes to beat Collins 3-and-2. Wright closed out the match with a 10-foot putt on No. 16.

Wright won her nine titles on five different courses.

Wright might have returned the next year to add to her record total, but she was going through a divorce and moved to Florida. McGary won her sixth title in 1970, and Collins won her first and only crown in 1971. Then Peggy Grant, DeDe Hoffman, Lisa Luken and Cathy Kratzert dominated play for the next 15 years. Michelle Hatfield won four titles from 1995 to 2004 and finished second six times, but no one has come close to Wright's mark.

**Also, in 2004, the greatest Fort Wayne Piston basketball player of them all, George Yardley, dies at age 75.**

August

**August 14**

**In 1916, the Fort Wayne Lawn Tennis Association is formed.**

Dr. Miles F. Porter was the first president of the organization, which was tasked with helping the Parks Department build and maintain city-owned courts. At that time, the only courts were privately owned. New courts were put up in various parks in sets of two or four. The first parks to receive courts were Foster, Swinney, Weisser, Memorial, McCullock, Rockhill, Lafayette, Packard, Lakeside and Hamilton. Two cement courts were built, one each at Weisser and Foster.

Laykold courts (hard courts today) were first built at Lafayette and Hamilton parks, each a battery of three courts. Weisser Park also had three clay courts which were worked every day to keep them in the best possible condition.

The Fort Wayne Lawn Tennis Association became the Fort Wayne Tennis Commission in 1944 when Mayor Harry Baals appointed the first members on July 17. The members were Herbert Foelber Sr., Jim Willson, Fred Fuestel, James Estes and John Higgins, the city recreation director.

Weisser Park remained the center of tennis in Fort Wayne until 1955 when there was a move to form the Fort Wayne Tennis Club and regroup at Swinney Park where there were five excellent courts. Ray Gorney, Paul Scherrer and Art Hammer were among the leaders. The city agreed to let the club use the courts, but the club was responsible for hiring a tennis pro to run the program, maintaining the courts and paying the light bill.

**Also, in 1959, the Fort Wayne Tennis Club became the Fort Wayne Tennis Center after a ruling by the IRS that all private clubs had to pay a 20 percent tax on membership.**

## August 15

**In 1926, Jim Thorpe plays baseball against the Lincoln Lifers.**

The legend of Jim Thorpe started in 1911 when he kicked four field goals and scored a touchdown to lead Carlisle to an 18-15 upset over Harvard in football. His team finished 11-1 and the next year won the national title. Then at the 1912 Olympics he won gold medals for both the pentathlon and decathlon, causing Sweden's King Gustav to say, "You, sir, are the greatest athlete in the world."

Thorpe became a professional in football and baseball and basketball. His Major League Baseball career ended in 1922, but Thorpe continued to play with the Oorang Indians as an outfielder. He played football with the Indians during the winter.

The Lincoln Lifers were a semi-pro baseball team managed by Bruff Cleary who regularly scheduled exhibition games against Major League teams as they were on their way to Chicago or Detroit on road trips. This time he scheduled the Indians for a game at League Park.

A huge crowd showed up to see the Lifers win the game 6-5 – partially thanks to Thorpe. He made three "neat" catches in center field, according to reports, but dropped an easy fly ball to left in the eighth inning which allowed the tying and winning runs to score. Thorpe also had a hit and scored a run during the game.

Lifers pitcher Chuck Noel struck out 12 Indians, and Tony Bergwald made a difficult game-ending catch for the home team.

**Also, in 1995, the Fort Wayne Golf Association starts its hall of fame by inducting Jim Kelley, Hilliard Gates and Jim Costin.**

**Also, in 2000, East Noble graduate Amy Yoder-Begley finishes 26th in the 10,000 meters at the Beijing Olympics.**

**August 16**

**In 1926, the New York Giants defeat the Lincoln Lifers 5-3.**

Fort Wayne has hosted about 20 exhibition games involving Major League teams over the years. During the 1920s, teams would often stop by on their way to a western road trip to Chicago.

John McGraw's New York Giants stopped by in 1926 and beat the semi-pro Lincoln Lifers 5-3 before a big crowd at League Park.

The game was close early on, with the Lifers holding a 2-1 lead after three innings, thanks to a Texas League double by Bill Ulrey. Then the Giants decided to give Lincoln pitcher Chuck Noel and attitude adjustment. Noel, who had been frequently complaining to the umpire about calls, gave up home run balls to Travis Jackson, Irish Meusel and Frankie Frisch, the "Fordham Flash." Frisch's belt was described as one of the longest possible in the park.

Jackson later hit his second home run to score the game-winning run, but by then Noel was out of the game after taking himself out in the fifth inning with no teammate warming up. Ralph Harwood gained respect by coming in to finish the game without complaining. He gave up only one run in four innings.

The Giants, who had won an exhibition game in South Bend 8-0 the day before, finished 74-77 that season, good for fifth place in the National League. The roster that year included veteran first baseman Bill Terry and a 17-year-old Mel Ott.

**Also, in 1991, Time Corners is eliminated from the Senior League World Series.**

## August 17

**In 1938, Olympic champion Jesse Owens races a horse at Pennsy Park and wins.**

After he returned from his triumph of winning four gold medals at the 1936 Olympics in Berlin, Jesse Owens came home to some controversy. Because he declined to compete for free in several international competitions, the governing bodies stripped him of his amateur status. To make a living, the former Ohio State star became his own promoter, traveling the country to participate in exhibitions.

One of those included a two-day stay in Fort Wayne in an event sponsored by the Fort Wayne Federation Baseball League. On the first night Owens ran hurdles around the bases in a race against one of the players before taking on some high school stars in sprint and broad jump competitions. The next night he raced against some college track stars before trotting against a horse.

Owens always said he didn't particularly want to race horses, but, "What was I supposed to do? I had four gold medals, but you can't eat four gold medals."

Local citizen Bill Borkenstein rode the horse in the 100-yard event.

"We brought in a fellow and his horse and put a saddle on the animal's swayback," Fort Wayne's "Mr. Baseball" Red Carrington recalled. "When they fired the gun, the horse reared up and by the time it came down, Jesse was halfway down the 100 yards."

Owens was undefeated during the two nights, running 9.8 in the 100-yard dash, 12.0 in the low hurdles and soaring 22-7½ in the broad jump.

"Owens proved himself an affable and popular center of attraction Monday evening and made an interesting talk to the fans about his track legacy," The News-Sentinel reported.

**Also, in 2004, Elmhurst graduate Mike Marchesano makes his Olympic baseball debut pitching for Italy.**

**Also, in 1953, the North American Vans semi-pro team beats the Chicago White Sox 5-4.**

**August 18**

**In 2009, Simon Castro throws the first no-hitter in TinCaps/Wizards history.**

Castro showed the form that would make him a potential Major League pitcher a few years later as he faced only one batter over the minimum and struck out nine Dayton Dragons over seven innings. The 5-0 win was the franchise's first no-hitter in its 17-year history.

The game was reduced to seven innings because the previous night's game had been suspended after four innings.

The only player who reached base was Dayton's Kevin Coddington who was hit by a pitch with two outs in the second inning. Castro responded by striking out the side in the third inning and the first two hitters in the fourth.

The TinCaps got two runs in the first inning to give Castro an early lead to work with. Daniel Robertson's sacrifice fly scored the first run, followed by a solo home run by Jaff Decker. Fort Wayne kept the pressure on Dayton when Allan Dykstra and Justin Baum hit back-to-back homers to lead off the second inning.

Castro finished off the no-hitter in the seventh inning by getting the Dragons to ground out, strike out and fly out. During the evening, Castro retired Dayton on nine strikeouts, three fly-outs, five ground-outs and two pop outs.

For the season, Castro finished 10-6 with a 3.33 earned run average. In 2011 the Padres traded Castro along with Pedro Hernandez to the Chicago White Sox for outfielder Carlos Quinten.

## August 19

**In 1945, Dottie Wiltse pitches and wins both games of a doubleheader for the Fort Wayne Daisies and meets her future husband, Harvey Collins.**

Wiltse beat the league-leading Rockford Peaches 5-1 and 1-0, and after the game Harvey was introduced to Dottie by long-time buddy Jimmy Haskins. The couple married March 10, 1946.

Before Dottie Collins became a Fort Wayne fixture, the tried to play high school softball in California and was banned for being a professional.

"The only thing I ever got when I played a fast-pitch softball game in California was a bag of peanuts," Collins said in 1994. "That was our pay. They really frowned at you doing anything outside of high school (during the 1940s) in Inglewood, Calif. All my friends played, but I was not allowed to play. The schools were very strict about that."

It was also extremely rare for a woman to play professional sports, but Collins became a pioneer as a pitcher in the All-American Girls Professional Baseball League. Collins tried out for the league in 1944 and was assigned to the Minneapolis Millerettes. She went 20-16 that year with a 1.88 earned run average for a last-place club, striking out 205 batters to lead the league.

The next season the team moved to Fort Wayne to become the Daisies. Wiltse went 29-10 with 17 shutouts and 293 strikeouts. She had a 22-20 record in the 1946 season with 294 strikeouts.

She struck out 16 in one game against Peoria. In 1947, the rules were changed to allow sidearm pitching and Collins had a 20-14 record. Collins went 13-8 during the 1948 season before taking a leave of absence to have her first child.

Collins made a comeback in 1950, this time throwing overhand, and went 13-8 before retiring at the end of the season. Her career record was 117-76 with a 1.83 earned run average.

After her retirement, Collins continued to compete and won the 1971 Women's City Golf Championship, also finishing second five times.

She died Aug. 12, 2008, in Fort Wayne.

**August 20**

**In 1909, the first city tennis tournament is held with Dr. Miles F. Porter winning the title over Dr. D.P. Weaver**

The Fort Wayne City Tennis Tournament is Fort Wayne's longest-lasting tournament, stretching further back than either the men's or women's city golf tournament, the city swimming meet or even the Little League City Tournament.

The first city championship was held at the Kekionga Golf Club on East Washington, now known as Memorial Park. There were no city tennis courts at the time so all matches had to be played on private courts of which there were about 50 in town.

This practice was followed until about 1920 when the tournaments were played on the clay courts at the Fort Wayne Country Club. The first city courts were at Weisser Park, a battery of four clay courts constructed for use by the general public.

Porter set a high standard for future champions by winning seven titles from 1909 to 1915. Les Ortlieb eventually broke Porter's record with eight from 1925 to 1933 and held the mark for nearly 60 years before Lee Ann Berning eventually won nine titles. Her record was broken by Ryan Recht who won his 10th title in 2010. Dudley Johnston also won seven titles from 1964 to 1970.

Berning continues to hold the record for women's singles titles followed by Amy Recht with seven, Kay Schoenefeld with six and Lorraine DePew-Aumiller with five.

**August 21**

**In 2007, Street & Smith's Sports Business Journal named Fort Wayne the No. 1 minor-league sports city in America.**

One of Fort Wayne's most noticeable traits is that nothing seems to change. For once, that's was major advantage.

Street & Smith's Sports Business Journal named Fort Wayne the No. 1 minor-league sports city in America in its Aug. 21, 2007, issue. Fort Wayne was ranked No. 7 the first time the magazine compiled the listing two years ago, and one of the major reasons for the jump up is because ... well, stability.

"They didn't improve on a whole lot of things, but just stayed consistent," the magazine's research director David Broughton said from his Charlotte, N.C., office. "The main strengths were consistency and tenure. I'd say it was Fort Wayne's stability that really made it go from No. 7 to No. 1."

That's no small feat, considering the constantly changing landscape of minor-league sports, where teams change as often as uniform styles. In fact, 71 cities in the survey lost at least one team. None of Fort Wayne's teams folded, attendance went up a little and no owner tried to hold the city hostage by threatening to move. It also didn't hurt that other cities in the upper Midwest around Fort Wayne are struggling to keep their sports franchises, and the next three cities behind Fort Wayne in the rankings each lost at least one team since the last ranking.

The magazine studied 242 markets covering 572 teams in 48 leagues. Cities were judged on tenure, attendance and economic rank. Tenure, or franchise stability, counted for 66 percent of a market's score. Attendance counted for 20 percent of the score and was based on average, percent capacity and percentage of overall population. The economic factors included fluctuations in unemployment, population and total personal income (TPI) average. Cities received a bonus for new facilities.

Fort Wayne fell to No. 2 in the 2009 rankings and to No.19 in 2011.

**August 22**

**In 2003, Elmhurst's football team ends its nation-longest 64-game losing streak by beating Bishop Dwenger 27-22.**

The only person who thought it was possible was Elmhurst coach Roosevelt Norfleet.

His Trojans were suffering through a state-record 64-game losing streak entering the 2003 season, including getting shut out 28 times. The last time the Trojans had won a game had been Sept. 27, 1996, when they beat Concordia 26-17. Since that game, the Trojans had lost the last four games of the 1996 season and then suffered through six consecutive 0-10 seasons, including scoring only seven points during the 1999 season.

Elmhurst was also 0-10 in Norfleet's first season in 2002, and their first game in 2003 was on the road at defending state champion and Class 4A No. 1-ranked Bishop Dwenger. The Saints were opening their season by playing at the newly renovated Zollner Stadium.

With Bishop Dwenger's top two running backs sitting out on team suspension, Elmhurst led 13-7 at halftime behind two touchdown catches from receiver James Hardy. With quarterback Mickey Owens hitting Hardy again and Charles Pearson with another scoring throw, the Trojans extended the lead to 27-7 before holding on as the Saints scored two late touchdowns.

"I told the kids before the game that we had a chance to shock the world, and, if not the world, the state, by beating the No.1 team in 4A," Norfleet said.

Elmhurst went on to a 3-7 record that season, and the next season ended a 32-game home losing streak but also started another losing streak. This one lasted 45 games.

**Also, in 1997, Class 2A No. 1 Harding beats 4A No. 1 Bishop Dwenger in football 21-14.**

**Also, in 2003, Harding wins a shootout with Snider 55-45 to end an 11-game losing streak to the Panthers.**

## August 23

**In 1992, the Men's Senior Baseball League begins play in Fort Wayne.**

Each summer Sunday afternoon since 1992, the members of the Men's Senior Baseball League play like boys again, the only concessions being aluminum bats and longer warm-ups before the game and the morning after.

The Men's Senior Baseball League started in 1986 in Long Island, N.Y., and now has affiliate leagues throughout the country. Local organizer Dan Eash read about the league in U.S. News & World Report and decided to organize a Fort Wayne league. Since the Fort Wayne league started, more than 1,000 players have participated.

The rules say every player must be older than 30, and everyone plays. All other baseball rules apply, though the strike zone has been slightly expanded to aid pitchers, many of whom haven't thrown competitively for at least eight years. The hardest part of the league is finding enough pitchers.

During that first day of play, Fort Wayne's Mr. Baseball Red Carrington threw out the first pitch, and then the Reds beat the A's 25-2 and the Yankees beat the Dodgers 19-15.

Along the way, there have been former Major Leaguers like Brent Gaff and Mike Roesler playing in the league, and several times local teams have gone to the league's World Series in Arizona.

In 2009 Eash was inducted into the MSBL Hall of Fame, becoming the third Indiana player to be inducted. The ironic thing is that he graduated from Bishop Dwenger in 1972 before the school started sponsoring a baseball team so he never played organized baseball from age 12 to 38.

**Also, in 1994, Rod Woodson is selected for the NFL's 75th anniversary team.**

**Also, in 1996, Homestead graduate Shawn Brown wins his first of two gold medals in the discus at the Paralympics.**

## August 24

**In 2008, Lloy Ball wins an Olympic gold medal at age 36 with the United States men's volleyball team.**

After a fourth-place finish in Athens in 2004, Woodburn-native Lloy Ball figured his career with the United States Men's Volleyball Team was over. The odd thing is, the further away he got from the American team, the more success he had playing overseas, winning pro-league titles in Greece, Italy and Russia. After winning the European Champions League title in the winter of 2008, the world's biggest title outside of international play, U.S. coach Hugh McCutcheon realized Ball was playing better than ever and asked him to return.

And then Ball showed the maturity he had gained. Throughout the Olympics, whenever the team got in trouble, he'd calm things down. He never yelled at teammates except to congratulate them. He became the team's steadying influence.

That calm helped the U.S. beat Brazil 20-25, 25-22, 25-21, 25-23 in the gold medal match in Beijing, China. The Americans trailed 20-17 in the fourth set.

"As much as this is an incredible feat, and one that I've been working on for so long, I know it won't change who or what I am. I still want to be a good dad, a great husband and son and teammate.

"It took me 36 years to get to be the man I am, and all this does is add another line on the resume and justify the sacrifice my family had to make. It's the most momentous thing in my sporting career, but it doesn't change who Lloy Ball is."

Ball finished with 90 assists and 10 digs as the Americans beat the defending Olympic champions, who were trying to become the first champion to defend its title since the Americans in 1988.

Before the Olympics, Ball was named the World League Most Valuable Player as the Americans won the title in Brazil.

**Also, in 1954, the Daisies beat the North American Vans men's team 10-9 before 2,700 fans at Memorial Park.**

Despite a rainy night, the game draws a larger crowd than the Van Lines' game the week before against the Philadelphia Phillies. The pitchers throw against their own teams.

**August 25**

**In 2007, Class 4A No. 1 Bishop Dwenger beats Class 2A No. 1 Harding 38-13.**

There have been seven times in Indiana high school football history where No. 1-ranked teams from different classes have met during the regular season. The last time was so exciting it was filled with lightning.

That's because school officials had to stop the game between Bishop Dwenger and Harding because of lightning strikes. The game was finished the next day with the Saints dominating.

This was the second game of the season after the defending state champion Hawks started as No. 1 in Class 2A. The Saints started No. 3 in Class 4A, but moved up after No. 1 Indianapolis Cathedral and No. 2 Concord both lost.

The Saints were led by John Goodman and the Hawks by Marquelo Suel, both of whom were playing quarterback as seniors after starring throughout their careers as receivers.

Bishop Dwenger stayed No. 1 throughout the rest of the season before losing in the semistate to Lowell to finish 13-1. Harding dropped to No. 6 the next week. The Hawks lost to Fairfield in the sectional to finish 5-5.

**Also, in 1965, Steve Hargan wins his first Major League game.**

He gave up six hits and three runs in six-and-a-third innings to beat California 6-3. Hargan, a South Side graduate, had an 87-107 career record with a 3.92 earned-run average in 354 games with the Cleveland Indians and Texas Rangers. In 1967 he was selected to play in the All-Star Game but was unable to because of an injury.

**August 26**

**In 1993, the Fort Wayne Senior Men's Baseball League takes on a team of Major League legends.**

Imagine the thrill the players from the Fort Wayne Men's Senior Baseball League must have felt during warm-ups. The league was just a year old at the time, but an elite team of players had been selected to play a group of traveling former Major League stars for a charity game to benefit the Northeast Indiana Easter Seal Society. Their goosebumps must have been the size of beach balls.

And then the game started. If they didn't know it already, the MSBL players knew for sure they were overmatched when former Cincinnati Reds great outfielder George Foster hit a home run that not only cleared the left field wall at Memorial Stadium, and the net above the wall, but also all four lanes of traffic on Coliseum Boulevard. It was likely the longest ball ever hit at the stadium, which was demolished in 2009 after the minor league baseball team moved downtown to Parkview Field.

Foster was one of 15 former Major League legends who came to town to face the MSBL Elite team, included former Cincinnati Reds greats Johnny Bench, Doug Flynn, Pedro Borbon and Bobby Tolan whose team dominated the 1970s when most of the MSBL players were kids. The other players included Bert Campaneris, Billy Almon, Paul Blair, Mark "Bird" Fidrych, Bill "Spaceman" Lee, Al Oliver, Rodney Scott, John Stearns and Mike Torrez.

A team with that many stars would have been nearly unbeatable during their prime as they showed the MSBL team with a 15-4 decision.

Torrez got the win with relief help from Fidrych, Lee and Borbon. The MSBL players got the thrill of a lifetime.

**Also, in 2000, the IPFW Soccer Showcase debuts.**

**Also, in 1994, coming off a 1-8 season, South Side upsets No. 1 ranked Bishop Luers 22-0 in football.**

## August 27

**In 1955, future French Open champion Nancy Richey wins the Fort Wayne City Tennis Tournament at age 13.**

George Richey was a Houston professional tennis coach who wanted to find a summer job close to Chicago so his daughter Nancy could play there in the National Girls 15-and-younger championship. Fort Wayne was a natural place so George taught for the Fort Wayne Tennis Club and Nancy reached the semifinals of the national tournament.

Then Nancy won the Fort Wayne women's city title in 1955, four days after turning 13, as her 8-year-old brother, Cliff, cheered her on after winning his first title, the Midget City Championships.

When the summer ended, the Richeys returned to Houston, and the kids began their touring careers in the early 1960s. They became the first brother and sister to be ranked in the top 10 together in 1965.

In 1966, Nancy played in the finals of the Australian Open, the French Open and the U.S. Open. She also played for the title of the 1967 Australian Open, the 1968 French Open and the 1969 U.S. Open.

Nancy won the 1967 Australian Open and the 1968 French Open, along with four Grand Slam doubles titles. Cliff never won a Grand Slam event, but he played in the semifinals of the French Open in 1970, and in the semifinals of the U.S. Open twice.

In 1970, Nancy was one of nine women who broke away from the United States Tennis Association and formed the Women's Tennis Association, which is the current professional tour. In 1976, she set a record by becoming the first U.S. woman to be ranked in the top 10 for 16 consecutive years. In 1975, she was ranked eighth in the world; she retired in 1979.

Cliff was ranked in the top 10 nationally throughout his career. He was the second-ranked American male in 1969, and climbed to No. 1 in 1970.

**August 28**

**In 2008, the Fort Wayne Wizards play their final game in Memorial Stadium.**

For the first 16 years of its existence, Fort Wayne's Class A minor league baseball team played its games at Memorial Stadium, located on the northeast corner of the Memorial Coliseum parking lot.

The final game was a little anti-climactic as Norwell graduate and Arizona Diamondbacks No. 1 draft pick Jarrod Parker dominated from the pitching mound for the South Bend Silverhawks. Parker allowed one hit and no runs, striking out seven in five innings before giving way to the bullpen in a 17-6 South Bend win before 6,106 fans.

One of the highlights of the night was seeing mascot Dinger finally win a race around the bases. Instead of facing, and losing to a youngster, this time Dinger sprinted past previously retired mascot Wayne the Wizard.

The 6,300-seat stadium opened April 19, 1993, costing $6.2 million to build. "The Castle" hosted 1,130 Wizards games (good for a 615-515 record) and 4,046,261 fans for an average of 3,581 fans per game. A total of 69 Wizards from the stadium era advanced to play in the Major Leagues.

After the Wizards, soon to be re-named the TinCaps, moved downtown to Parkview Field, Memorial Stadium was demolished on July 1, 2009 at an estimated cost of $2 million.

**Also, in 1953, the North American Vans beat the St. Louis Browns 7-4.**

A crowd of about 5,500 attended on a Monday night at Dwenger Park as Van Lines player Joe Unfried belted two home runs and drove in four runs. Tom Acker and Bob Upton scattered five hits to lead the pitching for the local squad. Upton struck out the side in the Browns' half of the seventh and eighth innings. Paul Florito also hit a homer to provide the final score.

**August 29**

**In 1945, the Zollner Pistons softball team wins its 50ᵗʰ game in a row.**

Whatever he tried, Fred Zollner wanted to be the best at it, whether it was running his pistons plant, his basketball team or his fastpitch softball team.

After the basketball team won its first world title in 1945, Zollner put the finishing touches on his softball team. Zollner signed pitcher Clyde "Diz" Kirkendall, Ed Robitaille, Sam Lombardo and Harold George from rival teams before the 1945 season started.

The other key players were catcher Bernie Kampschmidt, first baseman Hughie Johnston, second baseman Johnny Shaffer, shortstop Neal Barille and third baseman Robitaille. The outfield was usually made up from four of Lombardo, Chick Goldberg, Porky Slater, Louis Bertsos, Ron Burgette and Monday Cieselski.

The winning streak starts after a 2-0 loss to the Indianapolis Kingan Knights on June 8. One of the summer's highlights was winning the National Industrial Tournament title in Detroit over July 4 which guaranteed the Pistons a trip to the national tournament.

The Pistons broke the all-time record of 46 consecutive wins set by the South Bend Bendix Brakes team set in 1941. After out-scoring their opponents 346-35, Fort Wayne's streak finally ended with a 1-0 loss to Flint M and S Orange. The Pistons' pitchers, Leo Luken, Stan Corgan and Kirkendall, tossed 37 shutouts and nine one-run games, holding opponents scoreless in 451 of 464 innings.

The Pistons won their first world championship by beating Flint 1-0 behind Luken as Goldberg drove in Robitaille.

**Also, in 1995, the Wizards make the playoffs for the first time.**

**Also, in 1928, the women's city golf tournament begins.**

**August 30**

**In 1968, Branch Lew comes home after his nationwide tour following a Soap Box Derby national title.**

Because there were no Soap Box Derby races in Fort Wayne in 1968, Branch Lew's hometown is often listed as Muncie where he won a race against his brother to qualify for the national championships in Akron. Ohio. With the help of their father who was a runner-up in Fort Wayne races in 1937 and 1938, Branch 11, won the junior division and Robert, 14, the senior division.

When they raced in the championship heat, Branch won by a foot-and-a-half. He then advanced to Akron and beat a field of 242 other racers to win a $7,500 scholarship in the 31$^{st}$ running of the event.

Lew's father had studied wind tunnels to come up with a teardrop design made of fiberglass that was more efficient against the wind than wooden cars. At the time, Branch was 5-feet tall and weighed 83 pounds.

After the competition, the Lew family took a three-day tour of New York City before coming home in time for Branch to start the sixth grade at Glenwood Elementary School.

During the next year, Chevrolet included Branch in its marketing plans for the derby and he traveled throughout the country and Europe. He was also included in a movie about Soap Box Derby.

His victory encouraged local organizers to build a new track at Franke Park, and Robert won the title in 1969 to advance to Akron where he finished fifth.

**Also, in 2004, Lloy Ball and the U.S. Olympic volleyball team lose the bronze medal match to Russia.**

**Also, in a battle of No. 1-ranked football teams, Class 4A Wayne beats Class 2A Harding 28-14.**

**August 31**

**In 1973, the Summit Athletic Conference begins play.**

Before 1973, Fort Wayne's city schools played in a round-robin format called the Fort Wayne City Series. When Northrop and Wayne opened in 1971, the series split into North and South divisions for football with the winners meeting in an annual city championship game.

Central High School closed in 1971 and Central Catholic in 1972, but the city series finally changed in 1973 when Harding opened, pushing the number of schools to 10. The league included Bishop Dwenger, Concordia, Northrop, North Side and Snider in the North Division and Bishop Luers, Elmhurst, Harding, South Side and Wayne in the South Division.

The city series also saw some changes over the years as Concordia was also part of the Northeast Indiana Athletic Conference from 1953 to 1974, along with Elmhurst from 1959 to 1965. In fact, along with the city series, Central, North Side and South Side helped start the Northeastern Indiana Athletic Conference in 1927. They dropped out in 1929.

North Side was also part of the Northern Indiana Conference from 1942 to 1964.

With the closing of Elmhurst in 2010 and Harding in 2011, the SAC has remained with eight schools.

**Also, in 1995, the Wizards put their first playoff tickets on sale.**

The Wizards needed only three years to reach the playoffs, finishing 75-64 overall before losing to the Michigan Battle Cats in a two-game sweep during the first round of the Midwest League Playoffs.

**Also, in 1996, the Police Athletic League celebrates 25 years sponsoring youth football.**

# SEPTEMBER

## September 1

**In 2003, Rob Bowen makes his Major League debut with the Minnesota Twins.**

The Homestead graduate and a second-round pick in the 1999 draft played five years in the big leagues with Minnesota, San Diego, Oakland and the Chicago Cubs as a catcher. He retired in 2008 with 216 games, nine home runs and 43 runs batted in. He had a .209 career batting average.

While at Homestead, Bowen was an all-state player and was named Indiana Player of the Year by Gatorade and USA Today. After being drafted by the Twins, he rose through their minor league system and made the big league team late in the 2003 season.

During spring training in 2006, he was placed on waivers by the Twins, picked up by the Detroit Tigers and then released again. That gave the San Diego Padres a chance to sign him.

Another of Bowen's career highlights came in May 2006 when he hit a 10th-inning walk-off home run to beat the Cubs in San Diego. The next day he went 2-for-3 with a double to drive in the go-ahead run in the fifth inning of the Padres' 6-3 win over the Cubs.

The next season he was traded to the Cubs in 2007 by the San Diego Padres, along with Fort Wayne Wizards outfielder Kyle Burke, in exchange for catcher Michael Barrett and cash considerations.

The Cubs traded Bowen to Oakland for Jason Kendall in 2007, and was released by the A's on March 17, 2009.

Bowen was inducted into the Northeast Indiana Baseball Association's Hall of Fame in 2011.

**September 2**

**In 1947, the G.E. Club Voltmen win the first of their three National Semi-Pro Baseball Tournament championships.**

John "Red" Braden was a legendary manager of Fort Wayne semi-pro baseball teams, several times leading them to national and even world championships. The first time this happened was with the G.E. Club Voltmen in the 1940s.

The team was made up of local players and several former Major League players, such as pitcher Bill Brandt. When the Voltmen reached the championship game of the National Semi-Pro Baseball Tournament in 1947 in Wichita, Kans., Brandt beat the Golden Coors of Colorado 4-2. The Voltmen scored two runs in the first inning and wrapped up the win with two more in the eighth.

For the win, the Voltmen received a check for $10,000 and a four-foot high trophy which is currently on display at the Northeast Indiana Baseball Association museum and hall of fame in Auburn.

That victory started a dynasty as the Voltmen defended their title the next two years and won a fourth title under the sponsorship of the Capehard-Farnsworth Company in 1950. Even when they didn't win, Fort Wayne teams regularly contended for the national title.

Braden also led the Allen Dairy team to two national titles in 1956 and 1957. The highlight for that team was winning the Global World Series in Milwaukee.

During his tenure from 1944 to 1958, Braden scheduled 12 games against Major League teams in Fort Wayne, winning six. When the Fort Wayne Wizards came to town in 1993, he became the first person to buy a season ticket. He was inducted into the Northeast Indiana Baseball Association's Hall of Fame in 1965.

**Also, in 1993, LaTroy Hawkins loses the last game of the season for the Wizards to end his 13-game winning streak.**

**Also, in 2011, North Side ends Bishop Dwenger's record 38-game SAC football winning streak 26-16.**

## September 3

**In 1951, the Harlem Globetrotters draw a record crowd to Zollner Stadium.**

Before the Memorial Coliseum was built in 1952, with its 10,000 seats for basketball, the largest Fort Wayne crowd to see a basketball game was 6,732 for a game at Zollner Stadium between the Harlem Globetrotters and the United States Stars, which included several NBA players. There were no other gyms in the area capable of hosting even 4,000 fans at the time.

The Globetrotters featured Goose Tatum, former Fort Wayne star Bobby Milton, Marques Haynes and former IU star Bill Garrett. The U.S. Stars team consisted of George Mikan coaching and playing with a group of former college stars. The halftime entertainment was made up of vaudeville acts.

The Globetrotters won the game 46-40 as Josh Grider scored 17 points and Tatum 11. Tony Lavelli led the U.S. Stars with 13 points and Mikan scored eight. Milton scored only two points, hitting a long set shot in his return home.

The court was a tad bit slippery because condensation in the early going, but play picked up after a drying substance was used.

The previous biggest crowd for a basketball game was a Pistons' scrimmage that drew 4,300 to Zollner Stadium as part of a softball-basketball doubleheader earlier that spring. The record was easily eclipsed when the Pistons hosted the 1953 NBA All-Star Game to a sellout crowd.

**Also, in 1994, University of Cincinnati offensive lineman Jason Fabini makes a big impression on IU on his way to an outstanding NFL career.**

**Also, in 1993, the Wizards lose their first-ever playoff game.**

**September 4**

**In 2009, Rod Smith becomes the SAC football's all-time rushing leader.**

The Harding senior rushed for 217 yards and three touchdowns on 15 carries in a 63-7 win over Elmhurst. He broke the record on a 61-yard touchdown run in the third quarter to top the previous mark of 5,328 career yards by Wayne's Ray Byers who graduated in 2008.

Before going to Ohio State, Smith finished his career at Harding with 6,625 rushing yards and 66 touchdowns on an even 1,000 carries. During his senior season, Smith rushed for 1,855 yards and 19 touchdowns when he was also the Hawks' leading tackler. His career totals rank among the top 10 all-time high school numbers in Indiana.

Smith was an all-around athlete who was an all-SAC and all-area basketball player and a member of a state runner-up 400-meter relay team.

During his first two years at Ohio State, Smith has struggled to earn consistent playing time. As a freshman, he played in 11 games, rushing 29 times for 116 yards and a touchdown. As a sophomore, he played in nine games, rushing 32 times for 215 yards and two touchdowns, including a career-high 33-yard burst against Nebraska.

He started his college career with 74 yards on 18 carries against Akron. He also caught a 51-yard touchdown pass against Illinois as a sophomore.

## September 5

**In 1969, Woodlan beats Eastside 48-6 in the first ACAC football game.**

Heritage, Leo, Carroll, Adams Central, Churubusco, Norwell and Eastside joined Woodlan in forming the first ACAC football conference. One of the star players that season was an Adams Central running back named Rick Minnich.

The winners that first week were Woodlan over Eastside and Carroll over Norwell in conference games. Leo lost to Prairie Heights, Heritage fell to Manchester, Adams Central beat Parkway, Ohio, and Churubuso lost to Lakeland.

Everyone seemed to be trying to catch up to the Warriors. The Woodlan program started in 1962, and one of the assistant coaches that year was Leland Etzler, who became head coach in 1965. His first team finished 8-0-1, starting an amazing run until 1975 where the Warriors went 90-9-4 mark.

Adams Central finally broke the Warriors' run with an 8-0 win at Woodlan in 1969, giving the Jets their first ACAC title. Adams Central allowed only 37 points that season with four shutouts.

Woodlan and Heritage tied for the title the next season after tying 6-6 on the field in the last game of the season.

Things got more interesting in 1971. Norwell finished 4-0 in the South Division, but Woodlan, Leo and Churubusco all tied 3-1 in the North Division. The coaches voted Churubusco to represent the South Division in the championship game, and Norwell won 34-6.

There have been many great runs during the ACAC's history, including Woodlan in the 1980s, South Adams in the early-1990s, Heritage in the late 2000s and most recently Leo.

Woodlan played for the state title in 1981, followed by Churubusco's runner-up performance in 1983. Adams Central won the ACAC's first state title in 2000 in Class 1A, followed by Southern Wells in the same division in 2001.

Other long-time and great coaches in the conference included Minnich at Adams Central (236 wins), Kirk Sorg at South Adams (115 wins) and Bob Yager at Heritage (179 wins).

**Also, in 1995, Matt Lawton becomes the third Wizard to make it to the Major Leagues.**

**September 6**

**In 1954, the Fort Wayne Daisies play the final game in the AAGPBL.**

The Kalamazoo Lassies beat the Daisies 8-5 at Memorial Park to win the league's last championship series 3-2. Former Daisy June Peppas was the playoffs' Most Valuable Player after hitting .450 and pitching two of the Kalamazoo wins.

The league disbanded because of a lack of interest from owners willing to keep it going.

That was a shame especially for Daisies outfielder Jo Weaver, who led the league in hitting the last three seasons, including a .429 average in '54. She was only 18 when the league folded.

Weaver was a dominating player. When she was 14 years old in 1950, Weaver left Metropolis, Ill., with her sister Betty to try out for the Daisies. She was technically ineligible to play, but the Daisies didn't want to lose her, so Weaver hung out with the team all season.

She came back the next season to hit .276 in 48 games with 45 hits, and in 1952, Weaver won the first of three straight batting titles, hitting .344. The next year she hit .345 to win her second batting crown, but the next season was her best and perhaps the best year of the All-American Girls Professional Baseball League.

By mid-August of the 1954 season, Weaver led the league in batting average, runs scored, base hits, total bases and stolen bases. The 6-foot outfielder hit .429 with 29 home runs, 87 runs batted in, and had 79 stolen bases and 109 runs scored. It was the only time an AAGPBL player hit more than .400 for a season. She was the league's Player of the Year for 1954.

"She was a lovely lady," Collins said. "All the Weavers were very nice. They were quiet and the thing that amazed me more than anything, they didn't really believe they were that great. They never wanted to be in the limelight. They always wanted to sit in the back row and that amazed me because they were really fantastic ballplayers."

Weaver's career ended when the league folded after the 1954 season. She had a .359 career batting average in 329 games with 174 stolen bases. Weaver was inducted into the Northeast Indiana Baseball Association's Hall of Fame in 1999.

The Daisies won division pennants in 1952, 1953 and 1954, and also played in the title series in 1950, but could never win the playoff title.

## September 7

### In 2000, IPFW jumps to NCAA Division I.

This sounds like an easy decision and process, but it was like slogging across a campus covered by a foot of fresh snow.

Because so many schools were making the change to Division I in an attempt to share the wealth of the basketball tournament, the NCAA changed its rules to say that after Sept. 1, 1999, any new school had to wait eight years before becoming tournament eligible, increased from a two-year wait. Not coincidentally, the NCAA then put an April 27, 2000, deadline on schools switching divisions, enacting a two-year moratorium.

Initially, the NCAA ruled IPFW had missed the April 27 deadline as the school officially notified the NCAA of its proposed change by letter on May 30, 2000. IPFW successfully appealed, but was left with an eight-year waiting period to be eligible for post-season tournament play. IPFW appealed again, but relevant NCAA administrative committee left the appeal off the appropriate agenda, meaning the decision got pushed back a day. This time the NCAA said there would be a two-year waiting time.

That also created some immediate problems because the fall athletic season had already started and student-athletes in every sport had already enrolled. The switch to Division 1 meant some athletes' careers were immediately ended because the NCAA now required all IPFW athletes to be eligible by Division I standards, even though the IPFW fall teams had already started their seasons competing at the Division II level. More than 30 athletes were affected, and because school had already started, they were unable to consider a transfer to another Division II program.

It didn't help that some IPFW athletic officials had told the students their eligibility would be "grandfathered" in, but the NCAA later said there was no such grandfather rule. Even worse, many athletes said they never knew and were never told the ramifications of the switch to Division I and felt betrayed.

The move also ended the chances of the top 10-ranked women's volleyball team and the men's soccer team to make runs at Division II national titles.

## September 8

**In 2007, the Basketball Hall of Fame debuts a presentation highlighting Fort Wayne as the birthplace of the NBA.**

For more than 50 years, former Fort Wayne Pistons executive Carl Bennett had been saying Fort Wayne should be recognized as the birthplace of the National Basketball Association. While not declaring an official designation, the Basketball Hall of Fame in Springfield, Mass., decided to present an exhibit this summer telling Bennett's story.

Basketball Hall of Fame historian Matt Zeysing visited Bennett in Fort Wayne, recording his story and visiting the house at 2920 Alexander St. where Bennett says the initial meeting took place that led to the formation of the league.

Maybe the secrecy of the meeting has hurt Fort Wayne's notoriety. In the spring of 1948, Bennett, the Pistons' business manager and a member of the National Basketball League board of directors, met with Basketball Association of America President Maurice Podoloff.

The more-established NBL and the 2-year-old BAA were stuck in a bidding war over players. It was generally accepted that the NBL had the best players, and the BAA had the big-city markets. The BAA was basically set up in the East - with teams such as Boston, New York, Philadelphia and Washington - and the NBL ruled the Midwest. The NBL's key cities were Fort Wayne, Minneapolis, Rochester and Indianapolis.

Realizing the two leagues were killing each other, Podoloff called Bennett, hoping he would set up a meeting with Fort Wayne owner Fred Zollner, who was an NBL leader. Zollner told Bennett to handle it, and Podoloff snuck into Fort Wayne and met in Bennett's home with the idea the two leagues merge.

Podoloff and Bennett met Zollner at his Zollner Pistons plant office the next morning in a day-long meeting. The idea was to take the eight strongest BAA teams and join them with the four strongest NBL teams. An official meeting for the press was held in Chicago on May 10, 1948, announcing the four NBL teams jumping to the BAA for the 1948-49 season.

The remaining NBL members eventually sued the augmented BAA, which led to another merger and the renaming of the BAA to the National Basketball Association before the 1949-50 campaign. Unable to keep up financially, most of the remaining NBL teams from the second merger eventually dropped out, but the NBA name stuck.

**September 9**

**In 2001, Jason Baker makes his NFL debut with the San Francisco 49ers.**

Baker averaged 41.6 yards per punt during his college career at Iowa, including 42.5 yards as a senior, which ranked 17th in the nation. His most-impressive statistic was a three-to-one ratio on kicks downed inside the 20-yard line to touchbacks.

He averaged 39 yards per kick during his high school career, and was part of Wayne's Class 4A state title team in 1995 when he also played wide receiver and kicked field goals.

After college, Bakers signed as a free agent with the Philadelphia Eagles after also considering offers from Seattle and Green Bay. He was later cut an signed with San Francisco where he was named to the all-rookie team after averaging 40.8 yards per kick. He also had one game where he kicked seven times for a 49.1 average against the Carolina Panthers who remembered the performance and eventually signed Baker.

Baker had an 11-year pro career and the last seven were with Carolina. He was released March 14, 2012 in a salary cap move. Baker finished his Carolina career as the franchise leader in punts and punts downed inside the 20-yard line. He is second in career average (43.97 yards per punt).

During his NFL career, Baker played in 167 games with San Francisco, Philadelphia, Kansas City, Indianapolis, Denver and Carolina. He averaged 42.7 yards on his 798 career punts. His best season was averaging 45.7 yards in 2006 with Carolina which ranked third in the NFL. He led the league that season with 98 punts for 4,483 yards.

Baker also was very good to Fort Wayne. In 2006 he arranged for the NFL Pepsi Punt, Pass & Kick competition to come to his hometown, and the next year he introduced an NFL Youth Football's Junior Player Development camp. When the NFL dropped the program, Baker stepped up again and eventually this became known as the Jason Baker Football Camp and served more than 300 middle school athletes each year. Part of the camper's experience included a strong community service component.

## September 10

**In 1975, Bjorn Borg defeats Ilie Nastase in an exhibition at Memorial Coliseum.**

Fort Wayne has long been a hotbed of strong tennis action, but the most highly competitive match in city history involved Bjorn Borg facing Ilie Nastase before 3,921 fans at Memorial Coliseum.

Looking back through history, it would be easy to say that Borg would have been a heavy favorite, but actually, Nastase, 29, was just coming off a year-long run as the world's top-ranked player, while Borg, 18, was basically starting his pro career and had just won his second of six French Open titles and would not become the world's No. 1-ranked player for two more years. Jimmy Connors was the current No. 1 at the time of the match.

This time, Borg beat Nastase 7-6, 5-7, 6-2. Both players were having fun with each other and the crowd, often playing for laughs. In fact, Nastase kept up an entertaining dialogue with linesman J. Webb Horton most of the night, and often had fun teasing Borg about his two-handed backhand. Other times Borg would fake being upset when Nastase beat him with passing shots, but demonstrably motioning where he would have preferred where the ball had been hit.

The two squared off again that night in a mixed doubles match with Indiana Love players Carrie Meyer and Pat Bostrom. Borg and Meyer won the abbreviated match 7-6.

Borg's career took off the next season when he beat Nastase to win his first Wimbledon title. From 1978 to 1980 he won the French and Wimbledon tournaments each year.

**Also, in 1996, Colin Chin retires from the Komets.**

Chin finished with 746 games played, 285 goals, 422 assists, 707 points and 638 penalty minutes. On the franchise's all-time lists, he ranked in the top 10 in all but penalty minutes. Only Terry Pembroke, Eddie Long and Len Thornson played more games as a Komet than Chin.

The Komets retired Chin's No. 26 on Nov. 7, 2003.

"I grew up watching those guys," Chin said. "I know who they are. They're class people. There's a lot of people over a 52-year period who have played here, yet you only see a handful of guys whose numbers have been retired."

**Also, in 2005, Saint Francis destroys Indiana State on the football field.**

## September 11

**In 2012, Bob Chase is announced as winner of the Lester Patrick Award by the National Hockey League and USA Hockey.**

Chase, 86, was driving through the Tennessee mountains when NHL Commissioner Gary Bettman called to inform the Komets' broadcaster he was being honored for his dedication to American Hockey.

Starting in 1966, the Lester Patrick Award has been presented by the NHL and USA Hockey as a lifetime achievement award for service to the sport in the United States. Past winners include Wayne Gretzky, Gordie Howe, Bobby Orr, Phil Esposito, former NHL commissioners and Olympic gold medal-winning teams – basically a Who's Who of the Hockey Hall of Fame. This would be comparable to an actor receiving a lifetime achievement award at the Oscars.

One thing most of the winners have in common is they have been interviewed by Chase – whose real name is Wallenstein – during his 60 seasons calling Komets games. That's the longest run with any professional hockey team, breaking Foster Hewitt's run with the Toronto Maple Leafs from 1927 to 1963.

Eligible recipients are players, officials, coaches, executives and referees. The winner is selected by an award committee consisting of the president of the NHL, an NHL governor, a representative of the New York Rangers, a member of the Hockey Hall of Fame builder's section, a member of the Hockey Hall of Fame player's section, a member of the U. S. Hockey Hall of Fame, a member of the NHL Broadcasters' Association and a member of the Professional Hockey Writers' Association.

Chase received the statue that goes with the award on Oct. 15 at the 2012 U.S. Hockey Hall of Fame Induction Ceremony and Dinner. He shared the award with Washington Capitals president Dick Patrick, grandson of Lester Patrick.

Only five media members have previously been honored with the Patrick Award: broadcaster Dan Kelly, writer Stan Fischler, broadcaster Fred Cusick, broadcaster John Davidson and Chase protégé Mike Emrick.

**Also, in 2005, ABC legend and Bippus native Chris Schenkel passes away at age 82.**

During his 50-year career, there was nothing Schenkel didn't announce on television, from the NFL, Major League Baseball, the NBA, college football, boxing, the Olympics, the Masters, Triple Crown horse racing and professional bowling. Four times he was voted National Sportscaster of the Year.

**September 12**

**In 1986, run, jane, run Women In Sports Festival starts a record year of more than 3,000 participants.**

When the Fort Wayne Women's Bureau started run, jane, run as a fundraising women in sports festival in September 1981, the idea of Harriet Miller and Monica Wehrle, the event was a one-weekend affair held at Tah-Cum-Wah Recreation Center. The highlights were a 32-team softball tournament and a 16-team volleyball tournament along with a 5K run. Maybe the most fun event was an exhibition game featuring the first reunion of the Fort Wayne Daisies.

The goal was to find opportunities in sports for women, something the organization achieved with spectacular results. Within a few short years, more than 3,000 women were participating locally in a 10-day celebration, and the idea had spread across the country into other cities such as Toledo, Ohio; Muskegon, Mich.; Grand Rapids, Mich.; Tulsa, Okla., Cleveland, Ohio and Denver, Colo. The total number of participants in the early 1990s reached more than 10,000 annually.

Sports such as horseback riding, aerobics, fishing, triathlon, golf, bowling, tennis, soccer and lacrosse were eventually added. The event grew so large and was so popular the staff of the Women's Bureau was overwhelmed and asked for more help, eventually needing more than 300 volunteers for a single year.

One problem was as the more successful run, jane, run became, the less the younger athletes understood the need for the event. They took for granted that sporting opportunities would always be available, and the festival ended in 2001. So many of the athletes the event was trying to include were already competing in high school and college sports during September.

By the time the event finished, it was estimated more than $1.5 million had been raised for women's causes.

**Also, in 1998, Saint Francis plays its first college football game, winning 56-28 at Saint Xavier.**

## September 13

**In 1994, Bishop Luers graduate Angie Harris starts for Notre Dame's women's volleyball team.**

A natural leader, Harris helped the Irish climb as high as No. 6 in the national polls, Notre Dame's highest ranking ever. She also led Notre Dame to four straight undefeated Big East Conference championships and NCAA berths.

She was named a freshman all-American, three-time all-conference and three-time all-district, while also earning team Most Valuable Player honors as a senior. After earning Midwestern Conference Newcomer of the Year as a freshman, Harris was named the Big East Championships Most Outstanding Player as a sophomore.

Before she graduated with a sociology degree, Harris held team career records for aces and kills.

**Also, in 1994, the Fury select Damon Bailey with the 25th pick in the CBA draft.**

Sore knees hindered Bailey's play at pre-draft camps and caused his NBA draft stock to fall as the Indiana Pacers claimed him with the 44th pick in 1993. Knee surgery pushed Bailey's 1994-95 season back, and the Fury took a chance by drafting him.

"If he ever plays in this league, it would be a sin and a crime if he plays for anyone but Fort Wayne," Fury assistant coach Gerald Oliver told The News-Sentinel's Larry Everhart. "I'm excited. I've loved Damon for four years."

Fury officials knew there was no way Bailey would play for them that season, but they were hopeful there was a possibility in the future.

Bailey was first-team All-Big Ten last season with career-best and team-leading averages in scoring (19.3) and assists (4.3) while getting 4.3 rebounds per game. He was a third-team Associated Press All-American. Bailey finished fifth on IU's all-time scoring list, tied for second in assists, and sixth in three-point percentage, steals and free throws made.

**September 14**

**In 1950, the Fort Wayne Open PGA event begins.**

Lloyd Mangrum won with a 271 total, 13 under par at Orchard Ridge Country Club, and earned $2,600.

Sponsored by the Jaycees, the tournament lasted for seven years, the next six at the Elks Country Club where first-prize was $2,400 and the total purse was $15,000. The next years' winners were Jim Ferrier, Jimmy Clark, Art Wall, Doug Ford, Dow Finsterwald and Wall again.

The big winners during the seven-year run were Wall who earned $6,351, Middlecoff with $5,100, Ford $5,135, Clark $4,745 and Mangrum $3,070. Porky Oliver was next with $3,710 followed by Ferrier with $3,690 and Marty Furgoi with $3,542.

The only player out of 95 who played in the Fort Wayne Open who made money in all seven tournaments was Dave Douglas, and his total was only $2,884.

**Also, in 1996, the IU men's soccer team plays a match at Memorial Stadium against UAB.**

This may not sound like much, especially with a crowd of only 3,536 fans over two days, but this was the real start of the National Soccer Festival. Originally called the IPFW/Three Rivers Soccer Classic, the event matched IPFW, Indiana, Marquette and Alabama-Birmingham. Tickets cost $8 for a single session and $14 for both nights.

On the first day, IU beat Marquette 3-2 in overtime and UAB beat IPFW 8-0. On the final day, Indiana tied UAB 1-1, and Marquette edged IPFW 2-1.

## September 15

**In 1977, Steve Hargan pitches his last Major League game.**

Though he was only 15 at the time, most scouts said he didn't throw hard enough to be a major-league pitcher. Steve Hargan kept fighting to prove everyone wrong.

The 1961 South Side High School graduate signed with the Cleveland Indians in 1961 and started a steady climb to the majors that culminated in 1965. He was 13-5 with Portland when the Indians called him up, and Hargan won his first major-league game, 6-3 over the Los Angeles Angels.

Two years later, he was named to the American League roster for the All-Star Game. Unfortunately, he pulled a leg muscle in his last start before the game and could only hobble out for the introductions.

"It was probably my biggest thrill, just being there with these guys I admired when I was a kid," Hargan said in 1985.

That season he led the American League with six shutouts and had a 2.62 earned run average.

Injuries soon became a major part of Hargan's career. After going 13-10 in 1966 and 14-13 in 1967, he slipped to 8-15 in 1968 and 5-14 in 1969. He went back to the minors in 1970, but came back to Cleveland and posted an 11-3 record.

But the next year he faltered again and went 1-13, and the Indians sent him back to the minors in 1972 after he lost his first three games. Hargan kept pitching and joined the Texas Rangers in 1974. In three seasons with them, he went 29-27. His career ended in 1977 with brief stops in Toronto, Texas again and Atlanta and a 2-6 record.

Hargan's major-league career record is 87-107, with a 3.92 earned run average in 354 games.

He was inducted into the NEIBA Hall of Fame in 2003 and currently lives in Palm Springs, Calif.

**September 16**

**In 1956, the Fort Wayne Open ends a seven-year run.**

The last was probably the best as Art Wall Jr. claimed $2,400 by beating Gardner Dicksinson Jr. and Bill Trombley in a one-hole playoff at the Elks Country Club.

Trombley, who had led the first two rounds and was tied for the lead after the third round, took himself out of contention with a poor tee shot on the extra hole. Wall decided things when he hit second shot within six feet of the hole.

Ironically, Wall won the tournament in 1953 by also surviving a playoff, this time against Cary Middlecoff. In fact, Wall won only three tournaments in four years including his two victories in Fort Wayne. His first win in Fort Wayne allowed him to enter the 1953 Tournament of Champions in Las Vegas which he won and took home $10,000.

Wall had shot a 62 on the final day to create the tie, including an eagle on No. 16 and a birdie on No. 17.

Playing in four Fort Wayne tournaments, Wall won $6,431.

After that, purses began to grow, and Fort Wayne was forced off the PGA schedule.

That was the last PGA-affiliated golf tournament Fort Wayne hosted until 1990 when the Ben Hogan Tour came to town. Bobby Friend won the three-round tournament with a 201 to take home $20,000.

## September 17

**In 2009, the TinCaps win the Midwest League championship.**

Playing their first season at Parkview Field, and under a new nickname, the TinCaps started the year with a 10-game winning streak and stayed hot all season. They won the Eastern Division title in both halves of the season and swept the championship series in three games against Burlington. Fort Wayne finished with 101 victories for the year, tying the Midwest League record set by the Appleton Foxes in 1978.

It was a perfect summer as with a total of 378,529 regular-season fans, the team averaged more than 1,000 more per game at Parkview Field than it did the previous season at Memorial Stadium. The highlight was 8,206 fans at opening night who came out to check out the new ballpark.

Despite little time to promote because of an uncertain schedule, the TinCaps still averaged 4,215 fans for six playoff games - 25,289 total, pushing them over 400,000 in total attendance for the year. On Aug. 6, a Fort Wayne pro baseball record 8,752 fans came out to the game at a time when the TinCaps were winning 15 straight home games.

Merchandising was also up by about 40 percent.

After winning 45 games in the first half, the TinCaps went 49-21 in the second half to finish 101-48 for the season. Doug Dacsenzo became the all-time Wizards/TinCaps leading manager with 220 career wins.

Some of the playoff highlights included Robert Lara's 10th-inning home run to beat Great Lakes in the semifinals and send the TinCaps to the Midwest League finals, and Simon Castro threw the first no-hitter by a Wizards or TinCaps pitcher, and Erik Davis set a record with 16 pitching wins, breaking LaTroy Hawkins' mark of 15 set in 1993.

**September 18**

**In 1955, Arnold Palmer wins his first PGA check in the last Fort Wayne Open, $145.**

The interesting distinction here is PGA check, because Palmer won the Canadian Open in August for $2,400. By the time he got to Fort Wayne, Palmer had already earned $8,133 as a professional from various tournaments.

The 1954 United States Amateur champion played his first PGA tournament at the Fort Wayne Open. Playing at the Elks Country Club course, Palmer had rounds of 69-72-72-74 for a 287 total and tied for 25th place with Dick Mayer. The achievement was so monumental it was not mentioned in any of the local media reports.

According to the website ArnoldPalmer.com, Palmer came back in 1956 but withdrew after shooting 76 and 69 in the first two rounds.

Palmer came back to Fort Wayne to play in the 1961 Mad Anthonys where he dueled Gary Player in a match. Player, who had recently won the Masters, beat Palmer 66-69 to claim the $2,000 prize money. Palmer, who had set a record during the 1960 season by earning more than $75,000 on tour, earned $1,000. The crowd was estimated to be between 5,000 and 6,000 at Fort Wayne Country Club.

Palmer eventually won 62 tournaments on the PGA Tour, including seven majors, and 10 tournaments on the Champions Tour. He earned $1.9 million on the PGA Tour.

He was inducted into the World Golf Hall of Fame in 1974.

**September 19**

**In 1998, Saint Francis plays its first home football game.**

A week after beating Saint Xavier 56-28 in Chicago behind Antoine Taylor's 236 yards passing and four touchdowns, the Cougars came home for the first time and lost 40-18 to Taylor. The first Cougars team finished 2-8, but they accomplished a lot of good things such as setting the tone for a high-powered offense. The first squad averaged 290 yard passing to finish sixth nationally and 427 yards in total offense to finish 10th nationally.

Because there were so many young players on the team, it turned out to be the first and so far only losing season at St. Francis, as the Cougars came back to go 8-3 and win their first conference title. The second squad also made the NAIA playoffs for the first time, losing at Georgetown 38-0.

Since that first season, the Cougars have never had more than three losses in a year and 13 of the last 14 teams have qualified for the NAIA playoffs. The 2004, 2005 and 2006 teams all played for the national title. Six teams completed undefeated seasons, and the Cougars have been ranked in the NAIA national poll an amazing 167 consecutive weeks heading into the 2013 season. The Cougars also won 56 consecutive home games from 2001 to 2009.

After starting the program from scratch, Kevin Donley was named NAIA Coach of the Year in 2004 and 2005 and was inducted into the Indiana Football Hall of Fame in 2005. Donley has built a 149-34 overall record at St. Francis, including 81-13 in conference with 10 titles. He needed only 121 games to reach 100 wins as the Cougars' boss.

## September 20

**In 2000, Fort Wayne's first National Hockey League player, Fred Knipscheer, retires from hockey**

After suffering three concussions in three months, Knipscheer decided to hang up his skates after a seven-year professional career. He played his last NHL game in 1996, and then spent the next four seasons in the American Hockey League and the International Hockey League. His best season came in 1997-98 when he led the Utah Grizzlies with 21 goals and 53 points in 58 games. He finished his career by playing eight games with the Cincinnati Cyclones.

"I didn't play a lot of games in the NHL, but the memories I have are unbelievable," he said at the time of his retirement. "The things I've done are 1,000 times more than I could have ever imagined doing in hockey. The last couple of weeks I've just spent time going over some of those things. I can tell my kids some great stories."

He finished with 44 NHL games with eight goals and 12 points. He was also a thorn in the sides of the Komets, scoring nine goals and 12 points in 11 career games against his hometown team.

Knipscheer now lives in Indianapolis.

**Also, in 1998, the Komets sign Pokey Reddick for the third time.**

The ace goaltender actually played four separate times in Fort Wayne. He spent his rookie season with the Komets in 1984-85 and came back the next year to help the team reach the Turner Cup Finals.

He came back in 1991-92, after playing 131 games in the NHL, to help the Komets win their division. His breakout season and all-time legacy will be the 1993 Turner Cup playoffs sweep. He returned in 1998-99 to team with Bruce Racine in the nets as the Komets played their last year in the International Hockey League and joined them again in the United Hockey League for nine games in the 2002-2003 season in the United Hockey League before retiring.

**Also, in 1991, Wayne beats Snider in football for the first time since 1975.**

## September 21

**In 1954, the Zollner Pistons fastpitch softball team dissolves.**

It's too bad the Zollner softball team lost the final game it ever played, 4-0 to Detroit, because the Pistons won just about everything else. Over their 15 years of play, the Pistons were an amazing 1,253-189 for a winning percentage of .869. There were as dominating as any team in sports history.

That was part of the problem. They were so much better than their competitors, the games were getting boring. After finishing third in 1942 and second in 1944, the Pistons won three Amateur Softball Association world titles in 1945, 1946 and 1947. They then joined the National Softball League, the National Fastball League and the National Industrial Softball League and won nine regular-season titles in a row. In five of their last seven seasons they won more than 100 games.

The Pistons started play at Municipal Beach and free admission led the crowds of between 8,000 and 10,000 fans per game. They later moved the Dwenger Park and eventually owner Fred Zollner built Zollner Stadium.

Bernie Kampschmidt, Jim Ramage and Leo Luken played with the team all 14 years of its existence, and Hughie Johnston, Sam Lombardo, Ed Robitaille and Neal Barille played for more than 10 seasons.

Ten Pistons are enshrined in the National Softball Hall of Fame. They are Fred Zollner, Bernie Kampschmidt, Jim Ramage, Hughie Johnston, Clyde Kirkendall, Bill West, Herb Dudley, Sam Lombardo, Elmer Rohrs and Leo Luken.

**Also, in 1992, Homestead climbs to No. 6 in the state football poll.**

**Also, in 2001, New Haven football star Cory Jacquay rushes for 248 yards and five touchdowns against Columbia City.**

**September 22**

**In 1947, the Zollner Pistons win their third straight softball world championship.**

The Pistons made national news in two ways when they won their third straight world title in 1947. Bill West threw a no-hitter as the Pistons beat the Toronto Jewelers 4-0, and after the game team owner Fred Zollner announced the Pistons would no longer compete in the ASA.

There were various reasons for the move, as the ASA World Tournament came just before the National Softball League playoffs. The Pistons were also miffed at the ASA for banning Curly Armstrong from competing after the first tournament because he was also a professional basketball player. Armstrong had been allowed to compete in the tournament previously and had played in ASA-sanctioned games all season. After the world tournament was completed, Armstrong was allowed to complete the season in the National Softball League, which was also under ASA sanction.

Zollner had also decided to concentrate on trying to build the NSL in a national major league.

West was amazing in the championship game, striking out 17 and walking only two. The Zollner outfielders never had to make a play.

The offense was also good with Hughie Johnston belting his second home run of the tournament, and Chick Goldberg smacking three doubles and manager Bernie Kampschmidt three singles. Ed Robitaille and Billy Johnston each cracked a pair of singles.

The Pistons swept through the tournament without a loss for the second year in a row, scoring 22 runs and allowing only two, getting 38 hits and allowing only four. Three of their wins were no-hitters.

Zollner became the first men's team to win three consecutive titles. In five trips to the ASA championship over six years, their tournament record was 25-5.

The Pistons continued their season, winning the NSL playoffs to finish 113-19 record as West, Elmer Rohrs and Diz Kirkendall all won 28 games.

## September 23

**In 1945, the Zollner Pistons win their first world softball title.**

All we hear about today is how the Pistons dominated, but they didn't get that way until they won their first world title, and that was probably the toughest one they had to win.

After getting knocked out early in the 1941 world tournament, the Pistons came back in 1942 to finish third and in 1944 to finish second. Then, they almost finished second again.

This time their main opponent was Flint pitcher Charlie Justice who beat them 1-0, allowing only two hits to end the Pistons' 50-game winning streak (June 19 to Aug. 29). During the 50 games, the Pistons' pitchers threw 37 shutouts and nine one-run games. That loss set up a winner-take-all showdown in Cleveland at the Amateur Softball Association Championships.

The Pistons had beaten Flint and Justice 3-2 in 11 innings earlier in the tournament before losing the first game. The championship game was every bit as close. With Leo Luken throwing no-hit ball through the first five innings, his teammates finally got on the board in the fourth. Neal Barille lined a single to center and advanced to second on an infield out by Ed Robitaille. Then Chick Goldberg lined a single to right to drive in Barille for the 1-0 decision.

Flint got three hits off Luken in the sixth inning, but one of the runners got picked off second to end the threat. Luken allowed four hits, fanned five and walked one to improve his record to 35-0. The Pistons out-scored their opponents 33-6 during the tournament.

**Also, in 1995, Avilla Speedway closes.**

The speedway got its start in 1963 when Howard Bice bought many of the assets of the South Anthony Speedway and moved them to Avilla. The first event was held July 24, 1964, with races held each week during the summer. Among the great drivers who competed there include Don Gerardot and Don Garlits on the dragway, and Joe Wallace, Moose Myers, Little Joe Bennett, Jess Yates, Hank Lower, Terry Fisher, Rob Lash and Johnnie Walker on the speedway.

**Also, in 1981, the Fort Wayne Tennis Hall of Fame is started.**

## September 24

**In 2000, South Side's DeDee Nathan finishes ninth in the Olympic heptathlon competition.**

South Side's DeDee Nathan has had one of the most accomplished careers of any Fort Wayne athlete competing on the international level.

Nathan placed second in the heptathlon at the 2002 U.S. Nationals, seventh in the world championships in 2001 and won the USA Outdoor Nationals title in 2001. After missing the team by 1 second in 1996 in her second Olympic Trials, Nathan came back in 2000 to make the team and finish ninth in Sydney. She also became the first female IU track athlete to participate in the Olympics.

Nathan retired in 2002 to begin a coaching career as an assistant at Southern Illinois, but returned to training to make another Olympic try in 2012. That failed in in her fourth trip to the Olympic trials.

"I really want to go out there and make a difference in people's lives in other ways," she said. "I want to educate and help teens, and eventually I want to run a group home."

At South Side, Nathan led the Archers to back-to-back state championships in 1985 and 1986, setting records in the 300-meter hurdles. She also was part of a record-setting 1,600-meter relay team with Cathey Tyree, Angela Goodman and Trudy McCloud in 1983.

**In 1993, Class 2A No. 1 Bishop Luers beats Class 4A No. 1 Wayne 28-27.**

The Generals had finished second in Class 4A during the 1992 season, and the Knights won the Class 2A football title. Then No. 2-ranked Wayne beat Class 3A No. 1 Bishop Dwenger 16-7, and the Knights beat the Saints 28-27 in overtime the week before for Bishop Luers' first win over Bishop Dwenger since 1980.

Both teams were 4-0 heading into the game which turned out to be one of the best in Fort Wayne history. The game was tied 21-21 when Wayne running back Derrian Stanley's run set up a quarterback sneak by Heath Bunn's touchdown, but a bad snap on the extra-point try left the Generals with a 27-21 lead.

Bishop Luers kept its composure and a screen pass from Pete Krouse to Thomas Moriarity turned into a 40-yard touchdown to set up Zac Brough's game-winning extra point.

Both teams finished 11-2 that season, losing in the semistate round.

## September 25

**In 1982, Phyllis Weis is given the first Nancy Rehm Memorial Award.**

Shortly after the Fort Wayne Women's Bureau started the Run, Jane, Run Women In Sports festival in 1981, former Bishop Luers basketball star Nancy Rehm was shot and killed during a robbery at Indiana Tech. Rehm had helped Bishop Luers establish its tradition of strong girls sports and then had helped Indiana Tech win a state title during her first season with the Warriors.

The next year the women's bureau awarded the first Nancy Rehm Award honoring people for their work in the advancement of women's sports. Phyllis Weis was a long-time Catholic Youth Organization coach and physical education teacher at St. John's Catholic Church. Before Weis joined CYO, the only sport offered to girls was dodgeball, but she helped develop programs for volleyball, basketball, track and softball.

Among the people who received the award in the first 15 years were Mary Schreiber, Cheri Gilbert, Bobbi Widmann-Foust, Dona Schaefer, Mary Baumgartner, Emma Adams, Diane Thomas, Sis Arnold, Ruth Hall, Patricia Roy, Paula Pitcher, Phyllis Hebble, Diane Karst, Shirley Hallman and Jo Ann Roscoe.

That group was followed by Julie and Juby Hollingsworth, Kathy Kissinger, Brenda Robinson, Cathy Gerring, Ruth Riley, Shanna Zolman, Muffet McGraw, Jaclyn Leininger, Kim Mulkey-Robertson, Larry Westendorf, Tom Rehm, Dan Kline, Lori Culler, the Fort Wayne girls state finals committee, Dave Riley and Tiffany Gooden.

Because of waning funds and volunteer support, the Fort Wayne Women's Bureau ended Run, Jane, Run in January 2001, but the Nancy Rehm Award continues and is now presented annually at the Nancy Rehm Border Wars basketball game.

Rehm was inducted into the Indiana Basketball Hall of Fame in 2009.

**Also, in 1990, DeKalb ends Homestead's 13-year, 91-match conference winning streak in boys tennis.**

## September 26

**In 1946, the Pistons repeat as world softball champions.**

After finally winning the title in 1945, the Pistons made it look a lot easier the next year. During six tournament games, the Pistons scored 25 runs on 41 hits. Their opponents managed only one unearned run on 12 hits.

The pitching was amazing. Bill West threw a one-hitter during the championship game, a 2-0 win in 10 innings against the Chicago Match. West went 32-0 on the season, winning 16 games by shutout. Diz Kirkendall went 29-5 with two shutouts and Leo Luken finished 31-2-1. It added up to a total record of 92-7-1.

The Match and pitcher Jim Chambers gave them a battle in the title game. After a pair of disputed calls took away Zollner scoring chances, the Pistons finally scored in the 10<sup>th</sup> inning as Curly Armstrong hit a long home run to right field, and Ed Robitaille took advantage of a Chicago error to score an insurance run. West breezed through three Chicago hitters in the bottom of the inning to help the Pistons retain their place on softball's throne.

Another highlight of the season was playing a doubleheader in Toronto against the Tip Top Tailors at the Canadian National Exhibition. The Pistons won 5-1 and 5-0 before a crowd of 16,297, believed to be the largest attendance ever at a softball game.

**Also, in 1981, The Fort Wayne Women's Bureau hosts the first run, jane, run.**

**Also, in 1926, the Cincinnati Reds' Bubbles Hargraves goes 0-3 but still becomes the first catcher to win a batting title.**

**September 27**

**In 1988, Steve Bigelow places 10$^{th}$ in the Olympics.**

There are still times when Steve Bigelow gets recognized at the mall as a former Olympian. A former Big Ten champion and all-American at Michigan, Bigelow, finished 10th in the 200-meter backstroke at the Seoul Olympics at the age of 17.

"I see it as more of a reflection on my work ethic and my attitude on life in general more so than just my athletic ability," Bigelow said. "I think they read more into what type of person I am rather than what it took to get there. It still has a profound effect."

Bigelow tried to return to the Olympics in 1992, but lost in the trials despite swimming a faster time than the one he had in 1988. He made a brief run at the 1996 Olympics at age 23 before deciding to move on with the rest of his life.

That life is now in Grabill, working as a claims specialist for Meridian Insurance. He has a son, Kyle, and a daughter, Lauren.

"I still do some speaking engagements," he said. "A lot of people I used to swim with are now coaches, so I'll speak to their teams."

**Also, in 2008, the Fort 4 Fitness road race begins.**

**Also, in 1973, the NBA's Detroit Pistons beat the ABA's Indiana Pacers 121-98.**

When these exhibition games were played, the NBA leather ball was used for one half and the ABA's red, white and blue ball for one, along with the league's three-point line and 30-second shot clock. Billy Keller led the Pacers in this game with 24 points, and Bob Lanier topped the Pistons with 19.

**September 28**

**In 2012, martial arts legend Parker Shelton passes away at age 72.**

At age 12, Shelton left his Harlan, Ky., home and moved across the river to Cincinnati where he started training in martial arts. From that time, he wandered in search of a home until he came to Fort Wayne from St. Louis in 1965.

Shelton settled in to teach, eventually owning four area dojos. The Pineville, Ky., native fought professionally, including in Europe and Asia, to earn a worldwide reputation. (Imagine MMA matches without the pay-per-views but a stronger code and a bigger mythology around the fighters.) Though at 6-foot, 200 pounds he was often out-sized, the relentless Parker achieved the highest levels of judo and karate.

From 1972 to 1974 he was the nation's No. 1-ranked karate fighter and traveled to Europe and Japan and Korea for competitions. He also taught throughout the world after retiring as a fighter in 1978.

Besides being one of the top-ranked competitors in the world in judo and karate, Shelton also trained thousands of students. He was the first president of the United States Karate Association.

**Also, in 1991, Vaughn Dunbar rushes for 265 yards on 33 carries for IU against Missouri.**

Playing on a slippery, rain-soaked turf which prevented most players from cutting without falling, Dunbar broke 17 tackles to lead Indiana to a big win in the Hoosiers' season-opener. Dunbar carried 33 times and gained 336 all-purpose yards.

"Every time I got close to get my hands on him, he's gone. He's fast. He's a great back," Missouri lineman Mario Johnson told the Associated Press.

The performance established Dunbar as a Heisman Trophy candidate.

"'I have to single out Dunbar and the great job he did," said IU Coach Bill Mallory. "He played hard. I take my hat off to him."

**Also, in 1952, the Memorial Coliseum is dedicated.**

## September 29

**In 1999, Fort Wayne's Mr. Baseball, Red Carrington, dies.**

For more than 60 years, Carrington was the driving force behind Fort Wayne's amateur baseball. He served the Fort Wayne Baseball Federation from 1931, mostly as the organization's president.

Carrington was born in 1904 and graduated from Fort Wayne High School in 1922 before attending Indiana University. After he was laid off in 1931, Carrington became a scorekeeper for 50 cents a game, and was elected the Fort Wayne Baseball Federation's secretary in 1932. He moved up to the president's office in 1938 and held that title until his death.

He was also an administrator for the Indiana Amateur Baseball Congress for 40 years, and was a part-time scout for various Major League teams for more than 30 years.

After his death, the local Stan Musial League for players age 18 and older was renamed the Red Carrington League.

Carrington was always a character. Once asked about his nickname, he said, "If you look in the phone book, it says my name is Edward Red Carrington. My real name is Edward Ensign Carrington. I went by Ensign until I started school and my teacher said, `Is that your name or your title?' That was the first I knew of an ensign in the Navy. So I went by Edward after that. I was called Red because I had red hair when I was young, and if you had red hair, you were Red or Rusty."

On his half-century as a baseball guru: "I can't get out and do what I used to do. I used to rake the diamond and all that crap. Now I stick around and solve problems. I don't mind solving problems. Somebody has to. It's not that I'm so smart. But I know the rules, and I can clear up any questions. I even put in some of the rules myself."

On dealing with old age: "It's been a wonderful life. But I know all good things must end. I had a tavern once called the Third Base Tavern, the Last Stop Before Home. On my headstone, I want it to read: `He's off third and home safe at last.' "

Carrington was inducted into the Fort Wayne Baseball Oldtimers Association's Hall of Fame in 1966.

**September 30**

**In 1951, Ned Garver wins his 20th game with the St. Louis Browns.**

Garver is actually from Ney, Ohio, but he's spent so much time in Fort Wayne speaking at baseball functions he's practically adopted.

While playing for the St. Louis Browns, Detroit Tigers, Kansas City Athletics and Los Angeles Angels, Garver won 10 or more games eight times during his 14-year career that ended in 1961. He finished with a 12-157 record and 3.73 earned run average.

He was signed as a free agent by the Browns in 1944 and made his Major League debut on April 28, 1948. He played his final game on June 4, 1961 at the age of 35 for the Los Angeles Angels who released him a week later.

Garver also became one of only seven pitchers to win 20 games for a last-place club when he won 20 in 1951 for the St. Louis Browns, who lost 102 games. He's the only pitcher to do it with a winning record and on a team that lost 100 games. He also started the 1951 All-Star Game for the American League, and after the season Garver signed a $25,000 contract to become the highest-paid Browns player.

**Also, in 1951, during his only Major League game, Parnell Hisner faces Joe DiMaggio in his last career at-bat.**

A Monroeville native, Hisner was a rookie for the Boston Red Sox who had been called up AAA Louisville for the last two weeks of the 1951 season. He sat and watched all but the final game of a Boston collapse, as the Red Sox fell from contenders to 11 games out.

After Allie Reynolds had no-hit the Red Sox, Boston manager Steve O'Neill told Hisner he was starting the next day. He had the privilege of allowing DiMaggio's 2,214 regular-season and last hit.

Hisner pitched six innings, gave up seven singles, walked four, including DiMaggio his first time up, and lost 3-0. He also struck out Mickey Mantle twice.

# OCTOBER

## October 1

**In 1954, referee-turned-coach Charlie Eckman runs his first Pistons practice.**

After firing Paul Birch after the 1953-54 season, Pistons Owner Fred Zollner shocked everyone by hiring long-time the NBA referee as his next coach. Eckman, 32, had never coached at any official level before being named the Pistons' boss.

"Charley Eckman was my No. 1 choice from the very beginning," Zollner said in an official statement. "He meets our qualifications for the position. He has a thorough knowledge of basketball as it is played in the National Basketball Association because of his first hand association with all the teams in the league over a seven year period."

It turned out to be an amazingly successful gamble as Eckman led the Pistons to the NBA Finals in 1955 and 1956.

Eckman is the only man to have coached and officiated in the NBA Finals, and he surprised everyone by becoming a coach. Eckman was mainly known as an official in the 1940s and '50s, but coached the Fort Wayne Pistons for 2 1/2 years. In fact, he was their coach in 1957 when they moved to Detroit.

With a 43-29 record, the Pistons won the Western Division title and then beat the Minneapolis Lakers in four games to reach the NBA Finals where they lost to Syracuse in seven games.

The next season the Pistons won the division title again, this time with a 37-35 record. They overcame a 2-0 deficit to beat St. Louis for a return trip to the NBA Finals. This time they lost to the Philadelphia Warriors in five games.

## October 2

**In 1999, Fort Wayne Pistons owner Fred Zollner is inducted into the Basketball Hall of Fame.**

Zollner helped lead the NBA into the modern age as founder and owner of the Fort Wayne Pistons.

Zollner owned the Pistons when they won National Basketball League championships in 1943, 1944, 1945 and 1946. He also contributed to the inception of the 24-second clock, the six-foul rule and the widening of the free-throw lane.

Zollner helped found and nurture the early NBA, which was formed when four teams from the then-National Basketball League – Fort Wayne, Indianapolis, Minnesota and Rochester, N.Y. – merged with seven teams from the Basketball Association of America in 1948.

In 1952, Zollner was one of the first to buy an airplane to transport his teams to away games. The league's Western Conference trophy is named after Zollner, who died in 1982. Bennett, 83, coached the Pistons in the National Basketball League for six seasons beginning in 1941-42 and went on to be the team's general manager for seven more seasons.

The Pistons moved from Fort Wayne to Detroit in 1957, mainly because Zollner wanted the team to play in a larger market.

"The reason Fred belongs in, he wasn't the guy that put up the peach basket, but back in the 1940s and into the '50s and '60s, professional basketball was a real challenge to stay alive," said long-time Pistons official Carl Bennett. "Fred hung in there from 1941 on, and he helped most of the teams that were in the league in some way, either financially or organizationally, just to stay alive. It's nothing like the NBA is today, but back then is when the seeds were planted, and people like Fred stayed with it and made it happen."

## October 3

### Homestead's tennis team wins its 25th straight sectional in a row

Possibly the most dominant high school program in Northeast Indiana, the Spartans set a state record in 2009 by seeing their streak reach 30 before Canterbury knocked them off in 2010. Homestead started the streak with an emphasis on singles players with Joey Christoff, Steve Beier and Todd Hacker and then evolved into winning titles with doubles teams and depth.

The state record lasted until 2011 when Munster hit 31.

Homestead has won 30 sectionals, 27 regionals and 17 semistates since 1979. The only place the Spartans have come up short is in the state finals where they have finished second nine times, most recently in 2006. During their 17 trips to state, they have lost to the eventual champion in the semifinals or finals 16 times. Of those 16 times - all played at North Central High School in Indianapolis - they have lost to North Central 11 times and five times to other Indianapolis schools.
The Spartans hold state records for an ongoing streak of 30 sectional championships, 27 regional championships and six consecutive semistate appearances from 1992 to 1997.

"Beating Homestead is like beating Notre Dame," Clark said. "If you can do it, it makes your season. We have to prepare so people can't say that."

### Also, in 2003, Heritage beats Bluffton 35-16 to win third straight ACAC football title.

The Patriots put together a dominating run from 1998 to 2006, going 52-4 in Allen County Athletic Conference play. That included a 29-game winning streak that started Oct. 4, 2002 and ended Sept. 14, 2007. The streak faced a serious Leo challenge from 2008 to 2012, but the Lions' run was ended at 27 games.

Starting in 2001, the Patriots won six consecutive ACAC titles, sharing the 2002 crown with Leo.

October

**October 4**

**In 1972, the NBA's Detroit Pistons beat the ABA's Indiana Pacers 138-136 in double overtime.**

The only reason this game was played was because the National Basketball Association and American Basketball Association owners thought they were getting closer to a merger, which eventually came in 1976.

Though each summer the ABA champion would challenge the NBA champion to a "World Series of Basketball," but the NBA always declined. What they did take advantage of however, were preseason games, which drew more fans than normal exhibition games. Most of the games were played in ABA arenas or at neutral sites and rarely in NBA buildings.

The ABA teams wanted desperately to win and eventually ended up winning the all-time series 79-76. It was not uncommon to see players thrown out of the ultra-intense games.

This was one of those first games. The Pacers were the defending ABA champions after also winning title in 1970. They'd go on to win the 1973 title as well. The Pacers were led by all-time greats Roger Brown, Billy Keller, Mel Daniels and George McGinnis.

The Pistons were coming off a 26-56 season that saw them finish fourth in the Midwest Division, but Detroit was rebuilding around Dave Bing and Bob Lanier.

Detroit led by nine points halfway through the second quarter, but Indiana rallied to lead 60-57 at the half and remained in front 91-87 after three quarters. The score was tied 112-all at the end of regulation and 125-all after the first overtime. Then Detroit guard Harvey Marlott scored 10 of his 15 points in the second overtime.

Lanier scored 31 points and Bing 21 for the Pistons. Daniels scored 26 points and grabbed 24 rebounds and McGinnis scored 25 for the Pacers.

The teams met again in Fort Wayne a year later with the Pistons winning easily 121-98 as Lanier scored 19 points. Keller led the Pacers with 25.

**Also, in 1974, the Detroit Red Wings and Indianapolis Racers tie 3-3 before 3,600 fans in an exhibition game.**

## October 5

**In 2005, South Side ends Homestead's 17-year reign in the boys tennis regional.**

After the Spartans beat the Archers at the Homestead Invitational on Labor Day, South Side No. 2 singles player Jonathan Batuello started bugging coach Ryan Keirns to move him to doubles. Batuello felt he could give the Archers a much better match up against the Spartans by playing doubles.

Batuello teamed with Joe Reinke at No. 1 doubles and twins Alex and Andrew Harris remained at No. 2 doubles. That also put a lot of pressure on No. 1 singles player Derek Carpenter to keep winning.

The move worked as the Archers won their first tennis regional ever, beating the Spartans 3-2 at the Carroll Regional. Homestead led 2-0 after winning the matches at No. 2 and No. 3 singles before the Archers claimed the last three events. Batuello and Reinke won in straight sets, but the Harris twins had to rally to win in three sets after dropping their first set. Carpenter clinched the final and deciding point in his match.

It was Homestead's first regional loss since falling to Snider in1987. The Spartans had run off a string of eight championships before that, meaning they had a run of 25 regional titles in 26 years.

**Also, in 2001, South Side's football team survives a last-minute goal-line stand to beat North Side.**

**October 6**

**In 1906, Chick Stahl plays his last game in the Major Leagues.**

Chick Stahl was likely the first Major League star to come from Fort Wayne. He was born Jan. 10, 1873 in Avilla and moved to Fort Wayne when he was 12. He was also the second Fort Wayne man ever to manage in the big leagues.

Louie Heilbroner managed the St. Louis Cardinals at the end of the 1900 season to a 23-25-2 record. He was replaced at the start of the next season and remained as the team's business manager until 1908. What Heilbroner is really known for is starting baseball's first commercial statistical bureau, Heilbroner's Baseball Bureau Service which started publishing the Baseball Blue Book.

Stahl played semi-pro ball around the area for several years before being signed by Roanoke of the Virginia League in 1895. The Boston Beaneaters drafted him and Stahl made his Major League debut on April 19, 1897.

He turned out to be one of the most dangerous hitters of his time. Over 10 seasons, he hit .305 with 118 triples, 36 home runs and 622 runs driven in. He also stole 189 bases and hit 219 doubles. On May 31, 1899, he went 6-for-6 against Cleveland. Another highlight was hitting three triples in the World Series against Pittsburgh in 1903.

In 1901, Stahl jumped to the American League's Boston Americans, and in late August, 1906 he became the team's manager. He was supposed to continue the position the next year but resigned in March. On March 28 Stahl committed suicide. He's buried in Lindenwood Cemetery.

Stahl was inducted into the Fort Wayne Baseball Oldtimers Association's Hall of Fame in 1966.

## October 7

### In 2007, world-renowned basketball star Bobby Milton dies

Perhaps no one in Fort Wayne history has played more basketball games or in more places than Bobby Milton.

Milton's career started as a member of the Central High School team that came within one game of winning the state title in 1946. A 6-foot-1 forward, he scored 30 points in the afternoon semifinals to help the Tigers beat Flora 61-50 before they lost to Anderson and Jumpin' Johnny Wilson 67-53 in the title game.

Milton then joined Wilson at Anderson College to form one of the highest-scoring duos in the nation.

Milton joined the Harlem Globetrotters in 1949. He was with the team for 34 years, playing more than 8,000 games in more than 100 nations. He even played a game on the aircraft carrier Enterprise and played before a crowd of 175,000 at Olympic Stadium in Berlin in 1951. He once scored nine baskets in a row from half court.

Besides playing for the Globetrotters, he also served as the team's coach and later became the general manager after Abe Saperstein died.

Milton was inducted into the Indiana Basketball Hall of Fame in 1985 and was a member of the founding class of Fort Wayne's African-American Sports Hall of Fame in 2000.

"I'd do it all the same," Milton told The News-Sentinel's Bud Gallmeier in 1985. "I've done things most people have never done. And I've been to places most people never have. Those who have, usually are retired and too old to really enjoy themselves. I've enjoyed myself."

### Also, in 1987, Class 3A No. 1 Bishop Dwenger beats Class. 2A No. 1 Bishop Luers 24-21 in football.

This game was played in the rain and mud at Luersfield. Bishop Dwenger's defense used that to advantage, holding the Knights to 38 yards on 26 attempts. Steve Smeltzley completed 10 of 21 passes for 153 yards and two touchdowns to Tim Pelkington, and Dave Ludwig rushed for 123 yards on 23 carries and scored two touchdowns. The highlight for Bishop Luers was a 60-yard punt return for a score by Fred Moore.

## October 8

**In 1994, Michelle Hatfield becomes the first Fort Wayne golfer to win the girls state high school title.**

The Snider senior charged back from six strokes down to win by one shot with a two-round total of 152. A 3-foot putt on the final hole at Prestwick clinched a one-shot victory over Amber Amstutz of Leo and Angie Blythe of Evansville North. Amstutz equaled Hatfield's final-day 73, but a long iron shot on No. 18 landed in a pond and took her out of contention.

During the season, Hatfield hit 19 sub-40 rounds. Her worst scores were an 82 for 18 holes and a 42 for nine. She averaged 38.7 for nine holes.

Hatfield eventually won four Fort Wayne Women's City Titles and became the golf coach at Snider.

**Also, in 1963, John Ferguson becomes the first Komet to make it to the NHL.**

Ferguson came to the Komets in 1959 as a raw rookie left wing and quit playing in 1971 as one of hockey's greatest winners with five Stanley Cup rings.

In his book, "Thunder and Lightning," Ferguson wrote, "This may sound hard to believe, but the Fort Wayne Komets were the toughest team I ever had to make, throughout my entire career. They had a lot of veterans and very few spots for a rookie to crack the lineup."

Komets coach Ken Ullyot wanted the forward ever since Ferguson played against Ullyot's Prince Albert team in the Western Hockey League in the mid-1950s. Ferguson would later be known as perhaps the National Hockey League's toughest player ever, but he struggled mightily in the first half of the season in Fort Wayne, with only two goals by Christmas. He started playing much more physically in the second half and scored 30 goals as the Komets had their best season ever in 1959-60.

Ferguson spent only the one season in Fort Wayne, scoring 33 goals and 65 points with 126 penalty minutes. Then he moved to Cleveland of the American Hockey League for three seasons before joining the Montreal Canadiens in 1963.

## October 9

**In 1992, The News-Sentinel announces the dedication of the Gallmeier Cup to honor former sports editor Bud Gallmeier.**

Gallmeier covered the Fort Wayne Komets for 35 years before his retirement in 1990. The Gallemeier Cup honors the player who best exemplifies the spirit of Komets hockey through his play and community service.

When News-Sentinel Sports Editor Ben Tenny retired in 1972, Gallmeier was promoted and made an immediate impact.

"The thing that was always nice about Bud is that he was always fair to you, win or lose," said former Komets goalie Robbie Irons. "He knew when you had a bad game, but he didn't build his stories around the negative. He built around the positive. He was very fair and good to all the players that I've ever heard of."

Perhaps the most amazing thing about Gallmeier's reporting skills is the fact that he never used a tape recorder and rarely took notes when interviewing subjects. Occasionally, players said, they would look over at Gallmeier's notepad and see chicken scratches. When the paper came out the next day, they always wondered how he could be so accurate.

"'During an interview, he had the uncanny ability to enjoy a bottle or two of beer without taking notes and write a column the next day and quote you verbatim," said former Komet Lionel Repka. "I thought there was no way in h--- he could write anything, and boom, the next day he never missed a lick. His memory bank was like a steel trap."

**Also, in 1948, Emil Sitko rushes 24 times for 186 yards for Notre Dame against Michigan State.**

**Also, in 2009, Norwell breaks Homestead's 20-game NHC football winning streak.**

**Also, in 1998, Harding's Sean Casey scores six touchdowns in a win over Concordia.**

## October 10

**In 1920, Bill Wambsganss pulls off the only unassisted triple play in World Series history.**

Bill Wambsganss played in the major leagues for 13 years, but he has become known for only one thing.

Wambsganss became a baseball legend during the 1920 World Series when, as a second baseman for the Cleveland Indians, he completed an unassisted triple play against the Brooklyn Dodgers. During the fifth inning of Game 5 with baserunners on first and second, a sharp liner was hit to Wambsganss who caught it, stepped on second and then tagged the runner coming from first. It's the only unassisted triple play in World Series history.

"The only thing anybody seems to remember is that once I made an unassisted triple play in a World Series," Wambsganss once wrote. "Many don't even remember the team I was on, or the position I played, or anything. Just Wambsganss – unassisted triple play. You'd think I was born the day before and died the day after."

Following the World Series, Cleveland fans presented Wambsganss a medal to honor the triple play, but he lost it the following April while traveling by train.

Wambsganss was a great defensive player but also a pretty fair hitter. He finished with a career .259 average in 1,492 games. He hit a career-best .325 in 54 games with the Philadelphia Athletics in 1926. His best season during 10 years with Cleveland was .295 in 1918. His best season was probably 1924 when he hit .275 with career-highs with 174 hits and 93 runs scored.

Though he was born in Cleveland, Wambsganss grew up in Fort Wayne when his Lutheran minister father was transferred. He started to follow in his father's footsteps at Concordia College but decided to become a baseball player instead.

He dropped to the minors after 1926 and retired as a player in 1932. Wambsganss later came back to Fort Wayne to manage the Fort Wayne Daisies in 1945 and 1946. He was inducted into the Fort Wayne Oldtimers Baseball Association's Hall of Fame in 1962 and died Dec. 8, 1985, in Lakewood, Ohio, at age 91.

**Also, in 2008, the Chicago Bulls beat the Indiana Pacers 102-95 an exhibition game.**

## October 11

**In 1987, future St. Louis Cardinals pitcher Matt Kinzer punts for the Detroit Lions.**

Early in the 1990 Major League Baseball season, pitcher Matt Kinzer was watching a game from the Detroit Tigers' bullpen when a trivia question was asked on the JumboTron. "Who is the only person to play for both the Detroit Tigers and Detroit Lions?"

"I'm just shaking my head," Kinzer said. "The guys are all just guessing and no one got it. Four innings later when the answer comes, every head turns and looks at me. I just sat there and laughed."

Kinzer pitched nine games in the Major Leagues, but his one NFL game happened during the NFL strike in Green Bay against the Packers who won 19-16 in overtime. Kinzer, a Norwell and Purdue graduate, kicked seven times for a 34-yard average with a long of 42 yards. The Packers were only able to return four kicks for a total of 11 yards.

"In the NFL if you don't kick the ball out of bounds, they are going to kick you out of bounds," Kinzer said.

A former kicker at Purdue, Kinzer had not punted in three years because he was concentrating on his pitching career. Then Lions' linebacker and Fort Wayne-native Rosie Barnes called to say Detroit was looking for a new punter. The strike had not started at that point, and Kinzer was struggling in the minors so he figured, why not?

Kinzer impressed Lions' coach Darryl Rogers so much, a contract was offered the day of his tryout. He was watching the next game from the sidelines when Rogers told Kinzer he'd be kicking the next week. Then, the night before the game, the NFL went on strike.

The Lions honored Kinzer's regular NFL contract, and he kicked in the game. A week later the strike ended, and Kinzer came home to get ready for spring training. He received calls expressing interest from a few other NFL teams, but that's when his baseball career took off and he made the big leagues on May 18, 1989 with the St. Louis Cardinals.

**Also, in 1997, Larry Bird brings his Indiana Pacers to town to beat the Toronto Raptors 104-100 in an exhibition game.**

This was Bird's first win as a rookie coach, as Reggie Miller and Fred Hoiberg each scored 21 points in front of 8,200 fans.

**October 12**

**In 1993, No. 6 Snider beats No. 10 Northrop to win the SAC volleyball title.**

This has been a brilliant rivalry over the years, with great coaches and players on both sides, but it was rare when both teams were ranked in the top 10 at the same time.

An unranked Northrop team had beaten No. 4 Snider 15-12, 15-4 in the Summit Athletic Conference tournaments, but Snider came back to win the rematch 15-12, 15-12 to win the regular-season title.

This was an odd match, too because the Bruins led 10-4 and 12-10 in the first game. Northrop also led 5-1 and 11-9 in the second game before Snider rallied.

Jennifer Miller led the Panthers with 27 assists, two aces and two blocks, and Heather Cox hit 11 kills with two blocks. Holly Schneider led the Bruins with 17 kills and seven digs.

The Bruins must have learned something from the loss because they came back to beat the Panthers in the regional 15-13, 12-15, 15-13 to give Northrop its first-ever regional championship in volleyball.

**Also, in 1995, Komets defenseman Grant Richison survives a horrific motor cycle accident.**

While crashing his motorcycle into the back of a van on Jefferson Boulevard, Richison suffered a mild concussion, a torn-up, but not torn-apart, left knee, a sprained wrist and a broken pelvis. He missed the rest of the season, but came back to skate 51 games with the Komets in 1996-97.

## October 13

**In 2006, Bishop Dwenger beats Bishop Luers 35-0 to start the Saints' long Summit Athletic Conference winning streak which reached 38 games.**

The Saints won a record five consecutive Summit Athletic Conference titles. Bishop Dwenger had lost to Snider 13-12 on Oct. 6, 2006, a 10th consecutive loss to the Panthers.

Then coach Chris Szvarczkopf started building around players like John Goodman, Mick Mentzer and Tyler Eifert and the Saints started to dominate. The 2007 team was undefeated before losing to Lowell in the semistate, but the next year the Saints got revenge before losing the state championship game against Indianapolis Cathedral. Lowell won the semistate match in 2009 to end another Bishop Dwenger undefeated season, and in 2010 the Saints against lost in the state championship game, again against Cathedral.

The SAC winning streak was rarely challenged. Bishop Luers fell 28-21 in 2007, Snider lost 27-24 in early 2008 and the 2010 game against Snider needed overtime before it was decided 46-45.

North Side finally stopped the run with a 26-16 win on Sept. 11, 2012 at Chambers Field.

**Also, in 1973, South Bend St. Joseph's beats Bishop Luers 16-0 to end the Knights' 27-game unbeaten streak.**

This was the era that truly established the Knights as an area and state power in football. From 1969 to 1975, the Knights won nine games in five of seven seasons, and all of this came before there was a state playoff system. These teams were also known mostly for their defense, as Bishop Luers posted five shutouts in 1969, six in 1971 and five each in 1972 and 1973.

The unbeaten streak started after a 19-7 loss to Central late in the 1970 season. The run included a rare 0-0 tie against Central Catholic in 1971 and a 30-28 win over South Bend St. Joseph's in 1972. The 1973 team had allowed only seven points in its first five games before losing the game at St. Joseph's.

During this stretch, the Knights won City Series titles in 1969, 1971 and 1972 and Summit Athletic Conference titles in 1973 and 1975. The Knights finally got a chance in the state playoffs in 1983, finishing second in Class 2A after a 20-16 loss to Indianapolis Chatard.

**Also, in 1972, Northrop's Larry Kennedy scores a Fort Wayne-football record 46 points as the Bruins beat Wayne 46-22.**

Kennedy scored seven touchdowns and a pair of two-point conversions on his way to 243 yards rushing.

October

313

**October 14**

**In 2001, Homestead soccer coach Pat Teagarden claims his 300ᵗʰ career victory.**

The Spartans beat Bishop Luers 3-1 behind Lindsey Wiltshire's two goals to capture the Canterbury Sectional title.

A graduate of Bishop Luers and IPFW, Teagarden coached soccer for 35 years in the Fort Wayne area, including 24 years at Homestead. During his tenure at Homestead, the Spartans won nine sectional titles, eight regionals and made four state finals appearances, finishing second in 2001. In 1993 he was named the Indiana Soccer Coaches Association Coach of the Year.

Teagarden retired in 2005 to become an assistant coach at Saint Francis, and died in 2011 at age 59 after a long bout with cancer. The Pat Teagarden Field at Homestead was dedicated in 2011.

Teagarden was inducted into the Indiana Soccer Coaches Hall of Fame in 2008 and the Indiana Soccer Hall of Fame in 2011.

**Also, in 1990, Cathy Gerring wins $100,000 by winning LPGA World Championship.**

Gerring shot a 1-under-par 71 in the final round to edge Beth Daniel by one shot in Cely, France. She led through every round to take her third title of the year, and the check boosted her yearly earnings to $463,493, good for fifth on the tour.

She birdied four of the first five holes during the final round to increase her lead to seven shots.

**Also, in 1922, South Side beats Auburn 26-0 to win its first-ever football game.**

## October 15

**In 1993, defending Class 5A state champion Snider beats defending Class 2A state champion Bishop Luers 35-14.**

After starting the season 0-2, the Panthers came back to finish the regular season 6-2, including this win which ended Bishop Luers' hopes for an undefeated year. Still, the Knights did win the Summit Athletic Conference title.

The Knights were coming off a 13-1 season with Pete Krouse, Andy Boxberger, Pete Henry, Mike Reed and Marcus Stepp leading the way. Stepp was one of the top prep linebackers in the country. Bishop Luers faced a few tight games before this one, beating Northrop 28-27, Bishop Dwenger 28-27 in overtime, Wayne 28-27 in a battle of No. 1-ranked teams and Concordia 49-48 in overtime.

The Panthers were coming off a 14-0 record led by Willie Burton, Todd Ellinger, Brian Epps, Robert Ford, Contrell Johnson, Brett Rohrbacher, Jabar Robinson and Ryan Dohrman. Snider lost its first two games 21-19 against Bishop Dwenger and 26-24 against Wayne.

Snider defense controlled the line of scrimmage in the showdown of defending state champs, holding the Knights to 70 yards rushing. Willie Burton scored three touchdowns and Contrell Johnson two more for the Panthers. Boxberger was knocked out of the game in the third quarter, killing the Knights' comeback chances despite strong play from back-up Joe Bertels. Eric Shroyer caught passes for both of Bishop Luers' touchdowns.

The Bishop Luers game was Snider's best of the season which ended a week later with a 23-21 loss to Homestead in the sectional. The Knights fared a little better in the state tournament, beating Jimtown 29-26 in the regional before losing at West Lafayette 27-7.

## October 16

**In 2009, Jim Clark retires as the coach of the Homestead boys tennis team.**

Before Clark passed away in 2012 after a long battle with cancer, former Homestead great Joey Christoff asked his coach if he had any idea how many students he had worked with on a tennis court. Clark thought for a while and then came back with an answer of more than 6,000.

"My jaw dropped when I heard that," Christoff said. "I knew there were lots of lives he touched, but when you think of 6,000..."

During his career, Clark coached the Spartans to a state-record 31 sectional titles, 28 regionals and 18 trips to the state finals. Clark was named Indiana State Coach of the Year in both 1997 and 2009 and was inducted into the IHSTECA Hall of Fame in 1997. Clark was named the National Federation of Interscholastic Coaches Association Coach of the Year in 1997 and also was selected as Ball State's Alumni Coach of the Year in 1999, 2006 and 2009.

In 2011, Clark was inducted into the Fort Wayne Tennis Hall of Fame.

Among the individuals Clark coached are 1997 state champion Rick Phillipp, 1984 runner-up Todd Hacker and 10-time Fort Wayne Tennis Tournament singles champion Ryan Recht. He also coached mental attitude award winners Cameron Huffman (2006), Phillipp (1997), Raju Raval (1996), Tom Schneider (1994), Greg Ferkel (1992) and Christoff (1981).

After winning their first sectional title in 1997, the Spartans were killed by Peru in the regional and lost the 1978 sectional final to Wayne. During Clark's first season, the Spartans advanced to state, finishing third. Through they had many trips to state, they could never beat the Indianapolis schools on their home courts for the title.

"How can you complain?" Clark said in 2002. "I've always thought that I've never won a ring or a championship, but I've had some championship teams. How many coaches do you know who have been out there for years who have never won a sectional?

"When you go to the state finals 14 or 15 times, you get discouraged when you don't win it. That's so stupid. You've been so successful, had some great kids. How could you feel like you're not doing something worthwhile?"

**October 17**

**In 2004, after 153 Indy League races and nine first-place finishes, Kelley Racing runs its final race.**

The end didn't come on a racetrack but in a boardroom for Kelley Racing. On Feb. 9, 2005, Indy Racing League president Tony George purchased the remains of Tom Kelley's dream to end Fort Wayne's affiliation with big-time racing.

Kelley started his team on Oct. 23, 1996, when he announced he was buying three engines with plans to compete in the 1997 season. The team sponsored drivers Scott Sharp, Mark Dismore, Al Unser, Jr., Sarah Fisher and Tony Renna. Sharp won seven races, Dismore one and Unser one. The team also won the pole eight times.

Maybe the most-notable point came in 2001 when Sharp won the pole for the Indianapolis 500. Unfortunately, he crashed in the first turn. The team's best finish in Indianapolis was Renna placing seventh in 2003.

The best thing about Kelley Racing wasn't the wins or the drivers or the thrills during the racing, but the way Tom Kelley showed such grace while struggling so far to succeed. The sport allowed him just enough success to tease him, but he always reacted with class, and allowed Fort Wayne racing fans an inside look at the sport and the people in it. He set the tone, and his team members always followed his lead.

Though his team probably didn't win enough for his liking, Kelley gained respect from everyone he met in the sport and for his effort in it.

**Also, in 1919, Central loses 33-0 at Decatur in the first high school football game for a Fort Wayne team.**

## October 18

**In 1987, Class 5A No. 2 North Side beats Class 3A No. 1 Bishop Dwenger 36-20.**

"The Game of the Year" matching two undefeated teams didn't turn out that way, as the Redskins went up 36-7 before the Saints scored two late touchdowns.

The win gave the Redskins their third Summit Athletic Conference title, and they earned it by continually winning close games. During the rest of the regular season, North Side beat Snider 15-14, Bishop Luers 17-14, South Side 22-14 and Northrop 26-14 to set up the title showdown and a chance for redemption. A year earlier, North Side had been undefeated going into the final regular-season game against Snider and lost 56-10.

The Redskins never posted a shutout, but they had never given up more than 14 points in a game before the Saints scored a pair of fourth quarter touchdowns.

Junior Von Ganaway was the star in this game, rushing 31 times for 192 yards and two touchdowns. He also intercepted a pass to set up the Redskins' first touchdown.

With leading rusher Dave Ludwig missing the game with a knee injury, Saints' quarterback Steve Smeltzley tried to keep his team in the game by completing 10 of 18 passes for 184 yards. He threw for one score and ran another in himself.

North Side rushed for 309 yards and held Bishop Dwenger to 68.

This was an amazing era of North Side football under coach Dale Doerffler. From 1983 to 1991, the Redskins won 71 games and lost 22. Doerffler was the coach from 1980 to 1996 and compiled a 110-61 record.

**Also, in, 1981, Leo's Mike Augustyniak rushes 20 times for 80 yards to help the New York Jets beat the Buffalo Bills 33-14.**

## October 19

### In 1952, the Pistons play their first basketball game in Memorial Coliseum

Because the building was built for the Pistons, the lead in The News-Sentinel's story said, "Basketball in Fort Wayne comes into its inheritance."

The day was actually a doubleheader of exhibition games with the Pistons taking on the Milwaukee Hawks after the world champion Minneapolis Lakers played the Indianapolis Olympians.

The building's capacity for basketball was listed at 10,000, but only 4,821 fans showed up.

The Lakers pounded the Olympians 101-72, and then the Hawks beat the Pistons 71-67. The highlight for Fort Wayne fans was the arrival of Duke All-American Dick Groat to the Pistons' roster. The third pick overall in the 1952 draft, Groat scored nine points in limited action during his Fort Wayne debut to give Pistons a hint of what they could expect after he graduated from Duke around Christmas.

Groat played only 22 games for the Pistons that season, averaging 11.9 points and 2.7 assists, but his true love was baseball and he signed with the Pittsburgh Pirates. He played 14 years in Major League Baseball, getting 2,138 career hits and earning the 1960 National League Most Valuable Player Award as he led the Pirates to the World Series title over the Yankees.

The Pistons drew only slightly better for their regular-season home opener on Nov. 2 against the Lakers. They lost the game 81-69 before 5,683 fans.

## October 20

**In 1951, Drake's Johnny Bright is knocked out by a dirty play against Oklahoma A&M.**

A product of Central High School, Bright took a scholarship at Drake University to run track, with the condition that he could try out for the football and basketball teams. After sitting out the mandatory year of freshman ineligibility, Bright made the football team after two days. A few days after that, he became the focus of the offense.

As a sophomore, Bright rushed for 975 yards and threw for 975 yards to lead the nation in total offense as the Bulldogs went 6-2-1. He followed that with 1,232 yards rushing and 1,168 yards passing as a junior to set an NCAA record for total offense. The next season he was leading the nation in rushing and total offense with 821 and 1,349 yards, respectively when the Bulldogs played at Oklahoma A&M on Oct. 20, 1951.

As a sophomore in 1949, Bright became the first African-American player to play at Stillwater, but this game would be much rougher. After taking two late hits early in the game, Bright was well away from the play when he was blasted by Aggies defensive lineman Wilbanks Smith, lifting Bright off his feet. Despite suffering a broken jaw, Bright came back the next play to throw a touchdown pass, but another hit knocked him out of the game a few plays later.

Immediately after the game, Drake officials accused Oklahoma A&M of dirty play and being out to "get" Bright, but the Oklahoma A&M president said he saw nothing unusual with the play. Photos from the game by John Robinson and Don Ultang of the Des Moines Register showed the severity and won a Pulitzer Prize.

Bright came back to play two weeks later, rushing for 204 yards against Great Lakes Naval Station, to finish with more than 6,000 yards in career total offense. He averaged 236 yards per game and scored 384 points in 25 games, finishing fifth in the Heisman voting.

When the Missouri Valley Conference took no action against Oklahoma A&M, Drake eventually left the league.

**Also, in 1997, South Side's Derek Carpenter wins the state tennis championship.**

The senior reached his goal by beating Dalton Albertin of Lawrence Central 5-7, 6-2, 6-2 in Indianapolis. Carpenter finished his season 26-2 and his career 99-13.

## October 21

**In 1967, Merv Dubchak got off to a fast start with the Komets with five goals in his first two games.**

"Stubby" was already coming off his best season ever after scoring a remarkable 72 goals in 70 games during the 1965-66 season when he teamed with Bobby Rivard and John Goodwin to produce all kinds of records. Rivard scored 42 goals and 133 points, Dubchak 72 goals and 117 points and Goodwin 35 goals and 114 points. They were impossible to stop.

After scoring two goals in the Komets' home-opener against Dayton in a 7-2 win, Dubchak and the Komets started slowly the next day in Port Huron. Fort Wayne trailed 3-0 going into the third period before Dubchak sparked a comeback by scoring a hat trick during the third period. The Komets won 4-3. Dubchak also set up Goodwin's goal, and Len Thornson had three assists on Dubchak's markers.

Playing with Thornson at center after Rivard went to the American Hockey League, Goodwin and Dubchak again had very strong years. Thornson finished with a Komets' record 139 points, Goodwin 106 and Dubchak 98.

Dubchak finished with a 52-goal season, giving him an incredible 176 in three seasons. He played seven years with the Komets, scoring 321 goals in 367 games with 539 points. He also scored 24 goals and 49 points in 47 playoff games.

**October 22**

**In 1996, Tom Kelley purchases three engines in his initial move to field an IRL team in 1997.**

The president of the Kelley Automotive Group presented a check for $660,000 to representatives of Riley & Scott to order three chassis from the Indianapolis-based manufacturer with the intention of fielding an Indy Racing League team in 1997.

"I absolutely believe the Indy Racing League is a positive force for auto racing and the right way for open-wheel racing to grow and thrive in the future," Kelley told The News-Sentinel's Rich Griffis.

Kelley said he had been thinking about getting back into racing ever since George announced the Indy Racing League concept. With the lower-budget IRL, the venture was now more affordable.

The sale marked the return to racing for Kelley, who served from 1985 to 1987 as a distributor for March chassis, which competed in the now-rival Championship Auto Racing Teams series.
Kelley said affordability played a large role in his decision to return to racing.

"This opportunity would not be available to us in the old days," Kelley said, noting a single chassis for the CART series would cost over $450,000 and a single fully assembled car would require an investment of approximately $2 million.

The dream became reality when Kelley's first car, driven by Mark Dismore, qualified for the 1997 Indianapolis 500. Dismore was knocked out of the race on a lap 24 restart.

## October 23

**In 2009, Norwell's Klay Fiechter rushes for 307 yards and Harding's Rod Smith for 297 — in the same game.**

This might have been the quickest-played game in Northeast Indiana history as both teams stayed away from the pass and kept handing off to their stars.

Smith, playing in a Wildcat formation, took the first snap from scrimmage and ran 54 yards for a touchdown. On Norwell's first play, Fiechter ran 55 yards before he was pulled down from behind by Smith at the 5-yard line.

Smith finished with four touchdowns and Fiechter three. The key play in the game might have been a third-quarter fumble by Fiechter that led to the Hawks building a 28-13 lead. Smith finished with 32 carries, and Fiechter 39.

Fiechter finished the season with 2,126 yards rushing and 27 touchdowns, and Fiechter totaled 1,855 touchdowns and 19 touchdowns.

**Also, in 1987, Class 5A No. 2 North Side loses to No. 1 Penn 39-32 in two overtimes in the semistate.**

The Redskins led the Kingsmen 24-6 with less than seven minutes remaining when everything fell apart. A short North Side punt and then a fumble led to 11 Penn points and then a 35-yard touchdown pass with two minutes left tied the score and forced overtime.

When the Kingsman went up 39-32 in the second overtime, the Redskins received a penalty which meant they had to start their final drive 15 yards back. An interception on third down finished North Side's undefeated streak and season.

**October 24**

**In 1968, Sharon Wichman wins the gold medal in the 200 breast stroke.**

When Sharon Wichman started competing in the mid-1960s, there was a boys swimming team at Snider High School, but not one for girls. A few years later, Wichman said she was the only female swimmer she knew of at the time.

Quickly Wichman became a role model for other female athletes, as she won a gold medal in the 1968 Mexico City Olympics in the 200-meter breast stroke. Her time of 2:44.4 set an Olympic record, and she also won a bronze medal in the 100-meter breast stroke. Besides being the first American woman to win a gold medal in the event, at only age 16, Wichman became the first Fort Wayne athlete to earn an Olympic gold medal.

"For about a year, my world was wonderful," she remembered in 1997. She married David Jones in 1973. "I gave a lot of talks. People were so excited back then that I would tell them, when they asked me to speak, that I could do a Q & A. They'd ask questions for two hours. That keeps you going and excited."

After competing in the U.S. Nationals in 1971, Wichman decided not to defend her gold medal in 1972, saying she wanted to experience the normal life of a teen-ager.

"I didn't realize how goal-orientated I was until I tried to swim afterward," she said. "I had already done the only thing I ever wanted to do in swimming. Just to swim for swimming's sake was not what I wanted to achieve the rest of my life."

Wichman-Jones lives in Churubusco and has two sons. She often speaks to local groups about her athletic career and her 1985 decision to become a born-again Christian.

**Also, in 1970, Central beats Bishop Luers 19-7 in its last football game to clinch the Fort Wayne City Series title.**

## October 25

**In 1980, Bishop Luers ends North Side's 20-game football winning streak with an 8-6 decision at Spuller Stadium.**

This was a battle for the ages.

Both teams were 9-0 and still hoping for a chance at the state playoffs, which at the time were set up using a complicated ratings system. Bishop Luers already expected it would not be participating in the playoffs, while North Side still had a chance with a win.

Bishop Luers' defense won the game 8-6 by outlasting North Side's offense before more than 6,000 fans at Spuller Stadium. The Knights came into the game allowing four points per game, while North Side averaged 25. The Redskins out-gained the Knights 238-61 and had 15-2 advantage in first downs. Bishop Luers didn't earn its initial first down until there was only 4:34 left in the third quarter.

Tim Hines was the star for the Redskins, carrying 41 times for 185 yards to finish with 1,581 for the season.

North Side scored two touchdowns in the last minute that were nullified by penalties. A Redskins' fumble led to the Knights' touchdown, and a fourth-quarter blocked punt by Jeff Slater rolled out of the end zone for a safety to give Bishop Luers the lead.

The loss ended North Side's 20-game winning streak. The Redskins had been trying to break the city record of 20 games in a row set by Bishop Luers from 1971 to 1973.

There was talk of Bishop Luers playing undefeated South Bend St. Joseph's in an unofficial playoff game a week later, but the IHSAA squashed that effort.

**Also, in 1926, Babe Ruth plays an exhibition game with the Lincoln Lifers against the Kips.**

There's an urban legend about Ruth hitting a home run into a passing train car, but there's no official record of it. Ruth did hit two home runs and played every position but catcher in the game as the Lifers won 11-1 at League Park.

**Also, in 1952, the Fort Wayne Komets play their first game, losing to Toledo 4-0 before 4,956 home fans.**

**Also, in 1997, Homestead's Rick Phillipp wins the state tennis title.**

## October 26

**In 2000, Homestead graduate Shawn Brown wins his second Paralympics gold medal**

Brown lost his left leg at age 21 in 1992 in a grain elevator accident, and eventually came to accept it was the best thing that ever happened to him. The injury allowed him to meet his wife, a fellow Paralympic athlete who had lost a leg to cancer, they would not have had five children and he would not have had an opportunity to help so many others with similar afflictions.

Brown won his first gold medal in the discus at the 1996 Atlanta Paralympics where he set a world record. In Sydney he was able to repeat with a toss of 47.96 meters.

"I really can't find any single negative about it," he said in 2012. "Really, most everybody has that decision to make, that fork in the road. They really can travel and trust that what seems to be this devastating event in their life is really going to be a positive if they choose to mold it and find those positives."

Today, Brown is a certified and licensed prosthetist and orthotist and vice president of clinical services for SRT Prosthetics and Orthotics.

"When I think about all of the people whom I've had the ability to touch, hopefully in a positive manner, the loss of my leg was peanuts," he said. "I have a hangnail in comparison to what a lot of other people go through."

**Also, in 2003, Carroll's Trent Glassley and Brian Fleming win the state doubles tennis crown.**

The senior duo beat Munster's Scott Gray and Chad Holajter 6-4, 6-1 for the state title. Fleming and Glassley finished 27-1 for the season. The duo avenged its only regular-season loss against Bishop Dwenger during the sectional.

**Also, in 1974, the Fort Wayne Hoosiers begin play in the International Basketball Association.**

## October 27

**In 2002, Bishop Luers grad Angie Akers is named the AVP rookie of the year for women's beach volleyball.**

After graduating from Notre Dame, Angie Harris married football player Jeremy Akers and gave up volleyball after playing professionally for three months in Switzerland to become a stockbroker.

"I had the 9 to 5 and sometimes (longer), and it was not for me," Akers told The News-Sentinel's Chad Ryan in 2008. "I was absolutely going crazy, and that was a great job. My college roommate suggested, `Why don't we go try and play beach volleyball?' I was like, `Yes! Anything to get me out of the office.' "

Three years after she played, Akers earned more than $7,000 in her first year on tour and earned the rookie of the year honor.

Akers opened her own doors by moving to Southern California in 2002 for a pro beach volleyball shot even as her husband's NFL career was winding down. After stints with Dallas, Oakland and Denver, plus a season with NFL Europe in Germany and another with the ill-fated XFL, it was time for role reversal.

One of Akers' highlights was teaming with Brooke Hanson to finish seventh at the 2007 Pan American Games in Rio de Janeiro, Brazil. In 2009, she teamed with Tyra Turner to finish fifth at the FIVB World Championships in Stavanger, Norway. Akers also works as a runner and professional fitness runner. She was featured on the cover of Runner's World and ran the 2001 Boston Marathon in 3 hours, 24 minutes.

Today, Akers travels the world, competing in such places a Seoul, Rome, Shanghai, Moscow and the Hague. Akers has been competing in international volleyball for more than 10 years, earning more than $250,000 in prize money.

**Also, in 1934, South Side beats North Side 10-6 to win the first Fort Wayne City Series football championship.**

**October 28**

**In 1984, Bill Kratzert breaks a four-year slump by winning the Pensacola Open.**

The Elmhurst graduate birdied three of the last four holes for a two-shot margin over Ken Brown and John Mahaffey to pick up a check for $54,000, his largest check ever. The win came in the PGA's last official event of the season as Kratzert put together rounds of 67, 66, 71 and 66 for a 14-under par 270 total.

This was Kratzert's fourth career victory in nine years on the PGA Tour. His last win previous to this was July 13, 1980 at the Milwaukee Open.

**Also, in 2006, Bishop Dwenger's girls repeat as state soccer champions.**

The Saints beat North Central 2-1 to finish 22-0-2, the best record in school history. Bishop Dwenger scored 100 goals this season and allowed only 11 under the direction of coach Jason Wisniewski. Jordan Pawlik and Lauren Ottenweller scored in the championship game.

The Saints were dominant, but they also faced some tough challenges during the season, beating Canterbury 2-0 to win the sectional, Carroll 2-1 to win the regional, West Lafayette 1-0 in penalty kicks to win the semistate and then Portage 3-0 in the state semifinals.

**Also, in 2006, long-time cross country and track coach Barrie Peterson retires**

Peterson's Northrop teams won 16 regionals and advanced to state 21 times in 25 years.

**Also, in 1952, George Drysdale scores the first goal in Komets history during a 6-5 loss to Grand Rapids.**

## October 29

**In 2002, Eric Wedge is named manager of the Cleveland Indians.**

After his four-year Major League playing career ended because of injuries, Wedge started his five-year trek back to the majors as a coach. When the Sporting News named him its Minor League Manager of the Year in 2001 for his work with the Indians' AAA farm team in Buffalo, it was only a matter of time before Wedge got a call to manage a Major League club.

At age 34, Wedge became the youngest manager in the big leagues.

During his minor league career, Wedge was named Manager of the Year three times in five years, and his last two Buffalo teams posted a combined 178-108 (.622) record.

Wedge lasted seven years with the Indians before getting fired at the end of the 2009 season, compiling a 561-573 record. The highlight was winning the 2007 American League Manager of the Year Award. That squad finished one game from the World Series. All-time in Cleveland, Wedge ranks fifth on the team in wins, third in losses and fourth in games.

Wedge was inducted into the Northeast Indiana Baseball Association's Hall of Fame in 2009.

**Also, in 2005, Bishop Dwenger wins the girls state soccer title on penalty kicks over Zionsville.**

The Saints won their first of two-straight titles by beating Zionsville 2-1 on penalty kicks after a potential game-winning goal in overtime was waved off. A Zionsville player had booted the ball from midfield, but none of the officials could confirm the ball crossed the goal line before time expired.

After a lengthy discussion, the Saints dominated in the shootout as Dakota Helms, Blair Sorg and Lisa Underwood scored. Ironically, the Saints had defeated Homestead 3-2 in the regional after Sorg scored a last-second goal to force overtime. They also beat Carroll in a shootout in the sectional.

The Saints finished the season 21-3-1.

## October 30

**In 1988, Brandon Robinson of Heritage becomes the first Indiana high school running back to reach 7,000 yards during a career.**

During a sectional game against Eastbrook, Robinson rushed for 282 yards, two touchdowns, caught a 38-yard touchdown pass and returned a punt 60 yards for a score in the Patriots' 54-19 win. He entered the game needing 165 yards to break the state record of 6,895 yards set six years ago by Alex Smith of Franklin County. He needed 134 yards to pass Brett Law of Sheridan for second place. He passed both on a 94-yard touchdown run in the second quarter.

Robinson's career ended two weeks later. During a 35-6 loss to Jimtown in the regional, Robinson ran 25 times for 118 yards, and his last play as a high school football player was catching a touchdown pass.

He finished with a state-record 7,303 career rushing yards, gained 10,452 career all-purpose yards and was runner-up in the Mr. Football voting. He ran the ball 993 times and also caught 96 passes during his high school career. His senior season ended with 2,732 yards rushing, a state-best 210.1 yards per game average.

Robinson continued his college career at Purdue as a walk-on and later came back to Heritage as an assistant coach.

His career rushing record lasted two seasons as Otis Shannon of Indianapolis Cathedral topped it in 2000 when he finished with 7,560 yards. Nick Zachery of Sheridan also passed Robinson with 7,331 yards in 2008.

Harding's Rod Smith came the closest among Allen County runners to catching Robinson with 6,685 career yards when his career was completed in 2009. New Haven's Cory Jacquay finished with 6,318 career yards in 2001.

**Also, in 1984, an exhibition soccer match between the Chicago Sting and Minnesota Strikers draws only 1,368 fans to Memorial Coliseum.**

**October 31**

**In 1986, the Fort Wayne Flames beat the Toledo Pride 3-0 in their first game ever.**

A crowd of 3,625 showed up to watch the hometown team hold their opponents to a rare shutout.

The Flame played in the American Indoor Soccer Association, and team officials were hoping for a crowd of more than 6,000 for their first game. The first coach was Cliff Brown, and Pete Mahlock was the first general manager. The team was founded by Bob Britt, Fred Mathews, Jr., James Speed and Bill Fahlsing.

The AISA included teams in Canton, Chicago, Columbus, Hershey, Kalamazoo, Louisville, Memphis and Milwaukee.

Sold for its fast-paced, high-scoring style of play, the game was scoreless at halftime thanks to the goalkeepers, including Warren Lipka for the Flames who made nine of his 13 saves in the first two quarters.

Ed Puskarich scored the first goal in Fort Wayne's indoor soccer history on an assist from Lenny Armuth after his initial shot hit the post. Then Bobby Poursanidis and Ken Killingsworth scored in the fourth quarter. The Flames launched 23 shots.

The team continued to draw well, finishing fourth in the league in attendance with 2,269 fans per game, and finished with a 13-29 record. Brown was replaced five games in by Tony Alioto.

# NOVEMBER

## November 1

**In 1997, Canterbury's boys soccer team wins the state title after finishing second the season before.**

The first thing coach Greg Mauch did at the beginning of the season was make the Cavaliers watch a video of the 1996 state championship match that they lost to North Central 6-1. Ouch.

"It wasn't meant to be mean," Mauch said. "We just decided that was where we were starting from, and we wanted to improve from there. Whether reaching the championship game or getting waxed 6-1, one or the other has instilled a little bit of fire in these guys. They don't want to remember the 6-1 the rest of their life."

The Cavaliers beat Homestead 2-1 to win the sectional and then Concordia 4-0 to take the regional. Canterbury crushed Argos 2-0 and Warsaw 5-0 to earn another trip back to the state finals. The Cavaliers beat No. 3 Washington 4-1 to set up another state championship match, this time against Carmel, a team Canterbury had tied 0-0 during the regular season.

Canterbury controlled play for the first 25 minutes, but Carmel's Chris Tuleja had a perfect pass to Matt Glasser for the Greyhounds' first goal 16 minutes in. About nine minutes later, Nathaniel Shoaff tied it by blasting the ball into the upper-right corner of the net from about 35 yards out. With 28:40 remaining in the match, Dan Limburg, on a restart, passed to Luke Carpenter for the game-winning goal.

"No one can ever take this memory away from you," Mauch told his players. "You've done something wonderful. Say thank you to your teammates, all of your teammates, because now, you're the state champs."

Canterbury came back to win state titles in 1998, 2001, 2010 and 2011 while also finishing second in 2002.

## November 2

**Also, in 1960, Everett Scott dies in Parkview Hospital.**

Besides setting a Major League Baseball record with 1,307 consecutive games played, the Bluffton native had many other highlights during his career.

He played in five World Series - with Boston in 1915, 1916 and 1918, and in 1922 and 1923 with New York. He was a starter on four teams that won the World Series.

During the first game of the 1916 series, he saved the game for the Red Sox against the Brooklyn Dodgers. With the bases loaded in the ninth inning and the Dodgers threatening, Scott snagged Jake Daubert's line drive and threw him out from deep in the hole to preserve the victory.

The Red Sox beat the Chicago Cubs for the 1918 title – the last World Series victory the Red Sox have had - with Scott driving in the game-winning run in the third game. Scott set a World Series record by handling 36 chances in the six-game series without an error. He also set the record for a five-game series in 1922 with the Yankees by successfully handling all 29 chances.

He set the record for fewest strikeouts by a Yankees hitter in a season with 13, which Yogi Berra broke with 12 in 1959.

Besides playing with the Red Sox and Yankees, Scott played with the Cincinnati Reds, Chicago White Sox and Washington Senators. His big-league career ended in 1926, but he continued to play in the minors until 1929.During his 13-year major-league career, Scott had a .249 average with 1,455 hits.

After he retired, Scott moved to Fort Wayne to manage a pair of bowling alleys. He was also an excellent bowler.

Scott was inducted into the Fort Wayne Oldtimers Baseball Association Hall of Fame in 1962.

**Also, in 2007, a pair of South Side greats, Ralph Hamilton and De Dee Nathan, are inducted into the Indiana Athletics Hall of Fame.**

**Also, in 1963, the Komets display orange, black and white as their official colors for the first time.**

**Also, in 1952, the Pistons draw 5,683 fans for their first regular-season game in Memorial Coliseum.**

## November 3

**In 1974, the Fort Wayne Hoosiers basketball team begins play at home before 2,973 fans.**

The 1970s were a wild time in sports as pro leagues were popping up all over. There have always been more basketball players than teams in Indiana, but there haven't always been enough fans. That's what the International Basketball Association found out in 1974-75.

The Fort Wayne Hoosiers joined teams from Calumet, South Bend and Elkhart in the North Division, while Anderson and Lafayette played with teams from Dayton and Hamilton, Ohio, in the South Division. The league was the idea of Dayton attorney Richard Duncan.

This minor league was all about offense as usually the winning team scored at least 120 points. The Hoosiers made their home debut with a 132-105 win over the South Bend Bison before 2,873 fans. Steve Platt scored 47 points and Dick Harris 37 to pace Fort Wayne. Platt shot 39 times and Harris 31. Bill Smith added 17 points, Roy Charleswood 11 and Steve Heiniger 10.

Platt would end up leading the IBA in scoring at 34.1 per game, but the league never attracted as many fans as hoped and folded after one season.

The Hoosiers were run by colorful former News-Sentinel sportswriter and Pistons executive Phil Olofson who had become a promoter. Later, he became general manager of Memorial Coliseum before he died in 2008.

**Also, in 2010, former Pistons great Leo Luken shoots his age or better on a golf course for the 800th time. He was 92 at the time.**

**November 4**

**In 1948, Herm Schaefer makes his NBA debut and later helps the Minneapolis Lakers win the league's first playoff title.**

Everywhere he played, Herm Schaefer was a winner.

Schaefer played basketball at Central High School from 1935 to 1937 where he was a teammate of Paul "Curly" Armstrong. Both continued their careers at Indiana University, where Schaefer lettered from 1939 to 1941. During the 1939-1940 season, Schaefer and Armstrong helped IU win its first national championship, beating Kansas 60-42. Schaefer was IU's leading scorer in the tournament.

After being an All-American at IU in 1941, Schaefer was signed by the Fort Wayne Pistons as a player-coach at age 22. He averaged 8.6 points per game as a rookie. Schaefer played four years with the Pistons.

Schaefer's career was interrupted after his first two seasons by a call-up into the Navy.

He returned in 1945-46 to score 1.5 points per game, but was in full form in 1946-47 when he averaged 8.2 points per game for the Indianapolis Kautskys.

But Schaefer's pro career began to thrive when he joined the Minneapolis Lakers in 1947. He averaged 10.4 points per game in 1948-49, helping the Lakers to the Basketball Association of America championship.

In 1949-50, he worked primarily as a setup man for George Mikan and Jim Polland, and the Lakers won the first National Basketball Association title.

"I guess you'd call him a point guard today, but back then he was just a guard who brought the ball up and called the plays," Mikan wrote of Schaefer in his autobiography. "Herm played with his head – he was a smart player."

Schaefer died in Indianapolis on March 20, 1980, at age 61.

## November 5

**In 1927, North Side and South Side begin their football rivalry, one of the longest rivalries in the state.**

The rivalry has lasted 85 years, but it's not the longest-continuous rivalry in the state because the teams did not play in 1991 and 1992 because of the Summit Athletic Conference's rotating schedule. The Redskins lead the series 50-38-2 and that still doesn't add up to 85 because the teams played two times a year in 1943, 1944 and 1945 because of World War II and in 2004, 2005 and 2012 when they also met in the sectional.

For the first eight years, the series seemed a mismatch as North Side didn't win any of the games, at best managing a 6-6 tie in 1929. (The only other tie in the series came in 1948.)

Starting in 1937, North Side went on a 7-0 streak to tie the series 8-8-1. The series stayed close after that, being deadlocked at 25-25-2 after North Side won 22-20 in 1975. The Redskins pulled away in the late 1970s and 1980s to win 11 of 14 to take a 36-28-2 series lead.

South Side's worst whipping of the Redskins was 46-0 in 2002 and North Side's worst defeat of the Archers was 51-19 in 1955. Each team has also won 10 shutouts in the series.

In 1950, the Totem Pole was awarded to the regular-season winner for the first time with North Side taking it home after a 19-0 victory. Chain of medallions attached to the totem pole honoring winner began in 1995 (red with tomahawk for Redskins; green with arrow for Archers).

North Side leads the series 50-38-2 heading into the 2013 season after winning six of the last seven games.

**Also, in 1988, the All-American Girls Professional Baseball League was recognized by the Baseball Hall of Fame.**

Former Fort Wayne Daisy star Dottie Collins pulled back the curtain on the display for the 555 players whose names are listed on the display.

**Also, in 1994, Lia Oberstar and Leslie Place finish their senior seasons with a combined 10 state swimming titles.**

**November 6**

**In 1998, the IPFW women's volleyball team beats Lewis 3-0 to extend its home winning streak to 45 matches.**

Before it was ended after 46 matches on Nov. 13, 1998, the streak ranked third all-time on the NCAA Division II record list behind New Haven with 109 straight (from 1992-97) and Northern Michigan with 66 (1992-96). IPFW lost to Quincy in five games after starting middle hitter Rachel Brown tore her anterior cruciate ligament in a first-round match.

The last time IPFW lost at home was Oct. 7, 1995 to Northern Kentucky with the rally score going to 15-13 in the fifth game. What's amazing is that before starting the streak, IPFW had lost 10 of its previous 19 home matches.

IPFW has annually had strong teams, at that time winning the Great Lakes Valley Conference title eight times in 14 seasons. IPFW had won 20 or more matches seven of its last 10 years, and set an NCAA record at the end of that season with its 17th consecutive winning season.

That team finished with a 27-8 record as Laura Douglas and Tami Isch were named to the all-conference team, and Tim Heffron was named the conference coach of the year.

## November 7

**In 2009, Saint Francis loses its remarkable 56-game home winning streak to St. Xavier.**

It's ridiculous and amazing how dominant the Saint Francis football team was during the decade from 2000 to 2010.

A week after Daniel Carter became the all-time leading rusher in St. Francis history, he went down with a pulled hamstring on the eighth play of the game and so did the Cougars, losing 36-24. Despite that, the Cougars led 24-22 after a Rhys Barnhart field goal, but St. Xavier came back to score twice in the last two minutes of the game.

It was the first loss at Bishop D'Arcy Stadium since a 27-20 setback to Trine on Nov. 3, 2001, which also ended a 15-game home winning streak. A week later, Nov. 10, 2001, the Cougars started a 54-game regular-season winning streak that included both home and road games. That string ended Sept. 29, 2007 with a 30-20 loss at Ohio Dominican.

A 23-16 loss the following week to Taylor ended the Cougars' string of 10 consecutive years advancing to the NAIA playoffs.

**Also, in 1981, Harding's Kristi Walker wins the first girls cross country state title.**

Walker was the first great female distance runner in IHSAA-sponsored events, often beating the boys she was competing against. She won the 1,600 meters track state championship in 1980 and 1981 and won three state cross country titles. She won the first two girls state "invitational" titles in 1979 and 1980 and the first sanctioned cross country state title in 1981.

**November 8**

**In 1991, the Fort Wayne Fury make their CBA debut.**

With more than 2,700 season-ticket holders, a group of 15 owners, coach Gerald Oliver and players Travis Williams, Dan Palombizio, Lyndon Jones, Warren Bradley, Anthony Corbitt, Tony Karasek, Mark Peterson, Marvin Taylor, Carl Thomas, Clinton Smith and Victor Wells, the Fury couldn't wait to get started. Fort Wayne's seven-year attempt to land a Continental Basketball Association team was finally coming to fruition.

And 8,373 Fort Wayne fans showed up to see what it was like.

The only bad part was that the Columbus Horizon won the game 99-89. Still, it was a solid start to the Fury franchise.

Fort Wayne led 72-71 going into the fourth quarter, but Columbus guard Byron Dinkins scored 16 of his 23 points in the fourth quarter to help the Horizon pull away.

After arriving at 3:30 p.m., Smith scored 21 points, grabbed six rebounds and passed four assists. Bradley grabbed 13 rebounds and Jones scored 10 points with six assists and five steals.

The team finished 21-35, going 18-10 at home, and set a CBA record for attendance with an average of 5,844 fans. There were 26 players who wore the Fury uniform the first season.

**Also, in 1981, Mike Augustyniak rushes for 40 yards on 11 carries and catches three passes for 33 yards to help the New York Jets beat the Baltimore Colts 41-14.**

## November 9

**The Northeast Indiana Baseball Association inducts Ford Frick, Dave Switzer and Don Sherman into its hall of fame.**

The group has a long and interesting history, according to local sports historian and NEIBA Secretary Don Graham. A loose-knit group of former players gathered during the 1940s and in 1946 or 1947 started hosting and annual oldtimers game to benefit amateur baseball. In 1953, the formation of a local Hot Steve League of America was announced. Eventually the group was revamped and named the Fort Wayne Oldtimers Baseball Association.

At the groups Oct. 16, 1961 meeting, co-chairman Red Carrington and Elmer Wagner announced the formation of the Fort Wayne Baseball Hall of Fame with Lou Holterman and James "Hub" Hart being the first inductees. The nine-man Hall of Fame committee included Robert Parker, Ben Tenny, Robert Reed, Carl Hornberger, Jack Gassert, Paul "Gunnar" Elliott, Orley Blauvelt, Carrington and Wagner.

The group continued to operate until going on hiatus in 1992. A new group resurfaced in 1998, and in 2003 changed its name to the Northeast Indiana Baseball Association.

In 2002, the Dean Kruse Foundation's American Heritage Village invited the organization to house its long-sought museum and hall of fame at the facility in Auburn.

Among the famous former baseball personnel who have been inducted include Ned Garver, Ford Frick, Bubbles Hargrave, Carl Erskine, Pinky Hargrave, Red Braden, Everett Scott, Bill Wambsganss, Max Carey, Bruce Miller, Steve Hargan. Eric Wedge, Max Carey and 11 former Fort Wayne Daisies.

**Also, in 2002, the renovated Memorial Coliseum is rededicated before the Komets play Quad City.**

**Also, in 2012, NBC Voice of Hockey Mike Emrick joins his mentor Bob Chase and Robbie Irons in calling a Komets' game.**

**November 10**

**In 1991, Snider's girls volleyball team ends Muncie Burris's state-record 119-match winning streak.**

There have been two dominating programs in Indiana high school sports, Carmel in swimming and Muncie Burris in volleyball. Besides having a 119-match winning streak going, Muncie Burris was 40-0, and had lost only two sets all season.

One of those set losses was to Snider, and the Panthers were confident they could end the streak. Behind the serving of Kelly Harris and the blocking and hitting of Tiffany Gooden and Heather Cox, the Panthers crushed the Owls 15-5, 15-6.

Panthers coach Tom Beerman had his team prepared with detailed scouting reports and expert mental planning.

"There was no doubt that we were going to do it," Harris told The News-Sentinel's Monica Denney. "We were just so intense. It was just total intensity. I can't describe it... We knew where every player was every time. We just did everything perfect.'

Other key players on the team included Molly Dunderman, Heather Teagarden, Melissa Hartman and Terra Garoutte.

"'We passed great, and we knew everything we were going to do. We had their whole lineup in our minds. We knew every one of their players," Dunderman said. "After the (first) game, we knew we had it. We knew nothing was going to go wrong."

A week later, the Panthers pounded Martinsville and Mishawaka to earn their second state title and a top 10 national ranking from USA Today.

**Also, in 1987, IPFW's women's volleyball team beats Ball State for the first time, 3-2.**

This is likely IPFW's best Division II volleyball team as it finished 29-7, earned a top 10 national ranking and reached the second round of the NCAA Tournament. Some of the stars where Julie Hefty, Judy Yagodinski, Shari Hanna, Lisa Zehr, Joni Smith and Laura Pierson. Yagodinski, Hefty, Smith and Zehr have all been inducted into the IPFW Hall of Fame.

## November 11

**In 1950, Central Catholic beats Gary Edison 53-0 to clinch the city's second mythical state football championship.**

Fort Wayne may not have ever seen a team as this one as the Irish out-scored their opponents 368-37, and the starting defense gave up only two touchdowns all season. Because there was no playoff system, Central Catholic was named state champions by the United Press International and by the Litkenhous Poll.

The Irish shut out five opponents and only allowed two scores in a game once, in a 46-12 win over South Side. Tailback Phil Erhman scored 79 points as the city's top five scorers and seven of the top 20 played for Central Catholic.

Ehrman was a first-team all-state selection, and lineman John Becker made the second team. Denny Hatfield and Acy Chandler joined Ehrman and Becker on the first-team all-city squad, and Raleigh Myers, Herman Kroemer, Bob Kakle, Don Rushin, Dick Schuler, Bob Brown and Tony Martone all made the second team.

The Irish joined the 1940 North Side squad as the only state champions from Fort Wayne before the playoff system started in 1973.

The team was coached by Fordy Anderson.

The squad had a perfect combination of size and speed. The players up front averaged more than 200 pounds, which was rare for the day, and Ehrman, Brown, Chandler and Martone all had sprinters' speed.

Almost half of the seniors and a dozen players in all on the 1950 team went on to play college football.

**Also, in 1990, the IPFW women's volleyball team wins its fifth GLVC title in seven years.**

**November 12**

**In 1998, Rapper Master P makes the Fury and plays in eight games.**

Percy Miller, a 6-foot-4 guard really was a high school All-American who suffered a knee injury that appeared to end his college career before it even started. He played one year with the University of Houston as a walk-on who earned a scholarship, but he wasn't the same player. His agent knew Fury coach Keith Smart from their days in Baton Rouge, La., and Miller held his own on the court with the other players in the Fury's training camp.

Forbes magazine pegged Miller as the 10th-highest paid entertainer in the world, taking in $56.5 million during 1997.

"I've been loving basketball all my life," Miller told The News-Sentinel's Nate Trela. "High school player. College player. I've been there, and I've done everything else, so now it's time to get back to what I love to do."

After signing a contract for $1,000 per week, Miller played eight games with the Fury, averaging 1.9 points and 1.6 rebounds, scoring seven points and passing three assists and committing 25 fouls in 65 minutes.

Miller left the Fury in January to direct a movie.

He later played in the International Basketball League and played five exhibition games with the Toronto Raptors in 1999, averaging 2.6 points in 4.6 minutes.

**Also, in 1987, Snider beats Mishawaka to win Fort Wayne's first girls state volleyball title.**

## November 13

**In 1986, the Indiana basketball team scrimmages at Memorial Coliseum before a sellout crowd.**

This was a strange night for everyone involved. First, IU coach Bob Knight asked the crowd of 9,800 to give the officials a hand. Then he had the Hoosiers practice a 2-3 and then a 3-2 zone, staying away from his characteristic man-to-man defense. After the game, Knight even asked for more questions when someone suggested the press conference be cut off.

"This is my day to be nice to the press," he said.

Uh, huh.

On the court, Steve Alford, Rick Calloway, Keith Smart, Daryl Thomas and Dean Garrett showed hints of what they would become later that season as they led the Hoosiers to their fifth NCAA title. This was the first public display for junior college transfers Smart and Garrett.

The scrimmage was broken down into a pair of 20-minute games. Garrett scored 18 points with 11 rebounds and six blocks. Joe Hillman also scored 10 points and passed five assists.

"Garrett, where we are now, has come a lot further than I expected him," Knight told The News-Sentinel's Steve Warden. "He's caught on to what we're doing. He has good instincts about playing, particularly at the defensive end. Offensively, there are some things he has to learn. He doesn't get as involved in the offense as he has to, but he's really made some good strides."

As for the zone...

"We played some zone, and how effective we are in it, I don't know. Even if we don't play it, spending time on it has got to help us from an offensive standpoint. We always did pretty good against zones, but it ought to help us a bit more whether we use it in a game or not."

It certainly did, as the Hoosiers beat Syracuse and its match-up zone 74-73 for the national title.

**Also, in 1998, Brandon Robinson's Heritage career ends with 7,303 yards rushing.**

**Also, in 2003, IPFW's men's basketball team loses an exhibition to the Harlem Globetrotters 89-57.**

Terry Collins scored 25 points and David Simon 14 as the Mastodons were flogged by a group of former NBA players in front of 4,158 fans. The Globetrotters had already beaten Michigan State and defending national champion Syracuse earlier in the tour.

## November 14

**In 2007, Eric Wedge is named the American League Manager of the Year.**

The Northrop graduate became the first Cleveland manager to win the American League award after leading the Indians to tie Boston for the best record in baseball. At 39, he also became the third-youngest man to win the honor. Wedge received 19 of the 28 first-place votes and got 116 points in balloting by the Baseball Writers' Association of America.

Cleveland made its first playoff appearance since 2001, beating the New York Yankees in four games during the division series of the playoffs before losing to the Red Sox in Game 7 of the AL championship series. The Indians took over first place in the Central Division for good on Aug. 15 and achieved a Major League-best 31-13 to finish the season. Cleveland finished 96-66.

The Indians went 68-94, 80-82 and 93-69 in Wedge's first three years as manager before falling to 78-84 in 2006. After going 96-66 in 2007, the Indians went 81-81 in 2008 and 65-97 in 2009.

Wedge was fired after the 2009 season and became manager of the Seattle Mariners on Oct. 18, 2010, guiding them to a 67-95 mark in 2011. Seattle was 75-87 in his second season.

**Also, in, 1990, IU scrimmages at the coliseum for the last time.**

This was the sixth consecutive sell-out for the Hoosiers in Fort Wayne. Jay Edwards scored 35 points and Lyndon Jones 19 in their freshmen debut.

**Also, in 1987, Snider wins the city's first state volleyball title.**

The Panthers beat Mishawaka 15-6, 15-13 behind the play of Donna and Bonnie Gill, Kim Kumfer, Leslie Johnson Dawn Sterba, Jenny Herman and Keli Allison.

## November 15

**In 1970, K&K Insurance driver Bobby Isaac finishes seventh in the American 500 to clinch the NASCAR Grand National Series season championship.**

Today, this would be remarkable news, a locally affiliated driver wining the Sprint Cup championship, but in 1970 very few Fort Wayne fans followed NASCAR. K&K Insurance was named for Nord and Theodora Krauskopf and became the leading provider of specialty insurance programs for sports, leisure and entertainment risks. The company was founded in 1952 at 3015 Bowser Ave., the Krauskopf's home.

Besides selling insurance to race tracks, Nord Krauskopf decided to run a NASCAR team in 1966 with a five-year plan to win the championship, thus the car number was 71.

With Gordon Johncock driving, the team struggled through the first two seasons, but because so many NASCAR races were held on short tracks he decided to hire short-track specialist Bobby Isaac to drive. Isaacs won three races in 1968 and finished second in the points standings. He won 17 races in 1969 to finish sixth.

In 1970, Isaac switched from a Dodge Charger for the short tracks and a Dodge Daytona for the super-speedways. Isaac and James Hylton traded the points lead until Isaac put together a streak of 13 races with top-6 finishes to blast past everyone. Isaac clinched the title with one race to go on the schedule, finishing 22 points ahead of Bobby Allison for the closest margin in NASCAR's then-22 year history.

After having such drivers as Buddy Baker, Bobby Unser, Neil Bonnett, Dave Marcis, Bobby Allison and Johncock, K&K left the NASCAR circuit in 1977.

**Also, in 1940, North Side beats South Bend Riley 46-0 to clinch the city's first mythical state football championship.**

Coming off 9-1 and 7-1 records, the Redskins allowed only 18 points and scored 265. Their closest game was a 13-6 win over Central to avenge the previous season's only loss. Bob Cowan scored 155 points in eight games to set a state record. The Redskins were coached by Bob Nulf and the backfield included Mike Bojinoff and Bob Young.

**November 16**

**In 2001, Cory Jacquay's New Haven senior season ends with a state-record 3,366 rushing yards.**

Jacquay still holds the state record followed by Otis Shannon of Indianapolis Cathedral who rushed for 3,252 yards in 1999. Jacquay finished with 6,318 career rushing yards before continuing his career at Saint Francis.

Maybe his best game of the season came in the regional against NorthWood. Jacquay finished with 303 yards on 48 carries, at one point carrying 10 times in 12 plays to carry the Bulldogs 61 yards down the field for the game-winning touchdown inside the last two minutes.

"We couldn't bring him down at all," NorthWood coach Jesse Fink said. "I knew he was going to get the ball, but we couldn't stop him. They ran the same play three times in a row and we couldn't bring him down."

The Bulldogs' season ended the next week against Andrean in the semistate, but not before Jacquay also finished his season with 128 solo tackles, 57 assists and 14 tackles for loss as a linebacker. Despite those amazing numbers, Jacquay finished only third in the Mr. Football voting behind winner James Banks of Ben Davis and runner-up Jake Schiff of Evansville Mater Dei.

**Also, in 1991, Snider's girls win a second state volleyball title.**

After ending Muncie Burris's 119-match winning streak 15-5, 15-6 in the Wes-Del Semistate, the Panthers crushed Martinsville in the state semifinals and then Jasper 15-11, 15-2 in the championship match. Tiffany Gooden and Kelly Harris earned first-team all-state honors and Heather Teagarden and Molly Dunderman honorable mention for Tom Beerman's team.

Melissa Hartman, Terra Garoutte, Susie Sterba and Heather Cox were also stars on the squad that finished 40-1. The team's only loss came against Muncie Burris 15-9, 3-15, 15-11 at the Burris Invitational at Ball State in September when the Owls broke the state record with their 90th consecutive victory.

**Also, in 2001, IPFW loses to Morehead State 82-71 in its first NCAA Division I men's basketball game.**

## November 17

**In 1996, Lamar Smith rushes for 148 yards on 33 carries as the Seattle Seahawks beat the Detroit Lions.**

When Lamar Smith was at South Side High School, lots of people told him he was too short or too slow or too something to make it as a professional football fullback. Smith eventually made it to the NFL, but after a roundabout route.

After high school, he attended Northeast Oklahoma A & M Junior College and then the University of Houston on scholarship for his final two years.

Despite academic problems in his first season and shoulder problems in his second at Houston, Smith rushed for 1,262 yards and 11 touchdowns on only 207 attempts during the midst of the Cougars' run-and-shoot offensive display. He rushed for 845 yards as a junior, averaging 7.6 yards per carry, which led the nation. The highlight of his college career came as a senior against Michigan when he rushed for 120 yards and scored three touchdowns.

The Seattle Seahawks made him their third-round pick in the 1994 NFL draft. During a four-year career in Seattle, Smith's production was limited by a broken leg in 1997 and a back injury that knocked him out for the season in 1994. The back injury was the result of an auto accident that left teammate Mike Frier paralyzed. Because Smith was driving, he agreed to pay Frier $4 million.

Smith started his second season with the New Orleans Saints in 1999 after starting nine games in 1998.

The two best years of Smith's career were with Miami in 2000 and 2001 when he rushed for 1,139 and 968 yards. His career-best regular-season game came Dec. 30 in the playoffs against Indianapolis when he rushed a league-record 40 times for 209 yards and two touchdowns.

His career ended in 2003 with 4,853 rushing yards and 38 touchdowns on 1,322 carries. He also caught 159 passes for 1,255 yards and seven touchdowns.

## November 18

**In 1973, Indiana's men's basketball team holds its second Fort Wayne scrimmage.**

The Hoosiers surprised everyone at the end of the 1972-73 season by going 22-6 to win the Big 10 title and advancing as far as the Final Four where they ran into John Wooden's UCLA dynasty in the semifinals. Big 10 Most Valuable Player Steve Downing and John Ritter both graduated, but a strong class of newcomers included Scott May, Bob Wilkerson and Kent Benson.

Maybe there was a little disappointment as only 2,236 fans showed up at Memorial Coliseum on a Sunday afternoon. The white squad crushed the red 124-85.

After sitting out the year before because of poor grades, May showed what he could do by making 19 of 29 shots from the field and scoring 39 points. Green, a junior that season, scored 36. John Laskowski scored 25, Tom Abernathy 23 and Benson 21. Benson, a freshman at the time, had been Indiana's Mr. Basketball the year before while playing for New Castle.

On the strength of three returning starters, the Hoosiers were ranked among the top five teams in the country at the time and were playing without starting guard Quinn Buckner who was still with the IU football team. Jim Crews was the other starting guard. Crews scored 14 in the scrimmage.

The Hoosiers went on to finish the season 23-5, but lost a playoff game with Michigan for the Big Ten's NCAA Tournament berth. Indiana beat USC for the Collegiate Commissioners Association Tournament title.

**Also, in 1997, Keith Smart takes over as coach of the Fort Wayne Fury.**

## November 19

**In 1983, Bishop Dwenger wins the area's first football tournament state title.**

When the IHSAA started its football state tournament in 1974, it took a while for a Fort Wayne team to win the title. Bishop Dwenger lost to Carmel in 1978 and Snider lost to Carmel in 1981, the same year Woodlan was edged by Hamilton Southeastern.

The breakthrough finally came in 1983 as Bishop Dwenger finished 14-0, beating New Haven, Mississinewa, South Bend St. Joseph's and Indianapolis Roncalli to win the Class 3A state championship. The title game was decided 22-21.

The Saints' defense had eight shutouts that season and gave up more than 10 points in a game only three times.

**Also in 1974, Purdue and Walter Jordan and Eugene Parker come to town for their first Fort Wayne scrimmage.**

There were only 2,644 fans in attendance for the first Purdue men's basketball scrimmage in Fort Wayne, but the day was also noteworthy because it was the beginning of their Boilermaker careers for Summit City natives Parker and Jordan. Jordan scored 21 points to lead the Gold over the White 96-79 despite 11 points from Parker.

Parker had led Fort Wayne in scoring the year before at Concordia, and Jordan has led Northrop to a state title. Jordan hit his first six shots in the game, and Parker his first four as they alternated baskets early on.

Bruce Parkinson scored 20 points and Gerald Thomas 18 for the Gold. John Garrett scored 22 and freshman Wayne Walls scored 12 points for the White.

The News-Sentinel's Bud Gallmeier coached the Gold team, and the Journal Gazette's Carl Wiegman coached the white team.

**Also, in 1972, Indiana men's basketball plays its first scrimmage in Fort Wayne.**

## November 20

**In 2004, the JAM Fantasy Sports flag football team wins the national championship.**

The story started in 1998 when former Little League coach, Alois Johnson was looking for something to do on weekends. While on vacation, he found a flag football league in San Diego, and within two years, the college director at ITT and his wife Janel had turned Fort Wayne's JAM Fantasy Sports League into the nation's second-largest flag football organization with more than 40 teams and 500 players.

The league developed enough that one of the teams played in consecutive national championship games in Orlando, Fla. Corey Nelson (Carroll), Michael Starks (Concordia), Remound Wright (Bishop Dwenger) and Nick Myers (East Noble) were the cornerstones of that team who also became future high school stars. Most started playing at age 7.

In the 2003 finale in Orlando, Fla., Fort Wayne lost in overtime to Oakland. The other team members were Daryl Flowers (Northrop), Lamont Langford (South Side), Jake Kindig (North Side), Dustin Hall (South Side), Alex McKinstry (North Side) and Michael Richmond (North Side).

The next year, Fort Wayne returned to Orlando to blitz San Diego 26-6 for the championship. That team included Jonathan Harrison (Bishop Dwenger), T.J. Pruitt (Northrop), Bryson Scott (Northrop), Bryce Urschel (Concordia) and Corey Tom (Carroll).

The team was coached by Steve Hampton and assisted by Tim Harrison and Michael Starks Sr. Remound Wright II also coached in the league. Hampton was head coach in part because he didn't have a son on the team.

`That was the first place I learned teamwork," Michael Starks Jr. said. "We had a great group of kids who were committed to coming out and working hard every day. That's where my work ethic started. You really have to depend on your teammates and trust in them. I look back on it now and realize how fortunate I was to play with all those guys."

**Also, in 1962, the Montreal Canadiens beat the Komets 4-1 before 4,630 fans.**

**Also, in 1998, Homestead beats Penn to advance to the state title game.**

**November 21**

**In 1979 college coaches Digger Phelps from Notre Dame, Lee Rose from Purdue, Joe B. Hall from Kentucky and Eldon Miller from Ohio State watch Harding and Bishop Dwenger play boys basketball.**

The season was just starting, but this was a huge game for Fort Wayne basketball as it set the tone for the quality of the entire season.

Behind Mr. Basketball candidate Jim Master, the Hawks were ranked No. 1 in the preseason polls, and the Saints also had high expectations behind the play of 6-7 center Greg Eifert. Harding also had players like Brian Miles, Brian Hyde and Reggie Bryant, while the Saints countered with Casey Newell, Marty Secrest and Craig Cagnet.

Harding won the game 77-65 before a standing-room-only crowd of 3,200 as Master scored 34 points, hitting 14 of 20 shots from all over the floor. Miles grabbed 13 rebounds and Hyde 10.

"They're gonna be tough to beat with Master," Bishop Dwenger coach Bob Herber told The News-Sentinel's Kerry Hubartt. "We ran a diamond on him and double-teamed him and he still scored 34."

Newell scored 20 and Cagnet 18 for the Saints, as Harding's defense stifled Eifert into six of 17 shooting and 16 points after he picked up three fouls in the first quarter.

"Our kids did a good job of fronting him," Harding coach Harlan Frick said. "What a workhorse! How he gets up and down the floor for a man of 220 pounds!"

**Also, in 1953, Hilliard Gates starts work at WKJG;**

## November 22

**In 1950, the Pistons beat the Minneapolis Lakers 19-18 in the game that forced the NBA to adopt the shot clock.**

Thanks to one game, Fort Wayne's influence over the NBA will last forever.

The Fort Wayne Pistons helped push the NBA into the shot-clock era by showing how slow a game could be when they traveled to play the Minneapolis Lakers. The Pistons had never beaten the Lakers in Minneapolis (in seven tries), where the home team had won 29 consecutive games. Pistons coach Murray Mendenhall told his team before the game he wanted them to hold onto the ball.

"We didn't care," Pistons guard Boag Johnson said. "We knew it would be difficult to beat them up there. He said, `Look, they're zoning and playing under the basket. We'll just hold the ball.'"

The Lakers' front line featured a Hall of Fame trio. George Mikan was 6-feet-10 and the best player of his era, flanked by 6-foot-7 Vern Mikkelson and 6-foot-5 Jim Pollard. Minneapolis was in the midst of winning five NBA titles in six years. The Pistons' tallest players were the 6-foot-9 Larry Foust and 6-foot-6 Jack Kerris.

The stall plan worked, as the Pistons held the ball for as long as three minutes at a time and led 8-7 after the first quarter. Fort Wayne trailed only 13-11 at halftime. The Pistons stayed with the strategy and trailed 17-16 after three quarters..

A free throw by Foust tied the game 17-17 with 6:10 remaining, but Pollard hit a free throw a few seconds later to give the Lakers the lead. Then Minneapolis tried to stall in the final minute, but the Pistons hustled and forced a turnover.

Fred Schaus threw Foust the ball as he was coming toward the sideline away from Mikan and the basket. Foust flipped up a hook shot. The ball hit the backboard and bounced in. As the crowd of 7,021 went nuts, the Pistons raced to the locker room.

The shot clock was first used during the 1954-55 season.

**Also, in 1986 Rod Woodson plays both ways and dominates in an Old Oaken Bucket win over Indiana.**

Playing both offense and defense in his final college game, Woodson made 10 tackles and forced a fumble on defense and rushed 15 times for 93 yards and caught three passes for 67 yards on offense. It was the only time he played offense during his college career.

## November 23

**Also, in 2012, Bishop Luers wins its fourth consecutive Class 2A state football title.**

This was a strange season for many reasons for the Knights. They started off losing to Snider 10-7 on a last-second play, and then barely beat Northrop 21-17. A 20-3 loss at Toledo Whitmer and a forfeit against Wayne because of using an ineligible player meant Bishop Luers was 2-3. Coach Matt Lindsay was also fired after 26 years as head coach, a 229-99 record and nine state titles.

Former coach Steve Keefer was named as Lindsay's replacement, and he changed the team's offensive style, preferring to use a deep field of running backs to smash the ball down the field. The Knights won three of their final four regular-season games, and then kept on rolling.

Bishop Luers won its three sectional games easily before winning tough road games at Tipton and at Andrean for the regional and semistate titles.

Then the Knights raced to a 28-0 lead in the state title game before holding on to beat Indianapolis Ritter 40-28. Bishop Luers put the game away with 63- and 80-yard scoring drives in the fourth quarter. Jay Ion Smith rushed for 150 yards and three touchdowns on 21 carries.

The win gave the Knights four consecutive state titles to match Warren Central in 5A from 2003 to 2006 and Lafayette Central Catholic in Class 1A from 2009 to 2012.

**Also, in 1978, long-time News-Sentinel sports editor Ben Tenny passes away.**

**Also, in 2007, the Mad Ants bring pro basketball back to the city.**

**Also, in 1990, Bishop Dwenger beats New Palestine 56-14 for its second state title.**

**Also, in 2001, Bishop Luers gets revenge on Evansville Mater Dei.**

**November 24**

**In 1983, Roosevelt Barnes returns an interception 70 yards to help the Detroit Lions beat the Pittsburgh Steelers.**

About a decade before Deion Sanders thought of being a two-sport star, Fort Wayne's Roosevelt Barnes was a three-sport star. After playing basketball for four years and baseball for one season at Purdue University, Barnes decided to stay a fifth year and play on the football team as a linebacker and defensive back.

"When I got out of high school, I never thought I'd play football again," Barnes said in 1984. "It's something I never dreamed would happen."

Barnes was good enough that he started for the Boilermakers, making 32 tackles, and was drafted in the 10th round by the Detroit Lions. He played four years with the Lions on special teams, twice being voted the most valuable special teams player. His best season came in 1983 when he had 35 tackles, two interceptions and a fumble recovery.

In 1986, he was traded to the Indianapolis Colts but was cut during training camp. Eventually, Barnes returned to Fort Wayne to become a sports agent.

Barnes' athletic career thrived in Fort Wayne. At Wayne High School, Barnes dominated in football, basketball and baseball, becoming the first athlete to earn All-Summit Athletic Conference honors in three sports. As a senior in 1976-77, he scored 116 points on the football field and 444 on the basketball court as a guard and forward. He finished his high school basketball career with 1,300 points, 439 assists and a scholarship to Purdue.

Primarily as a backup guard, Barnes helped the Boilermakers to the NCAA Final Four in 1980, and to the NIT Final Four in 1979 and 1981. He also played baseball for one season at Purdue.

**Also, in 1989, Fred Moore rushes for 261 yards as Bishop Luers beats Tri-West 24-22 for the Class 2A state title.**

Moore was trying for the game-winning touchdown when he was knocked out of bounds at the 1-yard line with one second remaining. Tim Wilson came on to kick the game-winning 18-yard field goal.

**Also, in 2006, Harding beats Southridge 20-7 for the Class 2A state title.**

The Hawks' defense gave up only 48 points in six playoff games and held Southridge to 126 total yards.

## November 25

**In 1978, Leo's Mike Augustyniak rushes 23 times for 135 yards to help Purdue beat Indiana 20-7.**

Mike Augustyniak was having a wonderful senior season at Leo High School in 1974 when he snapped an ankle in his sixth game. Though Augustyniak had already rushed for 1,030 yards and had a 100-yard dash time of 10.1, no college offered the 6-foot-1, 195-pound fullback a scholarship.

So he walked on at Purdue University and, in 1977, earned a scholarship after rushing for 76 yards on 16 carries in the annual spring game. Used primarily as a blocking back, Augustyniak rushed for 308 yards as a junior and 295 as a senior.

Despite his low numbers, Augustyniak always did well against Indiana University. As a junior, he rushed for 135 yards on 23 carries in a 20-7 Purdue victory in 1978, and for 76 yards on 20 carries in a 37-21 Purdue win in 1979. Before deciding on Purdue, Augustyniak had visited IU but had been turned away.

Augustyniak's professional career might have ended after he was cut by the New Orleans Saints in 1980, but he bulked up to 226 pounds and tried out for the New York Jets in 1981. He fought his way into the starting lineup and rushed for 339 yards that season. He came back with 178 yards in 1982, starting seven games. He also played in three playoff games that season, rushing for 28 yards.

The 1983 season with the Jets turned out to be his last. Augustyniak rushed only 18 times for 50 yards. He was moved to second-string fullback behind Dwayne Crutchfield.

Augustyniak suffered an injured leg during preseason 1984 and his career ended.

He finished with 567 yards and seven touchdowns on 153 attempts. He also caught 52 passes for 404 yards and one touchdown.

**Also, in 1995, Wayne beats Franklin County 28-8 to win the Class 4A state title.**

After rallying through three playoff games to reach the state final, the Generals dominated defensively. Quavis Tate rushed for 138 yards in the title game and 2,212 for the season.

## November 26

**In 1990, Lloy Ball and Chris Beerman are named to Volleyball Month's all-time list of Fab 50 high school boys volleyball players.**

While Ball was just starting his career at IPFW, Beerman, a North Side graduate, had finished his All-American career at Ball State in 1990. The two-time All-American led the Cardinals to three NCAA Tournament appearances and became Ball State's all-time career leader in kills before becoming a successful women's college coach at Pittsburgh and Kentucky.

**Also, in 1992, the Komets lose to the San Diego Gulls 5-2.**

The Gulls were off to a 20-0-1 start and were on their way to building the best record in minor league hockey history. San Diego had 2,462 games' and more than 400 goals' worth of NHL experience. This score could have been worse, but goaltender Pokey Reddick stopped five San Diego breakaways.

"There's obviously a division in the league from teams that are .500 or over and teams that are below," Komets coach Al Sims said. "There's just not enough teams that are capable of beating that hockey team. I think we are, but we have to play a perfect game. And so does anybody else to beat them. San Diego is going to be up for those games. They only have to be up for three or four teams in the league, and they knew we were hot, and they were ready for us."

Things went a little differently at the end of the season.

**Also, in 1996, long-time North Side boys basketball coach By Hey is named into the Indiana Basketball Hall of Fame.**

After coaching for three years at Concordia, where he won 38 games, Hey moved to North Side where he won 419 games over the next 31 seasons. The highlights were a 1965 trip to the state finals and a 1978 team that was ranked No. 1 heading into the postseason on the strength of a 25-game winning streak that came to an end in the semistate.

## November 27

**In 1992, Snider wins its first state football championship, beating Ben Davis 24-21.**

After a snap by Ryan Hawley and a hold by Brad Rust, Seth Zeigel kicked a game-winning 34-yard field goal with 37 seconds left to give the No. 5-ranked Panthers the win. Courtney Davis gained 198 of Snider's 235 yards rushing, including a 68-yard romp during the third quarter to give the Panthers a 21-14 lead. Davis finished with 2,448 yards rushing for the season.

This was the first city title for a Fort Wayne public school since the IHSAA started its playoff format in 1973 after the Panthers finished second in 1981 and 1986. The Panthers were the only undefeated team in the state at 14-0.

**Also, in 2009, Bishop Luers beats Monrovia 24-17 for the Class 2A state title.**

The Knights finished the regular season 4-5, but that was just practice for the state title game as they trailed No. 2 Monrovia 17-7 in the second quarter before rallying. Quarterback James Knapke completed 10 of 16 passes for 140 yards. Besides finishing with 19 tackles on defense, Steve Kiermaier also scored the game-winning touchdown.

The Bulldogs took a 17-14 lead into the locker room at halftime. In the final two quarters, Monrovia would get the ball only two times, and both times the Knights dug deep and made huge stops on fourth downs to seal their victory.

**November 28**

**In 1890 an indoor baseball doubleheader is held at the Princess Rink.**

The Princess Rink was a roller skating facility at the corner of Fulton and West Main streets downtown. The games, played before about 200 fans, featured the Fort Wayne Baseball Club and the Princess Club. FWBC won the first game 10-6, and the Princess Club won the second 14-12 in 10 innings.

According to the Northeast Indiana Baseball Association newsletter Line Drives, the event had never been tried in Fort Wayne before but was popular in some bigger cites by this time. While the rules were much the same as those for the outdoor game, some modifications were necessary, such as 27 feet between bases and no stealing while the ball is being pitched. The ball was approximately 12 inches in circumference and very soft. The bat was about 30 inches long and shaped like a broom handle. All of this resulted in a much smaller field of play with each game being played in less than one hour, hence two games instead of just one.

**Also, in 2003, Harding loses a wild shootout for the Class 2A state title to Tri-West 41-36.**

The Hawks trailed 14-0, 21-6, 28-14, 35-21 and 41-29, but Harding senior Reggie Smith completed 15 of 29 passes for 235 yards and three touchdowns and rushed for 55 yards and another touchdown. He was matched by Tri-West quarterback T.J. Siple who completed 21 of 35 passes for 323 yards and four touchdowns.

Smith's favorite targets were slotback Dwight Coleman, who caught six passes for 54 yards and two touchdowns, and Selwyn Lymon who caught five balls for 136 yards and a touchdown. One of the Harding highlights in the game was Smith throwing an 86-yard touchdown pass to Lymon in the third quarter.

The key play of the game came with 3:04 left. After Harding's defense had finally stopped Tri-West on downs to force a punt, the Hawks were called for a roughing-the-punter penalty that gave the Bruins a crucial first down.

Tri-West finished 14-1 and Harding 13-2.

## November 29

**In 1986, Vaughn Dunbar rushes for 250 yards, but Snider loses the state football title to Carmel 20-17.**

As a junior at Snider High School in 1985, the tailback rushed for 1,646 yards and 20 touchdowns. During his senior season, he rushed for 2,568 yards and 40 touchdowns, including 252 on 28 carries against Carmel in the state championship game.

He compiled those numbers despite playing only about two quarters a game because the Panthers were so dominant.

The Panthers were a spectacular team that season. Dwenger and North Side came closest to Snider during that regular season, losing 42-14 and 56-10. Snider throttled Penn 28-0 in the sectional finals.

Led by linebacker Brock Rohrbacher, the Panthers held nine of 13 opponents to seven points or less. Among the other stars on the team were Solomon Emerson and Herb Jackson. The Panthers might have won the state title if quarterback Tim Haffner hadn't gotten hurt in the regional.

**Also, in 1985, Bishop Luers wins its first state title, beating Lawrenceberg 25-7.**

Since then, the Knights have won 11 state titles and played in 15 state championship games, compiling 17 regional and 21 sectional titles on their way to a .857 tournament winning percentage (114-19).

**Also, in 1986, DeKalb beats Franklin Central 28-7 to win the Class 4A state title.**

Rick Endsley scored three touchdowns, gaining 194 yards on 41 carries, as the Barons pounded out a state-record 24 first downs, rushing the ball 68 times. The offensive line included Scott Sproat, Mike Schmidt, Lance Timberlin, Danny McAnnich, Jim Wilson, Brian Raub and Denny West.

DeKalb gained only 16 yards passing on six attempts. Franklin Central ran only 32 offensive plays.

**November 30**

**In 1991, Bishop Dwenger wins two football championships in a row by beating Cathedral 34-27.**

After going 14-0 the year before and beating New Palestine 56-14 in the Class 3A state title game, the Saints came back with a 13-1 record and another state title. The Saints' only loss was to Wayne 25-14 which led to a three-way tie for the Summit Athletic Conference title with North Side, Bishop Dwenger and Wayne.

The game was tied at 27 with 1:34 remaining when Bishop Dwenger's Dan Murray grabbed a fumble out of mid-air and scored the game-winning touchdown.

The Saints were loaded with quality players like quarterback Chris Dittoe, receiver Euell Wilson, linebacker Kevin Carretta, lineman Jason Fabini, Chad Gagnet, Marc Tholen and Scott Jansen and running backs Brian Baker and Steve Martin.

The 1990 Saints gave up only 5.9 points per game, shutting out five opponents and holding four others to a touchdown or less. The 1991 Saints averaged 26 points per game. Baker rushed for 1,929 yards and 28 touchdowns in 1990, and Martin for 1,875 yards and 34 touchdowns in 1991.

**Also, in 1994, Lloyd Daniels scores a record 49 points, but the Fury lose to Omaha 137-136 in overtime.**

Daniels' 49 points broke Jay Edwards' Fury record of 45 set against Quad City in 1992. The 136 points is also a team record, breaking the old mark of 131 set against Columbus in 1993.

# DECEMBER

## December 1

**In 1956, Verle Wright competes in the shooting competition at the Melbourne Olympics.**

Verle Wright Jr. might be the only man who joined the Navy and later represented the Army as a marksman. After graduating from North Side High School in 1946, he enlisted in the Navy and used to shoot at Point Magu, Calif.

"I was out in the middle of nowhere, and there wasn't anything to do," he said. "I bought a .22 pistol and read a book on pistol shooting. I shot every evening for several months."

After leaving the Navy in 1948, Wright returned to Fort Wayne and shot in the Fort Wayne Rifle and Pistol Revolver Association, and then attended Indiana University. To help make ends meet, he joined the Army Reserves. He later was with the Army Reserves in Fort Wayne when he attracted attention as the state rifle champion.

Wright won the Army Reserves championship in 1953. In 1956, the Army told Wright it was forming a marksmanship unit, but he would have to go on active duty to participate. Later that year he made the Olympic team.

"I didn't do real well," he said. "I was inexperienced and finished about 12th or 13th. I was shooting against the Europeans, and I didn't have a lot of experience shooting outdoors. I also had a new rifle and didn't know how well it shot."

He rarely missed again, winning eight gold, seven silver and four bronze medals in international competitions. In 1958 he won the world championship in the 300-meter kneeling free rifle event with a world-record score. Wright retired from the Army in 1976 as major.

**Also, in 1941, the Zollner Pistons play their first National Basketball League game, beating the Chicago Bruins 48-44.**

**Also, in 1954, Larry Foust sets a Pistons' record by scoring 37 points against the Rochester Royals.**

**December 2**

**In 2006, St. Francis beats St. Xavier 42-20 to win a third straight trip to NAIA title game.**

Freshman running back Daniel Carter took the Cougars' second snap on offense 80 yards for a touchdown and St. Francis never trailed after that. The Cougars stopped St. Xavier on a fourth-and-1 at the 1-yard line on the next drive to take momentum away completely. St. Francis led 28-0 at halftime.

Quarterback Eric Hooks completed 14 of 16 passes for 245 yards and three touchdowns, and Carter finished with 194 yards on nine carriers, including another touchdown run of 81 yards in the second quarter. Bo Thompson caught six passes for 134 yards, including a 67-yard touchdown.

This was also the season when linebacker Brian Kurtz was named the NAIA Defensive Player of the Year after leading the Cougars in tackles.

Unfortunately, the No. 1-ranked Cougars stumbled in the NAIA championship game, losing to No. 2 Sioux Falls 23-19 at Savannah, Tenn. St. Francis finished the season 13-1.

The score was tied 13-13 at halftime, but Sioux Falls scored the first 10 points of the second half. The Cougars dominated the game with 349 offensive yards to 214, but gave up four turnovers, including three fumbles.

**Also, in 1967, South Side graduate Willie Long scores 55 points for the New Mexico freshman team in a 104-87 win over New Mexico Military Institute.**

## December 3

**In 2009, the IPFW women's volleyball team loses to Illinois in their first NCAA Division I Tournament experience.**

Throughout the history of the IPFW athletic department, volleyball has always been the strength of the program, and that continued with the first Division I NCAA Tournament berth. The Volleydons went 20-11 and won the Summit League title by winning at North Dakota State. That ended the Bison's 20-match home winning streak.

IPFW was led by Summit League Tournament Most Valuable Player Rebekah Roehm, a senior middle hitter. Stephanie Lamberti and Maya Schlindwein were also top offensive players thanks to help from setters Megan Steenhuysen and Shannon Reuter. Jamie Schwartz was one of the top liberos in the conference as well. Defensively, the middles Taryn Parker and Alli Hook and Tessa McGill was also one of the leaders in digs.

Despite all that depth, the Volleydons faced an Illinois team which was ranked No. 5 nationally and was playing at home. Illinois, 25-5, hit 43 kills on the night to win 25-15-, 25-16, 25-12 in Champaign. Michelle Bartsch belted a match-high 15 kills to lead the Illini.

The match served to further build Kelley Hartley Hutton's program. In 15 years, she has won more than 300 matches and led IPFW back to the NCAA Tournament in 2012.

**Also, in 1949, Emil Sitko plays his last game for Notre Dame against Southern Methodist.**

The Irish were tied 20-20 late in the fourth quarter. SMU kicked off as Sitko walked up to freshman quarterback Bob Williams. "OK, for a kid you're a good quarterback, but you give me the ball every play until I tell you different."

Sitko carried the ball every play until Notre Dame reached the SMU 3-yard line and then said, "It's OK now, kid, give it to someone else." Williams did, Notre Dame scored and won 27-20.

## December 4

**In 1984, Emil Sitko and Johnny Bright are inducted into the College Football Hall of Fame.**

Fort Wayne's Emil "Red" Sitko might be the finest offensive player who played during Notre Dame football's finest era.

The Central High School graduate rushed for 2,226 yards and 26 touchdowns from 1946 to 1949 as the Fighting Irish went 8-0-1, 9-0, 9-0-1 and 10-0 to win three national championships. Sitko was a first-team All-American in 1948 and 1949, and he won the Walter Camp Award as the nation's top player in 1949 when he rushed for 712 yards and nine touchdowns on 120 carries. He finished eighth in that season's Heisman Trophy voting behind teammate Leon Hart.

Sitko, who led Notre Dame in rushing all four years, measured only 5-foot-8 and 175 pounds but averaged 6.1 yards per carry.

"Emil wasn't very big as football players go - even for those days," Irish coach Frank Leahy once said. "But he was the fastest starting back I ever coached."

It's possible Bright had even better numbers.

As a sophomore, the Central graduate rushed for 975 yards and threw for 975 yards to lead the nation in total offense as Drake went 6-2-1. He followed that with 1,232 yards rushing and 1,168 yards passing as a junior to set an NCAA record for total offense. The next season he was leading the nation in rushing and total offense with 821 and 1,349 yards, respectively, when he suffered a season-altering injury on a late hit in a game at Oklahoma A&M (now Oklahoma State) during the 1951 season.

Bright came back to play one more game two weeks later, rushing for 204 yards against Great Lakes Naval Station, to finish with more than 6,000 yards in career total offense. He averaged 236 yards per game and scored 384 points in 25 games. As a senior he earned 70 percent of the yards Drake gained and scored 70 percent of the Bulldogs' points – despite missing three games. He finished fifth in the Heisman Trophy voting.

**Also, in 1963, Tom and Dick VanArsdale lead Indiana to a 108-102 win over Notre Dame.**

## December 5

**In 1986, Jody Beerman breaks the NCAA record for consecutive free throws.**

Beerman hit nine straight to lead Central Michigan past Bradley 91-88 in overtime. She eventually pushed the record to 57 straight with her first three free throws the next night before finally missing. Beerman's second streak started Feb. 19, 1986 and lasted 11 games. She led the nation in 1985-86 hitting 90.5 percent of her free throws.

During her career at Central Michigan, Beerman set school records for points in a season and in a career. During her senior season, she led the Mid-American Conference in scoring with 20.7 points and was also named academic all-American. When she finished, Beerman held five single-season and three career Chippewa records, including career assists.

Her free throw mark lasted until 2011 when Bowling Green's Lauren Prochaska made 70 consecutive shots.

**Also, in 1996, Bishop Dwenger graduate Lia Oberstar sets the U.S. record in the 200-meter backstroke.**

Oberstar broke the mark with a time of 2:07.88 seconds at the United States Open Swimming Championships in San Antonio.

"I've been looking forward to this meet for two months," Oberstar said. "I really wanted to break the American record. I can't believe that it all came together tonight."

Misty Hyman led for much of the race, but Oberstar made up ground in the last 50 meters.

After winning seven state championships at Bishop Dwenger, Oberstar continued her career at Southern Methodist where she won four NCAA titles and was named All-American 16 times. She was also held an American record as part of a 400 medley relay team.

**Also, in 1952, the Pistons softball and basketball squads become the first pro sports teams to have their own chartered place, a DC-3 dubbed The Flying Z.**

## December 6

**In 2012, Bishop Dwenger graduate Tyler Eifert wins the Mackey Award as the nation's top college tight end.**

After a spectacular senior season where he helped lead the Fighting Irish to the BCS Championship game, Eifert received the biggest award possible for a tight end. He finished with 44 catches for 624 yards and four touchdowns as a senior to improve his career totals to 134 receptions, 1,779 receiving yards and 11 touchdowns, which made him the all-time career leader in receptions and receiving yards by a Notre Dame tight end.

He had even better numbers during his junior season, catching 67 passes for 803 years and five touchdowns.

The John Mackey Award is given to the collegiate tight end who best exemplifies the play, sportsmanship, academics and community values of NFL Hall of Fame tight end John Mackey. The 2012 John Mackey Award recipient was determined by confidential balloting of the John Mackey Selection Committee.

Eifert was drafted by the Cincinnati Bengals with the 21st pick in the 2012 NFL draft.

**Also, in 2012, Bishop Luers' senior Jaylon Smith becomes the Fort Wayne area's first Mr. Football.**

The Notre Dame recruit was an all-state performer on both sides of the ball, finishing with 75 tackles, 20 tackles for loss and eight sacks as a linebacker and more than 1,200 yards rushing and 18 touchdowns as a running back. He also rushed for 150 yards and three touchdowns on 21 carries in the Class 2A state championship game, helping the Knights win their fourth title in a row.

Smith career totals included 6,625 yards rushing and 66 touchdowns while helping the Knights to a 48-11 (two of the losses being forfeits due to administrative errors) record in his four seasons.

Bishop Luers announced that Smith's No. 9 jersey with the Knights will be retired.

**Also, in 1995, East Noble's Brad Miller has his coming out party at Purdue with a big game against Oklahoma.**

## December 7

**In 1997, Nel Fettig wins her third NCAA soccer title with North Carolina.**

North Carolina shut out Connecticut 2-0 at UNC-Greensboro as Fettig served as the Tar Heels' team captain and was named NCAA Tournament Defensive Most Valuable Player.

Every summer as she was growing up, Nel Fettig spent as much time riding inside a car as outside it. The Bishop Luers High School student would travel around the country and even to Europe playing and practicing soccer, and she quickly became the most-dominating player on almost every field, either as an offensive force or a defensive presence.

In 1993 at age 17 she was the youngest player to compete in a U.S. Olympic Festival in San Antonio. That same year she became the youngest player ever on the United States' 20-and-younger women's national team.

When she wasn't playing soccer, Fettig was also a nationally ranked junior tennis player who could mix things up by switching from her left hand to using a right-hand serve without any loss of velocity. Sometimes she would switch hands during a short volley at the net to confuse opponents.

After leading Bishop Luers to three state high school Final Four soccer appearances and being named the National High School Player of the Year in 1994, Fettig chose national powerhouse North Carolina for college. The North Carolina coaches felt she could become soccer's version of Bobby Orr – the defensive player who keyed the offense.

The Tar Heels won three NCAA titles during Fettig's career, and she was twice named a first-team All-America defender. Twice she was named one of the 11 best defensive players in the country, and was also an Academic All-American.

Fettig played 102 games for North Carolina, scoring seven goals and 39 assists. She was a three-time All-American and was inducted into the Indiana Soccer Hall of Fame in 2008.

## December 8

**In 1985, Komets coach Robbie Laird puts himself into the lineup to fight Toledo's Chris McSorley.**

Robbie Laird had retired as a player the year before to become the Komets' coach, but when the team was hit hard by injuries, Laird activated himself on December 8, 1985. In a game against Toledo, Laird came off the bench to fight Toledo tough guy Chris McSorley during a 5-3 Fort Wayne loss.

Two days later, Laird was suspended by the IHL for one game. He played again December 12 against Flint, but then his three-game tryout contract expired and he needed to clear waivers before he could sign another contract.

Fearing the possibility of facing Laird as a player in the playoffs, Milwaukee General Manager Phil Wittliff claimed Laird, effectively ending his career.

"I was a little flattered, but mostly I was surprised," Laird said. "He must have been going off my past record and not my performance in those two games."

Laird played 577 games as a Komet, scoring 251 goals and 556 points while earning 1,298 penalty minutes. He also coached the team for four years, going 194-108-26.

He later became a long-time coach and scout in the Los Angeles Kings organization.

## December 9

**In 1997, plans are announced for the Lifetime Sports Academy.**

As part of its mandate to improve the area's quality of life through sports, the Fort Wayne Sports Corporation had been searching several years for an idea of how to become more involved in amateur youth athletics. Then during a meeting last summer, someone said they should try to teach every child how to play golf. That led to someone else suggesting adding tennis and swimming.

"These are sports you play for a lifetime," real estate developer Tom Jehl said. "Everybody's eyes lit up and said, `Let's go for it.' "

That's how the Lifetime Sports Academy was born, spearheaded by Public Safety Director Payne Brown, Parks Department Director of Leisure Activities Phil Bennett, Jerry Fox of The Journal Gazette and Jehl.

Because the members believed so strongly in the program, the Sports Corp. raised more than $200,000 and developed a partnership with the city government and the Fort Wayne Parks and Recreation Department. The parks department felt McMillen was being underused and would be the perfect location.

Through the program's first 16 years, more than 25,000 kids ages 8 to 18 have participated.

The academy got a huge boost in April 2003 with the completion of the Mad Anthony Threes, a nine-hole course built in part with funds donated by the Mad Anthonys Charity Classic for Children.

One of the best things about the program is that all the equipment is furnished, and there are even ways for children to earn a set of golf clubs. Golfers take lessons in hitting irons and woods, putting, chipping and pitching. Then they have to pass tests administered by the McMillen Park Golf Course staff before graduating. They receive a free set of clubs and are allowed to play the par 3 course for free anytime the course is open. The first year the course was open, nearly 300 children earned the right to play, and the course was used for nearly 2,500 rounds during its first two years.

**December 10**

**In 1960, Mike Emrick attends his first Fort Wayne Komets game.**

As he was growing up, Mike Emrick dreamed of becoming a baseball announcer until Dec. 10, 1960, when he attended his first hockey game, the Komets vs. the Muskegon Zephyrs. Emrick, then 14, and his brother Dan had watched hockey on TV through snowy reception because their home in La Fontaine (located just north of Marion) wasn't close enough to Indianapolis or Fort Wayne. They also listened to Bob Chase describe Fort Wayne games on WOWO, with Emrick jiggling the radio dial to give the signal a little extra strength.

After frequently bugging their parents to drive from La Fontaine to see a Komets game at Memorial Coliseum, the boys got their wish. Charles Emrick was a high school principal who also owned a music store.

A year after setting their all-time record for points and wins in a season, the Komets had lost four games in a row heading into the Muskegon game. The Zephyrs led 3-1 with 10 minutes left when Len Thornson scored to give the Komets a chance. Then Con Madigan tied it with 17 seconds remaining, skating backward around the rink to celebrate.

Neither team scored in overtime, but Emrick's highlight was watching Madigan fight Zephyrs' player-coach Moose Lallo with two seconds left. There was also organist Norm Carroll playing "Santa Claus is Coming to Town." Another favorite memory was watching Chase standing in the press box to lean over the WOWO banner and call the play.

Whenever possible, Emrick and his friends would drive up to be part of the Saturday night crowds. Eventually, he started taking along a tape recorder, sitting in the upper-deck corners to practice calling a game. Then he'd take the tape to Chase at WOWO, and they would talk about it.

Now Emrick is the best hockey broadcaster in the world, currently calling his 39th season of professional hockey, including 33 NHL seasons, 14 Stanley Cup Finals and six Olympics on his way to the Hockey Hall of Fame.

## December 11

**In 2004, Snider boys basketball takes on Lawrence North's duo of Greg Oden and Mike Conley at the coliseum.**

After finishing their work and their cleanup following Saturday's Snider-Lawrence North boys basketball game, the referees were leaving the Memorial Coliseum when one said, "That was fun, wasn't it?"

"We need more games like that," came the reply. "That was the way it ought to be."

A crowd of 4,654 watched the defending state champions pull away in the final minutes 71-61.

Oden finished with 15 points, five blocks and three assists, while running mate Conley stole the show with 21 points, 11 rebounds and seven assists.

Snider, which led 51-43 after three quarters, got 28 points and four assists from Ryan Sims, 15 points and four assists from Marques Johnson and 11 points from Ryan Hetrick. The Panthers proved they could play with anyone.

The Panthers were ranked No. 3 in the state and the Wildcats were No. 1 and were on their way to winning three straight Class 4A state titles.

Lawrence North also won the rematch with Snider in 2005, 89-45. Conley scored 26 and Brandon McDonald 20 as Oden sat out with an injury. Johnson led Snider with 14 points, eight rebounds and three assists and Hetrick scored 10.

## December 12

**In 1999, Phil Presser helps Indiana win another NCAA soccer championship.**

Though just a freshman, Presser played in 23 games that season to help the Hoosiers win their fifth national title.

Presser was a high school All-American and 1998 Indiana Player of the Year at Canterbury before going to Indiana where he was a four-year letter-winner at Indiana from 1999 to 2002 and helped the Hoosiers win a national championship as a freshman. A three-year starting midfielder and two-time All-Big Ten selection, Presser made three trips to the College Cup with the Hoosiers and helped IU to a 70-18-3 overall record during his career.

After starting for three years with the Hoosiers, he stayed in Bloomington as a graduate assistant, helping Indiana win the 2003 national title. Then he moved to Illinois-Chicago as an assistant coach for two years before coming back to Indiana for three years in 2006. He then spent three years as an assistant at Wisconsin before moving back to Indianapolis in 2013 to become director of the Indiana Fire Development Academy.

While at Canterbury, Presser was part of two state championship squads and a state runner-up team.

**Also, in 1999, Javon Witherspoon of Bishop Luers finishes second in the Mr. Football voting.**

Despite catching 68 passes for 1,128 yards and 12 touchdowns, Witherspoon lost to Indianapolis Arlington running back Derrick Ellis who rushed for 2,395 yards and 35 touchdowns.

## December 13

**In 2012, IPFW men's volleyball coach Arnie Ball is inducted into the AVCA Hall of Fame.**

When Arnie Ball started the IPFW men's volleyball program in 1979, everyone was mystified why he'd take on such a challenge. Even his family members wondered what he was doing.

A club program for two years before gaining varsity status, the team had to practice and play its matches at New Haven Junior High School or Harding High School because IPFW didn't have a gym. Ball started by converting basketball players into volleyball players until he could recruit volleyball players and turn them into All-Americans.

Along the way, he became one of only five men to win as many as 500 career matches, coached 15 All-Americans and led the Volleydons to six NCAA Tournament appearances. IPFW finished second in 2007 as Ball was named the ASICS/Volleyball Magazine Coach of the Year.

Early in his career, Ball also coached the IPFW women's team for eight years, winning four Great Lakes Valley Conference championships and posting a 231-102 career record.

He also coached United States teams in the Pan American Games and World University Games several times and won several medals coaching in the United States Olympic Festivals.

**Also in 1961, the Komets and Indianapolis Checkers combine for 227 penalty minutes during the third period.**

**Also, in 1958, South Side's Tom Bolyard sets the city scoring record with 43 points against Auburn.**

## December 14

**In 2003, Elmhurst's James Hardy sets a Fort Wayne record by scoring 57 points in a 100-97 overtime loss to Harding.**

Throughout the 2002-03 season, the focus was on Hardy's attempt to break the career city scoring mark held by Concordia's Tom Baack, but the Hardy didn't even know what the single-game scoring record was -- until he broke it.

Former Elmhurst star Steve Handy had scored 50 points against South Bend Washington on Dec. 21, 1968. Handy had broken the city record of 48 by South Side's Tom Bolyard set in 1959. Hardy also broke the Allen County record of 55 points set by Sammy Kreigh from Lafayette Central when he scored 51 points in 1963 against Union of Huntington.

This time, Hardy had 49 points at the end of regulation. While rallying the Trojans from a 10-point deficit at the end of the third quarter, Hardy scored 26 points in the fourth quarter. He scored another eight points in overtime, but the Trojans could not overcome Harding's balance. Brandon Foster led the Hawks with 33 points and Cody Thomas scored 26.

Ironically, Hardy's previous career-high in points had been 45 during his junior season – against South Bend Washington.

Hardy eventually eclipsed Baack's total of 1,623 and finished his high school career with 1,823 points. He didn't get to hold onto the record long, however, as Bishop Luers star Deshaun Thomas obliterated it in 2009 during his junior season and then extended it the next year.

**Also, in 2002, Joe Franke rescues the Komets' season as he beats the Elmira Jackals.**

Franke become the oldest player ever to play for the Komets, when he came off the bench to beat Elmira 4-3 in a shootout. He came into the game in the third period after Tom Lawson was called up and Pokey Reddick was injured. After dressing as an emergency back-up more than 30 times during his career, it was Franke's first actual game experience. The highlights were shown on ESPN, and now more than 20,000 people claim they were at the game even though the official attendance was 6,497.

Franke has the best winning percentage but worst goals against average of any goalie in Komets' history, not to mention the best T-shirt, "1-0 Joe."

## December 15

**In 1941, the Zollner Pistons sign Bobby McDermott, recognized as the best basketball player in the world.**

McDermott was voted the greatest basketball player of all time by coaches and managers in the National Basketball League in 1945. As the player-coach of the Fort Wayne Pistons, McDermott led the team to three straight National Basketball League championships in 1944-46.

McDermott's career ended in 1950, the year Collier's Magazine named him to the All-World team. He was killed in a Yonkers, N.Y., auto crash in 1963 at age 48, and was inducted into the Basketball Hall of Fame in 1988.

Widely acknowledged as the greatest two-hand set shot artist, McDermott joined the New York Celtics right out of high school. He played in Fort Wayne against the Pistons in 1940 and attracted the attention of Pistons owner Fred Zollner, who brought McDermott to Fort Wayne the next season.

McDermott led the Pistons in scoring for five straight years before he was traded during the 1947-48 season to the Chicago Gears.

**Also, in 2005, Northrop graduate Melissa Elmer celebrates being named a three-time all-American volleyball player at Nebraska.**

One of the best blockers in NCAA history, Elmer set Nebraska records for career blocks and block assists and became the first player in the country to lead the nation in back-to-back seasons in blocks. She's one of three players in Big 12 history to finish with more than 1,000 kills and 600 blocks in a career.

**December 16**

**In 2000, Northrop graduate Jenae Dowling wins the NCAA Women's Volleyball National Championship with Nebraska in a five-game win over Wisconsin.**

A co-captain in her last two years with the Cornhuskers, Dowling helped Nebraska win three Big 12 titles and the 2000 national title as a Libero. She was also a three-time academic all-conference honoree.

Amazingly, she walked on at Nebraska and played mostly as a serving and defensive specialist during her first three years as a Cornhusker. As a senior, she got more playing time and ranked among the team leaders with 203 digs.

Dowling was already committed to playing at NAIA school Cornerstone College, when a Nebraska coach visited Fort Wayne to recruit another Northrop standout, Melissa Elmer. After seeing Dowling play in a club practice, the Nebraska coach offered her a walk-on spot on the team and eventually a scholarship.

After graduating with a finance degree, Dowling served as an assistant coach at Kentucky for three years.

**December 17**

**In 1988, Angola's Mick Haley leads Texas to the NCAA women's volleyball title.**

Haley started his volleyball career at Ball State as a player under Don Shondell. Like his mentor, Haley became legendary as a coach. He led Kellogg Community College to two women's national junior college championships and the men's team to four. He moved to Texas in 1980 and guided the Longhorns to the AIAW national championship in 1981.

He built a 522-137 record in 17 years at Texas, including 150-10 in conference play, before leaving to take over the United States Women's National Team in 1997. That squad finished fourth at the 2000 Olympics in Sydney.

After the Olympics, Haley became took over the women's program at the University of Southern California. During his second season in Los Angeles, the Trojans won the NCAA Tournament and then repeated in 2003 with an undefeated season.

Haley won his 900th career match in 2012 and is 314-70 in 13 seasons at USC. His overall women's record is 1,087-258. His teams have won 17 conference titles.

**Also, in 2005, Concordia graduate Carolyn Farny wins the NCAA title with the Washington women's volleyball team.**

**Also, in 2005, St. Francis loses the national title game in a rematch to Carroll 27-10.**

**Also, in 1950, Dike Eddleman of Tri-Cities Blackhawks scores 48 points against the Zollner Pistons at North Side.**

**December 18**

**In 2004, St. Francis loses the NAIA football national title game 15-13 to Carroll.**

The game wasn't decided until Carroll's Matt Miller kicked a 32-yard field goal with 10 seconds left.

"We should have finished it," Saint Francis coach Kevin Donley said. "We had a phenomenal year, but you lose the national championship game, and it's so close... You feel like you should have won, and it takes time to recover. We will. We'll come right back. We'll be back here again."

The Cougars were 13-0 before losing the NAIA championship game. St. Francis was 25-2 over two seasons and both losses were to Carroll.

The powerful St. Francis offense was held to 268 yards in total offense, including 100 yards rushing after averaging 297 all season.

Quarterback Chris Bramell gave St. Francis a 13-12 lead with 1:13 to play on a 1-yard rush to complete a 17-play, 89-yard drive. Though he didn't have a time out remaining, that was too much time for Carroll quarterback Tyler Emmert to drive the Saints down the field. Emmert completed three of four passes for 49 yards and scrambled for another 11-yard gain to set up the field goal.

Because it was a first down, Carroll holder Zach Bumgarner spiked the ball for another chance after a bad snap. That gave Miller another chance on second down, and he drilled it.

Bramell completed 16 of 26 passes for 151 yards. The Cougars led 7-6 at halftime despite gaining only 82 yards.

Safety Jamie Holman led the Cougars' defense with 12 tackles.

Saint Francis had reached the title game by surviving a home game against Georgetown 12-7 in the national semifinals.

## December 19

**In 1894, future Major League Baseball Commissioner Ford Frick is born in Noble County's Wawaka.**

Best known for suggesting Roger Maris's 1961 home run record should be signified with an asterisk, Frick had a huge impact on Major League Baseball in many other areas.

After working as a teacher and later attending Fort Wayne's International Business College, Frick started working at the Journal Gazette as a police reporter and office boy. After graduating from DePauw University in 1915 and working as a journalist in New York, in 1934 he was elected president of the National League, and in 1951 he succeeded Happy Chandler as the third commissioner of baseball.

As president of the National League, Frick suggested a national baseball museum and hall of fame. He also stopped a planned protest by the St. Louis Cardinals against Jackie Robinson breaking the color barrier. Heading into the 1957 All-Star Game, he took on the Cincinnati fans who had flooded ballot boxes so much that eight Reds were named starters. Frick replaced two Cincinnati players and took the vote away from the fans for the rest of his term as commissioner.

Though he never publicly spoke about his reasons, Frick's most-lasting move was to separate Maris's record of 61 home runs over a 162-game schedule from Babe Ruth's record of 60 home runs in a 154-game schedule. While working as a sportswriter in New York, Frick had also served as Ruth's ghostwriter, and many suggested that showed bias.

Frick retired from baseball in 1965 and was elected into the National Baseball Hall of Fame in 1970. In 1978 the Ford C. Frick Award was instituted to honor baseball broadcasters for major contributions to the game. He died April 8, 1979 at age 83 in Bronxville, N.Y.

**Also, in 1967, Indiana basketball beats Notre Dame before 8,045 Memorial Coliseum fans.**

This was the last year the series was played in Fort Wayne because construction had been completed on Notre Dame's new Athletics and Convocation Center.

December

**December 20**

**In 1966, Indiana beats Notre Dame 94-91 before 4,039 Memorial Coliseum fans.**

After losing to the Hoosiers by 22 and 26 points in Fort Wayne the previous two seasons, Notre Dame coach Johnny Dee was hoping his 2-4 team could keep the score close. The Irish did that but might have done even a little better.

Bob Arnzen scored 38 points, but the Irish couldn't hold off a late Indiana rally. After IU's Vern Payne hit two free throws with 1:20 left to give the Hoosiers a 92-91 lead, Arnzen was fouled with 27 second remaining. He hit the first free throw but missed the second to leave Indiana on top.

Reserve Bill Russell hit two free throws in the final seconds to clinch the win for Indiana.

Payne and Berne-native Erv Inniger were the stars for Indiana, 4-2. With all three Indiana forwards sitting out because of foul trouble, the guards led the comeback as they combined for 30 points. Notre Dame led 87-79 with 3:59 remaining.

The key statistic was 22 turnovers for Notre Dame compared to 11 for Indiana.

Jack Johnson led Indiana with 18 points, and Russell added 16 off the bench.

Tom Caldwell came off the bench to score 23 for Notre Dame, and Dwight Murphy scored 13.

**December 21**

**In 1965, Indiana beats Notre Dame 107-81 before 10,003 fans.**

Fort Wayne was not a great place for Notre Dame to play in the 1960s. Because the Irish played in a 4,000-seat arena while the Athletics and Convocation Center was being built. Indiana was 7-1 against the Irish in Memorial Coliseum games, and Purdue was 2-1.

This game drew the most fans in the series, but the Hoosiers again dominated. Tom VanArsdale scored 21 points and twin brother Dick scored 11 to lead five Hoosiers in double figures.

Walt Sahm led the Irish with 13 points and 13 rebounds.

**Also, in 1968, Elmhurst's Steve Handy establishes a new city scoring record when he hits for 50 points against South Bend Washington.**

A 6-9 center, Handy had missed most of his sophomore and junior seasons because of injuries and illness. He broke the record of 48 set by South Side's Tom Bolyard in 1959. Handy made 21 of 31 field goals and eight of 12 free throws.

Elmhurst won the game 86-65 as Brett Able added 20 points.

**December 22**

**In 2004, Rod Woodson files his retirement papers with the NFL.**

When he was a sophomore at Snider High School, Rod Woodson quit the junior varsity football team.

"I believed that (if) you're not my parents, I don't need you yelling and screaming at me," Woodson said in 1999. "If you want me to do something, just tell me. That's the kind of attitude I had."

Eventually he was talked into going back out for the team by track coach Jim Gurnell, and, in an amazing twist of fate, Woodson became one of football's greatest players on the high school, college and pro levels.

Woodson dominated on both sides of the ball at Snider, leading the Panthers to the 1981 state title game as a junior. He also won four state titles as a track hurdler before moving on to play at Purdue, where he was an All-American in both football and track. He was named one of 100 greatest college football players of all time by College Football News in 2001

He reached his full potential in the NFL, where he played with the Pittsburgh Steelers, San Francisco 49ers, Baltimore Ravens and Oakland Raiders.

Woodson, 39, ended a 17-year NFL career that rivaled the best to ever play the game. He was the youngest member named to the NFL's 75th anniversary team in 1994, one of only five active players at the time. He was named to the Pro Bowl 11 times, the first player to be named at three different positions (kick returner, cornerback and safety). He won a Super Bowl title with Baltimore in 2001, only the fourth player to play in three Super Bowls with three different teams.

He holds the NFL records for interception returns for touchdowns and interception-return yardage and ranks third on the league's all-time interceptions list with 71.

Unfortunately, Woodson was unable to go out on his own terms. He was released by the Oakland Raiders in July 2004 after a knee injury limited him to 10 games in 2003.

**December 23**

**In 1956, Bill Russell makes his first appearance in Fort Wayne for the Celtics.**

Inspired by a crowd of 8,108, the Pistons won the game 95-87 as Russell played his second professional game.

The Pistons were led by 22 points from George Yardley, 17 from rookie Bill Thieben and 15 from Chuck Noble. The crowd broke the Pistons' regular-season mark of 7,900 set when Boston made a trip to Fort Wayne during the 1952-53 season.

The margin could have been a lot worse, but the Pistons made only 29 of 46 free throw attempts. The big difference was in the rebounding where Yardley led Fort Wayne with 14 and Mel Hutchins grabbed 12.

Russell played only 21 minutes, scoring five points on 2-of-8 shooting and grabbed eight rebounds. After he picked up his fifth foul in the third quarter, Celtics coach Red Auerbach decided to bench the rookie the rest of the game.

Bill Sharman led the Celtics with 26 points, making all 10 free throws, Jim Loscutoff scored 21 and Bob Cousy 13.

Boston actually led 82-77 with 5:40 left in the fourth quarter, but the Pistons scored the next 10 points.

There were almost a couple scraps during the game as Yardley and Cousy almost tangled in the third quarter after Sharman and Corky Devlin almost fought in the first half.

**December 24**

**In 1999, the Fort Wayne Fury beat the Connecticut Pride 116-109 before less than 900 fans.**

The Scrooge who had the idea of the Fort Wayne Fury and Connecticut Pride playing a game on Christmas Eve wasn't in attendance. He was probably home snuggling with his family. This was the only pro, college or high school game scheduled in the entire country that night.

The second-smallest crowd in the team's eight-year history witnessed the game. There were 3,217 tickets out but less than 900 fans in the seats. But those fans had a good time as the Fury made the most of the lousy scheduling by beating the first-place Pride 116-109.

"I thought we played hard," Fury coach Keith Smart said after thanking the crowd. "The guys had fun playing the game tonight. It was a really big game for us. We had enthusiasm, and it carried over and we had a good showing."

After telling Fury Vice President Scott Sproat earlier in the day he was going to score 30 points, Moochie Norris scored 30 but also ran a balanced offense. The Fury players continually drove to the basket, especially forward Antonio Lang who scored 29 points in his first game back after attending his grandmother's funeral in Alabama.

Before the game, the Fury added Lari Ketner to the roster to replace the released Darrin Hancock. Ketner scored 18 points, including 12 on dunks, and grabbed 11 rebounds.

He was needed in the middle because Yinka Dare was nowhere to be found. With the team's permission, Dare went home to Connecticut earlier in the week to handle some personal matters but was supposed to return Thursday.

Maybe even worse than playing on Christmas Eve, both teams had to hit the road to play on Christmas Day. The Fury played at Quad City and won 97-89.

## December 25

**In 1986, the Komets beat the Indianapolis Checkers 8-4 in their last Christmas Day game.**

The Komets used to play every year on Christmas, going 18-6-1, including 17-4-1 at home.

They stopped after 1986 when they pounded the first-place Checkers in front of 4,490 Memorial Coliseum fans.

Everyone wants to see a bench-clearing brawl for Christmas and the teams accommodated in the second period. Ejected for the Checkers were Brian Wells, Marc Magnutt, Byron Lomow and Harrold Schlamp. The Komets lost Mike Lekun, Bruce Shoebottom and Dale Baldwin. Indianapolis was called for 78 penalty minutes and Fort Wayne for 76.

It was a wild game all night. Fort Wayne led 3-0 after the first period on goals by Tony Camazolla, Lekun and Paul Pooley, but the Checkers rallied in the second on goals by George Gervais, Bob Lakso and Peter Laviolette.

The score was tied 4-4 before the Komets' Jim Burton scored with 1:41 left in the second period, and then Derek Ray scored with 1:01 left to give Fort Wayne a 6-4 lead. Ron Leef scored twice in the third period after missing the previous seven games with a knee injury.

The Komets went on to finish 48-26-9 and win the West Division behind 86 points from Steve Salvucci, 82 from Leef and 75 from Colin Chin.

**December 26**

**In 2012, James Blackmon Jr. scores 45 points to break the Summit Athletic Conference Tournament scoring record in a basketball game against Snider.**

After a poor-shooting first half, making only 2 of 10 shots, Blackmon got blistering hot in the second half.

"My dad (head coach James Blackmon) told me `That's your shot every time,'" Blackmon Jr. told The News-Sentinel's Jonathan Batuello. "I'll make those 90 percent of the time if I'm open. Just (needed) to get lower. I wasn't low on my shot (in the first half). I was standing straight up."

During the second half he did much better than 90 percent as Blackmon barely missed, scoring 40 points. He and brother Vijay scored all 21 of the Knights' points in the third quarter. Then in the fourth, Blackmon Jr. hit four three-pointers on top of multiple drives with an and-one attached. He broke former Bishop Luers teammate Deshaun Thomas' record of 43 points on an easy layup with under a minute to play.

After surviving the frantic second half, Snider won the game 101-87 as Devlyn Williams scored 16 of his 21 points during the last two quarters.

**Also, in 2012, the Mad Ants trade Walker Russell to Reno.**

Russell played with the NBA D-League team through its first six seasons, but the squad was off to a 3-10 start and needed to shake things up.

Russell, a 6-foot point guard, was one of the first Mad Ants and had an eventful and productive run with the franchise. He set a D-League record for assists in a season (508) in 2008-09, has led the team in scoring and assists at various times and in 2011-12 finally made it to the NBA at age 29. Russell played in 28 games in the second half of last season with the Detroit Pistons. He averaged 3.0 points and 2.1 assists per game while playing about 13 minutes per game. He scored a high of 15 points in a game against Atlanta and had six assists in a game against Milwaukee.

Russell was averaging 15.3 points and six assists per game this season with the Ants. Over six seasons and 143 Mad Ants games, Russell averaged 15.2 points and 8.1 assists per game.

**December 27**

**In 2003, No. 1 Lawrence North beats No. 2 Columbia City 56-55 in double overtime.**

The 2003 Indiana Hall of Fame Tournament in New Castle had an amazing field, especially for Columbia City. The Class 4A No. 2-ranked Eagles got the rare opportunity to play two No. 1-ranked teams in the same day.

During the afternoon semifinals, Columbia City played Class A No. 1 White River Valley. After training most of the first half and late in the third quarter, the Eagles rallied with a 29-8 run to win 55-48. Doug Sheckler led Columbia City with 14 points.

That set up a showdown against Class 4A No. 1 Lawrence North led by future NBA stars Greg Oden and Mike Conley. Both sophomores, Oden, a 7-foot center, would eventually earn Mr. Basketball honors and join point guard Conley for one year at Ohio State.

The deliberate-playing Eagles almost pulled off the upset, leading 38-34 going into the fourth quarter and by seven points with two minutes left in regulation before losing the heartbreaker.

Conley sank two free throws in the final minute to force the first overtime, and then Columbia City's Ryan Briggs scored 12 points for the Eagles and tipped in the basket to force the second overtime. Columbia City led 55-54 in the final moments, but Oden hit two free throws with eight seconds remaining to give the Wildcats the victory.

Eagles seniors Sheckler and Marcus Moore made the all-tournament team along with Conley and tournament Most Valuable Player Oden.

The teams met later that season in a rematch at the state finals, and this time Lawrence North showed its overall skill, taking a 19-2 first-quarter lead before winning 50-29 in the state championship game. Columbia City finished the season 25-4 and Lawrence North 29-2. Oden scored 13 points, grabbed 12 rebounds and blocked two shots in the championship game.

**Also, in 1975, the Summit Athletic Conference Holiday Tournament for basketball begins play.**

**December 28**

**In 2008, Jason Fabini plays the final game of his 11-year NFL career.**

When Jason Fabini joined the New York Jets in 1998, the rookie figured his personal streak of playing 44 straight games would end. Everyone knew how Jets coach Bill Parcells disliked playing rookies.

But Parcells loved his fourth-round draft pick, and he needed a new right tackle after incumbent offensive lineman David Williams was forced to retire with a back injury. Fabini became the Jets' first rookie starter at right tackle since Marvin Powell in 1977.

Except for a few injuries, the Bishop Dwenger graduate rarely came off the field, playing 152 games, including 129 starts, during his 11-year NFL career. He played eight with the Jets, one with Dallas and two with Washington before retiring in 2008.

One of the highlights of Fabini's career was being selected to the Jets' four-decade team by the fans in 2003.

From the time he was drafted, Fabini started 114 consecutive games for the Jets. The streak ended in 2005 when he suffered a torn pectoral muscle that knocked him out for the rest of the season.

"Being a couple years out, you do feel it," Fabini told The News-Sentinel's Reggie Hayes in 2011 when asked about the physical toll of playing football. "You don't realize it when you're playing. When you're playing, you'll do everything you can to get out on the field. People don't understand. Your job is really on the line every week. If you don't go out there and play, somebody else will and who knows if you'll ever get back in the lineup?"

## December 29

**In 1992, Scott Gruhl scores twice against San Diego to break the IHL's all-time goal-scoring record.**

Befitting the record, the final circumstances were almost as perfect as the play. Gruhl got to break the record at home before a sellout Memorial Coliseum crowd of 8,103, against the best team and the best goalie in the league as his family sat in the stands. Best of all, the goal was a slap shot and Gruhl said he got all of it.

After a face-off win by Colin Chin and a pass from teammate Jean-Marc Richard, Gruhl blasted a slap shot over the left shoulder of Gulls goaltender Rick Knickle with 2:37 left in the game. The goal broke the record held by former Komet and long-time Muskegon player Joe Kastelic.

Gruhl, who eventually finished his career with 663 minor league goals, held the record until Flint's Kevin Kerr beat it with his 664th on Jan. 7, 2005.

**Also, in 1964, the Boston Celtics get 40 points from Sam Jones to beat the Detroit Pistons 112-106 before 5,564 fans.**

Bill Russell scored 16 points and grabbed 30 rebounds for the world champion Celtics, and Dave DeBusschere scored 28 points and grabbed 20 rebounds for the Pistons.

**Also, in 1963, Jerry West scored 39 and Elgin Baylor 32 as the Los Angeles Lakers beat the Detroit Pistons 140-128 before 3,380 Memorial Coliseum fans.**

**December 30**

**In 2011, NASCAR star Tony Stewart wins again in the Memorial Coliseum Rumble series.**

There's a story why Tony Stewart keeps coming to Fort Wayne during most holiday seasons.

At 11:30 p.m. Dec. 26, 2004, Fort Wayne's Mike Fedorcak was lying in bed trying to forget about a midget race car's stubborn engine. It was the night before the annual Rumble in Fort Wayne at the Memorial Coliseum Expo Hall.

Then the phone rang. Who would call at 11:30 p.m.?

"Mike, I'm down here in Indianapolis playing poker with some buddies and I kind of want to buy your car," Tony Stewart said. "Is it for sale?"

Fedorcak had met Stewart around 1996, and in 2000 and 2001 Stewart ran unannounced in the Rumble in another of Fedorcak's cars, one called the "Munchkin."

Fedorcak had won races with the Munchkin all over the world, was the first man to win indoor races at the Memorial Coliseum before and after it was renovated. When tires showed up at his Yoder shot, that's how Fedorcak usually found out Stewart wanted to race in Fort Wayne.

"There are five of us here, and I bet these guys I could buy it before midnight," Stewart said, laughing. "Do you want to sell it?"

Because Stewart was a friend, Fedorcak offered it to him for $5,000 less than what he had been asking.

"You just helped me win $50 on this first bet," Stewart said. "We had another one going here where everybody wrote down what they think I'm going to pay for it. You just won another $50 for me because that was exactly what I said it would be."

It was midnight when they completed the deal, and Stewart asked if he could race the car the next day in Fort Wayne. Fedorcak got out of bed and started working. The car was ready to go by 9:30 a.m.

Stewart raced as "Mikey Fedorcak Jr." from "Gnawbone, Ind." The ruse ended when Stewart took his helmet off in the winner's circle.

## December 31

**In 1991, Vaughn Dunbar's brilliant football career at Indiana ends.**

Indiana crushed Baylor 24-0 at the Copper Bowl in Tucson, Ariz., as Dunbar finished with 106 yards on 28 carries and a touchdown to be named the game's most valuable player on offense. It was the first time since 1988 that Indiana had beaten a team with a winning record outside of Bloomington.

Dunbar finished the season with 1,805 yards, the most in a single season by an IU player and 11th best in the history of the NCAA. His career total for rushing yards is 3,029, third in IU history behind Anthony Thompson and Mike Harkrader, who both played four seasons to Dunbar's two. Dunbar ranks second among Big Ten rushers for a single season.

The Bears entered the game growling with a dominating defense that gave up only five touchdowns in its last 17 quarters of play. Opposing runners averaged just 2.9 yards per carry, but Dunbar gave his teammates confidence with some solid runs.

Hoosiers quarterback Trent Green completed 11 of 21 passes for 165 yards, Indiana gained 323 yards to Baylor's 269, rushing for 192 yards.

"You could tell they were really keying on old Vaughn," said IU Coach Bill Mallory. "That's all right. He's a great back and a great football player."

**Also, in 2010, the Komets beat Bloomington 5-1 as David Hukalo scores twice.**

The Komets are 37-14-6 all-time at home on New Year's Eve and have drawn more than 10,000 fans nine of the last 12s. They have gone 9-1-1 in their last 11 New Year's Eve games.

**Also, in 1950, Fred Schaus sets a Fort Wayne Pistons' record with 33 points against the Tri-Cities Blackhawks.**

# FUN FACTS

## MAJOR LEAGUE GAMES IN FORT WAYNE

### MLB exhibitions
July 27, 1920, Philadelphia Athletics vs. Lincoln Lifers. Athletics 9-2
August 18, 1920, New York Giants vs. Lincoln Lifers. Giants 3-1
September 1, 1920, Philadelphia Phillies vs. Lincoln Lifers. Phillies 13-4
June 29, 1921, Cincinnati Reds vs. Lincoln Lifers. Reds 5-1
Aug. 28, 1922, Philadelphia Phillies vs. Lincoln Lifers. Phillies 14-6
Aug. 16, 1926, New York Giants vs. Lincoln Lifers. Giants 5-3
May 6, 1927, New York Yankees vs. Lincoln Lifers. Yankees 5-3
July 30, 1931, Philadelphia Phillies vs. Pennsy AA. Pennsy 8-4
September 20, 1945, Cincinnati Reds vs. G.E. Club. Reds 9-2
July 8, 1946, Cincinnati Reds vs. G.E. Club. G.E. Club 7-6
June 25, 1947, Boston Braves vs. G.E. Club. Braves 11-5.
July 12, 1949, Chicago White Sox vs. G.E. Club. White Sox 3-2
July 11, 1951, Washington Senators vs. Midwestern Lifers. Lifers 1-0
August 28, 1952, St. Louis Browns vs. North American Vans. Browns 8-5
June 29, 1953, St. Louis Browns vs. North American Vans. Vans 7-4
August 17, 1953, Chicago White Sox vs. North American Vans. Vans 5-4
August 23, 1954, Philadelphia Phillies vs. North American Vans. Phillies 6-4.
May 5, 1994, Minnesota Twins vs. Wizards. Twins 8-4.
May 13, 1999, San Diego Padres vs. Wizards. Padres 6-4
April 30, 2001, San Diego Padres vs. Wizards. Padres 8-6
**(compiled by Don Graham)**

### NBA regular-season games (post-Fort Wayne Pistons)
February 9, 1959, Detroit Pistons 122, Cincinnati Royals 97
January 13, 1960, Detroit Pistons 114, New York Knicks 113
January 12, 1961, Detroit Pistons 124, Cincinnati Royals 112
March 10, 1961, Detroit Pistons 120, Philadelphia Warriors 103
November. 24, 1961 Detroit Pistons 142, St. Louis Hawks 135
December 26, 1961 Chicago Packers 108, Detroit Pistons 101
January 14, 1962, Detroit Pistons 118, Los Angeles Lakers 108
May 2, 1962, Cincinnati Royals 120, Detroit Pistons 112
December 9, 1962, Detroit Pistons 123, St. Louis Hawks 119
January 31, 1963, Los Angeles Lakers 127, Detroit Pistons 122
March 8, 1963, Detroit Pistons 131, San Francisco Warriors 123 OT
December 29, 1963, Los Angeles Lakers 140, Detroit Pistons 128
December 27, 1964, Boston Celtics 112, Detroit Pistons 106
February 11, 1965, Cincinnati Royals 130, Detroit Pistons 109
March 4, 1965, San Francisco Warriors 115, Detroit Pistons 110
December 30, 1965, Detroit Pistons 117, Los Angeles Lakers 114
January 27, 1966, Boston Celtics 131, Detroit Pistons 112
May 4, 1966, New York Knicks 121, Detroit Pistons 119
October 28, 1966, Detroit Pistons 129, Chicago Bulls 117
December 30, 1966, Philadelphia 76ers 137, Detroit Pistons 113

### NBA exhibition games
October 4, 1972, Detroit Pistons 138, Indiana Pacers 136 2OT
September 27, 1973, Detroit Pistons 121, Indiana Pacers 98
October 11, 1997, Indiana Pacers 104, Toronto Raptors 100
October 10, 2008, Indiana Pacers 102, Chicago Bulls 95

## National Hockey League exhibitions
February 18, 1957, Detroit Red Wings 11, IHL All-Stars 3
November 20, 1962, Montreal Canadiens 4, Komets 1
November 26, 1963, Montreal Canadiens 7, Komets 1
October 4, 1974, Detroit Red Wings 3, Indianapolis Racers 3

### Russian/Soviets vs. Komets
December 31, 1975, Spartak 7, Komets 4
December 7, 1989, Kiev Sokol 0, Komets 0
February 20, 1994, Komets 6, Russian Penguins 1
November 5, 1994, Komets 5, Soviet Wings 2

## Major college basketball games at Memorial Coliseum
March 10, 1953, NCAA Tournament regional: Notre Dame 72, Eastern Michigan 57; DePaul 74, Miami of Ohio 72
March 9, 1954, NCAA Tournament regional: Notre Dame 80, Loyola (La.) 70; Penn State 62, Toledo 50
January 10, 1958: Notre Dame 94, Valparaiso 69
December 20, 1960, Indiana 74, Notre Dame 69
January 2, 1962, Indiana 122, Notre Dame 95
February 19, 1962, Purdue 115, Notre Dame 62
January 2, 1963, Notre Dame 73, Indiana 70
January 21, 1963, Notre Dame 96, Purdue 86
December 4, 1963, Indiana 108, Notre Dame 102
January 21, 1964, Purdue 112, Notre Dame 103 2OT
December 21, 1964, Indiana 107, Notre Dame 81
December 21, 1965, Indiana 80, Notre Dame 58
December 20, 1966, Indiana 94, Notre Dame 90
December 19, 1967, Indiana 96, Notre Dame 91
March 23, 2004, NIT Tournament game: Notre Dame 77, St. Louis 66

## OLYMPICS
### Northeast Indiana Olympians
Bob Juday, Geneva, high jump, 1924
Dan Zehr, South Side, swimming, 1932
Don Lash, Auburn, track,1936
Verle Wright, North Side, rifle shooting, 1956
Sharon Wichman, Snider, swimming, 1968 (gold, bronze medals)
Matt Vogel, Snider, swimming, 1976 (two gold medals)
Mark Virts, New Haven, diving, 1980 (boycott)
Steve Bigelow, Fort Wayne, swimming, 1988
Lloy Ball, Woodlan, volleyball, 1996, 2000, 2004, 2008 (gold medal)
DeDee Nathan, South Side, track, 2000
Mike Marchesano, Elmhurst, baseball (Italy), 2004
Raul Papaleo, IPFW, beach volleyball (Puerto Rico), 2004
Amy Yoder-Begley, East Noble, track, 2008

# HIGH SCHOOL LISTS
## (Through winter 2013 season)

### Northeast Indiana basketball career scoring leaders - Girls

|     | Player             | School             | Graduated | Points |
|-----|--------------------|--------------------|-----------|--------|
| 1.  | Megan King         | Canterbury         | 2007      | 2,652  |
| 2.  | Tiffany Gooden     | Snider             | 1994      | 2,198  |
| 3.  | Leslie Johnson     | Northrop           | 1993      | 2,045  |
| 4.  | Tabitha Gerardot   | Canterbury         | 2010      | 1,944  |
| 5.  | Abby Salscheider   | Bluffton           | 1998      | 1,917  |
| 6.  | Jessica Ramsay     | West Noble         | 2002      | 1,746  |
| 7.  | Lindsey Swanson    | Canterbury         | 2003      | 1,649  |
| 8.  | Sha'La Jackson     | South Side         | 2007      | 1,647  |
| 9.  | Bailey Farley      | Canterbury         | 2013      | 1,636  |
| 10. | MaChelle Joseph    | DeKalb             | 1988      | 1,633  |
| 11. | Jody Beerman       | Heritage           | 1983      | 1,616  |
| 12. | Lacia Gorman       | Wayne              | 2011      | 1,604  |
| 13. | Jessica Rupright   | Norwell            | 2012      | 1,591  |
| 14. | Rachel King        | Bishop Luers       | 2001      | 1,588  |
| 15. | Leah Enterline     | Heritage           | 2003      | 1,584  |
| 16. | Lori Hissong       | Woodlan            | 1991      | 1,578  |
| 17. | Cindy Schweikhardt | Southern Wells     | 1990      | 1,575  |
| 18. | Abby Neff          | Lakeland           | 2008      | 1,541  |
| 19. | Allison Edgar      | Eastside           | 1995      | 1,520  |
| 19. | Amy Bechtel        | Fairfield          | 1996      | 1,520  |
| 21. | Tiffany Fisher     | Westview           | 2008      | 1,511  |
| 22. | Maria Recker       | DeKalb             | 1999      | 1,510  |
| 23. | Kris Booker        | Snider             | 1992      | 1,504  |
| 24. | Kindell Fincher    | Canterbury         | 2014      | 1,501  |
| 25. | Erica Schory       | Columbia City      | 1998      | 1,500  |
| 26. | Maria Marchesano   | Elmhurst           | 2001      | 1,466  |
| 27. | Liza Clemons       | Snider             | 2011      | 1,456  |
| 27. | Allison Kauffman   | Blackhawk Christian| 2011      | 1,456  |
| 29. | Mackenzie Warwick  | Norwell            | 2006      | 1,429  |
| 30. | Holly Schneider    | Northrop           | 1995      | 1,426  |

## HIGH SCHOOL LISTS
## (Through winter 2013 season)

### Northeast Indiana basketball career scoring leaders - Boys

|     | Player           | School             | Graduated | Points |
|-----|------------------|--------------------|-----------|--------|
| 1.  | Deshaun Thomas   | Bishop Luers       | 2010      | 3,018  |
| 2.  | Logan Irwin      | Whitko             | 2012      | 2,230  |
| 3.  | Seth Colclasure  | Bellmont           | Bellmont  | 2,207  |
| 4.  | Jeff Perlich     | Churubusco         | Churubusco| 2,109  |
| 5.  | Bryson Scott     | Northrop           | 2013      | 2,042  |
| 6.  | Luke Recker      | DeKalb             | 1977      | 2,008  |
| 7.  | Steve Anspaugh   | West Noble         | 1969      | 1,992  |
| 8.  | Ray Grocock      | Avilla             | 1956      | 1,838  |
| 9.  | James Hardy      | Elmhurst           | 2004      | 1,823  |
| 10. | Darin Archbold   | Norwell            | 1988      | 1,811  |
| 11. | Sean Kline       | Huntington North   | 2001      | 1,790  |
| 12. | Eschaunte Jones  | North Side         | 2007      | 1,759  |
| 13. | Michael Fosnaugh | Southern Wells     | 1997      | 1,752  |
| 14. | Jeff Stroman     | Garrett            | 1972      | 1,732  |
| 15. | Willie Long      | South Side         | 1967      | 1,697  |
| 16. | Bill Schwarz     | Columbia City      | 1960      | 1,646  |
| 17. | Kip Jones        | Bellmont           | 1985      | 1,628  |
| 18. | Tom Baack        | Concordia          | 1964      | 1,623  |
| 19. | Jim Master       | Harding            | 1980      | 1,592  |
| 20. | Brett Hughes     | DeKalb             | 1981      | 1,580  |
| 21. | Trent VanHorn    | Canterbury         | 2013      | 1,576  |
| 22. | Tony Miller      | Garrett            | 1969      | 1,573  |
| 23. | Jon Neuhouser    | Leo                | 1994      | 1,560  |
| 24. | Dan Shively      | Huntington Township| 1961      | 1,540  |
| 25. | Marques Johnson  | Snider             | 2006      | 1,538  |
| 26. | V.J. Beachem     | Harding/New Haven  |           | 1,538  |
| 27. | Terry Collins    | Snider             | 2000      | 1,520  |
| 28. | Brian Reeder     | Huntington North   | 2006      | 1,508  |
| 29. | Jamie Uptgraft   | Southern Wells     | 1994      | 1,508  |
| 30. | Eugene Parker    | Concordia          | 1974      | 1,503  |

## Football Career Rushing Leaders

|     | Player | School | Graduated | Total Yards |
|-----|--------|--------|-----------|-------------|
| 1.  | Brandon Robsinon | Heritage | 1998 | 7,303 |
| 2.  | Rod Smith | Harding | 2009 | 6,685 |
| 3.  | Cory Jacquay | New Haven | 2001 | 6,318 |
| 4.  | Doug Wasylk | Heritage | 2004 | 6,170 |
| 5.  | Ray Byers | Wayne | 2008 | 5,328 |
| 6.  | Konrad Mundon | East Noble | 2005 | 5,168 |
| 7.  | Rick Endsley | DeKalb | 1986 | 5,128 |
| 8.  | Te'Vaughn Hurse | New Haven | 2011 | 5,084 |
| 9.  | Fred Moore | Bishop Luers | 1989 | 5,015 |
| 10. | Kyle Mathewson | Churubusco | 2010 | 4,649 |
| 11. | Bryan Payton | Concordia | 2203 | 4,639 |
| 12. | Connor Kaczor | Leo | 2010 | 4,504 |
| 13. | Remound Wright | Bishop Dwenger | 2011 | 4,483 |
| 14. | Michael Ledo | Bishop Luers | 2000 | 4,479 |
| 15. | Larry Bostic | South Side | 2002 | 4,301 |
| 16. | Jason Nicodemus | Churubusco | 2013 | 4,227 |
| 17. | Vaughn Dunbar | Snider | 1986 | 4,218 |
| 18. | Courtney Davis | Snider | 1902 | 4,167 |
| 19. | John Nelson | Snider | 2011 | 4,139 |
| 20. | MiQuale Lewis | Snider | 2005 | 4,089 |

## Career coaching wins

### Girls basketball
1. Wayne Kreiger, Columbia City/Canterbury, 522
2. Dave Scudder, Bishop Dwenger, 388
3. Dave Riley, Northrop, 377
4. Mike Hey, Leo, 361
5. LaMar Kilmer, Snider, 356
6. Dave Miller, Bellmont/Concordia, 343
7. Scott Kreiger, Canterbury, 230
8. Eric Thornton, Norwell, 229
9. Tonya Burns-Cohrs, North Side/Woodlan, 219
10. Cary Blake, Adams Central, 216

### Boys basketball
1. By Hey, Concordia/North Side, 551
2. Bill Patrick, Whitko, 478
3. Glenn Parrish, Concordia, 414
4. Murray Mendenhall, Central, 396
5. Will Doehrman, Wayne/Leo/Arcola, 391
6. Al Gooden, Harding/New Haven, 373
7. Harlan Frick, Leo/Harding, 330
8. Marty Johnson, East Noble, 306
9. Jerry Lewis, Norwell, 304
10. Herb Banet, Central, 293

### Football
1. Leland Etzler, Woodkan, 287
2. Rick Minnich, Adams Central, 236
3. Matt Lindsay, Bishop Luers, 229
4. Russ Isaacs, Snider, 194
5. Andy Johns, Bishop Dwenger, 192
6. Bob Yager, Heritage, 179
7. Gary Scott, Norwell, 161
8. Cary Cavacini, Homestead, 143
9. Ron Frickey, Columbia City/Garrett, 137
10. Murray Mendenhall, Central, 134

## Indiana-Kentucky All-Stars

### Boys

Charles Stanski, Central, 1943
Robert VanRyn, Central, 1943
Murry Mendenhall Jr, Central, 1944
Bobby Milton, Central 1946
Dick Reinking, Monroeville, 1949
James Schooley, Auburn, 1949
Cal Grosscup, Auburn, 1952
Charles Lyons, North Side, 1955
Mike McCoy, South Side, 1958
Carl Stavreti, South Side, 1958
T.C. Williams, Central, 1960
Rod Schwartz, Berne, 1961
Bob Purkhiser, Bluffton, 1961
Tom Baack, Concordia, 1964
Mike Shumaker, Huntington North, 1964
Mike Weaver, Huntington North, 1964
Dave Moser, North Side, 1965
Chuck Bavis, Garrett, 1966
Willie Long, South Side, 1967
Bob Windmiller, Ossian, 1967
Mike Muff, Northrop, 1974
Walter Jordan, Northrop, 1974
Frank Thomas, North Side, 1976
Roosevelt Barnes, Wayne, 1977
Greg Eifert, Bishop Dwenger, 1980
Jim Master, Harding, 1980
John Flowers, South Side, 1981
Tracy Foster, Homestead, 1982
Lee Moore, Elmhurst, 1984
Kip Jones, Bellmont, 1985
Tony Jones, Northrop, 1986
Craig Riley, Harding, 1988
Nate Tubbs Jr., Wayne, 1989
Matt Dellinger, Wayne, 1992
Ryan Bond, South Side, 1993
Jon Neuhouser, Leo, 1994
Alan Eldridge, Wayne, 1995
Luke Recker, DeKalb, 1997
Charlie Wills, Angola, 1997
Chad LaCross, East Noble, 1997
Ben Corley, Wayne, 1998
Adam Ballinger, Bluffton, 1998
Vernard Hollins, North Side, 1999
Gabe Miller, Carroll, 2001
Sean Kline, Huntington North, 2001
Seth Colclasure, Bellmont, 2002
Adam Liddell, DeKalb, 2003
James Hardy, Elmhurst, 2004
Doug Sheckler, Columbia City, 2004
Adam Arnold, Bellmont, 2005
Grant Leiendecker, Homestead, 2006
Chris Kramer, Huntington North, 2006
Eshaunte Jones, North Side, 2007
Justin Jordan, North Side, 2009
Russell Byrd, Blackhawk Christian, 2010
Deshaun Thomas, Bishop Luers, 2010
Bryson Scott, Northrop, 2013
V.J. Beachem, New Haven, 2013

### Girls

Teri Rosinski, Norwell, 1977
Laura Augustyniak, Leo, 1978
Tonya Burns, Leo, 1981
Trish Phillips, Columbia City, 1982
Jody Beerman, Heritage, 1983
Cathey Tyree, South Side, 1983
Amy Hile, Bishop Dwenger, 1983
Leila Crossley, DeKalb, 1984
Jenny Eckert, Huntington North, 1986
Lori Meinerding, Northrop, 1987
Donna Gill, Snider, 1988
MaChelle Joseph, DeKalb, 1988
Nancy Hoover, Huntington North, 1989
Kris McGrade, Bishop Dwenger, 1990
Kamie Arnold, Huntington North, 1990
Leslie Johnson, Northrop, 1993
Tiffany Gooden, Snider, 1994
Krista Reinking, Bellmont, 1994
Lisa Winter, Huntington North, 1996
Candice Crawford, Homestead, 1997
Abby Salscheider, Bluffton, 1998
Vnemina Reese, South Side, 1998
Kelly Springer, Leo, 2001
Rachel King, Bishop Luers, 2001
Megan Dossen, Bishop Luers, 2002
Chanell Ridley, Concordia, 2007
Sha'La Jackson, South Side, 2007
Lindsay Enterline, Heritage, 2008
Lecretia Smith, Elmhurst, 2009
Sydney Weinert, South Side, 2009
Tabitha Gerardot, Canterbury, 2010
Andrea Newbauer, Concordia, 2010
Liza Clemons, Snider, 2011
Lacia Gorman, Wayne, 2011
Jessica Rupright, Norwell, 2012
Akila Sims, Snider, 2012
Arianna Simmons, South Side, 2013

### Local coaches

#### Boys

Bob Dille, Northrop, 1974 and 1975
Bill Patrick, Whitko, 1993
Marty Johnson, East Noble, 1997
Cliff Hawkins, DeKalb, 2004
Murray Mendenhall III, Wayne, 2007

#### Girls

Wayne Kreiger, Columbia City, 1989
Dave Riley, Northrop, 1991
Fred Fields, Huntington North, 1992
Fred Fields, Huntington North, 1996
Mike Hey, Leo, 1998
Teri Rosinski, Bishop Luers, 2003
Dave Miller, Concordia, 2011
Scott Kreiger, Canterbury, 2012
Juanita Goodwell, South Side, 2013

## High school state champions (through winter 2013 season)

## BOYS

### Baseball
DeKalb, 1980
Northrop, 1983
Class 1A: Blackhawk Christian, 2002
Class 3A: Norwell, 2003
Class 1A: Blackhawk Christian, 2005
Class 4A: Snider, 2006
Class 1A: Blackhawk Christian, 2006
Class 3A: Norwell, 2007
Class 2A: Bishop Luers, 2008
Class4A: Snider, 2009
Class 4A: Carroll, 2010
Class 4A: Carroll, 2011
Runners-up
South Adams, 1972
Northrop, 1981
Huntington North, 1993
Concordia, 1995
Class 4A: Carroll, 1999
Class 1A: Adams Central, 2001
Class 3A: Bellmont, 2002
Class 3A: Norwell, 2006
Class 2A: Heritage, 2007
Class 4A: Homestead, 2008

### Basketball
South Side, 1938
Central, 1943
South Side, 1958
Northrop, 1974
Class 2A: Harding, 2001
Class 2A: Bishop Luers, 2008
Class 2A: Bishop Luers, 2009
Runners-up
Central, 1936
Central, 1946
Huntington, 1964
North Side, 1965
Class 3A: Harding, 2002
Class 2A: Bluffton, 2002
Class 4A: DeKalb, 2003
Class 3A: Elmhurst, 2003
Class 4A; Columbia City, 2004
Class 3A: Bellmont, 2004

Class 1A: Blackhawk Christian, 2004
Class 2A: Harding, 2005
Class 2A: Harding, 2006
Class 3A: Harding, 2008
Class 4A: Snider, 2009
Class 3A: Norwell, 2012
Class 3A: Concordia, 2012

### Cross country
North Side, 1968
Runners-up
North Side, 1946
New Haven, 1960
North Side, 1961
North Side, 1965
Northrop, 1974
Norwell, 1978
Northrop, 1982
Northrop, 1997
Northrop, 2003
Carroll, 2008
Carroll, 2012

### Football
Class 3A: Bishop Dwenger, 1983
Class 2A: Bishop Luers, 1985
Class 4A: DeKalb, 1986
Class 2A: Bishop Luers, 1989
Class 3A: Bishop Dwenger, 1990
Class 3A: Bishop Dwenger, 1991
Class 5A: Snider, 1992
Class 2A: Bishop Luers, 1992
Class 4A: Wayne, 1995
Class 2A: Bishop Luers, 1999
Class 4A: East Noble, 2000
Class 1A: Adams Central, 2000
Class 2A: Bishop Luers, 2001
Class 1A; Southern Wells, 2001
Class 2A: Bishop Luers, 2002
Class 2A: Harding, 2006
Class 2A: Bishop Luers, 2007
Class 3A: Bellmont, 2008
Class 2A: Bishop Luers, 2009
Class 2A: Bishop Luers, 2010
Class 2A: Bishop Luers, 2011
Class 2A: Bishop Luers, 2012
Runners-up
Class 3A: Bishop Dwenger, 1978
Class 3A: Snider, 1981
Class 1A: Woodlan, 1981

Class 2A; Bishop Luers, 1983
Class 1A: Churubusco, 1983
Class 5A: Snider, 1986
Class 2A: Bishop Luers, 1991
Class 4A: Wayne, 1992
Class 4A: DeKalb, 1994
Class 3A: Bishop Dwenger, 1996
Class 2A: Bishop Luers, 1996
Class 5A: Homestead, 1998
Class 3A: Norwell, 1999
Class 2A: Bishop Luers, 2000
Class 5A: Snider, 2002
Class 4A: Bishop Dwenger, 2002
Class 4A: East Noble, 2003
Class 2A: Harding, 2003
Class 5A: Snider: 2004
Class 3A: Norwell, 2006
Class 4A: Bishop Dwenger, 2008
Class 4A: Bishop Dwenger, 2010
Class 5A: Snider, 2012

## Mythical state championships (based on polls)
North Side, 1940
Central Catholic, 1950

## Golf
Central Catholic, 1959
Northrop, 1984
Runners-up
Elmhurst, 1941

## Soccer
Canterbury, 1997
Canterbury, 1998
Canterbury, 2001
Canterbury, 2011
Canterbury, 2012
Runners-up
Bishop Luers, 1995
Canterbury, 1996
Canterbury, 2002
Homestead, 2009

## Swimming
None
Runners-up
Homestead, 2004
Homestead, 2006

## Tennis
None
Runners-up
Concordia, 1971
Homestead, 1980
Homestead, 1981
Homestead, 1984
Homestead, 1986
Homestead, 1992
Homestead, 1994
Homestead, 1995
Homestead, 2000
Homestead, 2006

## Track
North Side 1941
North Side, 1942
Central, 1944
North Side, 1956
North Side, 1957
North Side, 1963
North Side, 1965
South Side, 1968
Wayne, 1973
Snider, 1974
Northrop, 1997
Concordia, 1999
Northrop, 2004
Runners-up
North Side, 1938
North Side, 1939
South Side, 1941
North Side, 1953
North Side, 1966
South Side, 1972
South Side, 1978
South Side, 1980
South Side, 1981
Snider, 1982
Snider, 1983
Northrop, 1986
Concordia, 1997
Northrop, 1998
Northrop, 1999
Northrop, 2003
Northrop, 2006

## Wrestling
Bellmont, 1987
Bellmont, 1988

Bellmont, 1994
Runners-up
Bellmont, 1979
Bellmont, 1995
Bellmont, 1999
Bellmont, 2006

## GIRLS

### Basketball
Heritage, 1982
Northrop, 1986
Snider, 1988
Huntington North, 1990
Huntington North, 1995
Class 2A: Bishop Luers, 1999
Class 2A: Bishop Luers, 2000
Class 2A: Bishop Luers, 2001
Class 3A: Bishop Luers, 2002
Class 3A: Bishop Luers, 2006
Class 1A: Canterbury, 2008
Class 3A: Elmhurst, 2009
Class 1A: Canterbury, 2009
Class 3A: Concordia, 2010
Class 1A: Canterbury, 2010
Class 2A: Bishop Luers, 2011
Class 1A: Canterbury, 2012
Class 3A: Concordia, 2012
Class 1A: Canterbury, 2013
Runners-up
Class 2A: Bluffton, 1998
Class 4A: Snider, 1999
Class 3A: Columbia City, 2000
Class 4A: Snider, 2001
Class 3A: Bishop Luers, 2004
Class 2A: Bishop Luers, 2010
Class 2A: Bishop Luers, 2012
Class 4A: South Side, 2013

### Cross country
Concordia, 1983
Runners-up
Northrop, 1989

### Golf
None
Runners-up
Carroll 1981
Bishop Dwenger, 1998
Bishop Dwenger, 2003

### Gymnastics
Homestead, 1983
Homestead, 1984
Homestead, 1985
Bishop Dwenger, 1995
Homestead, 1996
Homestead, 1999
Homestead, 2001
Bishop Dwenger, 2003
Bishop Dwenger, 2005
Bishop Dwenger, 2006
Bishop Dwenger, 2012
Runners-up
North Side, 1977
Leo, 1980
Homestead, 1989
Bishop Dwenger, 1993
Bishop Dwenger, 1994
Bishop Dwenger, 1998
Bishop Dwenger, 2000
Bishop Dwenger, 2002
Bishop Dwenger, 2007
Bishop Dwenger, 2011

### Soccer
Bishop Dwenger, 2005
Bishop Dwenger, 2006
Bishop Dwenger, 2010
Runners-up
Homestead, 2001
Snider, 2004
Snider, 2008
Snider, 2009

### Softball
Class 1A: Eastside, 1998
Class 4A: Bishop Dwenger, 2010
Class 1A: Lakewood Park, 2012
Runners-up
Class 2A: Woodlan, 2011
Class 2A: Adams Central, 2012
Class 4A: Huntington North, 2012

### Swimming
None
Runners-up
Homestead, 2011

**Tennis**
None
Runners-up
Bishop Luers, 1980
Bishop Luers, 1982
Homestead, 1985
Homestead, 1987
Homestead, 1989
Homestead, 1995
Homestead, 1996
Homestead, 2004
Homestead, 2009

**Track**
Wayne, 1979
South Side, 1980
Northrop, 1981
South Side, 1985
South Side, 1986
Northrop, 1991
Harding, 1995
Harding, 1996
Northrop, 2000
Northrop, 2001
Northrop, 2002
Northrop, 2003
Northrop, 2004
Northrop, 2011
Runners-up
South Side, 1979
Wayne, 1980
Harding, 1983
South Side, 1984
Snider, 1987
South Side, 1988
Northrop, 1990
Northrop, 1992
Northrop, 2006
Northrop, 2012

**Volleyball**
Snider, 1987
Snider, 1991
Class 3A: Bellmont, 2007
Class 3A: Bellmont, 2010
Runners-up
Snider, 1973
Concordia, 1976
Carroll, 1988
Northrop, 1996

Class 4A: Northrop, 1997
Class 4A: Northrop, 1999
Class 3A: Bishop Luers, 2001
Class 3A: Bishop Luers, 2002
Class 3A: Concordia, 2003
Class 2A: Fairfield, 2010

## INDIVIDUAL STATE CHAMPIONS - Boys

### Cross country
Wayne Simon, North Side, 1946
David Redding, South Side, 1956
Henry King, Central, 1961
Phil Wysong, West Noble, 1970

### Golf
Fred Link, Elmhurst, 1941
Jon Oliver, Huntington North, 1997
Mike Schumaker, Columbia City, 2000

### Swimming
Shawn Cismowski, Kyle Laux, Joel Hageman, Justin Hoggatt, Homestead, 200 medley relay, 1998
Sean Gibson, Andrew Glassley, Michael Trent, Joel Usina, Concordia, 200 medley relay, 2001
Bart Wickard, Snider, 200 individual medley, 1997
Justin Hoggatt, Homestead, 50 freestyle, 1996, 1997, 1998
Mark Virts, New Haven, 1-meter diving, 1972
Luke Cox, East Noble, 1-meter diving, 1999
David Piercy, Homestead, 1-meter diving, 2006
Scott Place, Snider, 100 butterfly, 1991
Justin Hoggatt, Homestead, 100 butterfly, 1998
Blake Johnson, Homestead, 100 butterfly, 2011
Tim Bower, Snider, 500 freestyle, 1989, 1990
Timothy Glassley, Tyler Lemert, Michael Hartman, Daniel Hartman, Concordia, 200 freestyle relay, 2005
Adam Lill, Kyle Frebel, Christopher Jones, Andrew Hoffman, Homestead, 200 freestyle relay, 2006
Robert Rausch, Homestead, 100 breast stroke, 1993
Tyler Lemert, Concordia, 100 breast stroke, 2007

### Tennis
Singles
Fabio Souza, Northrop, 1993
Oliver Cantrell, North Side, 1996
Rick Phillipp, Homestead, 1997
Derek Carptenter, South Side, 2007

Doubles
Brian Fleming-Trent Glassley, Carroll, 2003

## Track

Kevin Craig, Wayne, 100, 1998
Rolondo Scott, Concordia, 100, 1999
Kesonn Lee, Northrop, 100, 2004
Scott Wims, Northrop, 100, 2006
Kevin Craig, Wayne, 200, 1995
Thomas Brashear, Huntington North, 200, 1997
Scott Wims, Northrop, 200, 2005, 2006
John Uecker, Bishop Dwenger, 400, 1991
Gustin Smith, Concordia, 400, 2000
Mark Keller, Northrop 800, 1983
Brock Smith, Homestead, 800, 1995
Michael Mazier, West Noble, 1600, 1983
Brett Tipton, Northrop, 1600, 1998, 1999
Steve Teusch, Wayne, 3200, 1996
Phil Yoder, East Noble, 3200, 1999
Robert Moldovan, Northrop, 3200, 2006
Andy Bayer, Leo, 3200, 2008
Rod Woodson, Snider, 110 hurdles, 1982, 1983
Charles Bailey, Northrop, 110 hurdles, 2004
Christopher Brautzsch, Wayne, 110 hurdles, 2006
Nathan Mueller, East Noble, 300 hurdles, 2011
Chris Tredway, Carroll, 300 hurdles, 2000
Ronald Elliott, Wayne, 300 hurdles, 2001
Mike Early, Mario Moore, Tony Jones, Enrie Davis, Northrop, 400 relay, 1986
Corey Eloms, Kamal Macon, Rolondo Scott, Tyrus Scott, Concordia, 400 relay, 1997
Kamal Macon, Gustin Smith, Terron Wharton, Rolando Scott, Concordia, 400 relay, 1998
Dominique Hill, Miqual Lewis, Dameon Talley, Justin Wynn, Snider, 400 relay, 2004
De'Andre Binion, Christopher Brautzsch, Keith London, Derek Washington, Wayne, 400 relay, 2005
Terry Stapleton, John Ramsey, Zachary Carr, Geoffrey Williams, Snider, 1600 relay, 1982
Shannon Grady, Robert Hardy, Cedric Jackson, Curtis Bynum, South Side, 1600 relay, 1999
James Hopkins, andrew Silkworth, Travis White, Scott Wims, Northrop, 1600 relay, 2005
David Coley, Kendal Frederick, Shauntis Lewis, Ethan Wappes, Snider, 1600 relay, 2010
Brad Miller, Matt Miller, Aaron Ruse, Patrick Miller, DeKalb, 3200 relay, 1996
Jordan Butler, Ryan Fritz, Ryan McNeil, Brett Tipton, Northrop, 3200 relay, 1997
Ryan Fritz, Terrell Goodspeed, Nathan Peffley, Andrew Schmitz, Northrop, 3200 relay, 1998
Mohammed Bangura, Tyvon Kelley, Ed Benson, Kersten Barnfield, North Side, 1,600 relay, 2012
Eric Claxton, Alexander Hess, John Hester, Jonathan Harper, Carroll, 3,200 relay, 2012
Luther Ellis, Bluffton, high jump, 1910
Schroff, Central, high jump, 1936
Henry Kulesza, Central, high jump, 1939
Dick Kilpatrick, South Side, high jump, 1942
Warren Anderson, South Side, high jump, 1952
Charles Lyons, Central, high jump, 1953
Travis White, Northrop, high jump, 2004
Tyrone McKinney, North Side, high jump, 2007
Bobby Brown, Northrop, long jump, 1980
Marcus Chamber, Snider, long jump, 1985
Corey Eloms, Concordia, long jump, 1997
Deutsch, Columbia City, pole vault, 1926
Don Osdale, New Haven, pole vault, 1964
Gary Thrapp, East Noble, pole vault, 1968
Gary Hunter, Northrop, pole vault, 1974
Brian Kimball, Northrop, pole vault, 1975, 1976

Ron Vernasco, Snider, pole vault, 1978
Dale Gerke, Leo, pole vault, 1983
Phil Yuska, East Noble, pole vault, 1984
Bob Shank, North Side, pole vault, 1987
Jo'l Gerardot, Northrop, pole vault, 1997, 1998
Ryan Schipper, Bishop Dwenger, pole vault, 2003
James Martzall, Northrop, pole vault, 2004
Jonathan Hall, Homestead, pole vault, 2006
Corey Shank, Northrop, pole vault, 2007, 2008, 2009
Myers, Auburn, shot put, 1935
Everett Tunget, South Side, shot put, 1950
Charles May, Huntertown, shot put, 1951
Tom Seifert, North Side, shot put, 1957, 1958
George Doehla, Harding, shot put, 1974
Gregg Hart, Homestead, shot put, 1990
Kurt Krick, Norwell, shot put, 1996
Aris Allen, North Side, shot put, 2009
Rob Goshert, Snider, discus, 1974
George Doehla, Harding, discus, 1975
Glenn Schneider, Harding, discus, 1984, 1985
Gregg Hart, Homestead, discus, 1988, 1989, 1990
Scott Starost, Carroll, discus, 1999
Taylor Treesh, DeKalb, discus, 2001
Events no longer contested
Max Ramsey, Central, 100 yards, 1943
Paul Bienz, Central, 100 yards, 1944
Ronald Huffer, New Haven, 100 yards, 1954
John Mitchell, Wayne, 100 yards, 1972
Robert Cowan, North Side, 220 yards, 1940, 1941
Max Ramsey, Central, 220 yards, 1943
Paul Bienz, Central, 220 yards, 1944
Robert Ewing, North Side, 220 yards, 1952, 1953
Ronald Huffer, New Haven, 220 yards, 1954
McMean, North Side, 440 yards, 1937
Roger Neighborgall, Garrett, 440 yards, 1941
Max Ramsey, Central, 440 yards, 1944
John Lumpp, South Side, 440 yards, 1968
Leon Tubbs, South Side, 440 yards, 1978
Lamont, Central, 880 yards, 1925
Richard Bell, South Side, 880 yards, 1928
Flemming, South Side, 880 yards, 1932
Donald Kemp, North Side, 880 yards, 1939
Charles Feistkorn, South Side, 880 yards, 1941
Frank Geist, North Side, 880 yards, 1957
Henry King, Central, 880 yards, 1961
Clymer, South Side, mile, 1932
Don Lash, Auburn, mile, 1933
Ashley Hawk, North Side, mile, 1941, 1942, 1944
William Griswold, North Side, mile, 1952
Steve Hibler, Concordia, mile, 1959
Richard Magley, Northrop, mile, 1973
Tom O'Connell, Bishop Dwenger, mile, 1978
Mike Bojinoff, North Side, 120 hurdles, 1941
William Stults, South Side, 120 hurdles, 1944
Sam Sims, Central, 120 hurdles, 1949
Carl Johnson, South Side, 120 hurdles, 1961

Jim Hallenbeck, North Side, 120 hurdles, 1965
Howard Doughty, North Side, 120 hurdles, 1966
Jeff Sroman, Garrett, 120 hurdles, 1971, 1972
John Mitchell, Wayne, 120 hurdles, 1973
Mark Cammack, Wayne, 120 hurdles, 1978
Warren Anderson, South Side, 180 hurdles, 1952
Daniel Howe, South Side, 180 hurdles, 1958
Jack Hallenback, North Side, 180 hurdles, 1959
Robert Hubbard, Central, 180 hurdles, 1962
Howard Doughty, North Side, 180 hurdles, 1965, 1966
Ken Wilson, DeKalb, 180 hurdles, 1971
John Mitchell, 180 hurdles, 1972
Wilfred Rouse, Wayne, 180 hurdles, 1974
Kenneth Cammack, Wayne, 180 hurdles, 1976
Mike Bojinoff, North Side, 200 hurdles, 1941
Archie Adams, North Side, 200 hurdles, 1948
Richard McComb, North Side, 200 hurdles, 1951
Ron Birchfield, South Side, 300 hurdles, 1980, 1981
Rod Woodson, Snider, 300 hurdles, 1982, 1983
Brian Yager, Carroll, 300 hurdles, 1995
South Side, 880 relay, 1933, 1934, 1941
Central, 880 relay, 1936, 1943, 1944
North Side, 880 relay, 1938, 1939, 1942
Daniel Howe, Terry Miller, Tom Pinder, Chris Stavreti, South Side, 880 relay, 1956
Steven Blumahn, Howard Doughty, Jim Hallenbeck, Paul Piano, North Side, 880 relay, 1965
Richard Burr, Ed Payne, William Pointer, Rod White, Wayne, 880 relay, 1974
North Side, mile relay, 1941, 1942, 1946
Ron Bowman, Dave Lang, Pete Lundell, Don Nuerge, North Side, mile relay, 1956
Frank Geist, Jim Hattery, Ron Bowman, Pete Lundell, North Side, mile relay, 1957

## Wrestling

Brock Norton, Carroll, 135, 2010
Taylor March, East Noble, 135, 2009
Billy Baker, Bellmont, 215, 2009
Justin Woods, Leo, 215, 2008
Matt Irwin, Bellmont, 135, 2006
Garlan Early, North Side, 119, 2003
Jason Woodson, Snider, 171, 2002
Gregory Wagner, Snider, 275, 2001
John Sheets, Bellmont, 103, 2000
Ben Sprunger, Bluffton, 130, 2000
Randy Pursley, Bluffton, 130, 1999
Anthony Lapsley, Snider, 145, 198
Anton Talamantes, Bishop Dwenger, 189, 1998
Anton Talamantes, Bishop Dwenger, 215, 1997
Jason Baker, Bellmont, 125, 1996
Tim Meyers, Bellmont, 130, 1994
Pete Knecht, Huntington North, 145, 1994
Rico Talamantes, North Side, 171, 1992
Eric Early, North Side, 103, 1991
Jermaine Brooks, Northrop, 160, 1991
Mark Bruner, Homestead, 160, 1990
James Starks, Northrop, 171, 1990
Matthew Koontz, Whitko, 112, 1989
Troy Bahler, Harding, 130, 1989
Paul Baker, Bellmont, 130, 1988
Paul Gunsett, Bellmont, 135, 1988
Paul Voight, Carroll, 155, 1987
Thomas Uhrick, Elmhurst, 167, 1987
Oliver Richmond, Elmhurst, 112, 1985
Elbert Starks, Snider, 132, 1985
Johnny Sewell, North Side, HWT, 1985
Oliver Richmond, 105, Elmhurst, 1984
Dan Brook, DeKalb, 167, 1984
Tom Bennett, Snider, 138, 1982
Brent Faurote, Bellmont, 98, 1981
Chris Mahlan, Bellmont, 185, 1979
Bill Schultz, Bellmont, HWT, 1977
Phil Ball, West Nobke, 185, 1976
Rob Goshert , Snider, 185, 1974
Patrick Weber, Huntington, 98, 1971
Phil Lengerich, Bellmont, 138, 1969

**INDIVIDUAL STATE CHAMPIONS - Girls**

## Cross country
Kristi Walker, Harding, 1981
Laura Didion, Northrop, 1983
Jamie Gorrell, Woodlan, 1986
Amy Yoder, East Noble, 1994
Alissa McKaig, Concordia, 2003
Adele Mitchell, Concordia, 2004

## Golf
Michelle Hatfield, Snider, 1994
Lauren Gant, Bishop Dwenger, 2000

## Gymnastics
Jill Beauchamp, Homestead, all-around, 1984
Laura Szczepanski, Bishop Dwenger, all-around, 1995, 1996
Shellen Goltz, Homestead, all-around, 2000
Irene Hattop, Homestead, vault, 1988
Alice Kruk, Bishop Dwenger, vault, 1994
Shanna Goltz, Hometead, vault, 1996
Elizabeth Minix, Bishop Dwenger, vault, 1998, 2000
Kristen Hines, Hometead, vault, 1999
Nicole Van Hoey, Bishop Dwenger, vault, 2002
Ericka Couch, Hometead, bars, 1984, 1985
Irene Studler, North Side, bars, 1987
Laura Szczepanski, Bishop Dwenger, bars, 1996
Brianna Neumann, Northrop, bars, 2004
Jeanna Van Hoey, Bishop Dwenger, bars, 2005, 2006
Brannon Springer, Concordia, bars, 2007
Kayla Heator, Fremont, bars, 2009
Alex Nickel, Angola, bars, 2012
Becky Carter, Concordia, beam, 1987
Christi Bowers, Carroll, beam, 1988
Laura Szczepanski, Bishop Dwenger, beam, 1995, 1996
Shera Shaw, Huntington North, beam, 1998
Shellen Goltz, Homestead, beam, 2000
Jeanna Glick, Snider, beam, 2005
Jeanna Van Hoey, Bishop Dwenger, beam, 2007
Jessica Baker, Huntington North beam, 2011
Alex Nickel, Angola, beam, 2012
Darinda Gres, East Noble, floor, 1984
Irene Studler, North Side, floor, 1987
Alice Kruk, Bishop Dwenger, floor, 1993
Laura Szczepanski, Bishop Dwenger, floor, 1994, 1995, 1996
Allyson Zipse, Homestead, floor, 2001
Hannah Osborn, Concordia, floor, 2007

## Swimming

Rebecca Wilson, Homestead, 200 freestyle, 1999
Leslie Place, Snider, 200 individual medley, 1993, 1994, 1995
Michala Kwasney, Snider, 200 individual medley, 1996, 1997, 1998, 1999
Heather Auld, DeKalb, 50 freestyle, 1997
Leslie Place, Snider, 100 butterfly, 1992, 1993, 1995
Michala Kwasny, Snider, 100 butterly, 1997, 1998, 1999
McKenzie Bagan, Homestead, 2009
Carolyn Horwitz, DeKalb, 100 freestyle, 1996
Lia Oberstar, Bishop Dwenger, 500 freestlye, 1992, 1993, 1994, 1995
Rebecca Wilson, Homestead, 500 freestyle, 1999
Jessica Skiba, Homestead, 500 freestyle 2007
Lia Oberstar, Bishop Dwenger, 200 backstroke, 1994
Erin Morris, Snider, 200 backstroke, 2002, 2003
Kelly Williams, Snider, 100 backstroke, 1993, 1994
Tori Bagan, Homestead, 100 backstroke, 2009, 2011

## Tennis

None

## Track

Sybil Perry, Wayne, 100, 1980, 1981
LaShonda Harper, Harding, 100, 1994, 1995, 1996
Joy Eloms, Concordia, 100, 2004
Tamara Adams, Northrop, 100, 2006
Brionna Thomas, Wayne, 100, 2012
Teresa Rozier, Snider, 200, 1982
LaShonda Harper, Harding, 200, 1994, 1995, 1996
Whittney Stuart, North Side, 200, 2001
Christina Whitt, Concordia, 200, 2002
Shauntel Elcock, Northrop, 200, 2003, 2004
Brionna Thomas, Wayne, 200, 2012
Sybil Perry, Wayne, 400, 1980, 1981
Terri Young, Harding, 400, 1983
Ellen Alkire, Homestead, 400, 2000
Shauntel Elcock, Northrop, 400, 2002, 2003, 2004
Rebecca Hardy, Wayne, 800, 1982
Molly Widmann, Snider, 800, 1997
Talia Barwick, Northrop, 800, 1998
Rholonda Ash, Harding, 800, 1999
Kristi Walker, Harding, 1600, 1980, 1981
Sherry Hoover, Woodlan, 1600, 1985
Alissa McKaig, Concordia, 1600, 2004
Kate DeSimone, Canterbury, 1600, 2009, 2010
Jamie Gorrell, Woodlan, 3200, 1987
Amy Yoder, East Noble, 3200, 1994, 1995, 1996
Kaylee McClanahan, Carroll, 3200, 2010
Shannon Kelley, Northrop, 100 hurdles, 2000
Tamara Adams, Northrop, 100 hurdles, 2004

Dee Dee Nathan, South Side, 300 hurdles, 1984, 1985, 1986

Deb Sauers, Columbia City, 300 hurdles, 1987

Crystal Anderson, Snider, 300 hurdles, 1990

Terri Wanamaker, Northrop, 300 hurdles, 1991

Shamora Moore, Wayne, 300 hurdles, 1996

Kim Parman, Leo, 300 hurdles, 1998

April Royal, Wayne, 300 hurdles, 2000

Kiwanna Johnson, Zanzy Moore, Lavette Harris, Stephanie Wattley, South Side, 400 relay, 1989

Dorothy Tinker, Tonya Shepherd, Sonya Shepherd, Monica Johnson, Northrop, 400 relay, 1990 Wilita McCarter, Ebony Jackson, LaShyra Harris, LaShonda Harper, Harding, 400 relay, 1995

Keli Walker, Ebony Jackson, Donishia Morrison, LaShanda Harper, Harding, 400 relay, 1996

Khyla Conway, Lakeita Rox, Monica Carter, Zakiya Robinson, Northrop, 400 relay, 2001

Christina Whitt, Joy Elombs, Amber Woodson, Amber Williams, Concordia, 400 relay, 2002

Tamara Adams, Lakeita Rox, Kyndal Carr, Zakiya Robinson, Northrop, 400 relay, 2003

Joy Eloms, Christina Whitt, Amber Williams, Rebekah Williams, Concordia, 400 relay, 2004

Cathy Tyree, Dee Dee Nathan, Trudy McCloud, Angie Goodman, South Side, 1600 relay, 1983

Lisa Martin, Dee Dee Nathan, Trudy McCloud, Angie Goodman, South Side, 1600 relay, 1984

Nicole Irby, Lorrenda Jordan, Amy Rising, Phyllis Williams, Snider, 1600 relay, 1987

Shalonda Davenport, Zanzy Moore, Kimwanna Johnson, Lynette Harris, South Side, 1600, 1989

Zakiya Robinson, Lakeesha Burnett, Kyndall Carr, Shauntel Elcock, Northrop, 1600 relay, 2002

Lakeesha Burnett, Tamara Adams, Natasha Fletcher, Shauntel Elcock, Northrop, 1600 relay, 2003

Alexis Scott, Makelle Skelton, Dejah Arnold, Demetra Taylor, Northrop, 1,600 relay

Sherri Dunn, Northrop, long jump, 1979, 1980

Terri Wanamaker, Northrop, long jump, 1991

LaShonda Harper, Harding, long jump, 1994, 1995, 1996

Aundrea Brown, North Side, long jump, 2002, 2004

Christy Richart, Huntington North, discus, 1992

Angie Joy, Huntington North, discus, 1994

Candice Crawford, Homestead, discus, 1996

Rachel Dincoff, DeKalb, discus, 2012

Cathy Tyree, South Side, high jump, 1980

Angie Bradburn, Norwell, high jump, 1984, 1985

Emily Loomis, Bishop Luers, high jump, 2001

Shanelle DeJournet , Snider, high jump, 2011

Davobnna Runkel, South Adams, shot put, 1986

Donna Gill, Snider, shot put, 1988

Katie Veith, Homestead, pole vault, 2004, 2006, 2007
Brianna Neumann, Northrop, pole vault, 2005
Nina Gutermuth , Leo, pole vault, 2011
Events no longer contested
Sybil Perry, Wayne, 100 yards, 1979
Delores Stewart, South Side, 440, 1979
Rosemary Junk, Northrop, 80 hurdles, 1976
Kelly Sparks, Northrop, 80 hurdles, 1977
Melinda Barfield, Wayne, 80 hurdles, 1979
Lorna Russell, Northrop, 100 hurdles, 1981
Sonia Perry, Northrop, 100 hurdles, 1983
Dee Dee Nathan, South Side, 100 hurdles, 1985, 1986
Deb Sauers, Columbia City, 100 hurdles, 1987
Sonya Shepherd, Northrop, 100 hurdles, 1990
Terri Wanamaker, Northrop, 100 hurdles, 1991
Kelly Elias, Tamara LaBorde, Gina Brown, Rosemany Junk, Northrop, 880 relay, 1976
Judith Anderson, Melinda Barfield, Jacklin Cooper, Sybil Perry, Wayne, 880 medley relay, 1979

## Club state championships

### Bowling
Team champions
Boys
Northrop, 2003
Huntington North, 2006
Huntington North, 2011
Girls
Huntington North, 2001
Huntington North, 2002
Snider, 2006
Snider, 2008
Individual champions
Josh West, Carroll, 2000
Jessica Fifer, Heritage, 2001
Lindsey Breumleve, Huntington North, 2003
Ashley Mann, Norwell, 2005
Tori McMillen, Elmhurst, 2006
E.J. Tackett, Huntington North, 2009
Sydney Brummett, Homestead, 2011
Abby Peters, Snider, 2012

### Hockey
Class 2A, Snider, 1977
Class 2A, Snider, 1978
Class 2A, Snider, 1985
Class 2A, Snider, 1986
Class 2A, Snider, 1989
Class 1A, Northrop, 1990
Class 2A, Homestead, 1990
Class 1A, Homestead, 1992
Class 2A, North Side, 1992
Class 1A, North Side, 1993
Class 2A, Homestead, 1995
Class 1A, New Haven, 1995
Class 1A, Snider, 1996
Class 1A, North Side, 1997
Class 1A, New Haven, 2000
Class 1A, New Haven, 2001
Class 1A, Northrop, 2002
Class 1A, Northrop, 2005
Class 2A, Northrop, 2006
Class 4A, Carroll, 2006
Class 1A, New Haven, 2008
Class 2A, Northrop, 2009
Class 1A, New Haven, 2010
Class 3A, Carroll, 2010
Class 4A, Carroll, 2011
Class 3A, Leo, 2012

## Mr. Basketball
Mike McCoy, South Side, 1958
Willie Long, South Side, 1967
Jim Master, Harding, 1980
Luke Recker, DeKalb, 1997
Deshaun Thomas, Bishop Luers, 2010

## Miss Basketball
Teri Rosinski, Norwell, 1977
Jody Beerman, Heritage, 1983
Lori Meinerding, Northrop, 1987
Tiffany Gooden, Snider, 1994
Lisa Winter, Huntington North, 1996
Jessica Rupright, Norwell, 2012

## Miss Softball
Amy Kendall, Northrop, 2002

## Mr. Baseball
Brad Weber, DeKalb, 1995
Jarrod Parker, Norwell, 2007
Will Coursen-Carr, South Side, 2012

## Mr. Football
Jaylon Smith, Bishop Luers, 2012

## Indiana Soccer Player of the Year
Boys
Phil Presser, Canterbury, 1998
Julian Jordan, Canterbury, 1999
Blake Sharpe, Canterbury, 2002

Girls
Kelly DeArmond, Homestead, 2001
Lisa Underwood, Bishop Dwenger, 2008
Jordan Pawlik, Bishop Dwenger, 2009
Sarah Killion, Bishop Dwenger, 2010

## CITY TOURNAMENTS

### Diving

1970 – Avalon
1971 – Avalon
1972 – Avalon
1973 – Avalon
1974 – Avalon
1975 – Avalon
1976 – Avalon
1977 – Avalon
1978 – Avalon
1979 – Avalon
1980 – Avalon
1981 – Avalon
1982 – Park Forest
1983 – Avalon
1984 – Avalon
1985 – Avalon
1986 – Avalon
1987 – Avalon
1988 – Avalon
1989 – Avalon
1990 – Lake Forest
1991 – Lake Forest
1992 – Avalon
1993 – Avalon
1994 – Avalon
1995 – Avalon
1996 – Avalon
1997 – Avalon
1998 – Avalon
1999 – Blackhawk
2000 – Blackhawk
2001 – Avalon
2002 – Arlington Park
2003 – Avalon
2004 – Sycamore Hills
2005 – Sycamore Hills
2006 – Arlington Park
2007 – Arlington Park
2008 – Sycamore Hills
2009 – Sycamore Hills
2010 – Arlington Park
2011 – Arlington Park
2012 – Arlington Park

### Swimming

*(Swimming started in 1961, but didn't name a team champion until 1971.)*

1971 – Lake Forest
1972 – Lake Forest
1973 – Lake Forest
1974 – Avalon
1975 – Avalon
1976 – Avalon
1977 – Lake Forest
1978 – Pocohontas
1979 – Pocohontas
1980 – Pocohontas
1981 – Pocohontas
1982 – Pocohontas
1983 – Pocohontas
1984 – Pocohontas
1985 – Lake Forest
1986 – Avalon
1987 – Avalon
1988 – Avalon
1989 – Avalon
1990 – Avalon
1991 – Avalon
1992 – Arlington Park
1993 – Avalon
1994 – Avalon
1995 – Arlington Park
1996 – Avalon
1997 – Arlington Park
1998 – Arlington Park
1999 – Arlington Park
2000 – Avalon
2001 – Avalon
2002 – Avalon
2003 – Avalon
2004 – Avalon
2005 – Avalon
2006 – Avalon
2007 – Avalon
2008 – Sycamore Hills
2009 – Sycamore Hills
2010 – Sycamore Hills
2011 – Sycamore Hills
2012 – Sycamore Hills

## Golf - Men

1926 – Guy Means
1927 – Guy Means
1928 – Bill Basset
1929 – Bill Basset
1930 – Bill Basset
1931 – Bill Basset
1932 – Will Catterton
1933 – Tony Bruggeman
1934 – Bob Ponsot
1935 – Enno Franke
1936 – Willie Adams
1937 – Parker Motter
1938 – Glen Miller
1939 – Fred Link
1940 – Fred Link
1941 – Hal Schmidt
1942 – Fred Link
1943 – Harry Offutt Jr.
1944 – Harry Offutt Jr.
1945 – Bill Link
1946 – Glen Miller
1947 – Harry Offutt Jr.
1948 – Bill Link
1949 – Bob Fowler
1950 – Parker Motter
1951 – Parker Motter
1952 – Bill Morris
1953 – Harry Offutt Jr.
1954 – Charlie Byrket
1955 – Parker Motter
1956 – Roy Hemsoth
1957 – Ken Rodewald
1958 – Harvey Collins
1959 – Phil Antibus
1960 – Tom Peipenbrink
1961 – Roy Hemsoth
1962 – Charlie Byrket
1963 – Bill Miller
1964 – Dave Schumaker
1965 – Dave Schumaker
1966 – Bill Miller
1967 – Dave Schumaker
1968 – Dave Schumaker
1969 – Dave Schumaker
1970 – Bill Schumaker
1971 – Bill Schumaker
1972 – Dick Bradow
1973 – John Churchward
1974 – T om Kelley

1975 – John Leeper
1976 – Tom Inskeep
1977 – Tom Kelley
1978 – Tom Kelley
1979 – Tom Kelley
1980 – Jim Houlihan Jr.
1981 – Chip Novak
1982 – Sam Till Jr.
1983 – Tom Kelley
1984 – Sam Till Jr.
1985 – Jeff White
1986 – Tom Kelley
1987 – Bill Blumenhurst
1988 – Tom Kelley
1989 – Steve Vernasco
1990 – Win Fisher
1991 – Tom Kelley
1992 – Mike Meehan
1993 – Bret Richards
1994 – Chip Novak
1995 – Sam Till Jr.
1996 – Dan Hall
1997 – Jim Joseph
1998 – Sam Till Jr.
1999 – Steve Vernasco
2000 – Tom Kelley
2001 – Jim Joseph
2002 – Steve Vernasco
2003 – Jim Joseph
2004 – Bret Richards
2005 – Chip Novak
2006 – Scott Pieri
2007 – Hartley McLeod III
2008 – Scott Pieri
2009 – Erich Johnston
2010 – Scott Pieri
2011 – Scott Pieri
2012 – Scott Pieri

## Golf - Women

| | |
|---|---|
| 1929 – Mrs. A.E. Bulson, Jr. | 1978 – DeDe Hoffman |
| 1930 – Mrs. A.E. Bulson, Jr. | 1979 – Cathy Kratzert |
| 1931 – Mrs. A.E. Bulson, Jr. | 1980 – Lisa Luken |
| 1932 – Mrs. Scott Snyder | 1981 – Cathy Kratzert |
| 1933 – Mrs. Scott Snyder | 1982 – Cathy Kratzert |
| 1934 – Lois Bond | 1983 – Lisa Luken |
| 1935 – Helen Hicks | 1984 – Peggy Gant |
| 1936 – Hillis Snyder | 1985 – Peggy Gant |
| 1937 – J ean Saint | 1986 – Jane Bair |
| 1938 – Leona Berghoff | 1987 – Julie Shumaker |
| 1939 – Laura Hart | 1988 – Lori Stinson |
| 1940 – Helen Greiner | 1989 – Lori Stinson |
| 1941 – Helen Greiner | 1990 – Mary Shupe |
| 1942 – Eleanor Allen Jr. | 1991 – Lori Stinson |
| 1943 – Helen Greiner | 1992 – Mary Shupe |
| 1944 – Jean Saint | 1993 – Mary Shupe |
| 1945 – Jean Saint | 1994 – Michelle Smith |
| 1946 – Jean Saint | 1995 – Michelle Hatfield |
| 1947 – Jean Saint | 1996 – Kasey Gant |
| 1948 – Jean Saint | 1997 – Michelle Hatfield |
| 1949 – Betty Graham | 1998 – Michelle Hatfield |
| 1950 – Jean Saint | 1999 – Molly Weissert |
| 1951 – Jean Saint | 2000 – Michelle Smith |
| 1952 – Barbara C. Squier | 2001 – Kim Moore |
| 1953 – Helen Greiner | 2002 – Jessica Till |
| 1954 – Barbara C. Squier | 2003 – Jessica Till |
| 1955 – Pat Wright | 2004 – Michelle (Hatfield) Gerbasich |
| 1956 – Molly Dunigan | 2005 – Michelle Smith |
| 1957 – Pat Wright | 2006 – Michelle Smith |
| 1958 – Pat Wright | 2007 – Camie Mess |
| 1959 – Pat McGary | 2008 – Sarah Prascsak |
| 1960 – Pat Wright | 2009 – Sarah Prascsak |
| 1961 – Pat Wright | 2010 – Kristi O'Brien |
| 1962 – Pat Wright | 2011 – Kristi O'Brien |
| 1963 – Pat McGary | 2012 – Amber Sieber |
| 1964 – Pat McGary | |
| 1965 – Pat Wright | |
| 1966 – Pat McGary | |
| 1967 – Pat McGary | |
| 1968 – Pat Wright | |
| 1969 – Pat Wright | |
| 1970 – Pat McGary | |
| 1971 – Dottie Collins | |
| 1972 – Mary Ann Lochner | |
| 1973 – Peggy Gant | |
| 1974 – Becky Miller | |
| 1975 – DeDe Hoffman | |
| 1976 – DeDe Hoffman | |
| 1977 – Peggy Gant | |

## Tennis
### Men's singles

1909 – Dr. Miles F. Porter, Jr. def. Dr. D.P. Weaver
1910 – Dr. Miles F. Porter, Jr. Runnerup not available
1911 – Dr. Miles F. Porter, Jr. Runnerup not available
1912 – Dr. Miles F. Porter, Jr. Runnerup not available
1913 – Dr. Miles F. Porter, Jr. Runnerup not available
1914 – Dr. Miles F. Porter, Jr. Runnerup not available
1915 – Dr. Miles F. Porter, Jr. Runnerup not available
1916 – Clinton Burton def. Dr. Miles F. Porter, Jr.
1917-1920 – No tournament played
1920 – Herbert Stephens def. Eric Gawhn
1921 – Clinton Burton def. Les Ortlieb
1922 – Herbert Stephens def. Les Ortlieb
1923 – Herbert Stephens def. Bill Plogsterth
1924 – Bill Plogsterth def. Herbert Stephens
1925 – Les Ortlieb def. Herbert Stephens
1926 – Les Ortlieb def. Wilfred Kruse
1927 – Les Ortlieb def. Wilfred Kruse
1928 – Les Ortlieb def. Jim Wilson
1929 – Les Ortlieb def. Jim Wilson
1930 – Les Ortlieb def. Jim Wilson
1931 – Howard Buck def. Joe Herr
1932 – Les Ortlieb def. Bill Dammeier
1933 – Les Ortlieb def. James Conway
1934 – Bill Herr def. Bill Dammeier
1935 – Jim Wilson def. Fred Feustal
1936 – Dick Shoaff def. Bill Herr
1937 – Jim Wilson def. Dick Shoaff
1938 – Bill Herr def. Jim Wilson
1939 – Bob Schelper def. Dick Shoaff
1940 – Bob Schelper def. Dick Doermer
1941 – Stan Weitz def. Dick Doermer
1942 – Paul Dammeier def. Stan Weitz
1943 – Stan Weitz def. Harold (Lefty) Workman
1944 – Stan Weitz def. Artie Hoffman
1945 – Art Hammer def. Artie Hoffman
1946 – Stan Weitz def. Paul Dammeier
1947 – Paul Dammeier def. Artie Hoffman
1948 – Artie Hoffman def. Paul Dammeier
1949 – Paul Dammeier def. Artie Hoffman
1950 – Ray Gorney def. Paul Dammeier
1951 – Bill Madamba def. Paul Dammeier
1952 – Paul Dammeier def. Artie Hoffman
1953 – Gene St. John def. Tom Hay
1954 – Ray Gorney def. Paul Scherrer
1955 – Ray Gorney def. Tommy Roberts
1956 – Ray Gorney def. Paul Scherrer
1957 – Ray Gorney def. Paul Scherrer

1958 – Paul Scherrer def. Ray Gorney
1959 – Paul Scherrer def. Ray Gorney
1960 – Harry Garnette def. Paul Scherrer
1961 – Paul Scherrer def. Harry Garnette
1962 – Paul Scherrer def. Dudley Johnston
1963 – Paul Scherrer def. Dudley Johnston
1964 – Dudley Johnston def. Jerry Swinford
1965 – Dudley Johnston def. Jerry Swinford
1966 – Dudley Johnston def. Jerry Swinford
1967 – Dudley Johnston def. George Bagnell
1968 – Dudley Johnston def. Rod Day
1969 – Dudley Johnston def. George Bagnell
1970 – Dudley Johnston def. Bruce Bolyard
1971 – George Bagnell def. Ronn Heathman
1972 – Bruce Bolyard def. George Bagnell
1973 – Ronn Heathman def. Bruce Bolyard
1974 – Bruce Bolyard def. Don Schmidt
1975 – Don Schmidt def. Luke Grossman
1976 – Luke Grossman def. Eric Bagnell
1977 – Luke Grossman def. Rick Seaman
1978 – Luke Grossman def. Tom Lazoff
1979 – Luke Grossman def. Tim Sullivan
1980 – Ronn Heathman def. Luke Grossman
1981 – Ronn Heathman def. Tom Lazoff
1982 – Tom Lazoff def. Ronn Heathman
1983 – Joey Christoff def. Steve Beier
1984 – Joey Christoff def. Steve Beier
1985 – Steve Beier def. Tim Sullivan
1986 – Todd Hacker def. Steve Beier
1987 – Steve Beier def. Todd Hacker
1988 – Steve Beier def. Luke Grossman
1989 – Luke Grossman def. Paul Cole
1990 – Steve Beier def. Luke Grossman
1991 – Luke Grossman def. Tim Sullivan
1992 – Steve Beier def. Jerry Gerig
1993 – Mike Rayburn def. Mike Insko
1994 – Steve Beier def. Luke Grossman
1995 – Jay Smithley def. Mike Andrews
1996 – Jay Smithley def. Steve Beier
1997 – Scott Miller def. Tim Sullivan
1998 – Jay Smithley def. Tim Sullivan
1999 – Ryan Recht def. Sean Keefer
2000 – Ryan Recht def. Joo Kim
2001 – Ryan Recht def. Martin Krbec
2002 – Ryan Recht def. Jake Parrish
2003 – Ryan Recht def. Jake Parrish
2004 – Ryan Recht def. Tim Hartman
2005 – Ryan Recht def. Sam Rocke
2006 – Derek Carpenter def. Ryan Keirns
2007 – Derek Carpenter def. Sam Rocke

2008 – Ryan Recht def. Derek Carpenter
2009 – Ryan Recht def. Hunter Schouweiler
2010 – Ryan Recht def. Derek Carpenter
2011 – Tom Murphy def. Jonathan Batuello
2012 – Tom Murphy def. Connor Andrews

## Women's singles

1927 – Peg Canode def. Velma Kohlmeyer
1928 – Esther Moli def. Veda Stevens
1929 – Veda Stevens def. Norma Leverency
1930 – Veda Stevens def. Velma Kohlmeyer
1931 – Veda Stevens def. Dolly Bell Ganthis
1932 – Veda Stevens def. Margaret Speigel
1933-1939 – No tournament played.
1940 – Jeanne Smith-Harter def. Marian Faux Fremion
1941 – Jeanne Smith-Harter def. Marian Faux Fremion
1942 – Jeanne Smith-Harter def. Marian Faux Fremion
1943 – Marian Faux Fremion def. Kathryn Vonderau
1944 – Florence Dammeier def. Wanda Hover
1945 – Edith O'Rourke def. Marian Faux Fremion
1946 – Edith O'Rourke def. Marion Faux Fremion
1947 – Joy Foelber Andrews def. Marion Faux Fremion
1948 – Marian Faux Fremion def. Joy Foelber-Andrews
1949 – Joan Obergfell-Couch def. Marian Faux Fremion
1950 – Joan Obergfell-Couch def. Joy Foelber-Andrews
1951 – Joan Obergfell-Couch def. Joy Foelber-Andrews
1952 – Lorraine DePew def. Alice Ann Murphy
1953 – Lorraine DePew-Aumiller def. Betty Hargan
1954 – Joy Foelber-Andrews def. Lorraine DePew-Aumiller
1955 – Nancy Richey def. Joy Foelber-Andrews
1956 – Lorraine DePew-Aumiller def. Joy Foelber-Andrews
1957 – Lorraine DePew-Aumiller def. Dottie Scherrer
1958 – Phyllis Nahrwold def. Lorraine DePew-Aumiller
1959 – Phyllis Nahrwold def. Lorraine DePew-Aumiller
1960 – Phyllis Nahrwold def. Lorraine DePew-Aumiller
1961 – Jackie Porter def. Phyllis Nahrwold
1962 – Jackie Porter def. Phyllis Nahrwold
1963 – Phyllis Nahrwold-Reisgies def. Marylin Retz
1964 – Kay Schoenefeld def. Phyllis Nahrwold-Reisgies
1965 – Kay Schoenefeld def. Amy Fremion
1966 – Lorraine Aumiller def. Anne Donnelly
1967 – Kay Schoenefeld def. Amy Fremion
1968 – Kay Schoenefeld def. Amy Fremion
1969 – Kay Schoenefeld def. Amy Fremion
1970 – No tournament due to lack of entries.
1971 – Kay Schoenefeld def. Lee Ann Berning
1972 – Lee Ann Berning def. Natalie Nichols
1973 – Lee Ann Berning def. Joanne Paul
1974 – Lee Ann Berning def. Kay Schoenefeld
1975 – Barb Teetor def. Joanne Paul

1976 – Lee Ann Berning def. Jane Littlefield-Martzell
1977 – Leslie Giffin def. Lee Ann Berning
1978 – Sue Weigand def. Cami Swanson
1979 – Lee Ann Berning def. Sue Weigand
1980 – Sue Weigand def. Mary Colligan
1981 – Sue Weigand def. Jane Filus
1982 – Mary Colligan def. Sue Weigand
1983 – Sue Weigand def. Jane Filus
1984 – Lee Ann (Berning) Reed def. Mary Colligan
1985 – Brenda Hacker def. Jane Filus
1986 – Brenda Hacker def. Lee Ann Reed
1987 – No tournament due to lack of entries
1988 – Babs Sullivan def. Suzie Gilbert
1989 – Lee Ann Reed def. Babs (Spidel) Sullivan
1990 – Lee Ann Reed def. Maria Sciole
1991 – Lee Ann Reed def. Holly Seaman
1992 – Johanna Hall def. Sarah Wagoner
1993 – Johanna Hall def. Molly Figel
1994 – Amy McClure def. Sally Smithley
1995 – Sommer Stier def. Michelle Evans
1996 – Natasha Joshi def. Sally Smithley
1997 – Natasha (Joshi) Nuerge def. Libby Gerding
1998 – Franchel Bennett def. Molly Figel
1999 – Franchel Bennett def. Sommer Stier
2000 – Natasha Nuerge def. Franchel Bennett
2001 – Michelle Evans def. Erin Carrel
2002 – Rachel Janssen def. Sachi Janek
2003 – Rachel Janssen def. Sachi Janek
2004 – Rachel Janssen def. Erin Carrel
2005 – Amy Recht def. Sachi Janek
2006 – Amy Recht def. Sachi Janek
2007 – Amy Recht def. Sally Smithley
2008 – Amy Recht def. Leah Barnes
2009 – Monica Purice def. Amy Recht
2010 – Amy Recht def. Leah Barnes
2011 – Amy Recht def. Audrey Rang
2012 – Amy Recht def. Marcy Huck

## Men's doubles

2012 – Michael Parker-Collin Williams def. Mike Sinish-Justin Parker
2011 – Josh Rifkin-Michael Parker def. Conner Andrews-Mike Andrews
2010 – Ryan Recht-Jay Smithley def. Derek Carpenter-Hunter Schouweiler
2009 – Ryan Recht-Jay Smithley def. Derek Carpenter-Hunter Schouweiler
2008 – Ryan Recht-Jay Smithley def. Derek Carpenter-Hunter Schouweiler
2007 – Derek Carpenter-Hunter Schouweiler def. Mike Sinish-Chad Hathaway
2006 – Derek Carpenter-Hunter Schouweiler def. Michael Parker-Scott Dredge
2005 – Rick Hanauer-Dan Brogan def. Ryan Keirns-Scott Dredge
2004 – Ryan Keirns-Scott Dredge def. Shaun Fisher-Adam Turner
2003 – Rick Hanauer-Dan Brogan def. Ryan Recht-Jacob Parrish
2002 – Ryan Recht-Jacob Parrish def. Mike Andrews-Tim Sullivan

2001 – Vince Williams-Martin Krbec def. Skye Heiney-Tim Sullivan
2000 – Rick Hanauer-Dan Brogan def. Ryan Recht-Scott Postlewaite
1999 – Ryan Recht-Jay Smithley def. Dan Brogan-Rick Hanauer
1998 – Dan Brogan-Rick Hanauer def. Tim Sullivan-Skye Heiney
1997 – Lovelle Crenshaw-Jay Smithley def. Scott Miller-Dan Brogan
1996 – Lovelle Crenshaw-Jay Smithley def. Steve Beier-Jerry Gerig
1995 – Jerry Gerig-Luke Grossman def. Scott Miller-Dan Brogan
1994 – Lovelle Crenshaw-Pat Downs def. Mike Insko-Dan Brogan
1993 – Steve Beier-Tim Sullivan def. Mike Insko-Dan Brogan
1992 – Steve Beier-Jerry Gerig def. Mike Insko-Dan Brogan
1991 – Luke Grossman-Tim Koehl def. Joe Altmeyer-Dan Brogan
1990 – Tim Sullivan-Steve Beier def. Pat Downs-Jim Solloway
1989 – Rick Hanauer-Paul Cole def. Byron Lamm-Grossman
1988 – Rick Hanauer-Todd Hacker def. Luke Grossman-Steve Beier
1987 – Tim Sullivan-John Zern def. Steve Beier-Rick Hanauer
1986 – Rick Hanauer-Todd Hacker def. J.Webb Horton-Bob Thompson
1985 – Tim Sullivan-Steve Beier def. Jan Reed-Rick Hanauer
1984 – Joey Christoff-Rick Hanauer def. Tim Sullivan-Jan Reed
1983 – Joey Christoff-Rick Hanauer def. Steve Beier-Tom Lazoff
1982 – Steve Beier-Tom Lazoff def. Tim Sullivan-Jan Reed
1981 – Ronn Heathman-J.Webb Horton def. Tom Lazoff-Steve Beier
1980 – Tim Tim Sullivan-John Frevert def. Todd Hacker-Ronn Heathman
1979 – Tom Lazoff-Luke Grossman def. Tim Sullivan-John Frevert
1978 – Tim Sullivan-Greg Crawford def. Schoenefeld-John Frevert
1977 – Tim Sullivan-Greg Crawford def. Schoenefeld-John Frevert
1976 – J. Webb Horton-Greg Crawford def. Don Frevert-Don Schoenefeld
1975 – Dennis Stoller-Greg Crawford def. Bob Nikels-Don Schoenefeld
1974 – Don Schmidt-Ronn Heathman def. unknown
1973 – Don Schmidt-Ronn Heathman def. Bruce Bolyard-Steve Phillipp
1972 – Steve Phillipp-Bruce Bolyard def. Don Schmidt-Don Lee
1971 – Dick Malsenbacher-Don Schmidt def. Don Schoenefeld-Ronn Heathman
1970 – Ronn Heathman-Don Shoenefeld def. Dudley Johnston-George Bagnall
1969 – Dudley Johnston-John Taylor def. Ronn Heathman-Don Schoenefeld
1968 – Dudley Johnston-George Bagnall def. Rod Day-Art Hammer
1967 – Dudley Johnston-George Bagnall def. Steve Williams-Leon Kennedy
1966 – Dudley Johnston-Paul Scherrer def. Jerry Swinford-Art Hammer
1965 – Dudley Johnston-Paul Scherrer def. unknown
1964 – Dudley Johnston-Paul Scherrer def. Ken Klossner-Larren Oren
1963 – Dudley Johnston-Paul Scherrer def. Larren Oren-Dick McGaw
1962 – Dave Shephard-Paul Scherrer def. Larren Oren-Art Hammer
1961 – Paul Scherrer-Dick McGaw def. Larren Oren-Dudley Johnston
1960 – Harry Garnette-Jim Porter def. Paul Scherrer-Art Hammer
1959 – Ray Gorney-Paul Scherrer def. Art Hammer-Charles Ludwig
1958 – Ray Gorney-Paul Scherrer def. Art Hammer-Roy Lindenberg
1957 – Ray Gorney-Paul Scherrer def. George Griffith-Porter
1956 – Ray Gorney-Paul Scherrer def. Porter-Roy Lindenberg
1955 – Ray Gorney-Paul Scherrer def. Dudley Johnston-Tommy Roberts
1954 – Ray Gorney-Paul Scherrer def. Jim Porter-Tom Hay
1953 – Tom Hay-Gene St. John def. Art Hammer-Hoffman
1952 – Hoffman-P. Dammeier def. Jim Porter-Lindenberg

1951 – Hoffman-P. Dammeier def. Bill Madamba-Lindenberg
1950 – Ray Gorney-Hammer def. Hoffman-P. Dammeier
1949 – Hoffman-P. Dammeier def. Jim Porter-Lindenberg
1948 – Hoffman-P. Dammeier def. Les Menxe-Roy Lindenberg
1947 – Hoffman-P. Dammeier def. Weitz-Art Hammer
1946 – Hoffman-P. Dammeier def. Arch McCall-Dick Benson
1945 – Reed-Hoffman def. Andy Bickett-Willson
1944 – Weitz-John Johnson def. Hoffman-Smith
1943 – Hoffman-Reed def. Harry Smith-Ralph Lindstrom
1942 – Ted Reed-Bryan Fenley def. Hoffman-Dammeier
1941 – Hoffman-P. Dammeier def. Willson-Shoaff
1940 – Artie Hoffman-P. Dammeier def. Shelper-Burns
1939 – Stan Weitz-Paul Dammeier def. Robert Shelper-Jim Burns
1938 – Willson-Shoaff def. J. Herr-Ortleib
1937 – Willson-Dick Shoaff def. J. Herr-Dammeier
1936 – J. Herr-Dammeier def. Willson-Don Troxel
1935 – J. Herr-Dammeier def. Willson-Allen Lomont
1934 – Dammeier-Bill Herr def. Joe Herr-unknown
1933 – Dammeier-Bill Herr def. Ortleib-Ron Smith
1932 – Dammeier-Buck def. Ortleib-Al Kruse
1931 – Dammeier-Buck def. Ortleib-Al Kruse
1930 – Otis Wyneken-Sam Fay def. Dammeier-Buck
1929 – Ortlieb-Willson def. Dammeier-Howard Buck
1928 – Bill Dammeier-Otis Wyneken def. Ortlieb-Willson
1927 – Ortleib-Willson def. Kruse-Seabold
1926 – Ortleib-Jim Willson def. Wilfred Kruse-Bob Seabold
1925 – Ortleib-Plogsterth def. Miller-Wilfred Kruse
1924 – Plogsterth-Ortleib def. Al Kruse-Jerry Miller
1923 – Burton-Plogsterth def. unknown
1922 – Ortleib-Plogsterth def. Herb Stevens-Ed Scheumann
1921 – Clinton Burton-Ortleib def. unknown.
1920 – Bill Plogsterth-Les Ortleib def. Porter-Parry
1917-1919 – No tournament
1916 – Porter-Weaver def. Clinton A. Burton-Murdock Milholland
1915 – Porter-Weaver def. unknown.
1914 – Porter-Perry def. unknown.
1913 – Porter-Perry def. unknown.
1912 – No records.
1911 – Porter-Skyrock def. Bond-Hunter
1910 – No doubles played
1909 – Dr. Miles F. Porter, Jr.-Dr. D.P. Weaver def. Zucker-Art Parry

## Women's doubles

2012 – Amy Recht-Raquel Vescoui def. Audrey Rang-Elizabeth Maxson
2011 – Amy Recht-Ingrid Ballus def. Stephanie Strong-Lauren Farnham
2010 – Amy Recht-Sachi Janek def. Alexa Rang-Audrey Rang
2009 – Amy Recht-Sachi Janek def. Sally Smithley-Natasha Nuerge
2008 – Amy Recht-Sachi Janek def. Sally Smithley-Sarah (Wagnoner) Goeglein
2007 – Amy Recht-Jade Johnson def. Rachel Janssen-Emily Lamport
2006 – Sachi Janek-Beth Miller def. Lisa Bartelheim-Hanna Hager

2005 – Sommer Butz-Alicia Wilkins def. Ashley Liles-Claire Liles
2004 – Emily Figel-Sommer Butz def. Maria Sciole-Sarah Rahrig
2003 – Rachel Janssen-Megan Doyle def. Erin Carrel-Allyson Logan
2002 – Molly Figel-Emily Figel def. Maria Sciole-Sarah Rahrig
2001 – Molly Figel-Emily Figel def. Rox Ann Krahn-Babs Sullivan
2000 – Franchel Bennett-Lee Ann Berning def. Molly Figel-Emily Figel
1999 – Franchel Bennett-Lee Ann Reed def. Molly Figel-Emily Figel
1998 – Franchel Bennett-Paula Willeford def. Babs Sullivan-Molly Figel
1997 – Libby Gerding-Natasha Nuerge def. Sally Smithley-Michelle Evans
1996 – Lee Ann Reed-Natasha Joshi def. Johanna Hall-Libby Gerding
1995 – Michelle Evans-Sarah Wagoner def. Sally Smithley-Babs Sullivan
1994 – Amy McClure-Kelley McClure def. Babs Sullivan-Sarah Ruoff
1993 – Johanna Hall-Libby Gerding def. Sommer Stier-Sarah Wagoner
1992 – Sarah Wagoner-Sommer Stier def. Babs Sullivan-Sarah Rahrig
1991 – Lee Ann Berning-Suzette Bible def. Babs Sullivan-Wendey Butzow
1990 – Babs Sullivan-Amy McClure def. Mary Edwards-Peggy Timbrook
1987 – Jan Weigand-Cara Beth Lee def. Wendey Butzow-Suzette Bible
1986 – Mary Colligan-Jane Filus def. Babs Spidell-Gina Krach
1985 – Babs Spidell-Caroline Zern def. Jeannie Fritz-Kelly Fritz
1979 – Lee Ann Berning-Sue Weigand def. Jan Weigand-Mary Colligan
1977 – Lee Ann Berning-Leslie Giffin def. unknown
1973 – Lee Ann Berning-Ann Donnelley def. Natalie Nichols-Jane Littlefield
1972 – Lee Ann Berning-Joan Paul def. Stephanie Shreeve-Jane Littlefield

## Mixed doubles

2012 – Michael Parker-Maja Furniss def. Connor Andrews-Amy Recht
2011 – Michael Parker-Maja Furniss def. Josh Rifkin-Jade Johnson
2010 – Ryan Recht-Amy Recht def. Brian Copice-Audrey Rang
2009 – Amy Recht-Ryan Recht def. Jade Johnson-Josh Rifkin
2008 – Amy Recht-Ryan Recht def. Jade Johnson-Josh Rifkin
2007 – Amy Recht-Ryan Recht def. Jade Johnson-Derek Carpenter
2006 – Derek Carpenter-Jade Johnson def. Michael Parker-Beth Miller
2005 – Amy Recht-Cameron Huffman def. Dan Brogan-Johanna Hall
2004 – Tim Hartman-Erin Wright def. Tony Mitson-Ashley Liles
2003 – Tim Hartman-Laura Phillipp def. Ryan Recht-Amy Recht
2002 – Ryan Keirns-Emily Figel def. Tony Mitson-Ashley Liles
2001 – Michelle Evans-Jerry Gerig def. Molly Figel-Ryan Keirns
2000 – Rick Hanauer-Franchel Bennett def. Ryan Keirns-Molly Figel
1999 – Rick Hanauer-Franchel Bennett def. Dan Brogan-Sarah Rahrig
1998 – Rick Hanauer-Franchel Bennett def. Dan Brogan-Sarah Rahrig
1997 – Jon Bemisderfer-Natasha Nuerge def. Jay Smithley-Sally Smithley
1996 – Jay Smithley-Sally Smithley def. Lovelle Crenshaw-Johanna Hall
1995 – Scott Miller-Michelle Evans def. Jay Smithley-Sally Smithley
1994 – Pat Downs-Amy McClure def. Mike Insko-Sommer Stier
1993 – Lee Williams-Johanna Hall def. Sommer Stier-Pat Downs
1992 – Rick Hanauer-Sarah Wagoner def. Lee Williams-Johanna Hall
1991 – Rick Hanauer-Lee Ann Berning def. Tim Sullivan-Babs Sullivan
1990 – Rick Hanauer-Lee Ann Berning def. Joel Harms-Meagan Everett
1987 – Vince Williams-Lee Ann Berning def. Maria Sciole-Joe Sciole
1986 – Babs Spidell-Dan Brogan def. Rick Hanauer-Julie Thompson

1985 – Steve Beier-Jan Weigand def. Jan Reed-Jane Filus
1982 – Jan Reed-Lee Ann Reed def. Tom Lazoff-Sue Weigand
1980 – Tim Sullivan-Cami Swanson def. Don Schmidt-Diane Mondini
1979 – Tim Sullivan-Lee Ann Berning def. Jan Reed-Peggy Graham
1978 – Rick Hanauer-Lee Ann Berning def. J. Webb Horton-Barb Teetor
1977 – Jerry Harms-Lee Ann Berning def. Ned Lee-Anne Donnelly
1974 – Luke Grossman-Lee Ann Berning
1973 – Luke Grossman-Lee Ann Berning
1972 – Art Scherer-Lee Ann Berning def. Rick Seaman-Renee Rousseau

## INDIANA STATE HALLS OF FAME
### (Northeast Indiana inductees)

### Baseball
Bruce Miller, Steve Hargan, Dean Stahly, Eric Wedge, Bubbles Hargrave, John Grantham, Dale McMillen, Norm Kramer, Jack Massucci, Don Sherman, Chris Stavreti, Gene Bottoerff, Red Carrington, Everett Scott, Bill Jones, Max Carey.

### Basketball
David Anspaugh, Decatur; Curly Armstrong, Central; Lori Augustyniak, Leo; Tom Baack, Concordia; Herb Banet, South Side/Central; Chuck Bavis, Garrett; Jody Beerman, Heritage; Carol Blauvelt, Heritage; Bob Bolyard, South Side; Tom Bolyard, South Side; Carl Braden, South Side; Tonya Burns, Leo; Bob Cowan, North Side; Bob Dille, Northrop; Lenore Doerling, Wakarusa; Fred Fields, Huntington North; Burl Friddle, South Side; Hilliard Gates; Ralph Hamilton, South Side; Bob Hammel, Huntington; Jim Hammel, Huntington; By Hey, Concordia/North Side; Dick Hickox, North Side; Amy Hile, Bishop Dwenger; John Hines, South Side; Jim Hinga, North Side; David Johnson, Columbia City; Walter Jordan, Northrop; LaMar Kilmer, Snider; Wayne Kreiger, Columbia City/Canterbury; Willie Long, South Side; Jim Master, Harding; Mike McCoy, South Side; Murray Mendenhall, Central; Murray Mendenhall Jr., South Side; Tony Miller, Garrett; Bobby Milton, Central; Steve Neff, Wakarusa; Eugene Parker, Concordia; Bill Patrick, Whitko; Steve Platt, Union Township; Nancy Rehm, Bishop Luers; Don Reichert, South Side; Dave Riley, Northrop; Teri Rosinski, Norwell; Patricia Roy, Harlan; Herm Schaefer, Central; Jim Schooley, Auburn; Steve Sitko, Central; Charlie Stanski, Central; Homer Stonebraker, Fort Wayne Hoosiers; Mike Weaver, Huntington; Ivan Wilhelm, Huntington.

### Football
Cary Cavacini, Homestead; Bob Cowan, North Side; Buzz Doerffler, Northrop; Kevin Donley, Saint Francis; Leland Etzler, Woodlan; John Gaughan, Bishop Dwenger; Bill Griffith, Snider/Wayne; Al Harants, Bellmont/Wayne; Mike Hawley, Snider; Terry Hoeppner, Woodlan; Dale Hummer, DeKalb; Andy Johns, Bishop Dwenger; Rick Minnich, Adams Central; Gary Scott, Norwell; Emil Sitko, Central; Kirk Sorg, South Adams; Fred Tone, Bishop Dwenger; Lundy Welborn, Central; Bob Yager, Heritage.

### Golf
High school: Gene Crosley, Homestead; Grant Schimmele, Fremont; James Thompson, Columbia City; Ken Wertz, Fremont; Bruce Oliver, Northrop; Keith Blythe, Bellmont.
Indiana PGA: Bill Kratzert III, Bud Williamson, Bill Schumaker, Gary Gant.

### Hockey
Colin Lister, Mike Stuckey, Mary Trabel, Roy Chin, Mitzi Toepfer, Bob Chase.

## Soccer

Greg Mauch, Rolf Anhaeuser, Klemens Zumbragel, Chuck Graham, Terry Stefankiewicz, Kuno Mirwaldt, David Tanner, Nel Fettig, Pat Teagarden, Greg Roberts, Rollie Clements.

## Softball

ASA: Bill House, Hughie Johnston, Bernie Kampschmidt, Leo Luken, Jim Ramage, Bill West, Fred Zollner, Vern Krauss, Elmer MacDonald, Cliff Gaze.
High school: Patricia Roy, Harlan; Joe Kroemer, DeKalb; Phyllis Vance, Huntington North.

## Swimming

Justin Hoggatt, Homestead; Leslie Place, Snider; Lia Oberstar, Bishop Dewnger; Michala Kwasny, Snider; Jennifer Gibson, Snider.

## Tennis

Brenda Hacker, Homestead; Jim Shull, Homestead; LaMar Kilmer, Snider; Tony Wright, Angola; Luke Grossman, Concordia; Jim Clark, Homestead; Lee Ann Berning, Concordia.

## Track and cross country

Rolla Chambers, North Side; Don Cotton, Huntington North; Phil Hostetler, Westview; Tom Knudson, Northrop; Terry Milton, Northrop; Barrie Peterson, Northrop; Dick Shenfeld, Homestead; Dean Slavens, Columbia City; Bill Walker, South Side; Roberta Widman-Foust, South Side; Angie Bradburn, Norwell; Laura Didion, Northrop; Sherri Dunn, Northrop; Jamie Gorrell, Woodlan; LaShonda Harper, Harding; Sherry Hoover, Woodlan; DeDee Nathan, South Side; Sybil Perry, Wayne; Megan Pierce, Concordia; Debbi Ramseyer, Norwell; Zakiya Robinson, Northrop; Deb Sauers, Columbia City; Delores Stewart, South Side; Cathey Tyree, South Side; Kristi Walker, Harding; Karen Wechsler, Huntington North; Amy Yoder, East Noble; Terri Young, Harding; Andy Begley, Westview; Paul Bienz, Central; Ron Birchfield, South Side; Shawn Brown, Homestead; Ken Cammack, Wayne; Mark Cammack, Wayne; Bob Cowan, North Side; George Doehla, Harding; Howard Doughty, North Side; Bob Ewing, North Side; Jo'L Gerardot, Northrop; Gregg Hart, Homestead; Ashley Hawk, North Side; Steve Hibler, Concordia; Dan Howe, South Side; Gary Hunter, Northrop; Brian King, Northrop; Henry King, Central; Kurt Krick, Norwell; Don Lash, Auburn; Will Luzar, Homestead; Rick Magley, Northrop; John Mitchell, Wayne; Glenn Schneider, Harding; Thomas Seifert, North Side; Robert Shank, North Side; Brock Smith, Homestead; Jeff Stroman, Garrett; Gary Thrapp, East Noble; Brett Tipton, Northrop; Leon Tubbs, South Side; Rod Woodson, Snider; Phil Wysong, West Noble; Carl Wiegman, Journal Gazette; Archie Adams, North Side; Nelson Detwiler, Wayne.

## Wrestling

Ed Fox, Carroll; Stan Hostetler, New Haven; Barry Humble, Adams Central; Fred Tone, Bishop Dwenger; Phil Lingerich, Bellmont; Chris Mahlan, Bellmont; Oliver Richmond, Elmhurst; Dr. John Doan, Decatur; Warren Eviston, Fort Wayne; Tim Myers, Bellmont; Brent Faurote, Bellmont; A.J. Kalver, Bishop Luers; Tom Bennett, Snider; Russ Isaacs, Snider; Paul Gunsett, Bellmont; Gary Giessler, Bellmont;

Troy Roe, Adams Central; Jim Bassett, Adams Central; Elbert Starks, Snider; Don Hunter, North Side; Denny Hayes, Bellmont; Ed Corazzi, Fort Wayne; Greg Moe, Garrett.

## Zollner Pistons in National Softball Hall of Fame

Bill West, Bernie Kampschmidt, Leo Luken, Hughie Johnston, Clyde Kirkendall, Jim Ramage, Sam Lombardo, Elmer Rohrs, Herb Dudley, Fred Zollner.

## Komets retired numbers

2 Guy Dupuis, 5 Terry Pembroke, 6 Lionel Repka, 11 Len Thornson, 12 Reg Primeau, 16 Eddie Long, 18 Robbie Laird, 26 Colin Chin, 30 Robbie Irons, 40 Bob Chase, 58 Ken Ullyot, 59 Colin Lister, 77 Steve Fletcher, Bud Gallmeier.

## Sportswriters and Sportscasters

Bob Chase, Jim Costin, Len Davis, Mike Emrick, Bud Gallmeier, Hilliard Gates, Fred Inniger, Dean Pantazi, Chris Schenkel, Ben Smith, Ben Tenny, Steve Warden.

## NORTHEAST INDIANA'S TOP 50 ATHLETES
**Published in The News-Sentinel in 1999**

1. Rod Woodson
2. Johnny Bright
3. George Yardley
4. Everett Scott
5. Len Thornson
6. Bobby McDermott
7. Don Lash
8. DeDee Nathan
9. Lloy Ball
10. Cathy Gerring
11. Bill Kratzert
12. Matt Vogel
13. Sharon Wichman
14. Emil Sitko
15. Eugene Hargrave
16. Dottie Collins
17. Willie Long
18. Bob Cowan
19. Eddie Long
20. Paul "Curly" Armstrong
21. Bill Wambsganss
22. MaChelle Joseph
23. Steve Hargan
24. Henry James
25. Gene Hartley

26. Bill West
27. Bernie Kampschmidt
28. Joanne Weaver
29. Herm Schaefer
30. Lionel Repka
31. Vaughn Dunbar
32. Walter Jordan
33. Bruce Miller
34. Lashanda Harper
35. Nel Fettig
36. Terry Pembroke
37. Steve Platt
38. Tom Beerman
39. Cathey Tyree
40. Jason Fabini
41. Tiffany Gooden
42. Lamar Smith
43. Leslie Johnson
44. Tom Bolyard
45. Roosevelt Barnes
46. Conan "Moose" Myers
47. Lee Ann Berning
48. Tom Kelley
49. Mike Augustyniak
50. Colin Chin

# About the Author

A native of Fort Wayne, Blake Sebring has been on the Fort Wayne Komets' beat for 23 seasons, covering more than 1,000 games, and is one of only four men to cover the team over 60 years for The News-Sentinel. Besides legendary sports editor Bud Gallmeier's 35 years, no one in newspapers has covered the Komets longer. He started working at The News-Sentinel at age 15 and has been living his dream ever since.

*Fort Wayne Sports History* is his seventh book. He is also the author of five sports nonfiction books, including *Tales of the Komets*, *Legends of the Komets*, *Live From Radio Rinkside: The Bob Chase Story* and *The Biggest Mistake I Never Made* with Lloy Ball. He has also written two novels, *The Lake Effect* and *Homecoming Game*. You can find out more at his personal website www.blakesebring.com.